REED ALL ABOUT IT!

Daily News from the Good News

Charles Allen Reed

Reed All About It!

Interior Formatting by: Ellen C. Maze, www.theauthorsmentor.com
Cover Design: Elizabeth E. Little, Hyliian Graphics, http://hyliian.deviantart.com
Front Cover Image Credit: www.123rf.com, photo 13619766 daynamore
Back Cover Paper Image Credit: http://ayelie-stock.deviantart.com/

ISBN-13: 978-1479189908
Also available in eBook publication

PRINTED IN THE UNITED STATES OF AMERICA

Dedicated
to
My Wife
Linda Vanderburg Reed

"Who can find a virtuous and capable wife?
She is more precious than rubies.
Her husband can trust her,
And she will greatly enrich his life.
She brings him good, not harm,
All the days of her life."
(Proverbs 31:10-12, NLT)

ACKNOWLEDGEMENTS

I am deeply grateful to all those who have encouraged me in the writing of this book, especially Denise George, bestselling author and co-founder of the Boot Camp for Christian Writers, for her encouragement and expertise. I am also indebted to Ellen C. Maze, author and founder of The Author's Mentor for her help with the editing and publishing process. Without these two wonderful ladies, this book would have been impossible. Thanks to both of you for your support and encouragement. You kept telling me it was possible, and I believed you!

A special word of gratitude is also expressed to Shirley McWhorter and Annelle Barbin; retired school teachers, faithful church members, dear friends, and proofreaders. Thanks for your time, effort, and patience with me throughout this whole project. You have been and are a blessing to me.

Finally, to my wife, Linda, the love and joy of my life. You have always believed in me and kept me going when I wanted to stop. Thank you for your love, prayers, and support. You are God's gift to me – a true pastor's wife!

PREFACE

Years ago young boys stood on the street corners of major cities across America and sold newspapers. Holding a bundle of newspapers under one arm while holding up a newspaper with the other arm, they shouted, “Extra! Extra! Read All About It!” That shout would be followed by calling out whatever major event had happened. They sold many newspapers to passersby that way. Newspapers print a variety of news including sports, politics, weather, classified ads, local as well as national and international news and even a comic section.

The night Jesus Christ was born in Bethlehem angels appeared to some shepherds who were staying in the fields keeping watch over their sheep. One of the angels said to the shepherds, “Do not be afraid; for behold, I bring you *good news* of great joy which will be for all the people” (Luke 2:10, NASB). The gospel of Jesus Christ is good news that needs to be shared with people everywhere. The Bible is filled with events and stories that appeal to people of all ages, telling the world of this “extra good news” that the Savior has been born.

Thirty-one years ago I began writing a weekly article for our local newspaper, *The Daily Sentinel.* When trying to decide what to name the column, my wife suggested, “Since our last name is REED, why not spell “READ” as “REED” and call the column, ‘REED ALL ABOUT IT!’?” That title has been the heading for the weekly articles ever since. In these articles I have used a combination of scriptures, illustrations, and humor to tell the good news of Christ and how it applies to our everyday life. Every effort has been made to footnote and document material.

During the depression era of our country, newspaper workers in New York City went on strike. The mayor, Fiorello LaGuardia, did not want the children of New York to be deprived of the comics (known as “funny papers”). Mayor LaGuardia endeared himself to the children of New York because he took the time to read the “funny papers” over the radio.

With all the serious news we read and hear about in our day, we need to laugh, so “A LITTLE HUMOR” was added at the end of each article. I believe God has a sense of humor. I believe He meant for us to laugh; after all, He made you and me, didn’t He?

Proverbs 17:22 reads, “A joyful heart is good medicine, but a broken spirit dries up the bones.” God Himself laughs (Psalm 59:8). Sarah laughed (Genesis 18:13-15). There is joy in heaven over one sinner who repents (Luke 15:4-10, 22-24). Ecclesiastes 3:4 reminds us that there is “a time to weep and a time to laugh.” Jesus said, “These things I have spoken to you so that My joy may be in you, and that your joy may be made full” (John 15:11).

When reading a newspaper I always read the comic strips. People who have read “REED ALL ABOUT IT!” have commented to me, “I always read your humor first,” but then, trying to explain themselves, they quickly added, “but I also read the article.” (Read the devotional for May 15 as an example). That’s okay with me. That’s why the humor is there.

Many have encouraged me to put these articles in print, thus the reason for this collection. It is my prayer that these daily devotionals will be both interesting and inspirational. It has been my goal to give a verse of scripture to meditate on each day, a story or illustration that applies this “extra good news” to daily living, and, of course, the humor to put a smile on your face and joy in your heart.

Table of Contents

JANUARY 1

HOW TO TRAVEL THROUGH THE NEW YEAR

"The highway of the upright is to depart from evil; he who watches his way preserves his life." (Proverbs 16:17, NASB)

Our journey into the New Year will lead us to many different encounters. We have never been this way before and never will be again. There will be new experiences to face, new problems to solve, new trials to endure, new temptations to meet, new sorrows to bear, new opportunities to grasp, new tasks to perform, and new blessings to enjoy.

Before anyone makes a long unfamiliar trip, he should prepare. If our journey over this new highway is to be successful, let me suggest some things we will need.

First, we will need **a guide book.** Some people refer to them as tour-guides. Guide books will contain information about the place you're planning to visit – places to see, what restaurants offer great meals, and of course, where to shop!

Likewise, we need a book that has directions for every day, comfort for every sorrow, and a solution for every problem. We have such a book; it's the Bible. Proverbs 119:105 reads, "Your word is a lamp to my feet and a light to my path." The Bible is not a book of the month, but of eternity!

Second, we will need **a personal guide.** I don't like to travel alone, especially if it's somewhere I have never been. This New Year is uncharted territory for us. We have never been this way before. It would be helpful to have an experienced guide to travel with us. There is Someone who is qualified to be our guide, the Holy Spirit. In John 14:16 we find our Lord's promise regarding the Holy Spirit: "I will ask the Father, and He will give you another Helper, that He may be with you forever." John 16:13 says, "But when the Spirit of truth comes, He will guide you into all the truth...." The Holy Spirit, who is Jesus in the Spirit, will be our guide, teacher, comforter, and friend as we travel throughout this New Year.

Third, we need **Christian friends** to make this trip courageously. Friends give to each other strength and encouragement. This is why we need the church. The church provides a fellowship to minister to one another. First Thessalonians 5:11 reads, "Therefore encourage one another and build up one another, just as you are doing." Charles Swindoll defines encouragement as "the art of inspiring others with renewed courage, spirit, or hope. When we encourage others we spur them on, we stimulate and affirm them."

Fourth, we will need **faith in God.** First John 5:4 reads, "For whatever is born of God overcomes the world; and this is the victory that has overcome the world – our faith." My favorite acrostic for the word F-A-I-T-H is, "For All I Trust Him." We can trust the Lord to always be there for us. Vance Havner wrote, "Faith has no value of its own, it has value only as it connects us with Him. It is a trick of Satan to get us occupied with examining our faith instead of resting in the Faithful One."[1] We may

---

[1] Dennis J. Hester, Compiler, *The Vance Havner Quote Book* (Grand Rapids: Baker Book House, 1986), 84.

not know what the future holds, but we know who holds the future. Enjoy the journey!

A LITTLE HUMOR: During the Christmas holidays a man walked up to the baggage check-in counter at the airport and saw a piece of mistletoe hanging right above the counter. He asked the clerk, "What's that for?" She replied, "That's so you can kiss your luggage good-bye!"

JANUARY 2

WHAT WE HAVE IS A COMMUNICATION PROBLEM

"Why do you not understand My speech? Because you are not able to listen to My Word." (John 8:43, NKJV)

A woman dialed the number of what she thought was the local record shop. A man answered. She asked, "Do you have 'Ten Little Fingers and Ten Little Toes in Alabama'?" The man had no idea that she was talking about a song. He said, "No, but I do have a wife and fifteen kids in Louisiana." She asked, "Is that a record?" He said, "I don't know if it is a record or not, but it sure is above average."

Communication — everybody's discussing it, studying it, practicing it. Yet, despite our improved communication skills, we may feel like the author who wrote, "I know that you believe you understand what you think I said, but I am not sure you realize that what you heard is not what I meant."

Good communication involves more than good speaking; it also requires good listening. Jesus, the master communicator, was often misunderstood. Although He spoke the truth clearly, His hearers jumbled up His message and then rejected it. "Why do you not understand My speech?" He quizzed them. Answering His own question, He replied, "Because you are not able to listen to My word" (John 8:43). Why were they such poor listeners? Not because Jesus failed to communicate but because they didn't want to hear the truth. And why didn't they? Because it made them face up to their need to change.

We have never really listened to Christ's words. We have never really taken His word and trusted that His way is the way to truth and to life. Even today, His voice is a still, small voice amid the noise of our time. But to those who will trust, Christ still speaks — words of counsel, words of forgiveness, words of hope but only to those who listen.

When we say, "God is getting through to me," it's not because He's communicating better but because we're hearing and willing to change. Let's always make listening to God one of our best communication skills.

A LITTLE HUMOR: A preacher walked up on the porch of a man chewing his tobacco and struck up a conversation with him. Always wanting to use every opportunity to witness to someone about the Lord, he asked him, "Are you a Christian?" The man replied, "No, the Christians live down the road about a mile." The preacher said, "Well, you don't really understand what I'm asking. Sir, are you lost?" "Lost?" he said, "why no. I've lived here all my life and I know right where I am." "No, no, said the preacher. "Are you ready for the judgment?" The old man said, "Well, when is it gonna be?" The preacher said, "Well, I don't rightly know. It might be today or it might be tomorrow." The old man said, "For heaven's sake, don't tell my wife. She'll want to go both days."

JANUARY 3

YOU GOTTA KILL THESE THINGS WHEN THEY'RE STILL SMALL

"Temptation comes from the lure of our own evil desires. These evil desires lead to evil actions, and evil actions lead to death." (James 1:14-15, NLT)

There is a silly story about a fellow who had spent his whole life in the desert. One day he came to visit a friend in town. The man who had lived in the desert had never seen a train or the tracks they run on. While standing in the middle of the railroad tracks one day, he heard this whistle – Whooee da Whoee! – but, he didn't recognize the sound as a train whistle. Predictably, he was hit – but only by a glancing blow – and he was thrown, head-over-heels, to the side of the tracks, with some minor internal injuries, a few broken bones, and some bruises.

After weeks in the hospital recovering, he was at his friend's house attending a party one evening. While in the kitchen, he suddenly heard the tea kettle whistling. He grabbed a baseball bat from the nearby closet and proceeded to batter and bash the tea kettle into an unrecognizable lump of metal. His friend, hearing the ruckus, rushed into the kitchen to see what had happened. He asked the man, "Why'd you ruin my good tea kettle?" The man replied, "Man, you gotta kill these things when they're small."[2]

That is the way sin is in our lives. Anger, resentment, self-destructive habits – we must deal with them while they are small – before we become captive to them. The Bible says, "If we confess our sins, He is faithful and just to forgive us our sins and to cleanse us from all unrighteousness" (1 John 1:9). Remember, too, the words of Jesus, "Most assuredly, I say to you, whoever commits sin is a slave to sin . . . Therefore if the Son makes you free, you shall be free indeed."(John 8:34, 36).

A LITTLE HUMOR: The Sunday School teacher had just concluded a review of the day's lesson. "And now, children," she inquired, "who can tell me what we must do before we can expect forgiveness of sin?" There was a pause, but finally one little boy spoke up. "Well," he mused, "first we've got to sin."

---

[2] *Dynamic Preaching*. October-December, 1998, Vol. 13, No. 4, page 59.

JANUARY 4

IT'S A JUNGLE OUT THERE!

"Be sober, be vigilant; because your adversary the devil walks about like a roaring lion, seeking whom he may devour." (1 Peter 5:8, NKJV)

Herb Caen of the *San Francisco Chronicle* once wrote, "Every morning in an African jungle, a gazelle wakes up. It knows it must run faster than the fastest lion or it will be killed. Every morning a lion wakes up. It knows it must outrun the slowest gazelle or it will starve to death. It doesn't matter whether you're a lion or a gazelle; when the sun comes up, you'd better be running!"

Animals in the wild realize that every day they are in a battle for their lives. We as Christians are also involved in a daily spiritual battle for our lives. First Peter 5:8 tells us that the devil is "like a roaring lion, seeking whom he may devour." The "whom" in this verse means us! The devil is the lion; we're the ones he's seeking to devour. God's plan to win the battle with Satan is revealed in James 4:7: "Submit yourselves therefore to God. Resist the devil, and he will flee from you."

How can we win this fierce and unrelenting battle? We can stand, we can walk, and we can run. First, **we can stand!** The Scriptures say, "Resist the devil, and he will flee from you." The word *resist* means to take your stand against the forces of evil. If you keep on resisting the devil he will flee from you. The Bible instructs us to "stand...withstand...stand" (Ephesians 6:10-13). Unless we stand, we cannot withstand. Our weapons are the Word of God and prayer (Ephesians 6:17-18), and our protection is the complete armor God has provided.

Second, **we can walk!** "Walk in the Spirit, and ye shall not fulfill the lust of the flesh" (Galatians 5:16). The word *walk* means keep on walking. A journey of a thousand miles begins with a single step. So it is with the Christian life. To walk in the Spirit is to live a life of continuous dependence upon the Lord.

Third, **we can run!** Paul wrote, "But put ye on the Lord Jesus Christ, and make not provision for the flesh, to fulfill the lust thereof" (Romans 13:14). The word *provision* suggests the idea of forethought. Don't give the flesh an opportunity to assert itself by putting yourself in a compromising situation. There is a time to fight and there is a time for flight. Joseph is a classic example of how to handle temptation in this way (Genesis 39:8-12). Sometimes the best resistance to temptation is a good pair of tennis shoes.

Interesting, isn't it? Either Satan will have you on the run, or you will have him on the run. This passage promises that if we submit ourselves to God and resist the devil, he will flee from us! Every morning when the sun comes up, you should take the offensive in your battle by surrendering control of your attitudes, thoughts and actions to Christ. Your spiritual survival depends on it.

A LITTLE HUMOR: A bruised and bleeding boxer staggered back to his corner after a tough round. His trainer splashed cold water on his face, stopped the bleeding, and rubbed him down while the manger spoke words of encouragement to him. The manager said, "Rocky, you're doing great. He hasn't laid a glove on you." Half dazed, the boxer looked up through glassy eyes and said, "If my opponent hasn't laid a hand on me, you'd better keep an eye on that referee because somebody out there is beating the daylights out of me."[3]

JANUARY 5

THE PEACE JESUS LEAVES

"Peace I leave with you, My peace I give to you; not as the world gives do I give to you. Let not your heart be troubled, neither let it be afraid." (John 14:27, NKJV)

My wife and I recently went on a British Airways airplane while on vacation. The captain was giving information and instructions before taking off. When he finished he said, "I will now leave you in peace." His remark reminded me of the words of Jesus, "Peace I leave with you." As those words filled my mind, the Lord gave me the following ideas about the peace that Jesus leaves each of His children.

First of all, there is the peace that comes at **CONVERSION.** Jesus is the Prince of Peace (Isaiah 9:6), and as such He is our peace (Ephesians 2:14). We who were once His enemies (Romans 5:10a) have been reconciled and are at peace with Him (Colossians 1:20).

Furthermore, His peace is produced in us by the power and presence of the **COMFORTER** who is the Holy Spirit (Galatians 5:22). Peace is not achieved by mental gymnastics. It is the work of the Holy Spirit as He controls that part of our being which the Bible calls the "spirit."

In addition, the peace Christ gives exceeds our **COMPREHENSION** (Philippians 4:6-7). Christ's peace is different from the world's peace. It goes beyond the understanding of the average person. It exceeds and surpasses all our own intellectual calculations and contemplations.

Finally, the peace Christ gives is developed by **CONCENTRATION**. Isaiah 26:3 states that the person who focuses his attention on the Lord will be given "perfect peace." The word "stayed" means "to lean on," "to rest upon," or "to support." The mind that is at peace is the mind that is supported by the Lord. We must discipline our minds to dwell on the Lord (Phil. 2:5; 4:8).

Vance Havner once said, "The world offers false peace to dull the senses, deaden the conscience, quiet the nerves, but it cannot give peace." That's exactly what Jesus meant: "My peace I give; not as the world gives . . . Let not your heart be troubled, neither let it be afraid." Do you have His peace?

---

[3] Paul W. Powell, *The Great Deceiver* (Nashville: Broadman Press, 1988), 11.

A LITTLE HUMOR: A man filling out an application in a factory was greatly perplexed at one question: "Person to notify in case of accident?" His decision: "Anybody in sight."[4]

JANUARY 6

HE WAS ASLEEP

"And do this, knowing the time, that now it is high time to awake out of sleep; for now our salvation is nearer than when we first believed." (Romans 13:11, NKJV)

Millions of people witnessed the swearing in of Barack Obama as the forty-fourth President of the United States of America. Tuesday, January 20, 2009, was a historical day for America because Barack Obama was the first African-American to become president. His election reminded me of another man who served as president, but it was one of the most unique in our nation's history.

President-elect Zachary Taylor (the 12th President of the United States, 1849-1850) was scheduled, according to the Constitution, to take office on March 4, but he refused to be inaugurated on that day. The fourth day of March fell on Sunday that year. Politicians pleaded in vain for the devoutly religious Taylor to change his mind. But Taylor wouldn't budge.

The Constitution forbade President James K. Polk from staying on another day. There was no alternative but for the Senate to elect a president to serve from Sunday noon to Monday noon, the time re-scheduled for Zachary Taylor to take office. The senators chose David Rice Atchison, head of the Senate to serve until Taylor was inaugurated.

The last week of the Polk administration was so hectic for Senator Atchison that he retired late Saturday evening after instructing his landlady "not to awaken him for any reason." She followed his orders. Senator Atchison slept through Sunday and on into Monday, past the time his twenty-four hours ended. The startling truth is that Atchison slept through his entire term of office!

The Bible admonishes us to take advantage of opportunities when they come our way. Paul wrote, "Awake, O sleeper. . . Make the most of every opportunity for doing good in these evil days" (Ephesians 5:14, 16, NLT). We each have a limited amount of time on this earth. Paul exhorts us to use as much of that time as possible for advancing Christ's purposes in this world. Don't sleep through your opportunity.

---

[4] Tal D. Bonham, *Another Treasury of Clean Jokes* (Nashville: Broadman Press, 1983), 19

A LITTLE HUMOR: In the days of the Puritans, when worship services lasted for hours and churches were not air conditioned, worshippers sometimes found it difficult to stay awake the entire service. So, churches had a man who often walked through the congregation with a long pole with a glass knob on the end. When worshippers began to nod, he would reach over with the pole, and using the glass knob, give them a solid thump on the head. One Sunday he thumped a nodding worshipper on the head, the man rose up, shook his head, and said, "Hit me again, I can still hear him."[5]

JANUARY 7

WHAT'S YOUR LOAD LIMIT?

"No temptation has overtaken you except such as is common to man; but God is faithful, who will not allow you to be tempted beyond what you are able, but with the temptation will also make the way of escape, that you may be able to bear it." (1 Corinthians 10:13, NKJV)

We've all seen load-limit signs on highways, bridges, and elevators. Knowing that too much strain can cause severe damage or complete collapse, engineers determine the exact amount of stress various materials and manufactured items can safely endure. Posted warnings tell us not to exceed the maximum load.

Human beings also have their load limits, which vary from person to person. Some people, for example can bear the pressure of trials and temptations better than others; yet everyone has a breaking point and can take only so much. British writer Oscar Wilde summed up the attitude of millions when he said, "I can resist anything except temptation." Unfortunately, resisting temptation has gone out of style in favor of "doing what comes naturally."

At times, circumstances and people seem to be pushing us beyond what we can bear. But the Lord knows our limitations and never allows any difficulties to enter our lives that exceed our strength and ability to endure. This is especially true when we're enticed to sin.

So when trials and temptations press down on you, take courage! Remember, your heavenly Father knows the limit of your ability to stand up under life's pressures. Someone has said, "If you give in to God, you won't cave in to sin." So draw upon His strength. No temptation will ever be greater than that!

A LITTLE HUMOR: "I have to have a raise," the man said to his boss. "Three other companies are after me." "Is that so?" asked the boss." What other companies are after you?" The man replied: "The electric company, the telephone company, and the gas company."

---

[5] Paul W. Powell, *A Funny Thing Happened on the Way to Retirement* (Tyler, Texas, 2000), 19.

JANUARY 8

DON'T BE LIKE OLD JOE

"Not forsaking the assembling of ourselves together, as is the manner of some, but exhorting one another and so much the more as you see the Day approaching."
(Hebrews 10:25, NKJV)

Do you bathe? On a regular basis? Here are ten reasons why one person said he never took a bath.

1. I was forced to wash as a child.
2. People who wash are hypocrites. They think they're cleaner than others.
3. There are so many kinds of soap. I could never decide which was right.
4. I used to wash, but it got boring.
5. I wash only on Christmas or Easter.
6. None of my friends wash.
7. I'll start washing when I'm older.
8. I really don't have time.
9. The bathroom isn't warm enough.
10. People who make soap are only after your money.

Silly excuses, aren't they? What about excuses for not going to church? Do you go to church? On a regular basis? If you don't, what are your excuses? They probably make about as much sense as the excuses the poor fellow above gave for not taking a bath.

When you were born into the family of God, you were a spiritual "baby." There are at least four things that an infant requires: food, fresh air, exercise and the help of others.

This is also true in the spiritual realm. We need *food* (the study of God's Word), *fresh air* (communion and prayer), *exercise* (service and witnessing), and *help* (fellowship with others). Any child of God who neglects any of these four things cannot expect to be well-rounded in his Christian life and experience.

All his life, Old Joe had never gone to church; no matter how much he was coaxed, he could never be persuaded to attend even on Christmas and Easter. "When it freezes in June," he would say, "then I'll go to church." One year it was unusually cold and stayed that way until late spring. The first part of June the mercury dipped to freezing for several nights. Everyone thought about Old Joe and what he had said. Perhaps this spell of cold weather would force him to attend church. It did! One Sunday Old Joe made his first appearance in church — while the organ played softly — six men carried him in! Don't be like Old Joe!

A LITTLE HUMOR: The only time the pastor ever sees some people in church is when they are hatched, matched, or dispatched!

JANUARY 9

A CHRISTIAN MADE OF IRON

"Above all, taking the shield of faith with which you will be able to quench all the fiery darts of the wicked one." (Ephesians 6:16, NKJV)

A spiritual war has been raging between good and evil ever since Adam and Eve disobeyed God and ate of the forbidden fruit (Genesis 3). Every day Christians are a part of that conflict. Satan and his demons fight against all believers. Satan never lets us rest. He never takes a day off. He never gets tired attacking. As believers, we must be alert constantly. We never know when he may attack.

On August 19, 1812, the U. S. Navy frigate *Constitution* earned the nickname *Old Ironsides*. During the War of 1812 the *Constitution* captured no less than a dozen British ships, and the success of the ship against the mighty British Navy was a tremendous morale booster for the young American navy. While the forty-four-gun frigate was engaged in battle with the *HMS Guerriere* off the coast of Nova Scotia, British cannonballs appeared to bounce off her thick wooden sides. An unidentified sailor exclaimed, "Her sides are made of iron." The inability of the eighteen pound British cannonballs to penetrate the sides of the *Constitution* was due to the fact that her hull, comprised of three layers of live oak (one of the most durable woods in the world), was twenty-five inches thick at the waterline.

Daily the devil bombards the believer. He hurls at us everything he can to get us to yield to temptation. He has but one objective – to sink us. Yet, clothed in the Armor of God "the fiery darts of the wicked one" do not hurt us. The believer is given a shield of faith to deflect all that is "fired" at him. Whether the attack of Satan comes as small as a "fiery dart" or as large as a cannonball, it is essential that we be properly protected. To face the enemy without the Armor of God is a sure recipe for defeat. Let us put on the Armor of God. Let the enemy be heard to say, "There's a Christian made of iron."

A LITTLE HUMOR: There was a man who was a chronic procrastinator. When asked why, he replied, "I inherited procrastination from my ancestors. They procrastinated so much that when they came to the New World, they arrived on the "Juneflower."

JANUARY 10

CALMING ANGER DOWN

"Wise people calm anger down." (Proverbs 29:8b, NCV)

In a west Texas town a few years ago, employees in a medium-sized warehouse noticed the smell of gas. Sensibly, management evacuated the building, extinguishing all potential sources of ignition – lights, power, etc.

After the building had been evacuated, two technicians from the gas company were dispatched. Upon entering the building, they found they had difficulty navigating in the dark. To their frustration, none of the lights worked.

It is assumed that one of the technicians reached into his pocket for a lighter, lit the lighter causing an explosion, sending pieces of it up to three miles away. Nothing was found of the technicians, but the lighter was virtually untouched by the explosion. The technician suspected of causing the explosion had never been thought to be as "bright" as his peers.

Years ago, Jim Croce, in his song, "You Don't Mess Around with Jim," used to sing about things that you don't dare do (pull the mask off the Lone Ranger, tug on Superman's cape, or spit into the wind). He might have done well to add, "You don't flick your BIC inside a building with a gas leak." In an explosive situation, the last thing you want to do is provide the spark.

We've all been around those kinds of situations (not literally, but figuratively) – where someone was angry, and it wouldn't take much to create an explosion. We have two choices in that setting, described by Solomon in this way: "A gentle answer will calm a person's anger, but an unkind answer will cause more anger" (Proverbs 15:1, NCV). I admire those people who have a calming effect on those around them, gently stifling the flames of anger before they burst into flames. "Wise people calm anger down" (Proverbs 29:8b, NCV). May God help us all to be wise.

A LITTLE HUMOR: Chicago Cubs outfielder Andre Dawson paid a $1,000 fine for disputing a strike called by umpire Joe West. On the memo line of his check Dawson wrote: "Donation for the blind."

JANUARY 11

UNLIMITED FORGIVENESS

"How often shall my brother sin against me and I forgive him? . . . up to seventy times seven." (Matthew 18:21-22, NASB)

One of my favorite comedians was the late Red Skelton. His characters included Clem Kadiddlehopper, Freddie the Freeloader, The Mean Widdle Kid, and the cross-eyed seagulls, Gertrude and Heathcliffe. His goal in life was to be known as a clown and to make people laugh. He always concluded his television show with his trademark line: "Good night, and God bless."

As funny as he was as a clown, in real life his was the story of a sad and lonely man who trusted no one and felt he had been cheated by some of his associates. "When anyone hurts us, my wife and I sit in our Japanese sand garden and drink iced tea," Skelton told *The New York Times* in 1977. "There are five stones in the garden – for sky, wind, fire, water and earth. We sit and think of five of the nicest things we can about the person who hurt us. If he hurts us a second time, we do the same thing. The third time, we light a candle, and he is, for us, dead."

This is not the forgiveness that Jesus spoke of in Matthew 18. True forgiveness does not put a limit on how often it is willing to forgive. Charles Swindoll has written: "Forgiveness is not an elective in the curriculum of life. It is a required course, and the exams are always tough to pass." C. H. Spurgeon spoke this great truth about forgiveness: "We must go to the cross to learn how to be forgiven. And we must stay there long enough to learn how to be forgiving."

A LITTLE HUMOR: A young boy picked the preacher up in the family horse cart for dinner and a visit at his parents' home. When asked what was on the menu, the boy replied, "Buzzard." "Buzzard?" the preacher asked, "Are you sure?" "Yep," the youngster replied. "I heard Maw tell Paw we was having that old buzzard for dinner tonight!"

JANUARY 12

CALLING ON THE LORD FOR SALVATION

"For whoever calls on the name of the Lord shall be saved." (Romans 10:13, NKJV)

Saturday, January 12, 2008, will be a date that I will always remember. It was on that date that I had the privilege of talking with my granddaughter, Samantha, about Jesus and to lead her in saying a prayer, asking Jesus to come into her life that she might be saved from her sins and have the assurance of eternal life. It was a most wonderful experience for her and me and for all the host of heaven too, for Luke 15:7 says, "I say to you that likewise there will be more joy in heaven over one sinner who repents than over ninety-nine just persons who need no repentance."

Now, Samantha wasn't a terrible sinner, but she was a sinner, just as you and I are. Sin is not knowing God; not caring about God, and wanting to do things our way rather than God's way. The Bible says all of us have sinned and fallen short of God's glory (Romans 3:23). Jesus died on the cross to save us from our sins (1 Corinthians 15:3), and when we call on Him to save us He does (Romans 10:9-10, 13).

I talked with my son, Samantha's father, later and he said as they were driving back home that Samantha asked if she could tell her friends what she had done. Of course, she could. All of us who have come to know Christ as Savior should share the good news with others that they might come to know Christ, too.

How about you? Have you asked Jesus to save you from your sins? That's what He came to do. He loves you. He died on the cross for you. And He will forgive you of your sins and transform your life. If you have not been saved, I encourage you to call on Him today. As the Bible says, "God is ready to help you right now. Today is the day of salvation" (2 Corinthians 6:3b, NLT).

A LITTLE HUMOR: A little girl was praying: "Dear God, I hope you take care of yourself. Because if anything happens to you, we would all be in a terrible mess."

JANUARY 13

ARE YOU HUNGRY?

"Blessed are they which do hunger and thirst after righteousness: for they shall be filled." (Matthew 5:6, KJV)

Ostriches are very unusual birds. They're great big and tall, about eight feet tall and weigh as much as 345 pounds. They are the largest living birds in existence today. Unlike most birds, ostriches can't fly. Their wings are too small. But ostriches can run very fast. Its long legs can carry it in 15-foot steps at speeds up to 40 miles per hour. Sometimes, for no reason at all, the ostrich will start running around in a circle. Its speed and its unusual good eyesight help the ostrich escape from its enemies, which are mainly lions and men.

There's something else ostriches do that is pretty unusual. They'll eat almost anything. Ostriches prefer to eat grass and fruit, but they'll also eat small rocks, pieces of glass, little mirrors, pieces of jewelry, just about anything they can get in their mouth. And all these strange foods don't seem to hurt ostriches. They would be very bad for you and me, but they're not too bad for the ostrich.

We laugh at the ostrich for eating everything it sees, even things that are bad for it, but we are just as guilty of taking bad things into our lives. We may not put bad things in our mouth and eat them, but we still take in bad stuff. When we listen to gossip and bad language, we're taking in bad stuff through our ears. When we watch TV shows or movies that have a lot of meanness or bad stuff in them, then we're taking in bad things with our eyes. And when we let sin into our hearts, and don't try to stop it, then we're taking bad things into our hearts.[6]

We are unlike each other in many ways: our fingerprints, personalities, color of hair and skin, family background, education, IQ, weight, and height. All differ in some degree. But all nations, races, families, and individuals are alike in one respect: all hunger and thirst. Jesus chose this common denominator to illustrate the fourth Beatitude: "Blessed are they which do hunger and thirst after righteousness: for they shall be filled" (Matthew 5:6, KJV). Jesus pronounced a blessing on those "who hunger and thirst for righteousness" and promises that "they will be filled."

In Greek mythology King Tantalus was punished for offending the gods. He was placed in a lake where the water reached his chin but receded when he tried to drink. Over his head hung branches of choice fruit, which likewise receded when he reached out to pick some. Tantalus became the symbol for teasing, and his name is the root of our verb tantalize.[7]

Not so in relationship to God. The promise is unqualified. Those who hunger, eat. Those who thirst, drink. God does not tease; He refuses to tantalize. His blessings are achievable and satisfying

A LITTLE HUMOR: Our favorite text at church is, "Bless the Lord, oh my soul, and all that is within me. Bless his holy name." Our favorite hymns are: "When the Rolls are Served up Yonder We'll Be There," and "God Be With You Till We Eat Again."

---

[6] *Dynamic Preaching.* January - March, 1999, Vol. 14, No. 1, 78.

[7] Robert J. Hastings, *Take Heaven Now!,* (Nashville: Broadman Press, 1968), 67.

JANUARY 14

WEAK HANDS, FEEBLE KNEES, AND LAME FEET

"Strengthen the hands that are weak and the knees that are feeble, and make straight paths for your feet, so that the limb which is lame may not be out of joint, but rather be healed." (Hebrews 12:12-13, NASB)

The context of our Scripture describes an individual running in a race. However, the runner is not in shape to run the race well. There are many believers that are spiritually out of shape. Their spiritual health is not well. In the words of verse 13, they need to be "healed."

In his devotional commentary on the book of Hebrews, William Barclay writes, "With this passage the writer to the Hebrews comes to the problems of everyday Christian life and living. He knew that sometimes it is given to a man to mount up with wings as an eagle; he knew that sometimes a man is unable to run and not be weary in the pursuit of some great moment of endeavor; but he also knew that of all things it is hardest to walk every day not to faint. In this passage he is thinking of the daily life and struggle of the Christian way."[8]

"Weak hands," or hands that "hang down" (NKJV) refers to a person who is beaten down, defeated, discouraged, and despondent. Who is there among us that doesn't get discouraged at times? We are told that one American in twenty is medically diagnosed as suffering from depression.

"Feeble knees" refers to one whose strength is depleted. The word *feeble* is translated sick of the palsy in Matthew 8:6, and there it speaks of one who is too weak to stand. Could this describe the spiritual condition you are in as a believer in Christ?

"Lame feet" speaks of a person who has a serious limp. He can barely walk much less run. The words *out of joint* mean to turn or twist out. The words speak of that which is out of joint, such as a dislocated hip, shoulder, etc. Perhaps the runner has tripped or stumbled over something in or on the track he was running. Is there anything in your life that could cause you to stumble? A habit? A temptation? Something you are watching? Something you are doing?

As a runner in the race of life, what kind of shape are you in? Are you running well? If your hands are hanging, if your knees are feeble, if your feet are lame, you need to come to the Great Physician and be healed.

A LITTLE HUMOR: A cross-country runner, suffering from a sudden spell of dizziness, stopped to sit a minute with his head resting on his knees. "Have you vertigo?" asked a curious passerby. "Yes! Two more miles," he said.

---

[8] William Barclay, "The Letter to the Hebrews" in *The Daily Study Bible* (Philadelphia: The Westminster Press, 1957), 204.

JANUARY 15

STANDING ON THE ROCK

"All drank the same spiritual drink, for they were drinking from a spiritual rock which followed them, and the rock was Christ." (1 Corinthians 10:4, NASB)

There is a scene in the action-packed movie, *Indiana Jones and the Last Crusade,* in which Indy's quest is to find the Holy Grail, the original chalice used by Christ at the Last Supper. In order to prove himself pure in heart, Indy must face life-threatening challenges that test his humility, his obedience, and his faith.

In the final challenge, Indy finds himself teetering on the brink of a deep, vast chasm. The way across, according to the legend, lies right before him. The problem is he cannot see it. He must step out in faith, with no tangible assurance of support. He must trust what his eyes cannot see. Fearful, but determined, Indy steps out and discovers himself standing on a rock bridge, solid and firm beneath his feet, but invisible to the eye.

Edward Mote loved his work as a cabinetmaker. For years he had worked for wages, but he eventually owned his own shop. He also had a hobby. He enjoyed writing articles and at times, poems. One Sunday he visited the home of a minister whose wife was near death. Groping for consoling words, he thought of a poem he had written. He quoted the lines to the dying woman, and at the conclusion of each verse he added his key line, "On Christ, the solid Rock, I stand; All other ground is sinking sand."[9]

When times and events challenge us, we Christians have a Rock on which to stand. That Rock is Jesus (1 Corinthians 10:4). I've stood on that rock, haven't you? Anyone who's ever trusted Christ for salvation has discovered Christ to be the solid Rock they needed. Anyone who's ever sat in a doctor's office and said, "Lord, I'm scared, but I'm turning this over to you. I know whatever comes I will always be under your watchful care," knows what it is to step out on that unseen bridge. It comes to us sooner or later, and it is then we discover whether or not we have faith in God. Once we've stepped out onto that Rock we can say with Edward Mote, "On Christ the Solid Rock, I stand; All other ground is sinking sand."

A LITTLE HUMOR: Life is going by too fast. It has even affected the animal kingdom. Three snails mugged a turtle. When someone asked the turtle what they looked like, the turtle said, "I don't know; it all happened so fast."

[9] Clint Bonner, *A Hymn is Born* (Nashville: Broadman Press, 1959), 68-69.

JANUARY 16

CLEAN UP YOUR GARBAGE

"If anyone considers himself religious and yet does not keep a tight rein on his tongue, he deceives himself and his religion is worthless." (James 1:26, NIV)

The National Park Service has discovered a way to keep bear incidents under control in Yellowstone and Glacier National Parks. They removed the garbage dumps that attracted bears. Now the parks offer stern warnings to tourists and campers: "Clean up your garbage and remove food items from your picnic table when you're through eating." This strategy keeps grizzly bears away. The way to control the bear problem is to control the garbage problem that incites it.

In the same way, cleaning up the garbage dump in your heart leads to controlled speech. We won't speak angry words if coveting, envy, anger, and jealousy are absent. Overcoming this problem takes more than the resolve to count to ten before opening your mouth; it takes cleaning sinful attitudes from your heart. Someone has said, "The most dangerous animal in the world has its den behind your teeth."

The Bible says, "If anyone considers himself religious and yet does not keep a tight rein on his tongue, he deceives himself and his religion is worthless" (James 1:26, NIV). The word *worthless* can be translated with six different English words: vain, empty, useless, futile, fruitless, or powerless. All of these English words suggest the same conclusion: a religion which does not control the tongue counts for nothing. The control of the tongue is the barometer which measures Christian maturity. Jesus expressed this idea. He said, "For out of the overflow of the heart the mouth speaks" (Matthew 12:34, NIV). The words "out of the overflow of the heart" indicate that a person's words reveal his or her character ("heart" referring to the inner person). The genuineness of our religion is manifest in the way we control our tongues.

The old country doctor always began his examination by saying, "Let me see your tongue." The tongue can reveal a lot about a person's character as well as his physical health. It is a good way to start the examination of anybody. "He, who guards his mouth and his tongue, keeps himself from calamity" (Proverbs 21:23, NIV). Cleaning out the garbage that's in one's heart is a good way to bring the tongue under control.

A LITTLE HUMOR: One woman said to a friend, "She told me you told her a secret I told you not to tell her." The friend responded, "I told her not to tell you I told her." "Well," the other lady responded, "let's just not tell her I told you she told me you told her."

JANUARY 17

A LITTLE KINDNESS GOES A LONG WAY

"Be kind to one another . . ." (Ephesians 4:32a, NKJV)

A man went into a roadside diner for breakfast. A cranky waitress came out, her hands on her hips, and demanded, "What do you want?" "Well," the man said, "I'd like some eggs and a few kind words." Speechless, the waitress just glared at the man and went back to the kitchen. After a few minutes, she came out with a plate of eggs and slapped the mess down in front of him. Looking first at the eggs and then back up at her, the man asked, "And where are my kind words?" "Don't eat them eggs," the waitress answered saucily and pranced back to the kitchen.

Everyone — including this man who just wanted some kindness with his breakfast — longs for kind words. A little kindness goes a long way in making an eternal impact for Christ. The Bible says, "Since you have been chosen by God who has given you this new kind of life, and because of His deep love and concern for you, you should practice tenderhearted mercy and kindness" (Colossians 3:12, LB).

A recent issue of *US News and World Report* reminded readers that this year is the 15th anniversary of the "Random Acts of Kindness" movement. In 1993, a Bakersfield College professor named Chuck Wall challenged his class to do a random act of kindness. Even churches took up the cause with significant results. Wall today reminds people that even the simplest acts can have a gigantic effect.

Every day we have many opportunities to treat others the way we would like to be treated. Let us live unselfishly today, so that as we close our eyes in sleep tonight, we can do so with the satisfaction that comes from showing kindness to others. A little kindness can go a long way.

A LITTLE HUMOR: There are two times when a man doesn't understand a woman — before marriage and after marriage.

JANUARY 18

A LIVE BOMB

"You shall not commit adultery." (Exodus 20:14, NASB)

For two weeks, Allen Gordon was a living bomb. He was on board a destroyer in the battle for the Coral Seas. An enemy plane was scraping the ship, and a 50-millimeter shell went into his chest, down through his stomach, and lodged in his hip. It was a live shell, five inches in length that did not explode.

A sign was placed across his chest that read: CAUTION: LIVE 50-MM SLUG INSIDE. He was placed in a hammock-like contraption and through rough seas, transported from the destroyer to a hospital ship. From there he was taken to New Caledonia. They waited two weeks while conducting an extensive study of his situation. Specialists were brought in and the shell was removed from Gordon's hip.

After the live shell was removed it was put in a gun and fired. It exploded when it went through a piece of tissue paper. It was that delicate and that dangerous.

Inside every person is a live shell, a live bomb. That bomb that is so explosive is the sex drive. When God created life, he gave us various desires and instincts such as the drive for food, water, and procreation. These are normal, God-given desires. But in our society we have taken the sex drive and have so distorted it that it has been driven out of proportion.

The eighth commandment states that we should not commit adultery. The word *adultery* means to contaminate, corrupt, debase, or make impure by the addition of a foreign or inferior substance. The sexual desire is God-given and should be enjoyed in the context of a marriage relationship of a husband and wife. Hebrews 13:4 reads, "Marriage is to be held in honor among all, and the marriage bed is to be undefiled; for fornication and adulterers God will judge" (Hebrews 13:4). The sexual desire is a "live bomb" and must be handled properly with the upmost care.

A LITTLE HUMOR: A young couple planning to marry met with the minister who was to perform their wedding ceremony. While filling out the form the minster required of them, the young man read aloud a few of the questions. When he got to the last one, which read, "Are you entering this marriage at your own will?" he looked over at his fiancée. "Put down, 'Yes'," she said.

JANUARY 19

A DEBT WE CANNOT PAY

"And the lord of that slave felt compassion and released him and forgave him the debt." (Matthew 18:27, NASB)

When Yahaya Wahab's father passed away in January of 2006, Yahaya cancelled his father's phone line and paid the final bill of 84 ringgit (approximately $23). Consequently, he was mildly surprised to receive another letter from Telekom Malaysia in April of 2006. He was completely and utterly shocked, however, after opening that letter. In fact, he said later that he almost fainted.

Inside was a bill for 806,400,000,000,000.01 ringgit, which is approximately $218 trillion. Also inside was a threatening letter, informing Yahaya that he must pay the bill within 10 days or face prosecution. It wasn't initially clear whether the monstrous charge was a mistake or if Yahaya's father's line had been used illegally after his death. What was immediately clear, however, was that the bill represented a debt that Yahaya would never be able to pay.

In His parable about forgiveness, Jesus talked about the inability of an individual to pay a debt he owed to the king. Out of the kindness of his heart the king forgave the man of his entire debt. There are several spiritual applications that come out of this parable but the main one is that we had a sin debt that we could not pay and God had compassion on us, sent His Son, the Lord Jesus Christ, to pay our debt by dying for us on the cross. When we turn to Him and ask for forgiveness for our sins, He graciously marks "Paid in Full" across our sins. We had a debt we could not pay; He paid a debt He did not owe! Hallelujah, what a Savior!

A LITTLE HUMOR: A long-winded preacher entered the pulpit with a bandage on his chin. Before beginning the sermon, he explained to the congregation: "When I was shaving this morning I was thinking about my sermon and cut my face." After the service one of his deacons said to him, "Next Sunday when you are shaving, I hope you will concentrate on your shaving and cut your sermon."

JANUARY 20

A GOOD WAY TO START

"And in the early morning, while it was still dark, He arose and went out and departed to a lonely place, and was praying there." (Mark 1:35, NASB)

Howie Childs, a retired minister, tells the story of how he learned to ice-skate on a frozen pond in Michigan. He and his son went out to the pond shortly before dusk hoping that no one in the neighborhood would see them learning to skate. They drove the car practically to the edge of the ice. Howie put his skates on while sitting in the front seat of the car. When he was ready he hollered to his son, "Are you ready to go?" His son said, "Dad, you go first."

Like many people Howie learned something about skating in an ice-skating arena. When you learn to ice-skate in an arena you begin by holding onto the rails. But on a frozen pond in Michigan there are no rails to hold onto. So Howie was thinking, "How do I get started? Maybe by holding onto the side of the car and giving myself a push." So he pushes off from the car and guess what happens? He lands flat on his behind. He tries to get up but can't — his feet keep slipping every which-way, and there are no rails to grab onto to help pull him up.

Just then some neighborhood kids from the church come by. They have been watching Howie struggling in vain to get back up on his feet. Finally, one boy shouts, "Preacher, if you want to stay up and skate, you have to get on your knees first."

That is not only good advice for ice-skating. It is also an important lesson for starting each day with the Lord's blessings. If we want to have a great day in the Lord, we must learn to start the day on our knees. Meeting the Lord early in the morning allows us the opportunity to spend some time with Him before activities of the day can interfere. This apparently was the practice of Jesus Himself.

It is good to seek the Lord early each day. The Lord Himself says, "I love them that love me, and those that seek me early shall find me" (Proverbs 8:17, KJV). "My voice You shall hear in the morning, O Lord; in the morning I will direct it to You, and I will look up" (Psalm 5:3, NKJV). If you want to stand up and stay up you have to begin the day on your knees.

A LITTLE HUMOR: An elderly woman was sitting next to a preacher on a plane and getting increasingly nervous about the thunderstorm raging outside. She turned to him and said: "Reverend, you are a man of God. Why can't you do something about this weather?" "Lady," he replied, "I'm in sales, not management."

JANUARY 21

A LAUGHING MATTER

"A merry heart does good, like medicine." (Proverbs 17:22, NKJV)

Robert Holden, a stress consultant, says a good belly-laugh exercises most of your body's muscles. Laughter releases certain chemicals throughout the system that serve as natural pain-killers and relaxants. A good chuckle also reduces muscle tension, restores a free breathing pattern, and gently expands circulation.

As far as we know, humans are the only creatures of God who enjoy humor. Laughter is a distinctive reaction of human beings. Hadden Robinson writes, "Laughter also can tell something about you. Show me what amuses you, and I can make a good guess about the sort of person you are. If you laugh at filthy stories, you give yourself away. If you scoff at virtue, you have embraced vice. If you laugh at another's failure or misfortune, you have a cruel streak inside of you. If you can laugh at your own stupidities and mistakes, you handle life with some skill."

I believe Christians have a greater capacity to enjoy healthy laughter than others. After all, we live with the promise of eternal life and with the knowledge that God can use even our setbacks to move us forward.

Proverbs 15:13 tells us that "a merry heart makes a cheerful countenance" (NKJV), and the Bible tells us to laugh for medicinal purposes: "A merry heart does good, like medicine" (Proverbs 17:22, NKJV). The Bible also says that the laughter of fools who are living only for this life is like the "crackling of thorns" that are burned in the fire (Ecclesiastes 7:6, NKJV). The "crackling of thorns" is drawn from the use of hay, stubble, and thorns for fuel. A fire of such material burned up more quickly than charcoal, but then it also died out quickly and left nothing but cold dead ashes. So it would be with frivolous laughter. It falls into the category of vanities.

Texas minister and educator William E. Thorn says: "Stop taking yourself so seriously. Some cannot see the humor in any situation. Humor is a good means of relieving tension, dispelling fear, and cooling anger. Try to develop humor as a personal trait. It will keep you from an overestimation of your own importance." Thorn quotes the Psalmist, "Then our mouth was filled with laughter, and our tongue with singing. Then they said among the nations, 'The Lord has done great things for them'." (Psalm 126:2, NKJV).

A Norwegian proverb says, "He who laughs — lasts." So, make it a point to indulge in at least one hearty laugh every day. If nothing funny comes along, laugh at yourself.

A LITTLE HUMOR: A small child with a bad cough was taken by her parents to a hospital emergency room. A nurse, examining the child's lungs with a stethoscope, told the child, "I have to see if Barney is in there." "I have Jesus in my heart," the child replied. "Barney is on my underwear."

JANUARY 22

A LOOK OF FAITH

"As Moses lifted up the serpent in the wilderness, even so must the Son of Man be lifted up; that whoever believes may in Him have eternal life. For God so loved the world, that He gave His only Son, that whoever believes in Him should not perish, but have eternal life." (John 3:14-16, NASB)

The whole world has been bitten by sin, and "the wages of sin is death" (Romans 6:23). God sent His Son to die for the whole world. How is a person born from above? How is he or she saved from eternal perishing? We are saved by believing on Jesus Christ. We must look to Him in faith.

On January 6, 1850, a snowstorm almost crippled the city of Colchester, England, and a teenage boy was unable to get to the church he usually attended. So he made his way to a nearby Primitive Methodist chapel, where an ill-prepared layman was substituting for the absent preacher. His text was Isaiah 45:22 – "Look unto Me, and be ye saved, all the ends of the earth." For many months this young teenager had been miserable and under deep conviction; though he had been reared in church (both his father and grandfather were preachers), he did not have the assurance of salvation.

The unprepared substitute minister did not have much to say, so he kept repeating the text. "A man need not go to college to learn to look," he shouted. "Anyone can look – a child can look!" About that time, he saw the visitor sitting to one side, and he pointed at him and said, "Young man, you look very miserable. Young man, look to Jesus Christ!" The young man did look by faith, and that was how the great preacher Charles Haddon Spurgeon was converted."

What happened to Spurgeon and many others can happen to you. If you have never repented of your sins and turned to Jesus Christ and placed your faith in Him, you can do that now and know the blessed assurance that your look of faith at Jesus Christ will mean eternal salvation for you. If you haven't done so, do it today! Look to Jesus and be saved!

A LITTLE HUMOR: Saint Peter greeted three doctors at the pearly gates and asked why he should let them into heaven. When the heart surgeon said he had saved over 600 lives, St. Peter said, "Okay." When the orthopedic surgeon said he had repaired the bones of thousands of children, St. Peter said "Okay." When the director of a health maintenance organization said that his organization had serviced more than 75,000 people, St. Peter said, "Okay, but you may only stay for three days!"

JANUARY 23

BUILDING SPIRITUAL MUSCLES

"Physical exercise has some value, but spiritual exercise is much more important." (1 Timothy 4:8, NLT)

Fitness guru Jack LaLanne, who inspired television viewers for decades to trim down, eat well, and pump iron long before diet and exercise became a national obsession, died January 23, 2011. He was ninety-six. When he turned forty-three, he performed more than one thousand push-ups in twenty-three minutes on the "You Asked for It" television show. At age sixty he swam from Alcatraz Island to Fisherman's Wharf in San Francisco – handcuffed, shackled and towing a boat. He maintained a youthful physique and joked in 2006: "I can't afford to die. It would wreck my image." His daily routine usually consisted of two hours of weightlifting and an hour in the swimming pool.

We ought to care for our bodies, and exercise is part of that care. Our bodies are God's temples to be used for His glory (1 Cor. 6:19-20) and His tools for His service (Romans 12:1-2). But bodily exercise benefits us only during this life; godly exercise is profitable now and for eternity. Paul did not ask Timothy to choose between the two. I think God expects us to do both. A healthy body can be used of God, but we must major on holiness.

The Greek word for exercise is *gumnazo* from which we get our English words gymnasium or gymnastics. It paints a picture of a strenuous workout routine. Just as a football squad goes through calisthenics, there are spiritual exercises that we ought to do: prayer, meditation, daily Bible reading, self-examination, fellowship, service, sacrifice, submission to God's will, and witnessing. All of these can assist us through the Holy Spirit to become more Godly.

A LITTLE HUMOR: A retired couple decided they should walk two miles a day to stay in shape. They chose to walk a mile out on a lonely country road so they would have no choice but to walk back. At the one-mile mark on their first venture, the man asked his wife, "Do you think you can make it back all right, or are you too tired?" "Oh, no," she said. "I'm not tired. I can make it fine." "Good," he replied. "I'll wait here. You go back, get the car, and come get me."

JANUARY 24

A REMARKABLE BOOK

"Above all, you must understand that no prophecy in Scripture ever came from the prophets themselves or because they wanted to prophecy. It was the Holy Spirit who moved the prophets to speak from God."(2 Peter 1:20-21, NLT)

A recent trip to New York City gave my wife and me our first opportunity to see the Statue of Liberty. What a breathtaking experience! The Statue of Liberty, which stands in New York Harbor, was made in Paris, France. It was cast in many parts of various sizes and shapes. When these parts were brought to America and assembled, the result was a statue of stately beauty. This was not unusual in that all of the parts were cast in a single place and were fashioned with the idea of forming one statue.

But suppose these parts had been fashioned by many men, living in different places during different periods of time, and with no common purpose. And suppose that when all these parts were brought together, they fit one into another to make a beautiful statue. That would have been highly unusual, in fact, it would have been miraculous. So it is with the Bible.

The Bible is made up of sixty-six different books that were written over 1600 years by more than forty different authors, and many of those who wrote did not have access to what the others had written. Yet the Bible is a united book. It is bound up in a common theme, the eternal purpose of God for the redemption of sinful man. It has a unity that is absolutely astonishing. One of the strongest arguments for the validity of the Bible is its unity.

Someone has written that "the doctrines of the Bible are holy, its precepts are binding, its histories are true, and its decisions are immutable. We read it to be wise, believe it to be safe, and practice it to be holy. Christ is its grand subject, our good its design, and the glory of God its end." The Statue of Liberty is a symbol of our freedom. Likewise, the Bible tells us that true freedom is found in Christ (John 8:36). The Bible is indeed a remarkable book!

A LITTLE HUMOR: A new preacher came to town and people walked by to greet him after the sermon. One lady came out and said, "You are something else." The next Sunday, she did the same thing, and the next again. Time after time, she would stop and say, "You are something else." He began to wonder what she meant by that. So one day, he asked one of his deacons if he knew. The deacon said he didn't but suggested that the preacher ask the lady what she meant. So the next Sunday, she walked out and said, "You are something else." He said, "I've heard you say that many times. What do you mean by it?" She replied, "You must be something else, because you're sure not much of a preacher."

JANUARY 25

A SENSE OF WHAT IS VITAL

"It is my prayer that your love may grow richer and richer in knowledge and perfect insight, so that you may have a sense of what is vital." (Philippians 1:9-10, Goodspeed)

There was once a man who wrote an epitaph for his tomb, "Born – a human being; died – a wholesale grocer." Here was his explanation, "I was so busy selling groceries that I did not have time to get married and have a family. There was a whole area of life crowded out by the grocery business. I was so busy selling groceries that I didn't have time to travel even though I had the money. I was so busy selling groceries I did not have time for the drama, for lectures, for concerts, or for reading. I was so busy selling groceries, I did not have time for community service – religious, social or political. All of these areas of life were pushed out by the grocery business. I was successful; I became a wholesaler. But I was so busy making a living I never had time to live."

I do not disparage the grocery business or any other place in the field of industry and commerce. Without them we could not live. But we cannot substitute the means of a livelihood for the meaning of a life.

Jesus had a sense of what is vital. You will remember his visit to the home of Mary and Martha. Mary kept herself in His presence while Martha found herself flustered and bothered by her various chores (Luke 10:38-42). To put it in today's language, Jesus said, "Martha, you are worried about providing so many things. Only a few things are needed, perhaps only one."

An article in the Rotary Club magazine several years ago began this way, "It is a good thing to have money and things money can buy, but it is good, too, to check up once in a while and make sure you haven't lost the things money can't buy."

In the pursuit of every worthwhile objective, there is a technique for attainment. Paul says that it is love. If there is love in the heart – love for God and love for others – a sense of what is vital will become a natural outgrowth.

A LITTLE HUMOR: The summer months in Texas can be some of the hottest months of the year. I recently read that it's been so dry in West Texas that the Baptist have started sprinkling, the Methodists are using a wet cloth, the Presbyterians are giving rain checks, and the Catholics are turning wine back into water. Now friends, that's DRY!

JANUARY 26

A SIMPLE ANSWER

"'Sirs, what must I do to be saved?' So they said, 'Believe on the Lord Jesus Christ, and you shall be saved' . . ." (Acts 16:30-31, NKJV)

While Benjamin Franklin was living in Philadelphia, Pennsylvania, George Whitefield, a young and notable evangelist was preaching there. Whitefield was such a godly man that one of his biographers wrote that he lived more in heaven than on earth.

Franklin was a great admirer of the English evangelist. Whitefield was very eager to lead Franklin to know the Savior. Thus, he wrote to Franklin, urging him to take seriously his need for salvation. Adding a personal note, Whitefield wrote something like this: "You will excuse this freedom. I must have something about Christ in all my letters."

It was this kind of earnest concern for people's salvation that motivated Paul. Acts 16:30-31 presents a simple answer to a simple question. The question? "What must I do to be saved?" The answer? "Believe on the Lord Jesus Christ, and you shall be saved."

The answer to that question has never changed. It was, is, and always will be the same. There are not many ways to be saved—only one way, only one Savior: the Lord Jesus Christ. Have you been saved?

A LITTLE HUMOR: A Sunday school teacher was discussing the Ten Commandments with her five and six-year olds. After explaining the commandment to "honor thy father and thy mother," she asked, "Is there a commandment that teaches us how to treat our brothers and sisters?" Without missing a beat one little boy (the oldest of a sizeable family) answered, "Thou shall not kill."

JANUARY 27

A SLAVE TO SIN

"Jesus answered them, 'Most assuredly, I say to you, whoever commits sin is a slave to sin.'" (John 8:34, NKJV)

Earnest Shackleton left England in August, 1914 on the ship *Endurance*, planning to cross Antarctica on foot with 27 other men. By January of 1915, when they were within 100 miles of land, the ship was trapped in ice. They were carried by the shifting ice pack farther from land. Shackleton and the crew lived on the ship until November, 1915, when the ice finally destroyed the ship and it sank. They then lived on the ice pack with supplies salvaged from the ship until April, 1916, when they sailed to Elephant Island in three lifeboats they had saved.

Shackleton left 22 men there and he and five others sailed for South Georgia Island, 800 miles through the planet's stormiest ocean, in a 22 1/2-foot boat. In August of 1916, Shackleton returned and rescued all the men. Shackleton never did accomplish his goal of crossing Antarctica on foot. He later died at 46 of a heart attack on South Georgia Island.

There is a gospel song that says, "Sin will take you farther than you want to go, sin will keep you longer than you want to stay, and sin will cost you more that you want to pay." The ice Shackleton encountered is like sin: it took them away from their goal, it kept them longer than they wanted, and it cost them the success of their expedition and the loss of their ship. Shackleton once commented on the ice's effect on the ship, saying, "She's pretty near her end. The ship can't live in this... what the ice gets, the ice keeps."

Jesus said, "Whoever commits sin is a slave of sin." Jesus also said, "If the Son makes you free, you shall be free indeed." Jesus broke the power of sin that enslaves and sets us free.

A LITTLE HUMOR: A young bachelor was once bothered by his aunts who would come up to him at weddings, poke him in the ribs and cackle, "You're next." They stopped after he started doing the same thing to them at funerals.

JANUARY 28

A SOUL IN CHAINS

"So if the Son makes you free, you will be free indeed." (John 8:36, NASB)

William Penn once wrote, "Men must be governed by God, or they will be ruled by tyrants." Penn was speaking politically, but his statement is also true spiritually. Lust is a tyrant. Greed is a tyrant. Superstition is a tyrant. Anger is a tyrant. Ambition is a tyrant. Sin is the tyrant that rules over people apart from Christ.

We all know that the drunkard becomes a slave to alcohol and that the drug addict becomes hooked on drugs. But the perfectionist can become so in love with details that he becomes cruel and irritable with those who have not attained a love for completeness. And the housekeeper can love for her house to be tidy – so tidy that she is unhappy when people relax and are at home in it.

Everywhere people have bad habits that they can't seem to break. They want to be free from these things, and they have said a thousand times that they are going to change, but they never do.

Herodotus, the historian, recorded that the Persian king, Darius, once sprained his foot while out hunting. He retained at his court the most distinguished members of the Egyptian medical profession. Their treatments, however, only aggravated the condition of his foot. Finally, someone told him of a certain Democedes of Croton who had unusual medical skills. Democedes at this time was a slave. He was brought into the king's presence, trailing chains and clad in rags. Democedes was able to soothe the king's foot and promoted its healing. As a reward, Darius gave Democedes two pairs of golden fetters.

Sin is like that. It leads eventually to bondage. Sometimes its chains are of iron, and sometimes they are of gold, but the same enslavement results. The only difference is the price of the chains.

But Jesus can set us free from the bondage of sin. We no longer need to live in slavery to Satan and wrongdoing. We can be free persons. We can know liberty in Jesus Christ.

A LITTLE HUMOR: A woman wanting to impress two old college chums, took them to dinner at an exclusive French restaurant and ordered for all three in flawless French. Handing the menu back to the waiter with a flourish, she asked, "Would you mind reading our order back to me?" "Oui, Madame. Number 4, Number 9, and Number 16."

JANUARY 29

A SPECK OF DUST

". . . for dust you are, and to dust you shall return." (Genesis 3:19, NKJV)

It is well for us to remember our humble origin. We are but as dust, the Scripture says. The late H. G. Bosch wrote a devotional on this verse a few years ago under the title "A Speck of Dust." In that devotional he wrote: "Modern science has recently emphasized this truth by confirming the fact that the atoms of which we are composed are almost all empty space! Each atom is similar to this solar system: a few specks of matter scattered through a comparably huge amount of sidereal nothingness. Therefore, they tell us, should all the space in the atoms of the body of a 200 pound man be removed and only the solid substance be retained, 'he would be no bigger than a particle of dust'!

"It is expedient that we should recognize with Job that we dwell here in 'houses of clay, whose foundation is in the dust' (Job 4:19)! This knowledge should make us reverence our Creator, humble ourselves and seek our salvation apart from our own transitory being, and finally make us aspire to that 'house not made with hands, eternal in the heavens.' (2 Corinthians 5:1)! All our boasting and vaunted greatness fall before these words: 'For He knows our frame; He remembers that we are but dust' (Psalm 103:14)!"[10]

The Scripture says, "Humble yourselves under the mighty hand of God, that He may exalt you in due time" (1 Peter 5:6). Evidently the crowns of heaven are not reserved for swell heads!

A LITTLE HUMOR: After church one Sunday, a little boy walked up to the pastor. "Pastor," he said, "I heard you say today that our bodies came from the dust." "That's right, I did," he said. "And I heard you say that when we die, our bodies go back to dust." "Yes, I'm glad you were listening." the pastor replied. "Why do you ask?" "Well you better come over to our house right away and look under my bed 'cause there's someone either coming or going!"

JANUARY 30

A STORM CELLAR FOR LIFE

"God is our refuge and strength, a very present help in trouble."
(Psalm 46:1, NASB)

As I write this article, breaking news tells of the violent storms that have torn through the southern Plains killing at least five people and injuring dozens more, leaving behind flattened homes, toppled semitrailers, and downed power lines. Several tornadoes were reported in Oklahoma and Kansas on Monday as the storms

---

[10] M. R. DeHaan and H. G. Bosch, *Our Daily Bread*, (Grand Rapids: Zondervan Publishing House, 1988), April 7.

moved through the area, dumping hail as big as baseballs. Our hearts go out to the people who have suffered from having to endure such a catastrophe.

Many times when storms hit, people need a safe place in which to hide. I remember that my grandfather had a storm cellar built in his back yard. It wasn't used very often, but when a storm occurred, it, was nice to have such a place. As a child I remember playing in it. It also served as a storage room. People don't build storm cellars today, at least not in our area, but it's a good idea. It's comforting to know that you have a safe place in which to hide when a storm comes.

The Bible talks about a safe place one can turn to when faced with the various storms of life. In Psalm 46:1 the Bible says, "God is our refuge and strength, a very present help in trouble." God is our refuge – He hides us. God is our strength – He helps us. These two go together: hide and help. God hides us so He can help us. Then we can return to the battle and face the storm.

The Old Testament contains 21 different Hebrew words for trouble. In Psalm 46:1 the word *trouble* means in tight places. If you are in a tight place today, let me suggest that you run by faith to Jesus. Go there and tell Him, "Lord, I want to go back to the battle, but you have to give me the strength." Then you can claim this marvelous promise of verse one.

Notice the conclusion in verse two: "Therefore we will not fear." When God is available as your refuge and strength, you have nothing to fear.

A LITTLE HUMOR: Two elderly gentlemen from a retirement center were sitting on a bench under a tree when one turns to the other and says, "Slim, I'm 83 years old now, and I'm just full of aches and pains. I know you're about my age. How do you feel?" Slim says, "I feel just like a new-born baby." "Really? Like a new-born baby?" "Yep. No hair, no teeth, and I think I just wet my pants!"[11]

JANUARY 31

A TRIP TO GOD'S WOODSHED

"Endure hardship as discipline; God is treating you as sons. For what son is not disciplined by his father? If you are not disciplined (and everyone undergoes discipline), then you are illegitimate children and not true sons."
(Hebrews 12:7-8, NIV)

A young man went off to a rather expensive university. The bills were coming in monthly to his parents. They were struggling to keep their heads above water. One day his mother received a letter from their son that read like this: "I'm writing to inform you that I have flunked all of my courses. I had an accident and totally wrecked my car. I owe the clothing store in town $2,000. I have been suspended for the next semester because of misconduct. I am coming home. Prepare Dad." His

[11] Paul W. Powell, *Laugh and Live Longer* (Tyler, Texas, 2008), 52.

mother wrote a one line letter back to him. It read: "Dear Son, Dad is prepared. Prepare yourself."

God is prepared to deal with His children when they sin. God has a woodshed, and if you are one of His children, before you get through this life you will make more than one trip to it. The author of the New Testament Book of Hebrews talks about God's woodshed: "Endure hardship as discipline; God is treating you as sons. For what son is not disciplined by his father? If you are not disciplined (and everyone undergoes discipline), then you are illegitimate children and not true sons" (Hebrews 12:7-8, NIV).

There are three ways God could deal with us when we sin. First of all, God could condemn us. Even after a person is saved, the first time he sins God could send him to hell. But God cannot do that, for the Bible says, "There is now no condemnation for those who are in Christ Jesus" (Romans 8:1, NIV).

Then again, God could condone us. God could stick His head in the sand and ignore our sin and overlook it. But God cannot and will not do that. God is a holy and just God who lets no sin go unpunished.

The third way God could deal with us, and does deal with us is, He can correct us. If God condemned us after we sinned, that would be pure legalism. If He condoned our sin, that would be liberalism. But the third way is God's way and that is the way of love. The Lord Himself said, "Those whom I love I rebuke and discipline" (Revelation 3:19, NIV).

We need to remember that the purpose of discipline is not to discourage us. Hebrews 12:5 reminds us that God's discipline is meant to encourage us. It is for our good (Hebrews 12:10) and it enables us to be productive in righteousness and peace (Hebrews 12:11). As His children we are to be holy, and He will discipline us when we are not; He will discipline us until we are.

A LITTLE HUMOR: A mom and dad were sitting and talking. Mom is reading the newspaper and she says, "According to this article, parents should set limits where children are concerned." Dad replies, "I agree, and my limit is two."

FEBRUARY 1

ENERGIZE YOUR LIFE THE RIGHT WAY

"But the Lord stood with me and strengthened me . . ." (2 Timothy 4:17a, NASB)

The front cover of the February, 2012 edition of *Reader's Digest* has these words: "Instant Ways to ENERGIZE YOUR LIFE!" The inside article presented twenty tips health pros beg you not to skip. The tips include such suggestions as drinking more coffee, go to bed early, take a walk, beware of diet candy, hit the yoga mat to relieve pain, etc. I'm sure these and the other suggestions mentioned in the article are meant to help us live a more energized life, and maybe they do. I'm certainly for a healthier and more energized life style. But there is another energy that is more valuable to you and that is a spiritual energy (or strength) that will help you live a more energized life for the Lord. The energy I'm referring to is that which comes from the Lord Himself.

In 1Timohty 4:17 the apostle Paul wrote that the Lord had stood with him and strengthened him even though others had forsaken him. The word *strengthened* refers to an inner strengthening; a supernatural infilling of divine power that literally super-charged him to bravely and victoriously face one of the most difficult times in his life. Paul is referring to the time he stood before the Roman imperial court to be tried. In that moment when he needed friends to testify in his defense, Paul discovered that every one of them had walked out and abandoned him. But the Lord stood by Paul's side and gave him an inner strength to face the crisis.

When Paul had been discouraged in Corinth, the Lord came to him and encouraged him (Acts 18:9-11). After he had been arrested in Jerusalem, Paul again was visited by the Lord and encouraged (Acts 23:11). During that terrible storm, when Paul was on board ship, the Lord had again given him strength and courage (Acts 27:22ff). Now, in that horrible Roman prison, Paul again experienced the strengthening presence of the Lord, who had promised, "I will never leave you, nor forsake you" (Hebrews 13:5).

That was encouraging to Paul and for us as well. God hasn't changed. If he strengthened Paul, He will do the same for you today!

Are you facing a disturbing situation today? Has something happened to make you feel lonely? Are you feeling weak spiritually and emotionally? If you will ask the Lord for help, He will step forward to assist you and fill you with the power you need to conquer the difficulty in your life. To be strengthened (or energized) you must pray, read your Bible and trust the Lord to give you strength and guidance each day. He didn't fail Paul, and He will not fail you.

A LITTLE HUMOR: An elderly couple, both 85, were involved in an automobile accident and died and went to heaven. Both of them had exercised their whole lives, eaten right, and taken care of themselves, but suddenly they found themselves in heaven as a result of their accident. St. Peter showed them around a beautiful mansion, swimming pool, Jacuzzi, and all of that. The man asked, "What is this going to cost us?" St. Peter said, "You don't understand. This is heaven." Then he looked out the window and said, "There is a beautiful golf course where you can play every day, and the course changes continually so that you will have new experiences." The man said, "That's wonderful! How much is it going to cost?" St. Peter said, "You don't understand. This is heaven." Then he took them to the club house and showed them all the food they had to eat, and the man said, "Oh my goodness, this is wonderful! But what about the light food, the cholesterol-free food?" St. Peter said, "You don't get it. This is heaven. You don't worry about health foods and cholesterol up here in heaven." With that, the old man took off his hat, threw it on the ground, and began to stomp on it, and St. Peter said, "What's the matter?" The man turned to his wife and said, "If it hadn't been for those bran muffins you've been giving me, I could have been here ten years ago!"[12]

FEBRUARY 2

CAN OTHERS SEE JESUS IN YOU?

"They took note that these men had been with Jesus." (Acts 4:13, NIV)

When God's presence shines through your life others are drawn to what they can see and sense. It happened to a short-order cook named Nicholas Herman. Dissatisfied with his life, he worried constantly about whether or not he was even saved. Then one day as he studied a tree he was struck by the same truth that David talks about in Psalm 1:3, that the secret to growing spiritually lies in being rooted and grounded in something (and someone) deeper than himself. So Nick decided to make his life an experiment in what he termed "the habitual, silent, secret conversation of the soul with God."

These days he's better known as Brother Lawrence, the name his friends gave him. Chances are you've heard of him and his writings. Although he spent his life in obscurity working in a kitchen, how he interacted with God has made people around the world long to know God like he did. After he died his friends compiled a book of his letters and conversations called *Practicing the Presence of God*. It's one of the most widely read books of the last four centuries. Jesus said, "If I am lifted up...I will make everyone want to come to me" (John 12:32, CEV). So the more you allow Him to express Himself through your life, the more others will be attracted to Him. The hymn writer, B. B. McKinney wrote:

---

[12] Paul W. Powell, *Laugh and Live Longer* (Tyler, Texas, 2008), 54-55.

"While passing through this world of sin,
And others your life shall view,
Be clean and pure without, within,
Let others see Jesus in you."

A LITTLE HUMOR: A mother knocked on her son's door one Sunday morning and said, "Get up, honey, it's time to get ready for church." The boy responded, "Oh, mother, I don't want to go to church today. Just let me sleep." The mother replied, "I don't care what you want. Get yourself out of bed, get dressed, and get down to church." He responded, "Mother, I don't want to go! Those people down there don't like me, and I don't like them. Just the other day when I was walking down the hall and around the corner, I heard some people talking about me. They were saying some awful things. Don't make me go." The mother responded, "I don't care about all that. You get yourself up. You're going." The boy responded, "Why should I go?" She said, "For two reasons. First, you're forty-five years old. And, second, you're the pastor and they're expecting you down there!"

FEBRUARY 3

CONTINUE

"Be my strong refuge, to which I may resort continually." (Psalm 71:3a, NKJV)

Three times in Psalm 71 the author speaks of his doing something "continually" (vv. 3, 6, 14). Also, three times he uses the term "all day long" (vv. 8, 15, 24). There were at least three things the author of this psalm said he would do continually.

First, he said he would continually turn to the Lord as his refuge (v. 3a): "Be my strong refuge, to which I may resort continually." To call God a refuge suggests that God is a shelter where a person may seek cover from a storm or hide from danger. All of us need someone we can turn to when we need help and encouragement. That someone for the Christian is the Lord Himself. He is our Refuge, Rock and Fortress all rolled up into one.

The second thing the author of this psalm said he would do continually is to praise the Lord: "My praise shall be continually of You . . . Let my mouth be filled with Your praise . . . I . . . will praise You more and more . . . also with the lute I will praise You . . ." (vv. 6, 8, 14, 22). David Jeremiah reminds us that when we are faced with a trial God will give us two gifts: a scripture for your mind and a song for your heart. The English preacher, Charles H. Spurgeon, said, "A man never grows nauseated through the flavor of praise being in his mouth all day."

The third thing the psalmist said he would do continually is to place his hope in the Lord: "I will hope continually" (v. 14), and in verse 5 he writes: "For You are my hope, O Lord God." Another word for hope is confidence. What an encouragement to know that we can place our confidence in the Lord to save us and to sustain us at all times.

The English preacher, F. B. Meyer, wrote a letter to a friend of his in which he said, "I do hope my Father will let the river of my life go flowing fully until the finish. I don't want it to end in a swamp." Neither do I, and I assume that would be your desire also. You can finish well if you continue to turn to the Lord as your refuge, praise Him, and place your hope in Him – all day long.

A LITTLE HUMOR: The pastor had announced his Sunday morning sermon topic: "The Second Coming of Christ." For dramatic appeal, with appropriate gesture, he proclaimed the Scripture, "Behold, I come quickly." For added emphasis, his voice rising, pointing toward the balcony, he said again, "Behold, I come quickly." And finally, the third time, with gesturing gusto, he lunged forward and shouted, "Behold, I come quickly" and, overbalanced, he fell into the orchestra pit onto the lap of a young female flutist. Red faced and flustered, he apologetically stammered, "I'm sorry, I'm sorry." "Oh, that's okay," said the gracious young lady. "You warned me three times."

FEBRUARY 4

DIG OUT THE ROOT OF BITTERNESS

"Be careful that no one becomes like a bitter plant that grows up and troubles many with its poison." (Hebrews 12:15, GN)

In some pastures there grows a weed called "bitter weed." A bitter weed is stringy and grows about a foot high with a small, compact, yellow flower. If a dairy cow eats bitter weeds, her milk will taste bitter. Obviously, farmers are anxious for their cows to avoid grazing on bitter weeds.

Entirely apart from a rural setting, bitter weeds grow in the pastures of life. Hebrews 12:15 states that a root of bitterness can spring up and cause trouble: "Be careful that no one becomes like a bitter plant that grows up and troubles many with its poison" (GN). Anger may come and go, but bitter feelings often remain for years. This is why the writer of Hebrews called it a "root of bitterness" (KJV). Like a root, bitterness can grow and spread for years, entangling our attitudes, feelings and thoughts.

The bitter root bears bitter fruit. Ironically, the one who suffers most is the one who lashes out at those around him. He becomes his own worst enemy. An ancient Roman story tells of Roman soldiers who became dissatisfied with their regiment and rations. They could not complain to Caesar, so they became angry with the gods. Many of them shot their arrows toward the heavens, hoping to hit the gods. Several of the soldiers were wounded or killed as their own arrows, with high velocity, fell back upon their heads. What an apt illustration of what bitterness does to a person. In Matthew 18:21-35, Jesus said if we refuse to forgive others, the gall of bitterness will torment us (verse 34), meaning we will experience intense inner torment. If we nurture feelings of bitterness we are little better than inmates of an internal concentration camp.

I have heard that Edwin Markham, the poet, reached the age of retirement and found out that his banker had defrauded him. He was ready to retire but was penniless. He came to the place where he could no longer write poetry. Because of his bitterness the candle of joy had been blown out in his heart. He was obsessed with the evil perpetrated against him by a man he had thought was his friend. One day he was sitting at his desk doodling, drawing circles on his paper, not writing poetry but only thinking of the man who had wronged him. Markham later testified that the Holy Spirit convicted him with, "Edwin, if you do not deal with this thing, it is going to ruin you. You cannot afford the price you are paying. You must forgive that man." The poet prayed, "Lord, I will, and I do freely forgive."

The root of bitterness was pulled out. The joy began to flow, and so did his mind and pen. He then penned perhaps his most famous poem, "Outwitted."

He drew a circle that shut me out --
Heretic, rebel, a thing to flout;
But Love and I had the wit to win:
We drew a circle that took him in!

There is the solution to bitterness. Someone has harmed you and wronged you. Bitterness has been so strong you could almost taste it as bile within your mouth. With the Spirit's spade root it out. Draw a circle that takes in those who have wronged you. Forgive them for Christ's sake!

A LITTLE HUMOR: It is said that on one occasion, Winston Churchill so angered Lady Astor that she said, "If I were your wife, I would give you arsenic to drink." Churchill angered her even more with his reply, "And if I were your husband, I would gladly drink it."

FEBRUARY 5

LAYING ASIDE FALSEHOOD

"Therefore, laying aside falsehood, speak truth, each one of you, with his neighbor, for we are members of one another." (Ephesians 4:25, NASB)

Many years ago, people did not wear hats. They wore hoods. Back then people wore different colors of hoods. The color of one's hood told his occupation. For example, if you were a minister, you wore one color hood. If you were a doctor, you wore another color of hood. You could tell the occupation of a person by the color of hood he wore.

The problem with that, of course, was that some people tried to pass themselves off as somebody they were not. So they wore a false hood. That is where we get the word "falsehood." What is a falsehood? It is something that is not true.

Telling lies ranks high among the common vices of mankind. The title of an article asked, "Are you a Liar?" It said, "You are, if you're like 97 out of 100 Americans. In fact, science says if you always tell the truth, you're abnormal."

This accords perfectly with Scripture, which says that the heart is deceitful above all things and desperately wicked (Jeremiah 17:9). One way human depravity displays itself most plainly is by lying. "Even from birth the wicked go astray; from the womb they are wayward and speak lies" (Psalm 58:3, NIV). Despite its prevalence, lying is a sin of speech that God forbids. "Lying lips are an abomination to the Lord, but those who deal faithfully are His delight" (Proverbs 12:22, NASB).

No Christian should be guilty of deliberate lying. Colossians 3:9 says, "Do not lie to one another, since you laid aside the old self with its evil practices."

Viewed as one of the "rags" that belonged to the old man, lying (or falsehood) must be banished from the Christian's life, and in its place "truth" must be cultivated. Christians are to "speak the truth with his neighbor." The motive in doing so is found in our mutual relationships within the body of Christ: "We are members one of another."

Telling falsehoods can get you into trouble. If you always tell the truth, people learn to trust you. They know that what you say is true – and they will know that Jesus lives in your heart.

A LITTLE HUMOR: The least credible sentences in the English language include the following: "The check is in the mail." "I'm from the government, and I'm here to help you." "Don't worry, I can go another twenty miles when the gauge is on 'empty'." "Can I have just five minutes of your time?" "...then take a left. You can't miss it." "...but we can still be good friends."

FEBRUARY 6

GOOD GRIEF OR GOOD HAPPINESS?

"A joyful heart makes a cheerful face." (Proverbs 15:13, NASB)

Good Grief! Charlie Brown, the round-headed kid whose "Peanuts" gang provided laughs for nearly fifty years, retired from the funny pages. Creator Charles Schulz, who had been diagnosed with cancer, retired January 4, 2000, the day after the final daily strip ran. The final Sunday strip ran February 13. Although Schulz officially retired, newspapers continue publishing comics from 1974, considered representative of his best works.

As far back as I can remember, whenever I read the newspaper, the first comic strip I looked at was "Peanuts." Like many other speakers I have used "Peanuts" to illustrate a spiritual truth I was sharing. Many lessons have been illustrated by all of the "Peanuts" characters and I would be hard pressed to select one as my favorite. I do remember one, however, that addressed the subject of happiness. It was a conversation between Charlie Brown and Linus. Linus says to Charlie Brown, "I think you're afraid to be happy, Charlie Brown. Don't you think happiness would be good for you?" Charlie Brown responds, "I don't know . . . what are the side effects?"

Charles Schulz did "some mighty good preaching" through his cartoon characters. Through the character of Linus we see that happiness is a good thing. All of us would like to have a little happiness in this life. In his book, *The Secret of Happiness*, Billy Graham reminds us that every person has a mysterious feeling inside himself that there is a fountain somewhere that contains the happiness which makes life worthwhile. Graham also reminds us that the word *blessed* as found in the Beatitudes (Matthew 5:1-12) could have been translated "happy," although it carries a far richer tone than the everyday content of our English word.

Genuine happiness does not come from having things or doing something. Real happiness comes from being in a proper relationship with God through His Son, the Lord Jesus Christ. It is God's intention that we be happy individuals. Through the death of Jesus Christ on the cross and our repentance from sin and the placing of our faith in Him for the forgiveness of sin, we discover genuine happiness. Happiness will produce a loving spirit in a person, the kind that is a joy to be around.

Thanks, Charles Schulz and Charlie Brown, for reminding us what the Bible says about happiness: there is "a time to laugh" (Ecclesiastes 3:4, NASB); "a joyful heart makes a cheerful face" (Proverbs 15:13, NASB); and, "a joyful heart is good medicine" (Proverbs 17:22, NASB). Good grief? No, good happiness!

A LITTLE HUMOR — A preacher entered the ice cream parlor for an ice cream cone. He asked the clerk, "What flavors do you have?" The clerk whispered hoarsely, "Strawberry, Chocolate, and Vanilla." The preacher asked, "Do you have laryngitis?" The clerk replied, "No, just Strawberry, Chocolate, and Vanilla."[13]

FEBRUARY 7

GET RID OF THAT DEAD CARCASS

"If I regard iniquity in my heart, the Lord will not hear me." (Psalm 66:18, KJV)

In his book, *Finishing Strong,* Steve Farrar writes about a certain man who wanted to sell his house for two thousand dollars. Another man wanted to buy it very badly, but he was a poor man and didn't have the full price. After much bargaining, the owner agreed to sell the house to the man for one thousand dollars. But the reduced price came with a stipulation. The owner would sell the house, but he would keep ownership of a large nail protruding from over the front door.

Several years later, the original owner decided he wanted to buy the house back. Understandably, the new owner was unwilling to sell. As a result, the original owner went out, found the carcass of a dead dog in the street, and hung it from the nail he still owned. Soon the house became unlivable, and the family was forced to sell to the owner of the nail.

The moral of the story: If we leave the devil with even one small nail in our life, he will return to hang his rotting garbage on it. You may own the entire house, but if you give the enemy access to just one nail in your life, you will ruin your life.

The Bible says, "If I regard iniquity in my heart, the Lord will not hear me" (Psalm 66:18, KJV). To "regard iniquity in my heart" means that I know that a particular sin is in my heart; I want it there; I like for it to be there; in fact, I cherish it

[13] *The Preacher Joke a Day Calendar 1998* (Lame Duck, Inc., 1997)

and nourish it and practice it from time to time. When we regard sin in our lives, we entertain the desire for sin, even though circumstances restrain our actions. It is to reflect upon past evil with pleasure rather than with sorrow. It is to know something is wrong, yet to neglect or refuse to correct it. You may have confessed all of your sins to the Lord but one -- your favorite one. If you harbor that sin in your life; if you nourish it and want it to stay there, it will not be long until Satan will hang his garbage on it. In 2 Corinthians 2:11, Paul talks about the devil getting an "advantage" over us. The word "advantage" is a military term describing the establishment of a beach head by an army from which it can operate. If given the opportunity, Satan will establish a beach head in our lives from which he can operate.

The only answer to the presence of sin in our lives is to confess it and ask for forgiveness. First John 1:9 reads, "If we confess our sins, he is faithful and just to forgive us our sins and purify us from all unrighteousness" (NIV). Let me ask you something. Is there a nail over the front door of your life? A nail that you have leased out to the enemy? If there is, you need to deed it over to Christ. Now.

A LITTLE HUMOR: A woman reported the disappearance of her husband to the police. The officer in charge looked at the photograph she handed him, questioned her, and then asked if she wished to give her husband any message if they found him. "Yes," she replied, "Tell him Mother didn't come after all."

FEBRUARY 8

GETTING THE BEST OF TROUBLE

"Call upon Me in the day of trouble; I will deliver you, and you shall glorify Me."
(Psalm 50:15, NKJV)

In his book, *Facing Life and Getting the Best of It,* Clarence E. Macartney wrote of the time when Robinson Crusoe was taken sick on his lonely island, and was faint in body and fainter still in spirit. Rummaging one day through an old chest which he had salvaged from the wreck, and searching for a medicine, he came upon a Bible. After he had taken the medicine, he opened the Bible, and the first verse upon which his eye fell was this:"Call upon Me in the day of trouble; I will deliver you, and you shall glorify Me" (Psalm 50:15, NKJV). This produced a great impression upon Robinson, and he began to hope that perhaps God would heal him of his sickness, deliver him from his solitary island, and bring him back to his native land and to his friends once more. Before he went to bed that night, he did what he had never done before, knelt down and prayed, and in his prayer asked God to fulfill the promise of that verse in his own life, and heal him of his sickness, and deliver him from his wave-washed island. After that he sank into an untroubled sleep.

Some days afterwards, as he was walking along the shore with his gun over his shoulder, his heart almost came to a stop, when he saw on the sand the imprint of a foot. He fled to his stockade and, climbing over the wall, pulled the ladder in after him in the greatest fear and terror. Then those same words came to him again, "Call upon Me in the day of trouble; I will deliver you," and as he remembered them his fear began to leave.[14]

We are all mariners on the sea of life, and sometimes cast upon islands of distress. When that happens, the thing to do is what Robinson Crusoe did, call upon God in the day of trouble. That was what Hezekiah did when he got the blasphemous letter from Sennacherib's lieutenant, threatening destruction to Jerusalem and to all the people of God. He took the letter into the temple, the place of prayer, and "spread it out before the Lord." God heard him and delivered him and Israel (2 Kings 19:14). That is what David did in his time of trouble: "In my distress I called upon God, and He heard me" (Psalm 18:6). That is what Paul did when the ship was sailing through the Mediterranean, and God sent His angel to the rescue (Acts 27:23-25). Prayer is to the soul in time of trouble what a life jacket is to the shipwrecked passenger.

A LITTLE HUMOR: Someone had placed a note just below the start button on the newly installed hot air hand drier in the restroom of their church. It read, "Press the above button to hear a pre-recorded message from our pastor."

FEBRUARY 9

A TRUE FRIEND

"A friend loves at all times, and a brother is born for adversity."
(Proverbs 17:17, NASB)

A newspaper cartoon showed a thief wearing a mask. His gun was pointed toward a frightened victim. In the next scene the robber is holding out a sack and saying, "Give me all of your valuables!" In the last scene the victim begins stuffing into the sack all of his friends. I don't know of anything more valuable, more blessed, more strengthening, and more encouraging than a true friend. There are at least three virtues of friendship found in Proverbs 17:17 and Proverbs 18:24b.

True friendship is selfless – "A friend loves . . . ." Certain people will claim to be your friend, and yet they will attach certain conditions upon their friendship. They will stipulate, "I love you if," or, "I love you when," or, "I will love you until," or, "I love you because." In other words, they are saying if I can satisfy their need they will be my friend. But it will not be a true friendship, because when the if, the when, the until, or the because is not exactly right, overboard they will go.

True friendship is steadfast – ". . . at all times." Someone has said, "A real friend is someone who comes in when the whole world has gone out." Do you want to find out who your friends are? Then make a mistake – not a little one, but make a big one, and see what happens. Most of the people you thought were your friends will desert you. It doesn't matter what you have done, a true friend will still be there.

---

[14] Clarence E. Macartney, *Facing Life and Getting the Best of It* (New York: Abingdon Press, 1940), 75-76.

True friendship is sacrificial – "There is a friend who sticks closer than a brother." (Proverbs 18:24b). Friendship is costly. The Indians have a word for *friend.* Translated into English it means one who carries my sorrows on his back. That reminds me of the Lord Jesus. "Surely our griefs He Himself bore, and our sorrows He carried . . ." (Isaiah 53:4). It cost the Lord Jesus to wear the title, *A Friend of Sinners.*

Jesus has all the attributes of a true Friend. He is a selfless Friend who first loved us (1 John 4:19). He is a steadfast Friend who will never leave you (Hebrew 13:5). He is a sacrificial Friend for "Greater love hath no man than this, that one lay down his life for his friends." (John 15:13). Even His enemies called Him, "a friend of sinners" (Matt. 11:19). No truer statement has ever been written than that which is found in the hymn, *What a Friend We Have in Jesus!* written by Joseph Scriven. Christ is, indeed, a true Friend!

A LITTLE HUMOR: A preacher thought that everyone in his church loved him. He had decided to accept the call to a new church. At the end of the worship service, he was telling his congregation that he would be leaving. He said, "I have always tried to do what Jesus wants me to do. Jesus brought me to this church, and Jesus is leading me away from this church. I know this is what Jesus wants me to do. Now if the choir director will please lead us in a closing hymn." The choir director stood up and said, "Let us stand and sing, 'What a Friend We Have in Jesus'."

FEBRUARY 10

DANIEL WEBSTER'S LOVE KNOT

"For I am convinced that . . . (nothing) . . . will be able to separate us from the love of God, which is in Christ Jesus our Lord." (Romans 8:39, NASB)

Daniel Webster, a 19th century lawyer and statesman, was courting his wife-to-be, Grace Fletcher. As he held skeins of silk thread for her, he suggested, "Grace, we've been engaged in untying knots; let us see if we can tie a knot which will not untie for a lifetime." They stopped right then and tied a random silk knot that would be almost impossible to untie. Grace accepted Webster's proposal.

After they passed from this world, their children found a little box marked "Precious Documents." Among the contents were letters of courtship and a tiny silk knot, one that had never been untied.

Those who know the love of Jesus can boldly say, "For I am convinced that neither death, nor life, nor angels, nor principalities, nor things present, nor things to come, nor powers, nor height, nor depth, nor any other created thing will be able to separate us from the love of God, which is in Christ Jesus our Lord." (Romans 8:38-39, NASB).

A LITTLE HUMOR: A new husband come home one evening to find his wife in tears. "You know the dinner I cooked for your tonight?" she asked. "The dog ate it." "Don't worry about it sweetheart," replied the husband. "We'll get another dog!"

FEBRUARY 11

ARE YOU READY FOR BIGGER THINGS?

"And so, God willing, we will move forward to further understanding."
(Hebrews 6:3, NLT)

Did you know that the hermit crab looks for a shell that fits him, then lives in it till he outgrows it? At that point he has to scurry along the ocean floor and find a bigger one; it's a process that repeats itself throughout his entire life.

When it comes to spiritual growth, Christians are to be hermits as well. It is important for Christians to be grounded in the faith, learning the elementary teachings about Christ, but having done that, we should move on to bigger things. We do not discard what we have learned as the hermit crab discards his shell; we simply build on what we have learned. Growing and learning as a Christian is like going to school; you don't start off at the high school or college level at the beginning, you start at the kindergarten level and move up the scale until you graduate.

An example of this is found in Luke 5 where Jesus tells Peter to "put out into the deep water, and let down your nets for a catch" (Luke 5:4). Peter was an experienced fisherman. He and his partners had fished all night. They knew how to fish. Yet Jesus challenged them to push away from the bank and go to deeper water. There they would catch so many fish they almost sank their boats.

To develop and grow spiritually you must be willing to move out of your comfort zone. Never become so "settled" that you can't go and move on when you need to. When God says it's time to move on, it's because there's another shell out there that will fit you even better. But you can't take occupancy till you vacate the old one. So how about it – are you ready for bigger things?

A LITTLE HUMOR: Two men were shipwrecked. One of them started to pray, "Dear Lord, I've broke most of the Commandments. I've been an awful sinner all my days. Lord, if you'll spare me I'll . . ." The other one shouted, "Hold on, don't commit yourself. I think I see a boat!"[15]

---

[15] Tal D. Bonham, *The Treasury of Clean Church Jokes* (Nashville: Broadman Press, 1986), 97.

FEBRUARY 12

AN EXPENSIVE TOLL ROAD

"And He was saying to them all, 'If anyone wishes to come after Me, he must deny himself, and take up his cross daily and follow Me'." (Luke 9:23, NASB)

Two of our children and four of our grandchildren live in the Ft. Worth and Frisco area. My wife and I have discovered that the fastest way to visit with each family is to use the toll roads when possible. To speed things up even more, we have purchased a Texas Toll Tag. It doesn't cost that much and sure beats having to stop at each toll booth and drop in the exact change. Whatever the cost, it's worth it just to see the grandkids!

When Dr. David Livingstone was working in Africa as a medical missionary, a group of friends wrote to him saying, "We would like to send other men to you. Have you found a good road into your area yet?" Dr. Livingstone wrote back and said, "If you have men who will only come if they know there is a good road, I don't want them. I want men who will come if there is no road at all." Livingstone wanted men who were willing to pay a price to follow Jesus.

Following Jesus sometimes involves a very difficult, or costly, "road." We must be willing to follow Jesus when conditions are not favorable and even downright bad. Are you willing to walk down the difficult road that Jesus leads you on today? Whatever the cost, it's worth the price.

A LITTLE HUMOR: A man and his wife were sitting in their living room, talking. He said to her, "Just so you know, I never want to live in a vegetative state, dependent on some machine and fluids from a bottle. If that ever happens, just pull the plug." She got up, unplugged the TV and threw out his beer!

FEBRUARY 13

HELP!

"Let us therefore come boldly to the throne of grace, that we may obtain mercy and find grace to help in time of need." (Hebrews 4:16, NKJV)

Tony Evans tells of the time he was trapped on an elevator. The immediate reaction of all of the people was panic. They were trapped, stuck, and couldn't get out. Some people were crying, "Help! Help! Help!" They were sincerely crying out for help. But it wasn't working.

Other folks were banging on the elevator door. Bam, bam, bam! No one was hearing all that noise, but those folks didn't care. They kept right on banging. Desperate people do desperate things. They were crying out.

Evans remained calm. He walked to the other side of the elevator and pulled out a latch, picked up the telephone and waited. A voice said, "Is there a problem?" He said, "We're trapped on the elevator between this floor and this floor. Can we get some help?" They responded, "We'll be right there."

Evans then made this application: "See, everybody forgot about the phone. We were so into being trapped that we forgot there was a phone link to the security department. Merely by picking up the phone, we were released from our hostage situation. All the human effort we put forth, banging and yelling, wouldn't work, but picking up the phone and asking for help did. We had to seek help using the connection."[16]

Hebrews 4:16 reminds us that we have a direct connection with God through prayer. When we are "trapped" in a problem, we can call upon the Lord and be assured that He will respond and send help "in time of need."

Today, take advantage of the privilege of prayer. Help is available for anyone who is willing to ask for it.

A LITTLE HUMOR: A young man was being interviewed for a job as a policeman. As his superior asked him questions about the various experiences he might have, he said to him, "What would you do if you were called upon to arrest your own mother?" Without hesitation, he said, "I'd call for backup."[17]

FEBRUARY 14

A WHOLE LOT OF LOVE

"Beloved, if God so loved us, we also ought to love one another."
(1 John 4:11, NASB)

If you've ever done a lot of cooking, you know the importance of the measuring cup. Measuring cups are used to measure different ingredients, like milk or sugar. If one cup of milk is needed, you pour in the milk up to the line that says "one cup." If you need two cups of sugar, you pour in the sugar up to the line that says "two cups." The measuring cup shows how much milk or sugar you have. It's very important to measure your ingredients right, or else your food won't taste good.

There is no measuring cup that we can use to measure how much God loves us. Do you know why? Because God loves us so-o-o-o much! There's no measuring cup big enough to hold all of God's love for us. It doesn't matter what age you are, what color you are, what language you speak, what kind of things you've done in life — God loves us all equally. In Ephesians 3:18-19 the apostle Paul wrote of his desire for us "to comprehend with all the saints what is the breadth and length and height and depth, and to know the love of Christ which surpasses knowledge."

We can't measure God's love with a great big measuring cup, but we can measure God's love for us by looking at Jesus. The Bible says that God loves us so

---

[16] Tony Evans, *Tony Evans' Book of Illustrations* (Chicago: Moody Publishers, 2009), 149.
[17] Paul W. Powell, *Laugh and Live Longer* (Tyler, Texas, 2008), 15.

much that He sent His Son, the Lord Jesus Christ to die for us (John 3:16). Karl Barth, famed theologian, was once asked, "What is the greatest thought you ever had? His answer: "Jesus loves me this I know, for the Bible tells me so."

Today is Valentine's Day. It is a day for us to express our love for those who are near and dear to us. Don't forget to tell your wife or husband how much you love them, and while you're at it, don't forget to tell God how much you love Him!

A LITTLE HUMOR: A man attended a marriage seminar in which the speaker encouraged husbands to tell their wives they loved them. He realized he had been negligent at that point and decided to do something about it. So, on his way home from work that day he stopped by the drug store and bought her a box of chocolates. He then went by the florist and got her a dozen long-stem roses. Then he walked in the house, handed her the gifts, threw his arms around her, and planted a kiss on her, and said, "Honey, I love you." She pulled away from him and said, "Oh, George, it's been a horrible day. Johnny got in a fight at school. The washing machine broke down. I burned supper. And now, you come home drunk."

FEBRUARY 15

WHY?

"And we know that God causes all things to work together for good to those who love God, to those who are called according to the will of God." (Romans 8:28, NASB)

On February 15, 1947 Glenn Chambers boarded a plane bound for Quito, Ecuador to begin his ministry in missionary broadcasting. But he never arrived. In a horrible moment, the plane carrying Chambers crashed into a mountain peak and spiraled downward. Later it was learned that before leaving the Miami airport, Chambers wanted to write his mother a letter. All he could find for stationery was a page of advertising on which was printed the single word "WHY?" Around that word he hastily scribbled a final note. After Chamber's mother learned of her son's death, his letter arrived. She opened the envelope, took out the paper, and unfolded it. Staring her in the face was the question "WHY?"[18]

How often have we asked that question: Why? Why God, why? Why me? Why her? Why now? An impossible question to answer completely, but here are a few thoughts.

The first is that "life happens." That doesn't sound too spiritual, but you can put your money on it. Life happens. We want a "why" to everything. But oftentimes there is no answer. Life happens

There is a second principle: Christian faith has little to do with what happens to us; Christian faith has everything to do with how we handle what happens to us. People of faith handle adversity differently from people who have no faith. We have

---

[18] *Dynamic Preaching*. July-September, 2000, Vol. 15, No. 3, 13.

resources that people without faith do not have. There is faith itself. We were made for faith — not for fear. And there is healing power in faith. We also have prayer. Prayer works. We don't always get what we ask for but God is responsive to our prayers. And we have the community of saints. We draw strength from bearing one another's burdens.

Ultimately, God is in control. We must ask ourselves the question: "Just how much do we trust God?" Can we trust Him when we have a crisis? Anyone can trust God when things are going our way, but what about those moments when even the universe seems aligned against us?

I don't pretend to know all the answers. I am a searcher, just as you are. But I do know this: in my seasons of highs and lows, I've noticed something peculiar. I rarely learn anything from pleasure, but I learn volumes from pain. Don't get me wrong. I prefer pleasure. Only a fool would prefer pain. But I've noticed that, whereas the highs make me glow, the lows make me grow. I have to believe that God put us in a world of both pleasure and pain, good and evil, highs and lows. The highs keep us going, but the lows keep us growing — emotionally, intellectually, and spiritually.

A LITTLE HUMOR: A little three-year-old boy did not enjoy baths. His mother coaxed, "Don't you want to be nice and clean?" He replied," Yes, but can't you just dust me off?"[19]

FEBRUARY 16

GLUTTONY: THE SIN OF EXCESS

"Do not carouse with drunkards or feast with gluttons, for they are on their way to poverty, and too much sleep clothes them in rags." (Proverbs 23:20-21, NLT)

A predator has entered our lives; one that started as soon as we were born. The predator is gluttony. Most people associate gluttony with overeating and that's true. But overeating is only one form of gluttony. Gluttony is the desire for excess: wanting more, bigger, better, more often, faster stuff. Some people can't have enough toys, sports, television, entertainment, sex, work, gambling, smoking, drinking, hoarding, or even too much studying and researching of a narrowly defined subject – the list is endless. Gluttony is about an excess of anything. The key term is "too much."

We must control our desires because excess desire is the driving force behind gluttony. When we lose control of our desires, we sin, feeding the god of too much, too fast, too eagerly. James 1:14 adds insightfully, "Each one is tempted when he is carried away and enticed by his own lust." The responsibility for our actions is upon each of us individually. Verse 15 of James 1 continues, "Then when lust has

[19] Tal D. Bonham, *The Treasury of Clean Jokes* (Nashville: Broadman Press, 1981), 37.

conceived, it gives birth to sin; and when sin is accomplished, it brings forth death." This is the process that leads to gluttony – and to death.

Any appetite that's out of control is dangerous, whether it is the appetite for food, sex, money, or power. If we are honest with ourselves, we tend to be gluttons out of control. We criticize too much. We gossip too much. We overeat. We overspend. We indulge in bad habits, thinking that one more time won't hurt.

The Bible offers some practical guidance on developing self-control. The theme of self-control can be found throughout the Bible, but it especially permeates Peter's epistles. Check out 1 Peter 1:13; 4:7; 5:8 and 2 Peter 1:5-6 as it reads in the New International Version (NIV) of the Bible. Peter not only talked about self-control, he practiced it rigorously. So should we.

A LITTLE HUMOR: The teacher knew there was a shortfall of intelligence after she asked the class to name the four major food groups. Suzie shot up her hand and quickly reeled them off: "Wendy's, McDonald's, Burger King, and Pizza Hut."

FEBRUARY 17

AS IF IT HAD NEVER HAPPENED

"Therefore, having been justified by faith, we have peace with God through our Lord Jesus Christ." (Romans 5:1, NKJV)

Imagine you are a race car driver in the Indianapolis 500 automobile race. How would you deal with the possibility of crashing, even dying, on that track?

According to one driver, you don't. "If a fatal accident occurs, you don't go look at where it happened. You don't watch the films of it on television. You don't deal with it. You pretend it never happened."

The Indianapolis International Speedway operation itself encourages this approach. As soon as the track closes the day of an accident, a crew heads out to paint over the spot where the car hit the wall. Through the years, a driver has never been pronounced dead at the race track. A trip to the Indianapolis Motor Speedway Racing Museum, located inside the 2.5 mile oval, has no memorial to the 40 drivers who have lost their lives here. Nowhere is there even a mention.

When a person repents of his or her sin and accepts Christ as Lord and Savior, that person becomes justified. The word *justified* is used to describe the act of God whereby He declares the sinner righteous. Romans 8:33 says that "God is the one who justifies". Justification is an act, not a process. There are not degrees of justification. Justification is permanent (Romans 8:31-34) and God is the only one who can justify a person. A minister, performing a wedding ceremony, pronounces the couple as "husband and wife." He doesn't "marry" them. He pronounces them married. A judge does not make a person guilty or innocent. A judge announces whatever the verdict of the jury might be.

Justification means sin is all past and gone – wiped out – not merely forgiven, not merely pardoned; it means clearing the slate and setting the sinner before God as a righteous person. God can do this because of the death of His Son, the Lord Jesus Christ, on the cross. An easy way to remember the meaning of "justification" is to re-pronounce it and say, "From the time I accepted Christ as my personal Lord and Savior, God has treated me "just-as-if-I-had-never sinned."

A LITTLE HUMOR: A preacher was speeding down the highway and was stopped by a highway patrolman. As the patrolman was preparing to write a ticket, the minister, hoping to appeal to his sympathy, said, "Officer, I hope you'll show me mercy. I am a poor preacher." The officer responded, "Yes, I know, I heard you last Sunday."

FEBRUARY 18

GOOD INTENTIONS

"They that were ready went in." (Matthew 15:10, NASB)

According to a report in the *Evangelical Press* sometimes back, it may be a little harder to go Hell this year. A bridge on the main road leading to Hell, Michigan, is badly in need of repair — a project that could close the road for three months. Business owners in the town fear that the disruption in traffic could force some stores into bankruptcy. "It'll close the whole town," complained Jim Ley, president of the Hell Chamber of Commerce. Officials acknowledge that the repair work will cause some disruption, but insist that plans to fix the road to Hell spring from good intentions. The road suffers damage each year when Hell freezes over.

I don't know where the phrase comes from that the road to Hell is paved with good intentions. It's not biblical, but certainly, it is accurate. Many who are in Hell never intended to go there. They intended to "get prepared" someday but "someday" never came around.

Jesus told about some very foolish people who waited until it was too late to get ready for a wedding. The story is found in Matthew 25:1-13.There were ten young women, five were wise and five were foolish. The wise women were considered wise because they had made adequate preparation for the arrival of the bridegroom. The foolish women were considered foolish because they had not made the necessary arrangements. Not being ready when the hour came, the foolish women were shut out. Verse ten says of the wise women, "They that were ready went in."

The road to hell is not a steep decline that you tumble into all at once. It is a gradual slope, paved by your delay. Why, sometimes you don't even know that you are going downhill. Delay is dangerous. To say "tomorrow" is to say "no." If the thief on the cross had said "Tomorrow," he would be in hell now. If Zaccheus of Jericho had said, "Lord, I'll think about it," he would never have made the decision for Christ. If blind Bartimaeus had not had spiritual insight enough to call to Christ when his one opportunity came, he would have spent the rest of his days spiritually and physically blind.

Delay won't make conditions better! A bad tooth won't get better if you put off going to the dentist. It will only get worse. If one has cancer, putting off a visit to the doctor will not improve the cancer but will only let the conditions become more serious. Delay is dangerous.

I don't know what kind of condition the road is in that leads to hell. I do know this: Good intentions are not enough. Jesus has put up a road block on the road to hell. It is a cross. Anyone who is willing to repent of his sins and put his trust in Jesus Christ as his only Savior doesn't have to go to hell.

A LITTLE HUMOR: A tourist driving down a country road came face to face with a sign that read, "Road closed — Do not enter." The road ahead looked pretty good to him, and having had great experiences as a traveler, he ignored the sign and pressed on. Five miles down the road he came to a bridge that was out, and he had to turn around and retrace his route. As he reached the point where the warning sign stood he read the words printed on his side of it: "Welcome Back, Stupid!"

FEBRUARY 19

LIVE WITH INTEGRITY

"The appeal we make does not spring from error or impure motives, nor are we trying to trick you. On the contrary, we speak as those approved by God to be entrusted with the gospel . . . You know we never used flattery, nor did we put on a mask to cover up greed – God is our witness." (1Thessalonians 2:3-5, NIV)

A writer for a newspaper in Toronto, Canada, undertook an investigation into the ethical practices of auto repair shops in his town. He took a spark-plug wire off of his engine, making the car run unevenly. He took the car to different shops and asked them to fix it. Time after time people sold him unnecessary repairs or charged him for repairs that were not done. Finally, he went to a small garage. A fellow named Fred came out, popped open the hood, and said, "Let me listen to that thing." After a few seconds, he told the reporter, "I think I know what's wrong." He reached down and grabbed the wire, announcing, "Your spark-plug wire came off." And he put it back on.

The reporter asked, "What do I owe you?"

"I'm not going to charge you anything," Fred said. "I didn't have to fix anything; I just reattached the wire."

The writer then told Fred what he was doing and that he had been charged all kinds of money by mechanics looking at that same wire. He asked Fred, "Why didn't you charge me anything?"

Fred said, "I am a Christian and believe that everything we do should be done to glorify God. I'm not a preacher and I'm not a missionary, but I am a mechanic, and so I do it honestly. I do it skillfully, and I do it to the glory of God."

Integrity is honesty. It is an uncompromising commitment to be trustful and trustworthy. Integrity brings glory to God.

A LITTLE HUMOR: A little girl went up to the front of the church to listen to the pastor's children's sermon. The pastor gathered the children around himself and noticed the beautiful new dress on this little girl. The pastor complimented the girl for her pretty dress and asked if it was new. The little girl leaned toward the pastor and spoke directly into his lapel microphone: "Yes, pastor, this is my brand-new dress. And my mommy says that it is even harder to iron this dress than to listen to one of your sermons."

FEBRUARY 20

JESUS IS THE ONLY DOOR TO HEAVEN

"I am the door; if anyone enters through Me, he shall be saved, and shall go in and out, and find pasture." (John 10:9, NASB)

What did Jesus mean when He referred to Himself as the "door"? It obviously teaches that there is only one door to heaven and that one door is Jesus Christ Himself. He is the sole way to God and to heaven. This point is evident from the nature of the sheepfold that Christ had in view – if it had more than one door, it would have been useless. John 10:9 speaks of three great benefits in accepting Jesus as the only door.

First, Jesus says that anyone who enters in will be saved. Saved from what? – the wrath of God (1 Thessalonians 1:10). When one repents of his sins and accepts Jesus Christ as His personal Savior, God forgives him of his sins based on the sacrificial death of Jesus and saves (rescues or delivers) him from the judgment of hell. He receives forgiveness of his sins and life everlasting.

Second, Jesus promises that anyone who enters in will be safe. This is the point of His reference to going "in and out." To be able to go in and out means security (Deut. 28:6; 1 Kings 3:7; Psalm 121:8). Jesus promises safety for those who trust Him.

Third, Jesus also promised that they would be satisfied for He said they would be able to go in and out and "find pasture." Palestine is a barren land for the most part, and good pasture was not easy to find. Consequently, to be assured of good pasture was to speak of prosperity and contentment, of health and happiness. It was in this sense that David wrote of the care of his Good Shepherd: "He makes me lie down in green pastures; he leads me beside the quiet waters. He restores my soul" (Psalm 23:2-3, NASB). Anyone who enters in by Christ will not lack any good thing.

One of the most moving scenes in the movie *Titanic* is when the great ship finally sinks and we see hundreds of people floating about in life jackets in the icy waters. In reality, every one of those people died – some 1,500 of them. Some died of hypothermia after only a few minutes. Stronger, more physically fit people lived perhaps an hour before freezing to death. The truth is they all died. The only ones who lived through that terrible tragedy were those who were in the lifeboats. The lifeboat was their only means of salvation from certain physical death. Jesus is our only means of salvation from certain eternal death. He is the "Door." Walk through, and you will be saved, safe and satisfied.

A LITTLE HUMOR: A hog farmer barged into the church office and said, "I need to see the head hog at the trough." "Sir," the receptionist answered, "If you are talking about our pastor, you may refer to him respectfully as "Pastor," or "Brother," but I wouldn't refer to him as 'head hog at the trough'." "Oh," the farmer said. "I just wanted him to know that I sold an extra $10,000 worth of hogs this year, and I'd like to donate the money to the building fund." "Just a minute," said the receptionist, "I think the Big Pig just walked in!"[20]

FEBRUARY 21

WHO'S RESPONSIBLE?

"When tempted, no one should say, 'God is tempting me.' For God cannot be tempted by evil, nor does he tempt anyone; but each one is tempted when, by his own evil desire, he is dragged away and enticed." (James 1:13-14, NIV)

Have you ever noticed that we gladly take credit for our accomplishments, but we often blame our failures on extenuating circumstances? For example, how many times have you heard someone say something like, "I'm sorry I lost my temper. It's because I'm so tired" . . . or "I'm under pressure". . . or "You were getting on my nerves." Our natural tendency is to blame someone or something else whenever we fail. It's not easy to accept responsibility for our failures.

In 1980 New York Mayor Ed Koch appeared on a local news program in the middle of the city's financial crisis. Koch had spent over a quarter of a million dollars to put up bike lanes in Manhattan, and they turned out to be a disaster. Cars were driving in the bike lanes, pedestrians were walking in them, and bikers were getting crowded out. It was a mess and many people in New York were irate about it. Koch was coming up for re-election, so a handful of journalists cornered him on a television show, planning to tear him to pieces for spending money foolishly when the city was nearly broke. One reporter said, "Mayor, in light of the financial difficulties New York City is facing, how could you possibly justify wasting $300,000 on bike lanes?" The stage was set for a half-hour confrontation. Instead, Koch said, "It was a terrible idea. I thought it would work, but it didn't. It was one of the worst mistakes I ever made." Then he stopped. None of the other journalists knew what to say or do. They were expecting him to squirm and make excuses, but he didn't even try. The next journalist stammered and said, "But Mayor Koch, how could you do this?" Koch said, "I already told you. It was a stupid idea. It didn't work." Then he stopped. There was still 26 minutes left to go on the news show, and the reporters had to find something else to talk about. The last thing they expected

---

[20] *The Preacher Joke a Day Calendar 1998* (Lame Duck, Inc., 1997).

that day was for the mayor to take responsibility for his actions.

The principle here is that we cannot blame our sin on anyone else. We are responsible for our own lives. It does no good to say, "I am a victim of my environment, or a victim of my circumstances, or a victim of genealogy, or a victim of bad luck." We can't be like the character in West Side Story who said, "I'm depraved on account of I was deprived."

This is what James meant when he talked about temptation. He wrote, "When tempted, no one should say, 'God is tempting me.' For God cannot be tempted by evil, nor does he tempt anyone; but each one is tempted when, by his own evil desire, he is dragged away and enticed." (James 1:13-14, NIV)

A LITTLE HUMOR: A minister selected a fifty cent item at a convenience store, but then discovered he didn't have any money with him. "I could invite you to hear me preach in return," he said jokingly to the clerk, "but I'm afraid I don't have any fifty-cent sermons." "Perhaps," suggested the clerk, "I could come twice."

FEBRUARY 22

MAKING SOMETHING GOOD OUT OF SOMETHING BAD

"And we know that God causes all things to work together for good to those who love God, to those who are called according to His purpose." (Romans 8:28, NASB)

On March 7, 1876, Alexander Graham Bell received a patent for the telephone. He was born in Edinburgh, Scotland, and from the age of eighteen, Bell worked on the idea of transmitting speech. Bell's telephone actually came about as the result of an accident.

Bell had built an experimental telegraph that began to function strangely one day because a part had come loose. The accident gave Bell understanding in how voices could be transmitted over wires. He constructed his phone, a transmitter and receiver, and had it patented. His experiments were successful when the first complete sentence was transmitted, "Watson, come here; I want you."

Many blessings have come from what appeared to be a tragedy. What first appeared to be an accident was later realized to be God's appointment. God has a way of taking the negative and making it a positive. Handley C. G. Moule said, "There is no situation so chaotic that God cannot from that situation create something that is good. He did it at creation, He did it at the cross, and He is doing it today." Today give thanks for God's promise that even the bad things turn out for our good.

A LITTLE HUMOR: Ever wonder . . . Why *abbreviated* is such a long word? Why is it that doctors call what they do *practice*? Why is the time of day with the slowest traffic called *rush hour*? Why isn't there mouse-flavored cat food? If con is the opposite of pro, is Congress the opposite of progress?

FEBRUARY 23

STAYING ON COURSE

"Your word is a lamp to my feet and a light to my path." (Psalm 119:105, NASB)

A wonderful invention that has helped many people who have wandered off course and don't know where they are, or who need directions to get somewhere is called the Global Positioning System (GPS). This unit utilizes signals from a system of satellites to calculate to within fifty feet the exact location of a person or a vehicle.

A similar device is needed as we travel on our spiritual journey. We can lose our bearings and get off course. Soon we realize we are going in the wrong direction, but we have a positioning system that will always tell us which way to go – the Word of God. If we consult it regularly, it will guide our path and keep us from straying.

I am told that at times a compass on a ship needs calibration. Over time, the hull of a ship builds up a magnetism that interferes with the ship's compass. True north is no longer true north. To remove this influence, the captain takes the ship over special coils. The Bible is your special coil for life. It will keep you on true north and keep you calibrated so that you are headed in the right direction.

A LITTLE HUMOR: The preacher had been disturbed by a person in the congregation who was a fast reader. "We shall now read the Twenty-third Psalm in unison," he announced. "Will the lady who is always by 'the still waters' while the rest of us are in 'green pastures,' please wait a minute until we catch up?"

FEBRUARY 24

LET THE LORD BLOT IT OUT!

"Repent therefore and be converted, that your sins may be blotted out . . ."
(Acts 3:19a, NKJV)

The words *blotted out* come from the time when ink had no acid in it. Modern ink has acid in it and thus bites into the paper. That's why to erase it you almost have to rub a hole in the paper. But ancient ink was not that way; it had no acid in it. It just lay on top of the page and dried. Because paper was very valuable in those days, it was used again and again. All that was needed to remove the old ink was to moisten it by wiping a wet sponge across the page. The page would then be as good as new. The words *blotted out* describe that process of wiping old pages clean and making them new again. It pictures for us just how complete God's forgiveness and cleansing is.

You can't unscramble an egg. You can't un-break a glass. You can't undo your sin. Sin is a knot that only God can untie. Repent and be converted and God, through Christ, will wipe the pages of your life clean for you and you can begin to write anew.

A LITTLE HUMOR: The night clerk in a hotel was surprised to see a guest walking through the lobby in a pair of pajamas. "Hey, there," he shouted, "what do you think you are doing?" The guest woke up and apologized. "I beg your pardon," he said. "I'm a somnambulist." "Well," said the clerk, "you can't walk around here like that, no matter what church you belong to."

FEBRUARY 25

OF BOTTLES AND BOOKS

"You number my wanderings; put my tears into Your bottle; are they not in Your book?" (Psalm 56:8, NKJV)

Did you know that God is keeping a journal about you? His journal is composed of bottles and books. According to Psalm 56:8, God watches our wanderings. The Revised Standard Version of the Bible renders the word "wanderings" as "my tossings" and the Moffatt translation renders it "my sleepless hours."

In Bible times it was customary for each family to own a "tear bottle." The tear bottle represented all the heartaches of life. It was with a tear bottle that Mary washed the feet of Jesus. Luke indicates that Jesus was deeply moved by her act of love and devotion (Luke 7:36-50).

Each of us experiences his or her own heartaches. Sorrows come to everyone. But what a comfort to remember that the God who knows the flight of the sparrow, the God who knows the flowers of the field, the God who paints the sunset knows and cares about your tears. He cares about you!

God sees when we weep. He sees and records our tears and files them for future reference. Malachi 3:16 refers to "a book of remembrance" that God keeps "for those who fear the Lord and who meditate on His name" (NKJV).One day God will show you the book and the bottle. He's going to say, "I knew when your heart was broken. I knew what you were going through. I've kept a record of it. Now, that sorrow shall turn into joy." And every one of your tears will become a jewel of beauty to the glory of God.

A LITTLE HUMOR: A missionary visiting a cannibal tribe asked the chief, "Do you people know anything about religion?" "Well, explained the chief, "we got a little taste of it when the last missionary was here."[21]

---

[21] Tal D. Bonham, *The Treasury of Clean Church Jokes* (Nashville: Broadman Press, 1986), 75.

FEBRUARY 26

OUR FUTURE REWARDS

"For we must all appear before the judgment seat of Christ, so that each one may be recompensed for his deeds in the body, according to what he has done, whether good or bad." (2 Corinthians 5:10, NASB)

The eighty-fourth Academy Awards of Motion Pictures Arts and Sciences was broadcast on February 26, 2012. Each year since 1929 the Academy recognizes the outstanding achievements by actors, directors, producers, and technicians. This year the best picture was *The Artist.* The best actress award went to Meryl Streep for her performance in *The Iron Lady.* The best actor award went to Jean Dujardin for his performance in *The Artist.*

For Christians, there is no earthly ceremony in which they are given rewards for their outstanding achievements. However, there is coming a day in which proper recognitions will be made. The future event is known as the judgment seat of Christ.

The Greek word used in 2 Corinthians 5:10 for judgment seat is *bema.* It was the place where the awards were given out to the winners in the annual Olympic Games. This judgment seat must not be confused with the Great White Throne from which Christ will judge the wicked (Revelation 20:11-15). Because of Christ's sacrificial death on the cross, believers will not face their sins (John 5:24; Romans 8:1); but we will have to give an account of our works and service for the Lord.

The Judgment Seat of Christ (*bema*) will be a place of revelation, reckoning and rejoicing. The word *appear* means to be revealed. As we live and work here on earth, it is relatively easy for us to hide things and pretend; but the true character of our works will be exposed before the searching eyes of the Savior.

The *bema* will also be a place of reckoning as we give an account of our ministries (Romans 14:10-12). If we have been faithful it will be a place of reward and recognition (1 Corinthians 3:10-15; 5:1-6). For those who have been faithful, it will be a time of rejoicing as we glorify the Lord by giving our rewards back to Him in worship and in praise.

Is the desire for reward a proper motive for service? Let Warren Wiersbe answer that question. He states, "The fact that God does promise rewards is proof that the motive is not a sinful one, even though it may not be the highest motive. Just as parents are happy when their children achieve recognition, so our Lord is pleased when His people are worthy of recognition and reward. The important thing is not the reward itself, but the joy of pleasing Christ and honoring Him."

A LITTLE HUMOR: Preachers are like athletes, they have good days and bad days. There are days when they strike out and days when they hit a home run. Recently a preacher at a convention had a good day. He felt as though he had "knocked their socks off." On the way to the hotel from the convention center, he said to his wife, "Honey, how many R-E-A-L-L-Y great preachers do you think there are in America?" She replied, "I don't know, but there's one less than you think."[22]

FEBRUARY 27

UP, UP, AND AWAY!

"You will keep him in perfect peace, whose mind is stayed on You, because he trusts in You." (Isaiah 26:3, NKJV)

Early on a July Saturday in Bend, Oregon, a colorful object was silhouetted against the rising sun. Floating slowly upward from his gas station property, Kent Couch, 48, sat back in his lawn chair and prepared to take in the view from 15,000 feet above the earth.

An old pro at improvised flight, Couch had logged two previous trips in his chair, suspended in air by 150 giant helium-filled balloons and 45 gallons of soda pop for ballast.

Nine hours and 236 miles after his ascent, Couch pulled out his "landing mechanisms" – a Red Ryder BB gun and blow gun with darts – and shot some of the five-foot-diameter balloons to get himself back to terra firma in Idaho.

"If I had the time, money, and people, I'd do this every weekend," Couch said. "Things just look different from up there. You're moving so slowly. The best thing is the peace and serenity."

I want peace as much as the next person, but I believe I could find a better place than 15,000 feet above the earth in a lawn chair held up by 150 giant helium-filled balloons.

Cleland B. McAfee wrote, "There is a place of quiet rest, Near to the heart of God, A place where sin cannot molest, Near to the heart of God." Being near the heart of God is a secure place of peace, and all you have to do to be there is to drop to your knees. James 4:8a reads, "Draw near to God and He will draw near to you." Remember, to find peace, you don't have to go up but down.

A LITTLE HUMOR: A mother with a fidgety seven-year old boy told how she finally got her son to sit still and be quiet. About halfway through the sermon, she leaned over and whispered, "If you don't be quiet, Pastor is going to lose his place and will have to start his sermon all over again!" It worked.

---

[22] Paul W. Powell, *A Funny Thing Happened On the Way to Retirement* (Tyler, Texas, 2000), 13.

FEBRUARY 28

GOD SEES YOUR OFFERING

"Jesus went over to the collection box in the Temple and sat and watched as the crowds dropped in their money..." (Mark 12:41a, NLT)

John A. Broadus, Baptist giant of a century ago was a preacher, teacher, denominational leader, scholar, and author with few, if any, peers. He was a professor at Southern Seminary from its opening in 1859 until his death 36 years later. Southern Baptists named the Broadman Press and the Broadman Hymnal for Broadus.

In a church Broadus was serving as pastor, he once stepped from the pulpit and walked with the ushers as they took the offering. He reached into the plate to examine the donations, reading checks and envelopes, examining and counting the money. With the congregation atwitter, the famous preacher returned to the pulpit and preached his greatest sermon on stewardship.

"My dear people," Broadus is quoted as saying, "if you take it to heart that I have seen your offering today and know just what sacrifices you made and have not made, remember that your Savior, God's Son, goes about these aisles with every usher. He knows whether or not we abound in this grace."

Broadus certainly had more courage than I to do something like that. You'll not find me looking over an usher's shoulder or checking the contribution ledgers to see who has given what, but the truth of the matter is that God's Son, the Lord Jesus Christ does. He knows not only what you give but why you give it and how you earned it and how much you are keeping for yourself. He is the ultimate One to whom we will be held accountable. So, let's give as though Jesus is watching, because He is!

A LITTLE HUMOR: A multimillionaire, who had never had any regard for God or his church, was on his deathbed. He called the pastor to his side and said, "Pastor, if I made the church the beneficiary of my will, if I left my entire estate to the work of God, do you think it would help me get into heaven?" The pastor replied, "I'm not sure, but I think it's worth a try."

FEBRUARY 29

GET SOME REST

"Come away by yourself to a secluded place and rest a while." (Mark 6:31, NASB)

For a few years in the Wild West, mail was dispatched across this country by a relay system known as the Pony Express. Occasionally an express rider would be attached by Indians. Because his big mount was stronger than the Indian ponies, the rider could spur his horse to a gallop and outrun his attackers before his horse would tire. This scenario wasn't repeated too many times before the Indians changed their plan of attack. Realizing they couldn't outrun the express rider, they wisely stationed some of their number every few miles along the route. Then, just when the rider had outrun the first group of attackers, the second band would appear, causing him to spur his horse on without rest. This tactic was repeated until at last the rider's horse would collapse from exhaustion.[23]

Sometimes we are like those Pony Express horses. We get one crisis resolved and here comes another. If it is not a child in trouble at school, it's an aging parent needing our attention. If it is not an unhappy client, it is an expensive car repair. One stressful thing after another. There is no rest for the weary, we say. And that is so.

Jesus knew it was important for people to get away from time to time. His apostles had been out preaching and teaching and healing and ministering to the public. And it was Jesus who suggested that they get away from the crowds for a while and rest. So many people were coming and going that they scarcely had time to eat (Mark 6:30-34).

As followers of Christ it is important for us to realize that Jesus advocated balance in life. Christianity has always been an activist faith in which the emphasis has been on taking up the cross, laying down your life, sacrificing yourself for the cause of Christ. And certainly, that is a major part of our faith. But it is possible to have an imbalanced Christianity. Jesus never meant for us to be so involved in doing good that we neglect our need for leisure, for rest, for family, for friends. As Vance Havner used to say, "If we don't come apart, we'll come apart!"

A LITTLE HUMOR: A man said, "I knew I was called to preach when I woke up one morning with a craving for fried chicken and didn't want to go to work."

---

[23] *Dynamic Preaching.* July-September, 2000, Vol. 13, No. 3, page 31.

MARCH 1

TO DECEIVE OR NOT TO DECEIVE

"Do not be a witness against your neighbor without cause, and do not deceive with your lips." (Proverbs 24:28, NASB)

On September 28, 1980, a story appeared in the *Washington Post* about the tragic ghetto life of Jimmy, an eight-year-old heroin addict. Reported by Janet Cooke, the story drew immediate attention by police and social workers. They searched for the boy but were unable to find him. Cooke refused to reveal any information about the boy, claiming that it would put the boy and her in danger. The Post submitted the story for consideration by the Pulitzer Prize Committee. When the story won, Cooke was asked to supply biographical information to the committee. The resume she provided was so full of errors that it cast doubts on the truth of the story. When questioned, Cooke finally admitted that the story was a hoax. The next day she publicly apologized and resigned.

Solomon speaks of deceiving others by the things we say and tell. The word *deceive* carries the idea of enticing and flattering. It would describe someone who desires to be accepted, and popular. He makes himself look better to others which leads him to tell stories that are not true. It would also be descriptive of someone taking a story and adding things to it to make it sound better or make him look better. Call such deception with your lips anything you want to, but it is nothing more than lying, and God makes it very clear how He feels about lying (Proverbs 6:16-17).

Whatever the motive or reason, lies are never condoned by God. Remember, a lie may make you look good at first, but it's how you look after the truth is known that you should consider.

A LITTLE HUMOR: A minister noticed a group of boys standing around a small stray dog. "What are you doing, boys?" "Telling lies," said one of the boys. "The one who tells the biggest lie gets the dog." "Why, when I was your age," the shocked minister said, "I never ever thought of telling a lie." The boys looked at one another, a little crestfallen. Finally one of them shrugged and said, "I guess he wins the dog."

MARCH 2

BE ON THE ALERT

"Be self-controlled and alert. Your enemy the devil prowls around like a roaring lion looking for someone to devour. Resist him, standing firm in the faith..."
(1 Peter 5:8-9a NIV)

Because of the terrorist attacks on America, the FBI will occasionally issue new terrorism warnings asking Americans and law enforcement to be on the highest alert for possible attacks from terrorists. One such alert was based on new information that was deemed credible. Attorney General John Ashcroft said, "We urge Americans in the course of their normal activities to remain alert and to report unusual circumstances and inappropriate behavior to the proper authorities." President Bush was asked whether the government expected more attacks. He responded, "We believe the country must stay on alert, that our enemies still hate us."

Such a warning reminded me of what Peter said regarding our enemy, Satan. As 1 Peter 5:8 warns us, we are to be on the alert at all times. We know that Satan is on the offensive; we just don't know when he will attack. Consequently we must be on guard at all times. Here are a few suggestions for being on the alert for Satan's attack.

First, remember that Satan is our enemy. He hates us. He wants to destroy us. He is committed to that end.

Second, remember that Satan is sneaky. He is the master deceiver. He hides, waiting for the appropriate time to ambush us. Temptations never appear what they really are — tools to destroy us.

Third, Satan is like a hungry lion, constantly on the prowl. He never sleeps. He never takes time off from his goal of our destruction.

Finally, remember that there is a way to defeat Satan. The secret to his defeat is in the person of the Lord Jesus Christ. First John 3:8 says that Jesus came into this world to "destroy the works of the devil." The word *destroy* means to demolish them, to undo them, to put an end to them. The word may suggest that the works of the devil (our sins) were like chains binding us. Christ came that He might shatter those chains and loose us from them.

Yes, we must be alert at all times, but we need not be afraid. The reason is "because greater is He (Jesus) who is you than he (Satan) who is in the world" (1 John 4:4). Having surrendered ourselves to the Lord Jesus Christ, we can resist the devil and stand our ground.

A LITTLE HUMOR: A man said to his friend, "I bought me a new hearing aid last week, and it is wonderful." His friend responded, "Oh, what kind is it?" The man (looking at his watch) said, "It's a quarter till three."

MARCH 3

ARE YOU GOING IN THE RIGHT DIRECTION?

"Jesus said to him, 'I am the way, and the truth, and the life; no one comes to the Father but through Me." (John 14:6)

The newspaper reported last year about a twenty-one-year-old German tourist who wanted to visit his girlfriend in the Australian metropolis of Sydney, but he landed more than 8,000 miles away near Sidney, Montana. It turns out he had mistyped his destination on a flight booking website. Dressed for the Australian summer in T-shirt and shorts, Tobi Gutt left Germany on Saturday for a four-week holiday. Instead of arriving "down under," Gutt found himself on a different continent and bound for the chilly state of Montana. "I did wonder, but I didn't want to say anything," Gutt told the newspaper. "I thought to myself, you can fly to Australia via the United States." Gutt's airplane ticket routed him via the U. S. City of Portland, Oregon, to Billings, Montana. Only as he was about to board a commuter flight to Sidney – an oil town of about 5,000 people – did he realize his mistake. The hapless tourist, who had only a thin jacket to keep out the winter cold, spent three days in Billings airport before he was able to buy a new ticket to Australia with 600 euros in cash that his parents and friends sent over from Germany.

It's possible to think you're heading toward one destination while all the time heading in the opposite direction. Many people on earth today think they're traveling to heaven, but they have the wrong ticket to the wrong destination. They don't realize it, and they have a false assurance of salvation. Are you sure you're going in the right direction?

A LITTLE HUMOR: Two men crashed in their private plane on a deserted South Pacific island. Both survived. One of the men brushed himself off and then proceeded to run all over the island to see if they had any chance of survival. When he returned, he rushed up to the other man and screamed, "This island is uninhabited; there is no food, there is no water. We are going to die!" The other man leaned back against the fuselage of the wrecked plane, folded his arms, and responded, "No, we're not. I make over $250,000 a week." The first man grabbed his friend and shook him. "Listen, we are on an uninhabited island! There is no food, no water, and we are going to die!" The other man, unruffled, again responded, "No, we are not! I make over $250,000 a week!" Mystified, the first man, taken aback with such an answer, repeated loudly and slowly, "For the last time I'm telling you, We are doomed! There is no water and no food. We are going to die! " Still unfazed, the other man looked the first man in the eyes and said, "Do not make me say this again. "I make over $250,000 a week and I tithe to my church . . . MY PASTOR WILL FIND ME!"

MARCH 4

GIVE TILL IT HELPS!

"Each one must do just as he has purposed in his heart, not grudgingly or under compulsion, for God loves a cheerful giver." (2 Corinthians 9:7, NASB)

Don't give till it hurts. Give till it helps. The story is told of a very wealthy man who had never been known for his generosity to his church. The church was involved in a big financial program and they resolved to pay him a visit. When the committee met with the man one afternoon, they said that in view of his considerable resources they were sure that he would like to make a substantial contribution to this program.

"I see," he said, "so you have it all figured out have you? In the course of your investigation did you discover that I have a widowed mother who has no other means of support but me?" "No," they responded, they did not know that. "Did you know that I have a sister who was left by a drunken husband with five children and no means to provide for them?" "No," they said, "we did not know that either." "Well, did you know also that I have a brother who is crippled due to an automobile accident and can never work another day to support his wife and family?" Embarrassingly, they responded, "No, sir, we did not know that either." "Well," he thundered triumphantly, "I've never given any of them a cent so why should I give anything to you?"

Like that man, most of us never give till it hurts or helps. It is interesting that people who tithe in the church never speak of it as hurting. My wife and I tithe and it has not made life painful for us in the least. We resolved from the first day of our marriage that we would be faithful stewards of all we have. It has been a joy and a blessing. Usually, it is the grudging giver who is the one who always registers the complaint: "At that church all they talk about is money." So let us get off of this notion of giving till it hurts. We can affirm that we give till it helps!

A LITTLE HUMOR: On one of their visits to the Holy Land, Mark Twain and his wife stayed in Capernaum near the Sea of Galilee. One particularly lovely night Twain decided to take his wife on a romantic moonlit ride on the Sea of Galilee. Dressed in his usual white Texas hat, white suit, and white shoes, Twain strolled down the pier with his wife. He asked a man who was sitting in a nearby rowboat how much he would charge to row them out into the water. Presuming this fine-looking man to be a wealthy Texan from the states, the oarsman said he would charge about twenty-five dollars. After thanking the man, Mark Twain was heard to proclaim as he and his wife turned away, "No wonder Jesus chose to walk!"

MARCH 5

GOSSIP? ME?

"A gossip tells secrets, so don't hang around with someone who talks too much."
(Proverbs 20:19, NLT)

According to a recent report on ABC's *Good Morning America,* four women in Hooksett, New Hampshire have gotten themselves in hot water for idle chatter. In fact, they have been fired, in part for gossiping and discussing rumors of an improper relationship between the town administrator and another employee that Hooksett residents now agree were not true. The administrator complained, and after an investigation the town council fired the women, finding, "Gossip, whispering, and an unfriendly environment are causing poor morale and interfering with the efficient performance of town business."

A gossip is one who repeats idle talk or rumors about others. The word "gossip" is not found in the King James Version of the Bible although the word "gossip" is found in more modern translations of the Bible such as the New Living Testament. In the King James Version one may find such words as "talebearer" (Leviticus 19:16), "whisperers" (Romans 1:29), and "tattlers" (1 Timothy 5:13). Probably no sin of speech has as many warnings against it as the sin of spreading rumors. So prevalent is this kind of tongue-wagging that Ogden Nash was prompted to claim that the human race could be divided into two classes: the gossipers and the gossipees.

"I like the parrot," someone has said, "It is the only creature gifted with the power of speech that is content to repeat just what it hears without trying to make a good story out of it." On Sunday a restaurant manager designated two rooms as a nonsmoking area to accommodate churchgoers who came in for a bite to eat after their evening service. A busboy there said he was glad to see the large number of nonsmokers. But then he added, "They may not smoke, but you ought to hear them gossip. If we had a non-gossip section, nobody would be there." The next time you are tempted to gossip about someone, bite your tongue!

A LITTLE HUMOR: The order of service at a church listed the sermon topic as "Gossip." Immediately following was the hymn, "I Love to Tell the Story."

MARCH 6

HAVE YOU EATEN LATELY?

"Blessed are those who hunger and thirst for righteousness, for they shall be satisfied." (Matthew 5:6, NASB)

Have you eaten any Oreo cookies lately? Tuesday, March 6, 2012, marked a momentous occasion in history – Oreo cookies' 100th birthday. That's right, Oreo fans around the globe have been twisting, licking, and dunking America's favorite cookie for an entire century. According to *The New York Times,* it all started on March 6, 1912, when the National Biscuit Company sold its first Oreo sandwich cookies to S. C. Thuesen, a grocer in Hoboken, New Jersey. Since they were first baked in 1912, more than 362 billion Oreos have been eaten worldwide.

Have you eaten any metal lately? According to a recent news release, three-year-old Payton Bushnell complained to her parents of symptoms that resembled the flu. Doctors took an X-ray and found thirty-seven "Buckyballs" magnets, clustered in her stomach. Successful surgery removed the magnets, and she is expected to fully recover.

Speaking of eating metal, several years ago *The Houston Post* reported that Michel Lotito of Grenoble, France, had eaten ten bicycles, seven television sets, several shopping carts, a coffin and six chandeliers. He ate a waterbed in Amarillo. He ate an airplane in Venezuela. *The Guinness Book of World Records* honored him as "The World's Greatest Omnivore." He ate the award.

Have you eaten any words lately? Radio talk show host, Rush Limbaugh has. Limbaugh responded to Georgetown law student, Sandra Fluke's testimony before Congress, that our government should require her school's health care plan to include contraception, by calling her inappropriate words. His remarks created a tremendous amount of criticism, the withdrawal of several key sponsors for his radio program, a mountain of criticism, and an apology from Limbaugh.

Have you eaten anything righteous lately? Righteousness, however, is not something you eat; it's a person – Jesus (1 Corinthians 1:30). To hunger and thirst after righteousness is to hunger and thirst after Christ. The deepest need of your life is a right relationship with God through Jesus Christ. According to Matthew 5:6 anyone who hungers and thirsts for righteousness shall be satisfied. The word for "satisfied" is translated as "filled" in the King James Version of the Bible and refers to being perfectly satisfied by all that Jesus Christ will mean to anyone who truly hungers and thirsts for Him.

A LITTLE HUMOR: A little girl called out several times after she went to bed for a drink of water. Finally, the mother said, "If you ask for a drink of water one more time I'm going to spank you." After a while the little girl said, "Mama, when you get up to spank me would you bring me a glass of water?"

MARCH 7

A SWING INTO HISTORY

"You are not your own; you were bought with a price. Therefore honor God with your body." (1 Corinthians 6:19-20, NIV)

Mark McGwire broke baseball's most revered record when he hit his 62nd home run of the season Tuesday night, September 8, 1998. It was a record that some believed would never be broken, certainly not after standing for 37 years. Roger Maris had hit 61 home runs in 1961. McGwire's bat, jersey, and the ball he hit are already in the Cooperstown Baseball Hall of Fame, next to Roger Maris'. There are several lessons taught by this historical occasion.

For one thing, think about the value of the ball. Before McGwire hit the ball it was just an ordinary ball, worth no more than any other. Once McGwire hit the ball, however, the value of the ball jumped tremendously. It was said that the ball could have brought up to one million dollars for the one who retrieved it. Likewise, when we were touched by the Lord Jesus Christ our value as a human being was changed tremendously. Before we accepted Christ as Savior, we were just ordinary human beings. But once Christ touched us we were instantly changed on the inside and became very valuable people in the eyes of the Lord. Jesus said that we are of more value than "many sparrows" (Matthew 10:31) or "sheep" (Matthew 12:12). The power of a touch to transform the value of an object or a person is miraculous.

A second observation has to do with the young man who retrieved the ball, Tim Forneris. Forneris is a Cardinals grounds-crew member. He ran it down and picked it up. He could have kept the ball and possibly have become a very wealthy man. But he rejected any suggestion of making money off the baseball. Instead, all he asked for was a life time pass to the Hall of Fame so he could see it any time he wanted. How unselfish. What an example for the rest of us to follow. Greed drives many people to "get all they can, can all they get, seal the lid, and poison all the rest." But not Forneris. Long may his unselfish spirit live. The word "greed" is not found often in

Scripture, but the Bible warns about the danger of living only to accumulate more of this world's goods. Greedy people always lose more than they gain.

A final lesson comes from the statement made by Tim Forneris when he presented the baseball to McGwire. Forneris leaned toward the microphone and said, "Mr. McGwire, I believe I have something that belongs to you." He then presented the baseball to the new "home run king." The Bible says that we belong to the Lord. We are His because He created us. We are His because He redeemed us when His Son, the Lord Jesus Christ, died on the cross for our sins. The Bible says, "You are not your own; you were bought with a price. Therefore honor God with your body" (1 Corinthians 6:19-20, NIV). The wisest thing we can do — the most unselfish thing we can do — is to recognize that our lives are not ours to do with as we please; they belong to the Lord. We must be willing to give them back to Him saying, "O Lord, I believe I have something that belongs to you — my life. I give myself to you unconditionally." When we do that, the Lord puts us into His "Hall of Faith" and we find ourselves alongside others who have experienced the same transforming touch by the Master's hand. Actions like that make a real "swing into history" or should I say, "a real swing into eternity"?

A LITTLE HUMOR: Two friends had played baseball together all their lives. One day, Joe and Frank made a pact that whoever died first would let the other know whether there is baseball in heaven. Frank passed away, and several days later Joe heard his friend's voice. "Joe," Frank said, "I have some good news and bad news. The good news is the baseball here is the best, the sun always shines, and the fields are glorious. The bad news is, you're the starting pitcher tomorrow."[24]

MARCH 8

HEAVEN IS A SPECIAL PLACE

"And he took me in spirit to a great, high mountain, and he showed me the holy city, Jerusalem, descending out of heaven from God. It was filled with the glory of God and sparkled like a precious gem, crystal clear like jasper." (Revelation 21:1-2, NLT)

On March 8, 1977, the Eisenhower Tunnel in Colorado was opened. Originally called the Straight Creek Tunnel but renamed in 1972 in honor of President Dwight D. Eisenhower, it is the highest tunnel in the world and the longest in the U. S. It took six years to complete the westbound side and four to complete the eastbound side. One million cubic yards of material were cleared and 190,000 cubic yards of concrete were used for each tunnel lining. One thousand, one hundred and forty persons were employed in three shifts working twenty-four hours a day, six days a week. Each tunnel has 2,000 light fixtures with eight-foot bulbs in each. The utility bill is about

---

[24] Paul W. Powell, *A Funny Thing Happened on the Way to Retirement* (Tyler, Texas, 2000), 113-114.

$70,000 a month. The cost of construction was $108 million.

One can only imagine what the cost of constructing the heavenly city would be. It would be difficult to estimate the cost of building a city in which streets are paved with pure gold, gates made of pearl, walls made of jasper, and the foundations are garnished with all manner of precious stones. Then when you realize that the size of the city is 15,000 times the size of London, ten times bigger than Germany it would be almost impossible to determine a construction cost. Can you imagine what the utility bill would be for such a place? We may never be able to determine a cost for building such a city but we do know the cost for living there. It cost the Lord Jesus Christ His life. We should give thanks that Christ loved us enough to die for us, and in addition to that, is building a new home for us to live in one day.

A LITTLE HUMOR: A couple bought a parrot at a pet store, and after they got it home, they discovered that the only vocabulary he had was "Let's neck." One day the preacher dropped in on them and heard the parrot. He advised them that he also had a parrot whose only vocabulary was "Let's pray." They decided to put the two birds together and see if they would start saying other things. Then the first parrot said, "Let's neck." The preacher's parrot responded, "Alleluia, my prayers have been answered!"

MARCH 9

YOUR SPIRITUAL BAR CODE

"By this all will know that you are My disciples, if you have love for one another."
(John 13:35, NKJV)

On October 7, 1952, Joseph Woodland and Bernard Silver were issued a patent for the "bar code". Silver was a graduate student at Drexel Institute of Technology in Philadelphia. A local food chain store owner had made an inquiry to the institute about a method of automatically reading product information at checkout. Silver joined with woodland and came up with a method of identifying patterns known as the bar code. The bar code was first used commercially in 1966, and in 1973 a Universal Product Code (UPC) was created. The first UPC scanner was installed at a Marsh's supermarket in Troy, Ohio. The first product scanned with a bar code was a pack of Wrigley's gum.

The bar code in simple language is a method of identifying a product. Jesus declared that disciples of Jesus Christ are identified by a type of "spiritual bar code": "By this all will know that you are My disciples, if you have love for one another" (John 13:35, NKJV). When people "scan" our lives, are we identified as disciples of Jesus Christ? Pray that your "bar code" reads, "This is a disciple of the Lord Jesus Christ." It's a great way to be known.

A LITTLE HUMOR: When Woody Hayes was coach of Ohio State University, he had an outstanding football player who was not very smart. He was in danger of losing his eligibility because of his grades, so Woody Hayes went to the player's biology teacher to appeal to him. He said, "I've got to have this player. You've got to pass him." The teacher agreed to give the student a simple test that anyone could pass. It consisted of one question. He asked, "Name the three vital parts of the body." The student replied, "That's easy. The head, the heart, and the bowels, of which there are five – A, E. I, O, U."

MARCH 10

WHERE CAN I BE SAFE?

"God is our refuge and strength, an ever-present help in trouble. Therefore we will not fear." (Psalm 46:1, NIV)

Where can I be safe? That is a question many people are asking. All of us want to know that our home is safe, our family is safe, that those we love are protected. Fear is a terrible thing.

No wonder the Bible says, "Fear not!" so many times.

One summer evening during a violent thunderstorm a mother was tucking her small boy into bed. She was about to turn off the light when her son asked with a tremor in his voice, "Mommy, will you sleep with me tonight?" The mother smiled and gave him a reassuring hug. "I can't dear," she said. "I have to sleep in Daddy's room." A long silence was broken at last by a shaken little voice saying, "The big sissy."

I'm not saying that we are becoming a nation of sissies, but people do seem to be more afraid than ever before.

Do you remember the song, *Who's Afraid of the Big Bad Wolf?* The song became enormously popular with Americans fighting the Great Depression in the 1930's. But how it became a hit surprised even its creators.

The song was in Walt Disney's animated cartoon, *Three Little Pigs,* which opened at New York's Radio City Music Hall in May, 1933. Disney expected a good response, but to his disappointment, critics and audiences were ho-hum about it. Then the lightning struck. After the movie was shown in other theaters, it suddenly caught on. Radio stations and band leaders were asking Disney for permission to play one of the songs featured in the film, *Who's Afraid of the Big Bad Wolf?*

Disney hadn't even arranged to publish the music, and to meet demands for sheet music, he had to send musicians with flashlights into darkened theaters to copy down words and music from the screen. The song soon swept the country as a plucky response to the grinding economic times. Even President Roosevelt said the movie was one of his favorites. Of course, this was during the time when Roosevelt was telling Americans that the only thing they had to fear was fear itself.[25]

Wouldn't it be wonderful never to be afraid again? Where shall we go where we will be safe? Where shall we turn so that we never live in fear again? The Psalmist tells us: "God is our refuge and strength, an ever-present help in trouble. Therefore we will not fear" (Psalm 46:1, NIV).

These words have brought comfort to millions of people across the centuries. There is a place that is safe. It is a place near the heart of God. When you are afraid and wonder where in the world you will be safe, be still. Stop for a moment, and reflect on God's great love for you.

A LITTLE HUMOR: A lady was flying with her infant daughter. When they landed, they were met in the waiting room by her father, who took the baby while she proceeded to the baggage claim area. Standing there alone waiting to claim her baggage, she was absent-mindedly holding the baby's pacifier. She noticed a flight attendant staring at her, then at the pacifier, then back at her. Finally, the flight attendant spoke: "Excuse me, Miss. Is this your first flight?"

MARCH 11

DON'T LET GO!

"For consider Him who has endured such hostility by sinners against Himself, so that you will not grow weary and lose heart." (Hebrews 12:3, NASB)

For many years Dr. Jeff Ray served as professor of preaching at Southwestern Baptist Theological Seminary in Fort Worth, Texas. He taught into the 1940's when he was more than eighty years of age. Trouble and tragedy etched their influence on the life of Jeff Ray.

Early in his adult life his first wife died, leaving him to serve as mother and father to his children. His sorrow was compounded when one day in the 1930's he received the news that a beloved son had died. This calamity, added to life's other burdens, threatened to drive the vitality out of Dr. Ray. For a time he quit teaching and preaching in area churches. Dejected and depressed, he was unable to develop interest in anything and was ready to say, "I cannot go on!"

Mrs. L. R. Elliott, wife of the seminary librarian, sent her husband to visit Dr. Ray with a scrapbook filled with poems and articles which had encouraged her. After Dr. Elliott's departure, the weary professor listlessly leafed through the pages of the scrapbook. A poem with the engaging title of "I Won't Let Go!" caught his attention. Realizing that he had been wanting to do just that, Dr. Ray read these words:

I want to let go, but I won't let go.
There are battles to fight,

---

[25] *Dynamic Preaching.* October-December, 1999. Vol. 14, No. 4, page 3.

By day and by night,
For God and the right –
And I'll never let go.

I want to let go, but I won't let go.
I'm sick, 'tis true,
Worried and blue,
And worn through and through,
But I won't let go.

I want to let go, but I won't let go
I will never yield!
What! lie down on the field
And surrender my shield?
No, I'll never let go!

I want to let go, but I won't let go.
May this be my song
"Mid legions of wrong –
Oh, God, keep me strong
That I may never let go!"
-- Author Unknown

After reading the poem, Dr. Ray closed the scrapbook, arose from his couch of grief and defeat and put behind him any thought of giving up and quitting. He returned to the classroom to teach and to pulpits to preach. For many years he distributed copies of this poem to his students. Many of them found encouragement from Dr. Ray's testimony and from the poem, so that they did not let go.

Perhaps today, you are going through a difficult time; if so, may you draw strength to never let go.

A LITTLE HUMOR: Unfortunately some people are like the one in the old Flip Wilson routine, in which someone asked Flip about his religion and he answered, "I am a Jehovah's Bystander." "A Jehovah's Bystander?" remarked his friend. "I never heard of a Jehovah's Bystander." Flip looked coy and said, "Well, they asked me to be a witness, but I didn't want to get involved."

MARCH 12

CONSUMED BY ZEAL

"Zeal for your house consumes me, and the insults of those who insult you fall on me." (Psalm 69:9, NIV)

Teddy Roosevelt, 26th U. S. President, wasn't afraid of many things as an adult.

But as a child he was terrified by Madison Square Church in New York City. He refused to walk into the great, dark sanctuary alone. Mittie Roosevelt, his mother, asked him why. He was afraid of "The Zeal," he said. The pastor said it might attack him at any time. His mother began reading aloud the biblical passages about zeal. When she got to Psalm 69:9, Teddy stopped her. The King James Version had it, "For the zeal of thine house hath eaten me up."

Let's talk about zeal. It's a seldom-used word these days. The dictionary defines it as "intense enthusiasm, as in working for a cause." Synonyms: passion, fervor.

What are some causes that attract zeal today? A favorite football team? A political cause? A new diet or exercise program?

Occasionally we encounter zealous Christians. The world doesn't know quite what to do about them and calls them "fanatics" or "Jesus freaks." They're modern-day zealots. The zeal of God's kingdom seems to "eat them up."

What would the world be like in this new year if we had a few more zealous disciples? Like the Marines, God is looking for a "few good men" – men who will be consumed by zeal for Him. Are you willing to be that kind of zealot?

A LITTLE HUMOR: An old man took his ugly dog for his regular Sunday walk in the park. He sat on the park bench while his dog played at his feet. They weren't bothering anyone. Soon another man appeared with his dog. Both the man and the dog had a mean, bulldog-type look on their faces. They were looking for a fight. The man and his bulldog began taunting the old man and his ugly dog. The younger man commanded his dog, "Spike!" and pointed in the ugly dog's direction. The old man said, "I wouldn't do that if I were you." Irritated by the passive old man's comment, he commanded his dog to attack. As the battle raged in cartoon fashion (lots of barking, dust flying, and dogs running in circles), the result was unexpected. Spike lay defeated, torn to pieces by the ugly canine. His humbled master said to the old man, "What kind of dog is that?" to which the old man replied, "Well, before I cut off his tail and painted him yellow, he was an alligator!"

MARCH 13

COOL OFF BY SUNDOWN

"If you are angry, don't sin by nursing your grudge. Don't let the sun go down with you still angry — get over it quickly; for when you are angry you give a mighty foothold to the devil." (Ephesians 4:26-27, LB)

Have you ever been angry? Foolish question, isn't it? Every normal person gets angry. A more proper question may be, how do you express your anger? Do you explode with harsh and ugly words? Do you sulk? Convey insulting looks? You can tell the size of a person by what makes him angry. Will Rogers mused, "People who fly into a rage seldom make a good landing." When does anger become sinful?

Anger becomes sinful if we are angry at someone without a just cause; when it is directed at people rather than at causes; when it comes from hurt feelings and injured pride; if it is a desire for revenge; if we harbor anger in our hearts; and, if we have an unforgiving spirit. The Bible says, "Do not be eager in your heart to be angry, for anger resides in the bosom of fools" (Ecclesiastes 7:9, NASB).

The Apostle Paul warns us, "Don't let the sun go down with you still angry." To harbor anger only gives the devil a "foothold" which means it gives him an opportunity to work. When a person has stubborn anger in his heart, he just says, "Devil, come on in. You're welcome. Here is your place." And that stubborn anger becomes the foxhole out of which the devil is going to snipe at your life. That stubborn anger becomes the beachhead from which the devil is going to attack and take more and more ground.

Look in Proverbs 14:29, "A patient man has great understanding, but a quick-tempered man displays folly". That means if you will just slow down, become slow to get angry, God will give you understanding. You will be able to think the situation through. You will be able to discern what it is that's making you angry and whether or not you have a right and a cause to be angry.

Alexander the Great was one of the few men in history who seem to deserve his descriptive title. He was energetic, versatile, and intelligent. Although hatred was not generally part of his nature, several times in his life he was tragically defeated by anger. The story is told of one of these occasions, when a dear friend of Alexander, a general in his army, became intoxicated and began to ridicule the emperor in front of his men. Blinded by anger and quick as lightning, Alexander snatched a spear from the hand of a soldier and hurled it at his friend. Although he had only intended to scare the drunken general, his aim was true and the spear took the life of his childhood friend. Deep remorse followed his anger. Overcome with guilt, Alexander attempted to take his own life with the same spear, but then was stopped by his men. For days he lay sick, calling for his friend and chiding himself as a murdered. Alexander the Great conquered many cities and vanquished many countries, but he had failed miserably to control his own spirit. Proverbs 16:32 says, "It is better to be slow-tempered than famous; it is better to have self-control than to control an army." (LB)

A LITTLE HUMOR: "Why haven't you mended the holes in these socks?" the husband demanded. "You didn't buy that new coat I wanted," replied the wife, "so I figured if you didn't give a wrap, I didn't give a darn!"

MARCH 14

A HAPPY HOME LIFE

"Wives, be subject to your husbands . . . Husbands, love your wives . . . Children, be obedient to your parents . . ." (Colossians 3:18-20, NASB)

There is no greater joy in life than a good marriage and a happy home. In the television movie, *Sweetheart's Dance,* two friends were talking of marriage. One's marriage was breaking up; the other was planning to be married. The one anticipating marriage asked his friend how marriage was. He replied, “Before I screwed up, it was great. When I was happy, I was twice as happy. And when I was sad, I was half as sad.”

There can be no greater blessing than a stable home life. Obviously, many homes lack happiness and stability. Today, approximately 50% of first marriages end in divorce; approximately 60% of second marriage; and 75% of third marriages. This turmoil in the family is taking a tremendous toil on our society. Someone quipped, “Most Hollywood marriages take place in the morning. That way, if things don’t work out, they haven’t wasted a whole day.”

It is possible to have a happy home life. Colossians 3:18-20 gives us the formula for such a home: “Wives, be subject to your husbands . . . Husbands, love your wives . . . Children, be obedient to your parents . . .” The key for this formula’s success is found in the word “Lord.” Notice these expressions: “as is fitting in the Lord . . . this is well-pleasing to the Lord . . . fearing the Lord . . . as for the Lord rather than for men . . . it is the Lord Christ whom you serve” (vv.18, 20, 22-24). When the Lord is given His rightful place in our relationships, then a home can be a happy one.

A LITTLE HUMOR: A couple came upon a wishing well. The wife leaned over, made a wish and threw in a penny. The husband decided he would make a wish, too. As he leaned over, he leaned too far and fell into the well. The wife just stood there looking down into the well and then finally said, “Well, I’ll be. It really works.”

MARCH 15

FACE TO FACE WITH JESUS

“For now we see in a mirror dimly, but then face to face . . .”
(1 Corinthians 13:12a, NASB)

The hymn writer Fanny Crosby gave us more than 6,000 gospel songs. Although blinded by an illness at the age of six weeks, she never became bitter. One time a preacher sympathetically remarked, “I think it is a great pity that the Master did not give you sight when He showered so many other gifts upon you.” She replied quickly, “Do you know that if at birth I had been able to make one petition, it would have been that I should be born blind?” “Why?” asked the surprised preacher. “Because when I get to heaven, the first face that shall ever gladden my sight will be that of my Savior!”

One of Miss Crosby’s hymns was so personal that for years she kept it to herself. Kenneth Osbeck, author of several books on hymnology, says its revelation to the public came about this way: “One day at the Bible conference in Northfield, Massachusetts, Miss Crosby was asked by D. L. Moody to give a personal testimony. At first she hesitated, then quietly rose and said, ‘There is one hymn I have written which has never been published. I call it my soul’s poem. Sometimes when I am troubled, I repeat it to myself, for it brings comfort to my heart.' She then recited while many wept, 'Someday the silver cord will break, and I no more as now shall sing: but oh, the joy when I shall wake within the palace of the King! And I shall see Him face to face, and tell the story saved by grace!'" At the age of 95 Fanny Crosby passed into glory and saw the face of Jesus.

Corinth was well known in commercial circles for its highly polished Corinthian brass, which was used extensively for mirrors, among many other things. But the best of these mirrors were highly imperfect, bearing only faulty reflections. In comparison to the direct sight of the eye, they were cloudy and dim. While we live on this earth we can only see Christ through the eye of faith, but someday, when we leave this world and go to heaven, we will see Jesus face to face.

A LITTLE HUMOR: A little girl asked her mother, "How did the human race start?" The mother answered, "God made Adam and Eve and they had children, and so all mankind was made." Two hours later, the girl asked her father the same question. The father answered, "Many years ago, there were monkeys from which the human race evolved." The confused girl returned to her mother and said, "Mom, how is it possible that you told me the human race was created by God, and Dad said they developed from monkeys?" The mother answered, "Well, dear, it is very simple. I told you about my side of the family and your father told you about his."

MARCH 16

FULL OF THE RIGHT STUFF

"Therefore, brethren, seek out from among you seven men of good reputation, full of the Holy Spirit and wisdom, whom we may appoint over this business."
(Act 6:3, NKJV)

The 1983 movie *The Right Stuff* was one of the nominees for best picture. The story is based on Tom Wolf's best-selling book of the same name. It is the story of the men who had "the right stuff" that qualified them to be astronauts.

Stephen was a man who was full of "the right stuff" in spiritual matters. Acts 6:8-10 mentions five things about Stephen.

First, Stephen was full of the Holy Spirit (Acts 6:3, 10). To be filled with the Holy Spirit is to be controlled by the Holy Spirit. The Bible commands that we be filled with the Holy Spirit (Ephesians 5:18).

Second, Stephen was full of wisdom (Acts 6:3, 10). Wisdom comes from the guidance of the Holy Spirit through God's Word. Stephen was well grounded in the Word as chapter 7 of Acts 6 reveals. If you want to be wise, knowledgeable, and discerning in spiritual matters, get to know your Bible. James 1:5 encourages us to ask for wisdom, and James 3:17-18 describes heavenly wisdom.

Third, Stephen was full of faith (Acts 6:5). Stephen was inspired, illuminated, and strengthen by his faith. It was his faith in Christ that made him eloquent, bold and Christ-like. Without faith it is impossible to please God (Hebrews 11:6).

Fourth, Stephen was full of grace (Acts 6:8a).This was not only saving grace and sufficient grace, but it was grace that caused his face to give the appearance of an angel (Acts 6:15). From the life of Stephen, we can see that when the grace of God is operative in our lives, the result is charm in character.

Fifth, Stephen was full of power (Acts 6:8b). Jesus said, "Without Me you can do nothing" (John 15:5) Stephen proclaimed the gospel with great power (Acts 1:8; 7:51-53) and prayed with great power (Acts 7:59-60).

Stephen was full of the Holy Spirit, wisdom, faith, grace, and power. He was a well-rounded saint indeed; a man full of "the right stuff." We too can be people "full of the right stuff" if we follow his example.

A LITTLE HUMOR: A couple drove down a country road for several miles, not saying a word. An earlier discussion had led to an argument and neither of them wanted to concede their position. As they passed a barnyard of mules, goats, and pigs, the husband asked sarcastically, "Relatives of yours?" "Yep," the wife replied, "in-laws."

MARCH 17

EXERCISING YOUR SPIRITUAL MUSCLES

"Physical exercise has some value, but spiritual exercise is much more important, for it promises a reward in both this life and the next." (1 Timothy 4:8, NLT)

The late Merv Griffin was an entertainer, pianist, and television personality. He also created such game shows as *Wheel of Fortune* and *Jeopardy*. Several years ago, he had a television program called *The Merv Griffin Show*. The guest on one particular program was a body builder. During the interview Merv asked, "Why do you develop those particular muscles?" The body builder simply stepped forward and flexed a series of well-defined muscles from chest to calf. The audience broke into applause. "What do you use all those muscles for?" Merv questioned. Again the muscle-bound man flexed, and biceps and triceps grew to impressive proportions. "But what do you use those muscles for?" Merv persisted. The body builder was bewildered. He didn't have an answer. His muscles were just there for show.

The Greek word translated *exercise* gives us our English word *gymnasium*. Gyms are full of people exercising to develop their muscles. Believers should be just as intent on developing their spiritual well-being. First Timothy 4:7b reads, "Spend your time and energy in training yourself for spiritual fitness" (NLT).

Paul was not belittling bodily exercise. Exercise does help to keep arteries open and cholesterol down and in warding off strokes and heart attacks. Physical fitness has value, but it is relatively unimportant compared with spiritual exercise. If we stop exercising the spiritual man, we will fail to reach our ultimate objective, which is to manifest godliness.

A LITTLE HUMOR: A little girl learned the multiplication table and thought she had exhausted mathematics. With a twinkle in his eye, her grandpa asked, "What's thirteen times thirteen?" Turning to him with scorn in her eyes, "Don't be silly, grandpa; there's no such thing!"

MARCH 18

A BAD NEWS BAY

"The devil, who deceived them, was cast into the lake of fire and brimstone..."
(Revelation 20:10a, NKJV)

A bay in North Carolina is called "Nag's Head." There's an interesting story about how the bay got its name. Back in the 1700's thieves (called "wreckers") made their living by luring unsuspecting ships to the rocky bottom of this bay. They would tie a lantern to a pole and fasten the pole to a horse's back so that the lantern hung in front of the horse's head (that's where the name "Nag's Head" came from). When they knew a ship was in the area, the wreckers would lead the horse back and forth on the beach. Pilots on the ships would mistake the moving light for a signal of safety and guide their vessels into the treacherous bay. The deception inevitably led to a shipwreck, and the wreckers would simply gather up the goods that washed ashore in the hours that followed. To this day much of the furniture in homes of that area came from the plunder at Nag's Head Bay, taken from ships that had been destroyed by the lure of a deceptive light.

The Bible says that Satan is "crafty" (Genesis 3:1), meaning he is skilled in underhandedness and deception. As the great deceiver, he is able to transform himself into an angel of light (2 Cor. 11:14). He wants to use his deceptive light to lure you into "bays" of destruction which at first appear harmless, and even secure.

In James 1:14 the Bible says that a person is "drawn away" and "enticed" to sin. The words *drawn away* mean lured and the word *enticed* means ensnared. These words are taken from the language of fishing. The imagery is that of a fish swimming in a straight course and then drawn off toward something that seems attractive, only to discover that the bait has a deadly hook in it.

The devil is clever. He realizes that if a person knows the truth about sin's consequences, he would never sin. He would never tell a person that if he plays around with drugs or alcohol and abuses them that he could become addicted to these things and ruin his life. He is a master deceiver and hides the truth about sin until after the person has committed it.

We must watch out for the great deceiver. He provides "bays" which seem harmless enough at first, but there are dangers underneath their waters which you can't see. That's part of Satan's game. Remember, his plan is to wreck your life and steal all he can. Which bay is Satan's "Nag's Head" in your life?

A LITTLE HUMOR: Two boys were leaving church after hearing the pastor's sermon about the devil. One boy asked the other, "Do you believe all that stuff about the devil?" "No," said the second little boy, "It's just like that Santa Clause stuff. It's really your father!"

MARCH 19

A SPECIAL TRANSFER

"But as many as received Him, to them He gave the right to become children of God, to those who believe on in His name." (John 1:12, NKJV)

Back in 1891, Robert Louis Stevenson, author of such classics as *Dr. Jekyll and Mr. Hyde* and *Kidnapped,* gave a rather odd gift to the daughter of a friend of his. This friend, Henry Ide, once joked that Christmas was not the happiest day of the year in his household. His fourteen-year-old daughter, Annie, had been born on Christmas, and she always complained that she got cheated out of a separate birthday party. So Robert Louis Stevenson came up with the idea of giving away his birthday. He drew up a legal document transferring all the "rights and privileges" of his birthday, which fell on November 13th, to Miss Annie H. Ide. From that day forward, Annie celebrated her birthday on November 13th.[26]

Robert Louis Stevenson was not the first to transfer all his "rights and privileges" to someone else. In a sense Jesus became mortal that he might transfer some of His immortality to us. Jesus became human that He might transfer the spark of divinity to us. Jesus became a servant that He might transfer us to the status of sons and daughters. Or as John put it: "The Word became flesh and made his dwelling among us. We have seen His glory, the glory of the One and Only, who came from the Father, full of grace and truth" (John 1:14, NIV). No wonder we feel a need to celebrate. Happy birthday, Jesus!

Did you know that *Happy Birthday* was one of the first songs performed in outer space? It was sung by the Apollo IX astronauts on March 8, 1969. But it was not the first song sung by astronauts. That honor goes to *Jingle Bells* which was sung by the crew of Gemini VI on December 15, 1965. They accompanied themselves on harmonica and bells.

It is appropriate that a tune associated with the birth of Jesus would be the first to be sung in outer space — even though it is primarily a secular tune. But even that festive song was not the first to ring out in the heavens. That honor goes to an unknown tune whose lyrics go something like this: "Glory to God in the highest, and on earth peace, good will to men." It was the angels' way of singing "Happy Birthday, Jesus." God's own Son had come into the world.

---

[26] Webb Garrison, *A Treasury of Christmas Stories* (Nashville: Rutledge Hill Press, 1990), 13-16.

A LITTLE HUMOR: A woman returned home from a holiday shopping spree with her arms loaded with packages. Her husband met her at the door and said, "What did you buy? With prices as high as they are, I'll bet you spent a fortune. I hate to think what has happened to our nest egg?" "I'll tell you what happened to our nest egg," his wife said defensively as she began to put her packages on the dining room table. "The old hen got tired of sitting on it."

MARCH 20

NOW THAT I AM SAVED, I WILL . . .

"But grow in the grace and knowledge of our Lord and Savior Jesus Christ."
(2 Peter 3:18a, NASB)

For people to be born and never grow into maturity is a terrible waste. Yet something like that happens in spiritual life all the time. People through faith in Christ become a part of the family of God. But many fail to grow from that initial experience of birth to maturity in the Christian life. I use the word **S-A-V-E-D** as an acrostic to encourage you as a believer in Christ to go beyond your conversion experience and "grow in the grace and knowledge of our Lord and Savior Jesus Christ."

S – Search The Scriptures Daily. Acts 17:10-11 speaks of a group of people of Berea who "examined the Scriptures daily." There is no substitute for a day-by-day studying of God's Word. The Bible requires serious attention and diligent study if it is to be enjoyed.

A – Attend Church Regularly. Hebrews 10:23-25 refers to the habit of many first century Christians coming together on a regular basis in order to "stimulate one another to love and good deeds . . . and encourage one another." Billy Graham has said, "Without the fellowship of believers, a newly born Christian has a tendency to wither."

V – Vow To Confess Christ. Matthew 10:32-33 records the words of Jesus encouraging His disciple to confess Him before others, and if they would He would confess them before His Heavenly Father. We must never be ashamed to let others know that we love the Lord Jesus Christ and follow Him.

E – Engage In Constant Prayer. F. B. Meyer said, "The great tragedy of life is not unanswered prayer, but unoffered prayer." Paul Powell writes, "One of the tragedies of most modern disciples is that they are trying to live without prayer. That's why we are weak and anemic in our spiritual lives." Jesus said to His disciples "that all times they ought to pray and not to lose heart" (Luke 18:1).

D – Depart From All Sin. The Psalmist wrote, "Search me, O God, and know my heart . . . and see if there be any hurtful way in me, and lead me in the everlasting way." (Psalm 139:23-24). The apostle Paul wrote, "The grace of God has appeared, bringing salvation to all men, instructing us to deny ungodliness and worldly desires and to live sensibly, righteously, and godly in the present age" (Titus 2:11-12).

Since your conversion to Christ, have you been growing in His grace and knowledge? If not, why not make a commitment to follow these five suggestions and start growing today.

A LITTLE HUMOR: A small country church was having a "baptizing" in a river on a cold January day. A revival meeting had just concluded. The preacher asked one baptismal candidate, "Is the water cold?" "Naw!" he replied. One of the deacons shouted, "Dip him agin' preacher, he's still lyin!"

MARCH 21

TOO MANY DECISIONS

"If you want to know what God wants you to do, ask Him." (James 1:5a, LB)

"Be sure to get the right one." Those were the last words my wife said to me as I left to go the grocery store. She was sending me to buy a box of detergent. "I want Tide detergent without bleach. If it has bleach in it, it will say so on the package." "Fine. I can handle this," I thought to myself. Then I remembered the experiences of the past when invariably I would get the wrong thing.

Once again I found myself standing in the grocery aisle looking for Tide detergent – without bleach. What she didn't tell me was there are many different kinds of Tide detergent. As I looked at the shelves I discovered there was Tide with a "Clear Breeze" scent, Tide with a "Mountain Spring" scent, Tide with "A Touch of Downey," Tide with a "Cold Water Fresh Scent," and Tide with a "New Scent Glacier." Now what do I do? Thank God for the cell phone! A quick call home should help. But then I discovered you can't get a reception inside the building. You have to go outside to make the call, but at least you can call home. Sure enough that phone call saved my life!

Some times in life when we have to make decisions about certain matters, we may not know what to do. That's when we discover the answer is just a prayer away. James 1:5 tells us "If you want to know what God wants you to do, ask Him." So the next time you need help in making a decision, ask God for help. He's waiting for you to call.

A LITTLE HUMOR: There was a line of men standing in front of the Pearly Gates, waiting to get in. A sign overhead read: "For Men Who Have Been Dominated By Their Wives All Their Lives." The line extended as far as the eye could see. There was another sign nearby: "For Men Who Have Never Been Dominated By Their Wives." One man was standing under it. Someone went over to him and asked, "What are you standing here for?" The man said, "I don't know. My wife told me to stand here."

MARCH 22

BE PATIENT

"Therefore be patient, brethren, until the coming of the Lord. The farmer waits for the precious produce of the soil, being patient about it, until it gets the early and late rains." (James 5:7, NASB)

On November 1, 1512, Michelangelo's paintings on the ceiling of the Sistine Chapel were revealed to the public for the first time. Considered Michelangelo's greatest project, the frescoes on the chapel ceiling show nine scenes from the Old Testament – three scenes of God creating the earth, the story of Adam and Eve, and Noah and the flood. Twelve Old Testament prophets and classical prophetic women called sibyls surround each scene. Michelangelo began painting the frescoes on the ceiling in 1508 and completed the work three years later in 1511. The paintings were done while lying on his back on a scaffolding high above the chapel floor.

For the most part, we are not very patient. When it comes to seeing things done, we want to see results immediately. Yet, oftentimes, the greatest works are those that require patience. In our Scripture for today, James spoke of the patience of the farmer. The fields have been plowed, and the seed has been sown, but the farmer knows that he cannot expect a harvest the next day. It takes time. When it comes to the work of God, we all want to see immediate results; but we must never forget that once we have sown the seed, results may not come until later. Today, don't lose heart. Keep sowing the seed. The ceiling of the Sistine Chapel was not done overnight.

A LITTLE HUMOR: A pastor and his wife were shopping in an antique store. Their efforts at witnessing had revealed that the owner was a member of a Baptist church. The pastor's wife asked, "Why don't you come hear my husband preach sometime?" "I can't do that, ma'am," said the dealer. "I've been going to hear my pastor preach for ten years thinking he might say something. If I miss once, that just might be the Sunday he would say something."

MARCH 23

DON'T FRET

"Fret not . . ." (Psalm 37:1, 7-8)

Psalm 37 begins with a personal and practical admonition: "Fret not." The word *fret* means to burn; to become heated up; to be incensed. Someone has said that the previous generation was called "the jet set" and the present generation is called "the fret set." How do we calm a fretful spirit and bring peace to a troubled heart?

First, **TRUST IN THE LORD** (v. 3). C. H. Spurgeon said, "Faith cures fretting." When you fix your eyes on the Lord and trust and obey Him, that fretful spirit quiets down, and peace comes to your heart.

Second, **DELIGHT IN THE LORD** (v. 4). The word delight means to find your joy and satisfaction in Christ. We delight in the Lord when we delight in His Word (Psalm 1:2) and His Will (Psalm 40:8).

Third, **COMMIT YOUR WAY TO THE LORD** (v. 5). To commit something to God means to give it to Him. And, when you give it to the Lord, don't take it back!

Fourth, **REST IN THE LORD** (v. 7a). Other translations render the word rest as be still, or be silent. The phrase "all shook up" was made popular by the late Elvis Presley. Christ gives us His peace that we will not be shaken.

Fifth, **WAIT PATIENTLY FOR THE LORD** (v. 7b). To wait on the Lord doesn't mean that we sit around and do nothing. It means to have hope; look to God for all we need.

Don't fret today. Trust, delight, commit, rest, and wait for the Lord. God takes care of His own.

In his book, *Three Steps Forward, Two Steps Back*, Charles Swindoll writes that "Elvis Presley said shortly before his death that he would pay a million dollars for one week of a normal life of peace, to be able to move up and down the streets of his city without harassment."[27]

The psalmist said, "Do not fret; it leads only to evildoing" (Psalm 37:8b, NASB). When we are in a stressful situation, we can say with confidence, "We will not be moved. We will not be 'all shook up,' because the God of hope and peace is with us."

A LITTLE HUMOR: A little boy went to the grocery store and asked the clerk for a box of detergent. The clerk asked the boy why he needed detergent. "I want to wash my dog," he replied. "Well, son, this detergent is pretty strong for washing a little dog." The little boy replied, "That's what I want. He's mighty dirty." He took the box of detergent home, and about a week later he returned. The store clerk, recognizing him, asked him about his dog. "Oh, he's dead," said the boy. "Oh, I'm sorry," replied the clerk. "I guess the detergent was too strong." "I don't think the detergent hurt him," said the boy. "I think it was the spin cycle that got him."

MARCH 24

DON'T FLIRT WITH TEMPTATION

"Watch and pray, lest you enter into temptation. The spirit indeed is willing, but the flesh is weak." (Matthew 26:41, NKJV)

The movie, *Lord of the Rings: Fellowship of the Ring* has revived interest in Tolkein's fantasy. It also has people talking about truths the book addresses. Much discussion centers on the ring itself. The ring is the most powerful of several rings that are abroad in their fantasy world. It can make the wearer invisible. It also seduces those who wear it.

---

[27] Charles R. Swindoll, *Three Steps Forward, Two Steps Back* (Nashville: Thomas Nelson Publishers, 1980), 41.

By strange circumstances, the ring comes into the possession of Bilbo Baggins, a noble, peace-loving creature called a Hobbit. He took it from a nasty, beastly creature named Gollum. At the beginning of the book and movie, Bilbo is urged by his old friend Gandalf to give up the ring. Even though the ring is evil, by and large, it seems, Bilbo is uncorrupted. Yet, when told to give it up, he resists and gets angry.

It finally comes to Bilbo that he is becoming more and more like the loathsome Gollum, even beginning to talk like him. The ring has come to affect him after all. To his surprise, he learns that the evil Gollum was once a creature very much like himself. With some reluctance he surrenders the ring. So it is with all temptations. The longer we flirt with it and harbor it, the more it begins to corrupt us.

We cannot avoid being tempted. Even Jesus was tempted. But we don't have to flirt with temptation. Jesus warns us of the need to "watch and pray, lest you enter into temptation." Don't see how close you can get to sin without getting into trouble – rather, see how far you can stay away. Listen to the warnings of God's Word, and don't forget the pain of past mistakes. Learn from them. When you flee temptation, be sure you don't leave a forwarding address.

A LITTLE HUMOR: "Opportunity knocks only once," one preacher warned his flock, "but temptation bangs on your door for years."

MARCH 25

GOD IS STILL ON THE PHONE

"Let us therefore draw near with confidence to the throne of grace, that we may receive mercy and may find grace to help in time of need." (Hebrews 4:16, NASB)

Years ago, congregations frequently sang a chorus that goes like this:

God is still on the throne,
And He will remember His own;
Though trails may pass us
And burdens distress us
He never will leave us alone.

The story is told of a little boy who, when introduced to this chorus for the first time in his Sunday School, came home and told his mother, "We learned a new song in Sunday School today." "Oh, said his mother, "what was it?" "God is still on the phone," said the little boy. Well that wasn't exactly what he had been taught, but the thought contained in those words was equally true. Though God reigns from a majestic throne, He is accessible to us at all times of day and night. The lines of communication that lead from us to Him are never blocked and never "down." The throne of God, you see, is not only a throne of righteousness but a throne of grace as well.

The word *grace* suggests kindness, goodness, and favor and indicates that we can be assured when we approach the Lord we do not have to be afraid of His wrath or judgment. Rather, we may approach Him with *confidence.* The word *confidence* means freedom of speech. The idea is there is such trust between two people that one may share with the other anything that may be on his heart and not be afraid that his trust will be betrayed. He is assured that the one to whom he speaks loves him and will support him no matter what.

I like that. I also like what Charles Spurgeon said of prayer. He compared it to the pulling of a rope that rings a bell: "Prayer pulls the rope down below and the great bell rings above in the ears of God. Some scarcely stir the bell . . . others give only an occasional jerk. But he who communicates with heaven, is the man who grasps the rope boldly and pulls continually with all his might."[28]

When you pray to God you will not find a "busy signal." The line between ourselves and God is always open. "God is still on the phone." Have you "called" Him lately?

A LITTLE HUMOR: Seven-year-old George came out with a loud shrill whistle during the minister's sermon one Sunday. After church, his mother scolded him and asked, "Son, whatever made you do such a thing?" "I asked God to teach me to whistle, and he did just then," answered the boy.

MARCH 26

GETTING OLDER AND FLYING HIGHER

"For a thousand years in your sight are like a day that has just gone by, or like a watch in the night." (Psalm 90:4, NIV)

You've probably heard the amazing story of Herb Keller and Southwest Airlines. They're the ones who brought fun back into flight. When you step onto a plane guided by the folks at Southwest, you'rc liable to hear just about anything. Here's a sample.

Toward the end of a flight, you'll hear this over the intercom from a flight attendant: "Ladies and Gentlemen, we have a very special person aboard today. He's 85, today's his birthday, and he's never flown before today." Everyone is clapping politely and nodding by this time. The attendant continues: "So as you de-plane, be sure to wish our PILOT a happy birthday."

As children, we're exhilarated by the passing of time. We count the days until our birthdays, thrilled by the idea of being a year older. We look forward to each new year.

Somewhere in that twilight zone between young adulthood and middle age, we develop a new attitude toward aging. The world begins to circle the sun a bit too

---

[28] Michael P. Green (Editor), *Illustrations for Biblical Preaching* (Grand Rapids: Baker Book House, 1989), 273

rapidly for our taste. We want to slow things down and savor them a bit. It certainly doesn't help that our culture has always glorified youth.

It's difficult for us to take in the fact that time is one more creation of the Lord. He Himself never ages, but guides and cares for His creation from outside time and space. As the psalmist explains, "For a thousand years in your sight are like a day that has just gone by, or like a watch in the night" (Psalm 90:4, NIV).

We, too, are eternal creatures. Old age and death are not, for us, enemies to be feared; they bear a sign that says, "To be continued." We will spend all of eternity in His presence, no longer limited by the frailties of this life.

That should be our reference point as we reach the end of one more year. Time flies, but so do we! We soar higher and faster toward a sure destination, borne on wings of His love.

A LITTLE HUMOR: At a drugstore, a wife wanted to buy shaving lotion for her husband. "What kind?" asked the clerk. "Well," explained the wife, "he's seventy years old. Have you any of that 'Old Spouse'?"

MARCH 27

BIRD LEGS?

"And He withdrew from them about a stone's throw, and He knelt down and began to pray." (Luke 22:41, NASB)

Birds sleep on their perches, but they never fall off. When a bird bends its legs at the knee, the tendons cause the claws to contract and grip like a steel trap. They will not let go until their legs are straightened again. The bended knee gives the bird the ability to hold onto his perch tightly.

As Christians we can learn a valuable lesson from a sleeping bird. Just as the greatest strength and security comes from the bended knee of the bird, so it is for us. The bended knee for us represents prayer. Our power as Christians to hold onto the qualities of God such as honesty, purity, thoughtfulness, and honor lies in our prayer life. For us constant communion with God is the key to becoming what He wants us to be.

The story is told of a group of people who had just completed the dangerous ascent of the Weisshorn. One of them, anxious to see over the top of the peak and not aware that the gale always blowing there would sweep him over the cliff, had thoughtlessly jumped to his feet. "On your knees, sir! You are safe here only on your knees," shouted the guide as he pulled the inexperienced mountain climber to the ground. In that place of danger, he was safe only on his knees. In like manner, we are safe only on our knees when we pray.[29]

---

[29] Leslie R. Smith, *From Sunset to Dawn* (New York: Abingdon Press, 1954), 86.

How are you doing with your prayer times? Are you taking more time to pray or praying throughout the day when an issue or problem arises? Hold onto God. He is holding onto you.

A LITTLE HUMOR: A college student felt he was very prepared for the final exam in ornithology (the study of birds). To his surprise, the test was different than he had expected. The professor placed twenty-five pictures on the front board and each picture contained one set of bird's-legs. The professor explained that each student was to identify all twenty-five birds by examining the picture of their legs. The student was enraged, he bolted to the front of the classroom, and contested the legitimacy of such a test. The professor held his ground and told the young man he could either take the test like everyone else, or fail the class. The student loudly declared, "I'd rather take an F than take this ridiculous test!" The professor said, "Very well, I'll be glad to give you an F. What's your name?" The young man gleefully pulled up his pant leg and said, "You tell me!"

MARCH 28

BELLS THAT NEVER STOP RINGING

"You shall make on its hem pomegranates of blue and purple and scarlet material, all around on the hem, and bells of gold between them all around: a golden bell and a pomegranate, a golden bell and a pomegranate, all around on the hem of the robe."
(Exodus 28:33-34, NASB)

Have you ever heard of Big Ben, that big clock tower in London? Actually neither the clock nor the tower are Big Ben. Big Ben is the 13.7-ton hour bell itself, the largest bell ever made by the Whitechapel Bell Foundry in London.

Over a century and a half, Big Ben has kept near perfect time, only falling silent or behind on rare occasions. During WW I, the bell was silenced for two years so as not to attract attention from the German zeppelins. In 1949, a flock of starlings decided the clock's minute hand made an impressive perch. Their combined weight slowed the hand by 4.5 minutes. In 1962, heavy snow accumulated on the clock's hands, causing the bell to ring in the New Year about ten minutes late.

The bells described in Exodus 28:33-34 are bells that were a part of the High Priestly robe worn by the High Priest as he ministered in the Holy of Holies of the Tabernacle. The sound of the bells sewn on the hem of the High Priest robe signaled those waiting outside the Holy Place that their representative ministering before the Lord was still alive and moving about, fulfilling his duties of interceding on their behalf.

Hebrews 4:14 reminds us that ". . . we have a great high priest who has passed through the heavens, Jesus the Son of God . . ." and that ". . . He always lives to make intercession for them" (Hebrews 7:25). As our High Priest, Jesus is able to save completely any and all who believe and never stops interceding for us. Listen! Can't you hear those bells ringing?

A LITTLE HUMOR: A cowboy was sitting on a barstool one night, minding his own business, when a fellow came in and sat down beside him. Without any warning, the man reached over, whacked him across the back of his neck with the edge of his hand, knocked him from the stool and down on to the floor. He got up, looked at the man, and said, "What was that?" The man replied, "Judo from Japan."

The cowboy continued with his drink, minding his own business, when the man next to him, for no reason at all reached over and hit him across the back with his forearm, knocking him from his stool and to the floor again. The cowboy got up, brushed himself off, and said, "What was that?" The man replied, "Karate from Korea."

Without a word, the cowboy went outside, came back in a minute, and hit the guy that had hit him, so hard that he knocked him off the stool, rendering him unconscious for five minutes. When he finally came to, he looked at the cowboy and said, "What was that?" The cowboy replied, "Tire tool from Wal-Mart."

MARCH 29

BIRTHMARKS OF A BELIEVER

"The disciples were first called Christians at Antioch." (Acts 11:26, NASB)

Every family has certain definitive physical characteristics. You know that some people are in a particular family because of the size or curvature of their nose. You know that others are members of a particular family because of the size of their frame. Likewise, there are some birthmarks of the believer.

The child of God is **a child of conviction.** First John, chapter five, verse 1 reads, "Whoever believes that Jesus is the Christ is born of God."(NASB). Faith is the birthmark and lifestyle of a believer. A Christian does not overcome the world by trying but by trusting. Notice that the object of a Christian's faith is the Lord Jesus Christ (vv. 1, 5). One's faith is no greater than the object of his faith.

The child of God is **a child of compassion.** Again, John writes in his first epistle, "Whoever loves the Father loves the child born of Him" (1 John 5:1, NASB). Jesus said the world would be able to recognize us as His disciples by our love for other believers (John 13:34-35).

The child of God is **a child of compliance.** He obeys God in every area of his life: "By this we know that we love the children of God, when we love God and observe His commandments" (1 John 5:2, NASB). God's commandments are not "burdensome" (v. 3). A Christian does not look upon the keeping of God's commandments as a duty or a burden. It is a joy and a privilege to keep God's commandments. The more you love God the more you will delight in keeping His commandments.

The child of God is **a child of conquest.** In verses four and five of 1 John, John writes: "For whatever is born of God overcomes the world; and this is the victory that has overcome the world – our faith. And who is the one who overcomes the world, but he who believes that Jesus is the Son of God." The word *overcome* means to conquer, to have victory. God wants us to be victors, not victims; to soar, not sink, and to overcome, not to be overwhelmed.

Vance Havner once wrote of the victory that is ours as believers: "It is *total* victory over sin, death, and the grave. It is *daily* victory. Every heart ought to be a 'victory garden.' And it is *final* victory."

A LITTLE HUMOR: A lady, trying to control her dry hair, treated her scalp with olive oil before washing it. Worried that the oil might leave an odor, she washed it several times. That night when she went to bed, she leaned over to her husband and asked, "Do I smell like olive oil?" "No," he said, sniffing her. "Do I smell like Popeye?"

MARCH 30

DIVINE HELP FOR ALL TIME

"Behold, God is my helper; the Lord is the sustainer of my soul."
(Psalm 54:4, NASB)

The word *helper* can be translated as mainstay (chief support). As God was the mainstay for David, likewise He is our mainstay. Of all the resources one has for assistance in life, there is none greater than that which comes from God Himself. He has been our helper in the past; He is our helper during this present time; and, He will be our helper in the future.

PAST HELP – "*Hitherto* hath the Lord helped us" (1 Samuel 7:12, KJV). With Samuel we raise our "Ebenezer," and thus marshal the scattered forces of memory as we recall the times when God has been faithful to help us. We can testify that in times past our lives have been full of trials and tribulations, but through it all God has woven threads of mercy and grace. We give Him the glory, and we also give Him our hearts' fullest confidence. In Him we confide. On Him we rely. He has always been there for us.

PRESENT HELP – "God is our refuge and strength, a very *present* help in trouble" (Psalm 46:1, KJV).The word *trouble* means in tight places. Who hasn't been in a tight place? If you are in a tight place today, let me suggest that you run by faith to Jesus. He will hide you. He will help you At times in life we need a refuge. It's not a sin to hide, but it is a sin to stay hidden. God hides us so that He can help us. Then we can return to the battle and face the storm.

FUTURE HELP – "*Tomorrow* . . . ye shall have help" (1 Samuel 11:9, KJV). The promise of future help is reassuring. The help of God, like the love of God, is vitally bound up in the believer's heart and life. Neither height, nor depth, nor any other creature, shall be able to separate us from it. God has promised His help, His unfailing help, His ever-present help for the future.

Isaac Watts, often called the father of English hymnody, wrote of God's help in his wonderful hymn, *O God, Our Help in Ages Past.* Considered to be one of the grandest in the whole realm of English hymnody, the first stanza reads, "O God, our help in ages past, Our hope for years to come, Our shelter from the stormy blast, And our eternal home!" God is a wonderful helper – past, present and future.

A LITTLE HUMOR: A little boy asked his daddy who was the preacher, "Daddy, every Sunday morning when you come out to preach, I see you sit up by the pulpit, and you bow your head for a long time. What are you doing?" The father replied, "I'm asking the Lord to give me a good sermon to share with the people." The little boy then asked, "Well, why don't he?"

MARCH 31

DO YOU HAVE AN INSTRUCTOR?

"The Helper, the Holy Spirit, whom the Father will send in My name, He will teach you all things, and bring to your remembrance all things that I said to you."
(John 14:26, NKJV)

The photographer for a national magazine was assigned to get photos of a great forest fire. Smoke at the scene was too thick to get any good shots, so he frantically called his home office to hire a plane. "It will be waiting for you at the airport!" he was assured by his editor.

As soon as he got to the small, rural airport he noticed a plane was warming up near the runway. He jumped in with his equipment and yelled, "Let's go! Let's go!" The pilot swung the plane into the wind and soon they were in the air. "Fly over the north side of the fire," said the photographer, "and make three or four low level passes." "Why?" asked the pilot. "Because I'm going to take pictures! I'm a photographer, and photographers take pictures!" said the photographer with great exasperation and impatience. After a long pause the pilot asked, "You mean you're not the instructor?"

Who do you look to for counsel and instructions? Sometimes we turn to people for counsel who have no more to offer than we do. The Lord knew we would need instructions, and He has adequately provided it for us in His Word and in the person of the Holy Spirit.

The Bible is a tremendous source of counsel and instruction. Several years ago, these words appeared on the cover of a telephone directory: "Look in the book first." It was a reminder to check its pages for numbers before calling the operator. Before we meet any challenge or seek the Lord's blessing on our lives, we should look first in His Book for His direction and guidance. The apostle Paul wrote, "All Scripture is given by inspiration of God, and is profitable for. . . instruction in righteousness, that the man of God may be complete, thoroughly equipped for every good work" (2 Timothy 3:16-17, NKJV). The word *instruction* originally referred to training a child. Scripture provides positive training in godly behavior. As we face life today with its many demands, let the Bible be your instructor.

The Holy Spirit is also a wonderful source of counsel and instruction. Before he left His disciples, the Lord Jesus Christ said to them, "The Helper, the Holy Spirit, whom the Father will send in My name, He will teach you all things, and bring to your remembrance all things that I said to you" (John 14:26, NKJV).

I read about a man who carried a tiny little folder in his Bible case. Inside the folder was a microfilm reproduction of the entire Bible. All 1,245 pages and 773,746 words were printed in a space just a little more than one square inch. But the man couldn't make out one word of it! Holding it up to the light or putting it against a dark background wouldn't help. Only with the aid of a high-powered microscope could it be read. The Bible cannot be understood without the aid of the Holy Spirit. The apostle Paul said we have received "the Spirit who is from God, that we might know the things that have been freely given to us by God" (1 Corinthians 2:12, NKJV). Christians, who have the Spirit of God living within them, have an inward interpreter who helps them to understand what the Bible means. We Christians have our own private instructor.

A LITTLE HUMOR: A little boy who saw his friend's grandmother reading her Bible, asked: "Why does your grandmother read the Bible so much?" "I think she's cramming for her finals," he replied.

APRIL 1

THE BIGGEST FOOL OF ALL

"The fool has said in his heart, "There is no God." (Psalm 14:1, NASB)

Today is April Fools' Day. According to an article in *Biography* magazine (April, 1999), the most popular theory as to how April Fools' Day began dates back to the 1500's, when the Gregorian calendar was adopted, changing the first day of the year from April 1 to January 1. Those who forgot about the change were said to have been the first April Fools. Over the centuries, playing pranks on April became a tradition.

The Greek word for "fool" is *moron* from which we get our English word "moron" (literally, an adult with the intelligence of an average child 8-12 years old). It can refer to the acts of a person who failed to show judgment, or who exhibited a general "deficiency of intellectual and spiritual capacities."

There once lived a king who gave a scepter to his court jester and crowned him as the official "Royal Fool" and said to him, "Should you ever meet someone who is a bigger fool than yourself, I give you the authority to give him your scepter." Years passed and the king lay dying. He called everyone to his bed side to say goodbye. When it came the jester's turn the king said to him, "I am going away on a long journey." The court jester asked him, "Where are you going?" "I do not know," answered the king. "How long will you be gone?" he asked. "I do not know," responded the king. "What preparations have you made for this journey?" Again the king said, "None whatsoever." Handing his scepter to the king, the court jester said, "Years ago you gave me this scepter and crowned me the "Royal Fool" of your court. You said should I ever meet someone who is a bigger fool than myself, I had the authority to give it to him. I give this scepter to you, for in all of my folly I am not as great a fool as you."

Someday you and I will go on a long journey. That journey begins with death. The most foolish thing we can do in making preparations for that journey is nothing. The Bible teaches that a person will go to one of two places at death: heaven or hell. Preparation for going to heaven requires repentance of sin and faith in the Lord Jesus Christ as one's personal Savior. Preparation for hell is to reject Christ and to deny the existence of hell.

On this April Fool's Day I pray that you have made adequate preparations for heaven. Jesus Christ died on the cross for your sins. He rose from the dead and today requires that all men everywhere repent of their sins and trust Him as their Savior (Acts 17:30-31). If you have not done so, I encourage you to pray this prayer: "Dear Father in heaven, I admit I am a sinner. Please forgive me of my sin and sins. I believe that Jesus Christ is the Son of God and that He paid for all my sins with His blood on the cross. I call on His name to save me. I now receive His life. I believe Jesus is living in me; that I am forgiven, and now I am a Christian. Because of His free gift of eternal life I will go to be with Jesus when I die. Thank you, Lord, for saving me. Amen."

A LITTLE HUMOR: The pastor shocked the congregation when he announced that he was resigning from the church and moving to a drier climate. After the service a very distraught lady came to the pastor with tears in her eyes, "Oh, Pastor, we are going to miss you so much. We don't want you to leave!" The kindhearted pastor patted her hand and said, "Now, now, don't carry on. The pastor who takes my place might be even better than I." "Yeah," she said, "that's what they said the LAST time too!"

APRIL 2

THE RAILROAD OF REDEMPTION

"For there is one God, and one mediator also between God and men, the man Christ Jesus." (1 Timothy 2:5, NASB)

Years ago a railroad was constructed that spanned the continental United States from East to West and from West to East. It was called the "Transcontinental Railroad." Six years after the groundbreaking, laborers of the Central Pacific Railroad from the west and the Union Pacific Railroad from the east met at Promontory Summit, Utah. It was here on May 10, 1869, that Leland Stanford, a grocer, future governor of California, founder of Stanford University, and one of the Big Four investors in the transcontinental railroad, drove the last spike (or golden spike) that joined the rails of the transcontinental railroad. As soon as the ceremonial spike had been replaced by an ordinary iron spike, a message was transmitted to both the East Coast and West Coast that simply read, "DONE." The country erupted in celebration upon receipt of this message.

Centuries earlier there was another spike that was driven into a piece of wood – in fact, several spikes were used – that made the greatest connection in the entire universe. It occurred when Jesus Christ was nailed to a cross on Mount Calvary. In 1 Timothy 2:5 we read, "For there is one God, and one mediator also between God and men, the man Christ Jesus." The only silver on the cross was the silver of His tears. The only gold, the gold of His priceless blood. When He died, Jesus did not say the word "DONE," but He did cry out, "It is finished" (John 19:30). The price of redemption was complete and man could make a connection with the living God because of what Jesus had accomplished on the cross.

If you go to heaven, you'll not get there on the wagon of works. You'll not climb the ladder of logic. You'll not ride on the rocket of reason. You will get there on the Railroad of Redemption – the ole T & O — "Trust and Obey, for there's no other way to be happy in Jesus, but to trust and obey."

A LITTLE HUMOR: A minister was preaching on the subject of heaven when he suddenly stopped and asked, "Is there anyone here who wants to go to heaven?" Everyone in the congregation stood up except one little boy. Surprised, the preacher asked, "Son, don't you want to go to heaven?" The little boy said, "Yes I do pastor, but I can't go right now. My mother told me to come home right after church."

APRIL 3

IT'S STILL THE BEST POLICY

"Pray for us, for we are sure that we have a good conscience, desiring to conduct ourselves honorably in all things." (Hebrews 13:18, NASB)

During the fourth century B. C. there lived in Athens a philosopher known as Diogenes the Cynic. He appeared in the streets of Athens in broad daylight carrying a lighted lantern and peering intently into the face of everyone who passed by. When asked what he was doing, he solemnly replied, "I am searching for an honest man."

If Diogenes lived today he would be in no less a dilemma. It seems that honesty has evaded our society as it did his. In a recent book entitled *The Day America Told The Truth* a survey conducted by the authors revealed that 91% of Americans lie regularly and 1 out of 5 say they cannot make it through a single day without lying. A few years ago, *U.S. News and World Report* published an article referring to America as "A Nation of Liars" and reported that 54% of those surveyed said that people are less honest today than they were ten years ago.

More recently we have had the need for honesty driven home by the sex scandal of Washington, D. C. and the constant lying that has gone on for months. It's time for us to sound again the trumpet call for honesty. We need to be reminded that honesty is still the best policy; that there is still virtue in a person being beyond reproach; that we need people who are truthful, trustworthy, and upright.

God wants us to tell the truth. In reciting the commandments to the rich young ruler, the Lord Jesus included this one. He said, "You shall not bear false witness" (Matthew 19:18). And in Proverbs 6, listed with seven things the Lord hates are "a lying tongue," and "a false witness who speaks lies" (vv. 17, 19). Lying is sinful. And, as with all violations of God's standards for our behavior, it must be avoided.

Sports Illustrated magazine ran an unusual story about a Little League game in Wellington, Florida. Tanner, a seven-year-old first baseman, fielded a ground ball and tried to tag a runner going from first base to second. When the young lady umpire Laura, called the runner out, Tanner immediately ran to her side and said, "Ma'am, I didn't tag the runner." She reversed her call and sent the runner to second base — and Tanner's coach gave him the game ball for his honesty.

Two weeks later, Laura was again the umpire and Tanner was playing shortstop when a similar play occurred. This time she ruled that Tanner had missed the tag on a runner going to third base, and the runner was safe. Tanner just looked at her. Without saying a word, he tossed the ball to the catcher and returned to his position. Laura sensed something was wrong. "Did you tag the runner?" she asked Tanner. His reply was simply, "Yes."

Everyone was shocked when the umpire called the runner out. The coaches of the opposing team protested until she explained what had happened two weeks earlier. "If a kid is that honest," she said, "I have to give it to him. This game is supposed to be for kids."

What is more important, winning or being honest? The glory of winning lasts for a moment, but integrity will last for a lifetime. Although doing the right thing will certainly not always be popular, God will bless those who speak the truth and honor Him.

A LITTLE HUMOR: The minister of a church was called by the IRS about a $1,500.00 contribution claimed by a member. "Did he really give that amount?" asked the IRS investigator. The minister hesitated a moment and then replied: "Well, I'd rather not say just now, but if you will call back tomorrow, I'm SURE the answer will be yes!"

APRIL 4

IF YOU ARE GOING TO BE A FOOL, BE THE RIGHT KIND

"We are fools for Christ's sake . . ." (1 Corinthians 4:10a, NASB)

The Bible has a lot to say about fools. In the Book of Proverbs forty-five times the word "fool" is used and another twenty-nine times "fools" or "foolish." You might ask, "Why would the Bible talk so much about fools when Jesus said you should never call a person a fool?" The answer is found in the context of Matthew 5:22. Jesus was saying that you should not call someone a fool in a spirit of anger and hate.

The word "fool" in the Bible does not refer to a person who is mentally deficient. In the Bible a fool is the person who is morally and spiritually deficient. The problem is not with the head – but the heart. And the fool is a fool by choice.

It is possible to reduce the causes of folly to two principle choices. First, the fool is one who has willfully determined not to follow the way of wisdom (Proverbs 1:20-25). Second, one becomes a fool by trusting in himself. Proverbs tells us that the fool is self-confident, trusting in his own wisdom, rather than in God (12:15; 28:26). A Yiddish proverbs says, "Don't approach a goat from the front, a horse from the back, or a fool from any side."

The only fools who are "wise fools" are Christians, because they're "fools for Christ's sake" (1 Corinthians 4:10). The world calls them fools, but in trusting Jesus Christ and committing their lives to Him, they've made the wisest decision anybody can make. I believe it was Donald Grey Barnhouse, who on a ship with a group of Christians who were singing and praising the Lord, when another person who had been watching and listening to them referred to them as fools. Barnhouse heard what he said and replied, "Fools? Yes we are fools. We are fools for Christ. Whose fool are you?"

A LITTLE HUMOR: A young preacher was scheduled to give a special sermon at the evening hour, but in the afternoon he began to get hoarse. He asked an older preacher what to do to relieve it. The elder minister advised, "Get some brandy and pour a little in a glass and fill the rest of the glass with water. Take it into the pulpit and as you preach, just sip it a little at intervals and your voice will clear up."

After the sermon was concluded, the young preacher asked the older minister how he liked it. "Well, in all candor, I didn't," he replied. "You didn't?" asked the young preacher. "Why didn't you?"

The older minister answered, "I have my reasons. In the first place, I didn't say gulp it, I said sip it. Second, the Sermon on the Mount was not preached in New York City. Third, there are 10 Commandments not fourteen. And in the fourth place, when David killed the giant Goliath, he used a sling and a stone – he didn't stomp his insides out."[30]

APRIL 5

I CAN'T TAKE MY EYES OFF YOU

"God knows about everyone, everywhere. Everything about us is bare and wide open to the all-seeing eyes of our living God; nothing can be hidden from him to whom we must explain all that we have done." (Hebrews 4:13, LB)

In the movie *The Truman Show*, Truman Burbank believes his life is no different from anyone else's. He has one life to live, just like the rest of us. But one day he begins to notice peculiar things happening. For example he notices things that happen exactly the same way every day. This causes him to get suspicious that something strange is going on. What he doesn't realize is that every second of his life from the day he was born has been telecast live to the entire planet. He is the star of *The Truman Show,* the most popular television show in the world, which broadcasts every aspect of his life around the clock. From the moment he wakes up until he goes to bed at night, the world eavesdrops on Truman's life through the aid of five thousand hidden cameras. Finally Truman comes to the life-changing realization that an unseen audience is watching his every move.[31]

The Truman Show is just a movie. It's not real. But the Bible does teach that God is watching every one of us. He knows about everyone, everywhere. There is nothing that escapes His watchful eye. There are at least three things that God sees and knows about us.

First, our sins are perfectly known to God. No acts of wrong, no thought of wrong, no desires of wrong are hidden from Him. Strange, isn't it, that we are not embarrassed to do before God that which would cause us to shamefully blush if such

---

[30] Paul W. Powell, *A Funny Thing Happened on the Way to Retirement* (Tyler, Texas, 2000), 106-107.
[31] *Dynamic Preaching.* January-March, 2002, Vol. 17, No. 1, 17.

were known to our neighbors?

Secondly, God knows all of our needs as well as all of our sins. There isn't one single area of personal need unknown to God. He knows our physical needs, our social needs, our mental needs, our moral needs, our spiritual needs.

Finally, our knowledge of the future is limited, but the future is naked before God. A very apt statement is true: "We do not know what the future holds, but we do know who holds the future." God knows the end from the beginning.

When Isaac Watts was a little child, he was visiting in the home of a very old lady. She asked him to read a framed text that hung on the wall, "Thou, God seest me" (Genesis 16:13). Then she said, "When you are older, people will tell you that God is always watching you to see when you do wrong so he can punish you. I do not want you to think of it that way, but I want you to take the text home, and to remember all your life that God loves you so much that he cannot take His eyes off you."

A LITTLE HUMOR: A little boy was attending his first wedding. After the service, his cousin asked him, "How many women can a man marry?" "Sixteen," the boy responded. His cousin was amazed that he had an answer so quickly. "How do you know that?" "Easy," the little boy said. "All you have to do is add it up, like the preacher said, '4 better, 4 worse, 4 richer, 4 poorer'."

APRIL 6

YOUR KING COMES

"...the whole multitude...began to rejoice and praise God...saying: 'Blessed is the King who comes in the name of the Lord!'..." (Luke 19:37-38, NKJV)

Belle Starr was one of the few women outlaws in the Old West, and so she gained widespread notoriety. One day, Judge Isaac Parker was attempting to try a case, but he couldn't get the courtroom's attention. Even the members of the jury had wandered from the jury box to stare out the courtroom windows. What was the source of all the excitement? Outlaw Belle Starr was riding by on her horse, and everyone in town wanted to catch a glimpse of her. The judge had to call a five-minute recess to deal with the distraction.

I can imagine a similar distraction on the day Jesus entered Jerusalem. He was no outlaw, of course, even though the law would put Him to death. But His time had come. His entrance into Jerusalem riding on a donkey was in fulfillment of the prophecy of Zechariah 9:9 (NKJV), which states: "Rejoice, greatly, O daughter of Zion! Shout, O daughter of Jerusalem? Behold, your King is coming to you; He is just and having salvation, lowly and riding on a donkey, a colt, the foal of a donkey."

At His birth Jesus came into a world that would reject Him. As He entered Jerusalem, He entered a city that would reject Him. But at this stage of His entrance, the people are still singing His praise. In fact, they are so boisterous, they make the Pharisees uneasy.

The Pharisees said to Jesus, "Teacher, rebuke Your disciples" (Luke 19:39, NKJV). To which Jesus replied, "I tell you that if these should keep silent, the stones would immediately cry out" (Luke 19:40, NKJV).

Matthew 21:9 records the people welcoming the Lord with the word *Hosanna* which means "save us!" It was common in Bible times to spread garments in the path of princes and kings, especially at their coronation. The phrases "Hosanna" and "Blessed is he who comes in the name of the Lord!" (Matthew 21:9, NKJV) come from Psalm 118:25-26, one of the "Hallel" or praise psalms (Psalm 113-118) used every Passover. These Jewish hymns would be as familiar to the Jewish people as Christmas carols are to Christians.

Christ was welcomed with hallelujahs and hosannas. The Pharisees objected, but it was too late. The drama for our redemption must be played out – the drama that gives hope to sinful humanity. Our Lord's commitment to our redemption is worth our praise also.

A LITTLE HUMOR: A six year old boy came home from a Palm Sunday worship service proudly carrying his palm. When his parents quizzed him on his Sunday school lesson for the day he enthusiastically said, "Jesus came to Jerusalem on a donkey. And the happy people waved their palm branches and sang, 'Ho, Suzanna'."

APRIL 7

THE CRUX OF THE MATTER

"So he then handed Him over to them to be crucified." (John 19:16, NASB)

The attack on America and the World Trade Center by Muslim terrorists on September 11, 2002 was terrible. While trying to find anyone who might have survived the attack, rescue workers found a steel beam that once supported the World Trade Center building six. The steel beam was in the shape of a cross. After discovering the beam that had been shaped by the blast, rescue and construction workers moved it to a special site where some volunteers wrote religious messages on it, and a Roman Catholic priest blessed it. Discovery and display of the cross were reported to bring comfort to numerous workers on the rubble pile.

The cross of Christ, when recognized as the ***crux*** of the matter regarding our salvation, does bring hope and comfort to those who cling to it.

May we say with George Bennard:

On a hill far away stood an old rugged cross,
The emblem of suffering and shame;
And I love that old cross where the dearest and best
For a world of lost sinners was slain.

Oh, that old rugged cross, so despised by the world,

Has a wondrous attraction for me;
For the dear Lamb of God left His glory above,
To bear it to dark Calvary.

In the old rugged cross, stained with blood so divine,
Such a wonderful beauty I see;
For 'twas on that old cross Jesus suffered and died,
To pardon and sanctify me.

To the old rugged cross I will ever be true,
Its shame and reproach gladly bear;
Then He'll call me some day to my home far away,
Where His glory forever I'll share.

So I'll cherish the old rugged cross,
Till my trophies at last I lay down;
I will cling to the old rugged cross,
And exchange it someday for a crown.

A LITTLE HUMOR: A little boy was trying to raise some money by collecting old bottles, going door-to-door in his neighborhood. When he came to the home of a woman who was the "town grouch," the little boy asked, "Do you have any coke bottles?" "No," she replied with a scowl. Then he asked, "Do you have any old whiskey bottles?" "Young man," the woman replied, "do I look like the type of person who would have old whiskey bottles?" He studied her for a moment and then asked, "Well, do you have any old vinegar bottles?"

APRIL 8

MORE POWER TO YOU

"That I may know Him and the power of His resurrection. . ."
(Philippians 3:10a, NASB)

One little boy said he knew that Jesus died when he went to hang the power lines. The teacher said, "What do you mean?" He handed her a picture. The teacher looked at the picture of Jesus carrying a cross, and to the boy it looked just like the utility poles in his yard. He assumed Jesus worked for the electric company. The teacher had earlier explained that the picture was of Jesus dying. He had combined the ideas, thinking Jesus died when He was hanging power lines. That's not bad theology because when He died and came back, He gave us resurrection power. He died hanging a power line from you to God.

The Life Application Bible has this footnote for Philippians 3:10: "When we are united with Christ by trusting in Him, we experience the power that raised Him from the dead. That same mighty power will help us live morally renewed and regenerated lives. But before we can walk in newness of life, we must also die to sin. Just as the resurrection gives us Christ's power to live for Him, His crucifixion marks the death of our old sinful nature. We can't know the victory of the resurrection without personally applying the crucifixion."

There was a man who had a trusty old pickup. He told the funeral director he wanted to be buried with his old pickup. The funeral director said, "Why would you want that?' The man said, "I've never seen a hole that this pickup couldn't get me out of." Well, there's one hole your pickup won't get you out of. It's called the grave. You need more power than a pickup to have a good ending to the grave question. Easter is when God gave the power to us – the power to answer the grave question of life.

Easter gives us another opportunity to thank our Savior for the victory that is ours over sin, death and the grave.

A LITTLE HUMOR: A drunk was walking through a cemetery and accidently fell into a newly dug grave. He tried several times to climb out but couldn't. He decided to wait till morning and perhaps someone would find him and help him out. It wasn't long until he fell asleep. A second drunk also came walking through the cemetery, and he too fell into the same grave. He started trying to get out but to no avail. The first drunk woke up, saw what the man was trying to do and said to him, "You'll never get out of here." But he did!

APRIL 9

HEAVENLY CLOTHING FOR EARTHLY LIVING

"...put them all aside...and have put on..." (Colossians 3:8, NASB)

If you are a soldier, you must dress the part; if you are a football, basketball, or baseball player, you must dress the part; if you are a carpenter, you must dress the part; if you a professional business person, you must dress the part; likewise, if you are a Christian, you must dress the part.

In Colossians 3:5-9 Paul lists the sins that must be "put off" by the Christian and in verses 10-14 he lists virtues that the Christian is to "put on." The sins we are to put off include "anger, wrath, malice, slander, and abusive speech from your mouth" (v. 8). The virtues we are to "put on" include "a heart of compassion, kindness, humility, gentleness and patience" (v. 12). These sins and virtues are to be taken off and put on as one would take off dirty clothes and put on clean ones.

The Duchess of Windsor, for whom the king of England surrendered his throne, often made the list of the ten best-dressed women in the world. Elsa Maxwell, Washington socialite, once asked the duchess why she devoted so much time and attention to such frivolous things as clothes. She replied that her husband had given up everything for her. "If anyone looks at me when I enter a room, my husband can feel proud of me. That's my chief responsibility," she replied.

Our Lord Jesus Christ gave up everything for us. Our greatest ambition in life should be to so live that He can be proud of us.

A LITTLE HUMOR: A little girl was asked to describe the parts of man. She said, "Man has three parts: the branium, the chester, and the abominable cavity. The branium holds the brain, the chester holds the heart, and the abominable cavity holds the bowels, of which there are five: a, e. i. o, and u."

APRIL 10

GOING TO THE EXTREME!

"Then He touched their eyes, saying, 'It shall be done to you according to your faith'." (Matthew 9:29, NASB)

A high school drama class was performing at a local theater. Somehow an accident occurred, and a hole was cracked in the stage floor. Carefully the performers avoided the damaged area until Joey, jugging bowling pins, accidentally stepped through the hole up to his knee. He apologized to the audience for his clumsiness which caused a heckler to shout, "Don't worry, Joey . . . It's just a STAGE you're going through!"

We all go through stages, don't we? One of the stages that some sports enthusiasts enjoying going through is a fondness for extremes. Note the popularity of extreme sports — sky diving, ice climbing, skateboarding, paragliding, and who knows what's next.

The people known as Generation X introduced us to extreme fashions. Not only extreme clothes — but also ornaments attached to the body. All kinds of body parts are pierced including eyebrows, navels, tongues, and more private parts. All that sounds a little extreme to me, but that's the point, isn't it?

Going to extremes is nothing new. Some of the greatest people who have ever lived have been risk-takers. Think of people who have placed footmarks on our history. People like John Glenn, Alan Shepherd, Krista McAulliff, Charles Lindbergh, Amelia Earhart, Christopher Columbus, Martin Luther, Galileo, Augustine, and Saint Paul.

Think what risk-takers Jesus' followers were in those first centuries after His ascension into heaven. They faced the possibility of death daily for their faith. But they still persisted. If there is any sin that you and I are guilty of, it probably is that we play it too safe when it comes to our faith. We have made being a Christian so convenient and so comfortable that our faith has lost its edge. A faith that demands too little will not grab hold of the passion that many people need in their lives.

A missionary society wrote to the great missionary David Livingstone deep in the heart of Africa and asked, "Have you found a good road to where you are? If so, we want to know how to send other men to join you." Livingstone wrote back, "If you have men who will come only if they know there is a good road, I don't want them. I want men who will come if there is no road at all."

Christ is still looking for men and women like that today, people who will come if there is no road at all. Better than extreme sports; more exciting than extreme fashions; God is looking for men and women who have extreme faith.

A LITTLE HUMOR — A preacher was wired for sound with a lapel mike, and a long cord. As he preached, he moved briskly about the platform, jerking the mike cord as he went. Then he moved to one side, getting wound up in the cord and nearly tripping before jerking it again. After several circles and jerks, a little girl in the third pew leaned toward her mother and whispered, "If he gets loose, will he hurt us?"

APRIL 11

GOOD AND BAD LAUGHTER

"For everything there is a season, a time for every activity under heaven . . . A time to cry and a time to laugh . . ." (Ecclesiastes 3:1, 4, NLT)

Doctors and psychologists tell us that laughter is good for us. This is undoubtedly true, because the Bible says that "a cheerful heart is good medicine" (Proverbs 17:22, NLT).

But the Scriptures distinguish between good and bad laughter. The author of Ecclesiastes declared that the laughter of people who have no place for God in their lives has no more value than "thorns crackling in a fire" (Eccl. 7:6). God disapproves of any humor that belittles people or makes light of immorality. Sin is never a laughing matter.

Joe E. Brown was a top-notch movie and Broadway comedian of the World War II era. When entertaining American troops in the South Pacific, he was asked by a soldier to tell some "dirty jokes." He responded, "Son, if telling a dirty story is the price I must pay for your laughter, then I'm not interested. I've never done an act that I couldn't perform before my mother, and I never will." I wish comedians of today would realize that.

C. H. Spurgeon had a vivid sense of humor. He was once scolded by an irate woman for his humor in the pulpit. Spurgeon responded, "Madam, if you only knew how much I held back, you would give me more credit than you are giving me now!" May our prayer be, "Lord, give us a merry heart. Help us to be discerning so that we will laugh for the right reasons and about the right things."

A LITTLE HUMOR: "Lady, if you'll give us a quarter, my little brother will imitate a chicken." "What will he do? Cackle like a hen?" "Oh, no. He wouldn't do a cheap imitation like that. He'll eat a worm."[32]

---

[32] Tal D. Bonham, *Another Treasury of Clean Jokes* (Nashville: Broadman Press, 1983). 7-8.

APRIL 12

GOD IS SUFFICIENT!

"And who is sufficient for these things?" (2 Corinthians 2:16, NKJV)

Paul asks a personal question in 2 Corinthians 2:16: "Who is sufficient for these things?" By "these things" he means the demands and sacrifices of the Christian life. Who is sufficient for living a creative, victorious Christian life?

But Paul does more than ask the question; he gives us the answer: "Our sufficiency is from God" (2 Corinthians 3:5b, NKJV). We have no power of our own, no wisdom of our own; but we belong to the One who is the very power and wisdom of God! Christ is sufficient for a person's spiritual needs. We draw upon His fullness of grace, according to John 1:16; and Philippians 4:13 declares that the believer can "do all things through Christ" who strengthens him.

In 2 Corinthians 12:9 Paul testified that God said to him, "My grace is sufficient for you, for My strength is made perfect in weakness" (NKJV). The word *sufficient* means adequate. Referring to God's grace, Dr. Melvin Worthington has written, "Christians live by God's grace, learn by God's grace, labor by God's grace, look for His coming by grace, manifest loyalty by God's grace. Believers are saved, schooled, sanctified, secured, and satisfied by God's grace. The truth of God's grace should cause praise and thanksgiving."

No matter what spiritual demands are made upon you, your Saviour is sufficient to meet them. Christ can enable you to be an effective witness at work, a good family member at home, a winsome neighbor on your street. Don't depend on your own strength today. Depend on the sufficiency of Him who is all-sufficient for every spiritual need in your life.

A LITTLE HUMOR: Several children were playing together, when one said, "My dad is an artist. He takes paint, splashes it on a canvas, calls it 'pop art', and sells if for $100." A little girl said, "My daddy is a composer. He puts dots of ink on little lines, calls it 'music', and sells it for $200 a page!" A third youngster said, "That's nothing. My dad's a preacher. He waves his arms, yells and spits, calls it a 'sermon' and it takes four men to carry all the money!"

APRIL 13

GOD ISN'T IN A HURRY

"But let patience have its perfect work, that you may be perfect and complete, lacking nothing." (James 1:4, KJV)

The great nineteenth-century preacher Phillips Brooks was renowned for his gentle spirit and enormous patience. But one day a friend walked into his study and found him pacing back and forth, terribly agitated. He was shocked. "Dr. Brooks! What on earth is the matter?" he asked. "I'm in a hurry," he said, "but God is not!"

Isn't that the way it so often seems to be with God? You desperately want something that you don't have, something apparently legitimate and worthwhile. And you're forced to wait for it. Do you ever think that God is taking his own sweet time with you?

Patience was one of the first lessons we had to learn in childhood. The child who does not learn to be patient is not likely to learn much of anything else. It takes patience to learn to read, to spell, to write, and to master multiplication tables. It even takes patience to grow! God has ordained that maturity is a slow process, not an instant experience.

Impatience is usually a mark of immaturity. At least James felt that way. "But let patience have its perfect work, that you may be perfect and complete, lacking nothing" (James 1:4, KJV). Little children think you have arrived at your destination when you stop for the first stoplight. A short wait in the doctor's office is unbearable.

"Do not be like the horse or as the mule," warns Psalms 32:9, and it is a warning that we need. The mule is stubborn and has a tendency to hold back. The horse is impulsive and wants to rush ahead. Personality differences may enter in here, but we all have the same problem — it is difficult to wait on God.

God is always at work for the good of His people, and He is working in all things (Romans 8:28). This includes the things that perplex us and that pain us. The only way God can teach us patience is to test us and try us, and the only way we can learn patience is to surrender and let God have His way. God has His times as well as His purposes, and to miss His times is to delay His purposes.

"Why has God made me this way?" a suffering saint once bitterly asked her pastor. Gently, he replied, "God has not made you — he is making you." The school of patience never produces any graduates, and it never grants any honorary degrees. We are always learning, always maturing. The best thing you and I can do is to stop looking at our watches and calendars and simply look by faith into the face of God and let Him have His way — in His time.

A LITTLE HUMOR: A couple walked into a pet store and were greeted by a parrot who said, "Hey Mister, you're stupid and your wife is ugly." The couple marched back to the manager's office and said, "Your parrot insulted us!" The manager stormed over to the parrot, grabbed him by the neck, and said, "Don't say that they are stupid and ugly again or I will feed you to the snakes!" The couple accepted the manager's apology, yet as they were leaving, the parrot calls out, "Hey mister!" "What?" replied the man. "You know . . ."[33]

[33] *The Preacher Joke a Day Calendar 1998* (Lame Duck, Inc., 1997).

APRIL 14

IT'S IN YOUR JEANS!

"Let us put aside the deeds of darkness and put on the armor of light. . .clothe yourselves with the Lord Jesus Christ and do not think about how to gratify the desires of the sinful nature." (Romans 13:12, 14)

Charles Barbee wore a mask when he walked in to rob a Spokane, Washington, bank in 1996, but in court, FBI agents put his blue jeans at the scene. Now, Barbee is serving time. Using photographs taken by the bank's security cameras, the head of the FBI photo analysis unit found more than two dozen distinctive features that matched a pair of J. C. Penny blue jeans taken from Barbee's closet.

That it could be proven that those jeans were worn while the crime was committed is part of a new research technique conducted by the FBI Crime Lab's special photographic unit. Blue jeans, investigators are finding, fade and wear out in distinctive ways, offering a sort of textile fingerprint. The investigator said, "If you look at the seams or hems on blue jeans, you'll find it is pretty bumpy. It comes from when the jeans are sewn together. The operator is pushing material through a little bit at a time. It bunches and stretches in a wave pattern, and you get little humps and valleys. When the dye wears away on the hump, what is left is white material with blue fabric in the valleys. The humps and valleys — known as wave patterns — are critical because the distance between them can be measured and charted, sort of like a bar code."

Leaving one's sins and accepting Christ as one's Lord and Savior is often compared in the Bible to changing one's clothes. For example, in Romans 13 the apostle Paul wrote, "Let us put aside the deeds of darkness and put on the armor of light. . .clothe yourselves with the Lord Jesus Christ and do not think about how to gratify the desires of the sinful nature" (verses 12 and 14). The words *put aside* mean to take off as one would take off dirty clothes and the words *clothe yourselves* mean to put on as a garment.

Vance Havner said, "One might as well try to wear two suits at once as to try wearing the armor of light without shedding the works of darkness." We cannot wear both the garments of sin and the robe of righteousness. We can only wear one.

We would be wise to remember the words of Edward Mote, "When He shall come with trumpet sound, Oh, may I then in Him be found; Dressed in His righteousness alone, Faultless to stand before the throne." Having on the right clothes when Jesus comes will determine whether you will be sentenced to hell or freed to enjoy heaven. It's all in your "jeans."

A LITTLE HUMOR: A husband and his wife were having financial troubles. He decided that the family should go on a very strict budget. He gave his wife instructions that she should not be buying any clothes for a while. The next week she came in with a very expensive outfit. He reprimanded her and said, "Honey, why in the world did you do that?" She said, "The devil made me do it." He replied, "Why didn't you say to the devil, 'Get thee behind me, Satan'." She replied, "I did. And he said, "It looks good from the back, too."[34]

APRIL 15

MUCH GIVEN, MUCH REQUIRED

"Much is required from those to whom much is given, and much more is required from those to whom much more is given." (Luke 12:48b, NLT)

Not all people have equal opportunities, and not all people have equal abilities. We like to say, "All men are created equal," but it simply is not so. We may be equal under the law and we may be equal before God, but we are not equal in any other way, especially in our abilities. But whatever abilities God gives to us, He holds us accountable for them. All we possess we have received as a trust from Him.

John D. Rockefeller, Sr., one of our nation's first billionaires, was a devout Baptist. He believed that the ability to make money was a gift from God to be developed and used to the best of one's ability for the good of mankind. And, he practiced what he preached. He gave away more than $550 million during his lifetime. But Rockefeller did not wait until he became rich to become generous. He gave a tithe (10%) of all he had from the time of his conversion. He believed he was a steward of all he had. Jesus taught the same thing when He said, "Much is required from those to whom much is given."

In his book, *Taking the Stew out of Stewardship,* Paul Powell writes, "If I could persuade you to begin tithing today, I would be doing you one of the greatest favors of your life. 'But,' you say, 'things are so tight with me economically.' Good! The harder it is to tithe the more it will mean to you. 'But,' you say, 'I don't see how I can make ends meet.' Good! That means it will take faith for you to do it. And, without faith it is impossible to please Him. 'But,' you say, 'I have other obligations.' Good! It will demand that you establish priorities and exercise discipline. It comes to this, in life we do what we want to do. Everything else is just an excuse."

---

[34] Paul W. Powell, *A Funny Thing Happened On the Way to Retirement* (Tyler, Texas, 2000), 97.

A LITTLE HUMOR: A pastor wired all his pews with electricity. One Sunday from his pulpit he said, "All who will give $100 toward the new building fund, stand up." He touched a button and twenty people sprang up. "Fine, fine," the preacher beamed. "Now all who will give $500, stand up." He touched another button and twenty more jumped to their feet. "Excellent," he shouted. "Now all who will give $1,000, stand up." He threw the master switch and electrocuted fourteen deacons.[35]

APRIL 16

UNCHANGED ORDERS

"You will receive power when the Holy Spirit has come upon you; and you shall be My witnesses both in Jerusalem, and in all Judea and Samaria, and even to the remotest part of the earth." (Acts 1:8, NASB)

A few years ago my wife and I had the privilege of going to Washington, D. C. with our church group. While there we visited Arlington National Cemetery and witnessed the changing of the guards at the Tomb of the Unknown Soldier. The tomb is protected by soldiers who stand guard 24 hours a day, 365 days a year. Every hour on the hour, a new soldier reports for duty. When the new guard arrives, he receives his orders from the one who is leaving. The words are always the same: "Orders Remain Unchanged."

The same could be said of the orders that Jesus gave to His disciples. Just before He ascended to heaven, He told His followers, "You shall be My witnesses . . . even to the remotest part of the earth." He also said, "Go therefore and make disciples of all the nations" (Matthew 28:19).

From that day to this day, Christian to Christian, generation to generation, the good news of Jesus Christ has been proclaimed. We too must tell others that Jesus Christ is the Son of God, that He died on the cross to pay the penalty for our sins, and that salvation is granted to all who put their faith in Him.

Much has changed in the 2000 plus years since Jesus chose His first disciples and started the church. But regarding the command to spread the good news of Christ, these words can still be said: "Orders remain unchanged."

A LITTLE HUMOR: A preacher was completing a temperance sermon. With great emphasis he said, "If I had all the beer in the world, I'd take it and pour it into the river." With even greater emphasis he said, "And if I had all the wine in the world, I'd take it and pour it into the river." And then finally, shaking his fist in the air, he said, "And if I had all the whiskey in the world, I'd take it and pour it into the river." When the sermon was completed, he sat down. The song leader stood and announced, "For our closing song, let us stand and sing Hymn number 518, 'Shall We Gather at the River'."[36]

---

[35] Tal D. Bonham, *The Treasury of Clean Jokes* (Nashville: Broadman Press, 1981), 97.

[36] Paul W. Powell, *Laugh and Live Longer* (Tyler, Texas, 2008), 33.

APRIL 17

HELPFUL FRIENDS

"Now when David had come to Mahanaim, Shobi...Machir...and Barzillai...brought beds, basins, pottery, wheat, honey, flour, parched grain, beans, lentils, parched seeds, honey, curds, sheep, and cheese of the herd for David and for the people who were with him, to eat..." (2 Samuel 17:27-29, NASB)

Three men (Shobi, Machir, and Barzillai) were helpful friends to David at a time when he needed friends. When they came to David, they came at the right time and with exactly what David and his people needed. Verse twenty-seven says that David was at Mahanaim. The first time Mahanaim is mentioned was when Jacob returned home after twenty years of exile. Angels met Jacob at Mahanaim and ministered to him (Genesis 32:1-2). Just like the angels who came and ministered to Jacob, these three friends came and did angel's work in David's life.

One of the all-time greats in baseball was Babe Ruth. His bat had the power of a canon and his record of 714 home runs remained until Hank Aaron came along. The Babe was the idol of sports fans, but in time age took its toll, and his popularity began to wane. Finally the Yankees traded him to the Braves. In one of his last games in Cincinnati, Babe Ruth began to falter. He struck out and made several misplays that allowed the Reds to score five runs in one inning. As the Babe walked toward the dugout, chin down and dejected, there rose from the stands an enormous storm of boos and catcalls. Some fans actually shook their fists. Then a wonderful thing happened. A little boy jumped over the railing, and with tears streaming down his cheeks, he ran out to the great athlete. Unashamedly, he flung his arms around the Babe's legs and held on tightly. Babe Ruth scooped him up, hugged him, and set him down again. Patting him on the head, he took his hand and the two of them walked off the field together.

That's the kind of friend we need – the kind that will stand with us and help us rather than hurt us. That's exactly the kind of Friend we have in Jesus. He came in when we had no hope. He gave us just what we needed when we needed it. He did, not the work of an angel, but the work of a Savior. He gave His all and never stopped to consider the cost or ask for repayment. Thank God for the greatest Friend of all!

A LITTLE HUMOR: A preacher was giving his message when he noticed two girls were passing notes and not paying attention. He wanted to correct them without embarrassing them so he stopped preaching and said, "There are two people not paying attention to this message. If you will see me in my office after the service, I will be accepting your apology. After the service, four deacons came to him to apologize.

APRIL 18

IT'S NOT OVER UNTIL IT'S OVER

"But we were hoping that it was He who was going to redeem Israel . . . 'O foolish ones, and slow of heart to believe . . .'" (Luke 24:21a, 25a, NKJV)

In the 1982 NBA championship series between the Los Angeles Lakers and the Philadelphia 76ers, the Lakers jumped out to a commanding 3-0 lead. They needed to win only one more victory to clinch the crown. But the 76ers refused to give up. In the interview with a sports writer Dr. J (Julius Ervin) was asked if his team was willing to concede the series. He expressed the optimism of his whole ball club when he said, "It's not over until it's over." The saying of Dr. J caught on and now people everywhere say, concerning events where defeat looks eminent but there is still a glimmer of hope, "It's not over until it's over."

That, I believe, is the message of Easter. God can bring life out of death, victory out of defeat, resurrection out of crucifixion. So, don't close the books on a life too soon. Don't throw in the towel prematurely. Don't walk away from a problem before you ought to. If God is in it, it's not over until it's over. Nothing is over until God gets through with it. He specializes in turning tragedy into triumph, and turning Calvaries into Easter mornings.

No matter how final death may look, remember the message of Easter: It's not over until it's over. God raised Jesus from the dead and one day He will raise us up also. Now, because of His resurrection we can live until we die, and then we can live forever.

A LITTLE HUMOR: Three friends from the local congregation were asked, "When you're in your casket, and friends and congregation members are mourning over you, what would you like them to say?" Artie said, "I would like them to say I was a wonderful husband, a fine spiritual leader, and a great family man." Eugene commented, "I would like them to say I was a wonderful teacher and servant of God who made a huge difference in people's lives." Al said, "I'd like them to say, 'Look, he's moving!'"

APRIL 19

WHEN GOD IS GIVEN A CHANCE

"And we know that in all things God works for the good of those who love him, who have been called according to this purpose." (Romans 8:28, NIV)

God works in "all things" – not just isolated incidents – for our good. This does not mean that all that happens to us is good. Evil is prevalent in our fallen world, but God is able to turn every circumstance around for our long-range good.

Years ago a tornado struck the prairies of Minnesota, killing many, injuring hundreds, and almost demolishing the town of Rochester. An elderly doctor and his two sons, just out of medical school, worked for days aiding the stricken. Their heroic work did not go unnoticed. Financial backing was offered to build a hospital, provided the doctor and sons would take charge. In 1889 they opened a clinic which soon attracted wide attention. Today people come from all walks of life to the Mayo Brothers Clinic. Out of disaster came blessing. William Cowper wrote:

God moves in a mysterious way
His wonders to perform,
He plants His footsteps in the sea,
And rides upon the storm.

When sometimes situations seem out of control, our vision should focus on the overruling activity of God. God is not working to make us happy, but to fulfill His purpose. Romans 8:28 is not a verse that can be claimed by everyone. It can be claimed only by those who love God and are called according to His purpose. Those who are "called" are those the Holy Spirit convinces and enables to receive Christ. Such people have a new perspective, a new mind-set on life. They trust in God, not life's treasures; they look for their security in heaven, not on earth; they learn to accept, not resent, pain and persecution because God is with them. If given the chance, God can and will work out all things for the good of those who love Him.

A LITTLE HUMOR: Whatever you need to do, you need to do it now. A boy and a girl returned to the girl's home after their first date. Standing at the front door, the boy asked nervously, "May I kiss you?" There was no reply. Again he asked, "Can I kiss you?" No reply. A third time. "Can I kiss you?" Still no reply. "Are you deaf?" said the boy. "Are you paralyzed?" the girl asked.

APRIL 20

THE BLACK BART OF THE SOUL

"For God has not given us a spirit of fear, but of power and of love and of a sound mind." (2 Timothy 1:7, NKJV)

Black Bart terrorized the Wells Fargo stage line for thirteen years, roaring like a tornado in and out of the Sierra Nevada, spooking the most rugged frontiersmen. During his reign of terror between 1875 and 1883, he is credited with stealing the bags and the breath away from twenty-nine different stagecoach crews. A hood hid his face. No victim ever saw him. No sheriff could ever track his trail. He never fired a shot or took a hostage. He didn't have to. His presence was enough to paralyze.[37]

He reminds me of another thief: one who is still around. You know him. Oh, you've never seen his face. You couldn't describe his voice or sketch his profile. But when he's near, you know it in a heartbeat.

If you've ever been in the hospital, you've felt the leathery brush of his hand against yours. If you've ever sensed someone was following you, you've felt his cold

---

[37] *Dynamic Preaching*, April-June, 2008, 75.

breath down your neck. If you've awakened late at night in a strange room, it was his husky whisper that stole your slumber.

It was this thief who left your palms sweaty as you went for the job interview. It was this con man who convinced you to swap your integrity for popularity. And it was this scoundrel who whispered in your ear as you left the cemetery, "You may be next."

He is the Black Bart of the soul. He doesn't want your money. He doesn't want your diamonds. He won't go after your car. He wants something far more precious. He wants your peace of mind, your joy. His name? FEAR! His task is to take your courage and leave you timid and trembling. Fear of death, fear of failure, fear of God, fear of tomorrow. His arsenal is vast. His goal? To create cowardly, joyless souls.

Let's not live in the shadow of fear, but in the light and victory of our Lord Jesus Christ. He "has not given us a spirit of fear, but of power and of love and of a sound mind."

A LITTLE HUMOR: While a pastor was taking his morning walk he came across a woman pushing a baby carriage up a hill. She was struggling with it a bit, so he offered to push it up the hill for her. It was a rather unwieldy baby carriage, so it was no easy job to get it to the top. Once they had reached her house, the woman thanked the pastor for his help. The pastor asked, "Do you mind if I take a little peek at the precious baby that I've been pushing all this time?" The woman laughed and said, "Pastor, this ain't a baby we been struggling with. It's my husband's weekly beer supply!"

APRIL 21

ANSWERING LIFE'S MOST IMPORTANT QUESTION

"Sirs, what must I do to be saved?" (Acts 16:30b, NKJV)

From time to time I like to share how a person may become a Christian. In Acts 16 one may find the account of a jailer in Philippi who asked of Paul and Silas life's most important question: "Sirs, what must I do to be saved?" Saved from what? Sin. I suggest six "steps" one may follow in order to be saved from sin:[38]

1. Realize God's Love For You.

"For God so loved the world, that He gave His only begotten Son, that whoever believes in Him should not perish but have everlasting life." (John 3:16, NKJV)

2. Recognize Your Sin Before God.

" For there is no difference; for all have sinned and fall short of the glory of God." (Romans 3:22b-23, NKJV)

3. Rejoice That God Desires to Save You.

"For this is good and acceptable in the sight of God our Savior, who desires all

---

[38] Steve Gaines, *Morning Manna* (Gardendale, Alabama: Hope For Your Future Publishing, 2003), 389-390.

men to be saved and to come to the knowledge of the truth." (1 Timothy 2:3-4, NKJV)

4. Remember What Jesus Did for You on the Cross.

"For Christ also suffered once for sins; the just for the unjust, that He might bring us to God, being put to death in the flesh but made alive by the Spirit." (1 Peter 3:18, NKJV)

5. Repent of Your Sin.

"Repent therefore and be converted, that your sins may be blotted out, so that times of refreshing may come from the presence of the Lord." (Acts 3:19, NKJV)

6. Receive Jesus as Your Savior by Faith.

"But as many as received Him, to them He gave the right to become children of God, to those who believe in His name." (John 1:12, NKJV)

Would you receive Christ as your Savior now? If so, pray a prayer like this:

"Lord Jesus, thank you that you love me. I know I am a sinner. I believe that you died on the cross to forgive my sin. I repent of my sin and surrender my life completely to You. I ask You to save me right now, Lord Jesus. Come into my life. Wash me with Your blood. Fill me with Your Spirit and make me whole. Write my name in Your eternal Book of Life. Help me to live for You for the rest of my life on earth, and then take me to heaven when I die. In Jesus' name I pray. Amen."

Now What?

If you have prayed this prayer for the first time the next thing for you to do is to make it public by joining a church and being baptized. Baptism doesn't save you. Christ saves you. Baptism is an outward sign of what has happened to you on the inside and is an act done in obedience to the Lord Jesus Christ.

As a new Christian you need to be in a place and with people who can be a support for you as you grow in your new faith. Find a church where the Bible is preached and Christ is recognized and worship.

A LITTLE HUMOR: A minister who was very fond of pure, hot horseradish always kept a bottle of it on his dining room table. He offered some to a guest, who took a big spoonful. When the guest finally was able to speak, he gasped, "I've heard many ministers preach hellfire, but you are the first one I've met who passed out a sample of it."

APRIL 22

ASK!

"Ask, and it will be given to you; seek, and you will find; knock, and it will be opened to you." (Matthew 7:7, NKJV)

In 1962 a fourteen-year-old boy by the name of Robert White wrote to President John F. Kennedy's personal secretary, Evelyn Lincoln, requesting the President's autograph. Within a few weeks Evelyn Lincoln honored the boy's request by sending him a facsimile of Kennedy's signature in the mail. That began a relationship of correspondence that lasted thirty-three years. Impressed with White's passion for presidential history, Mrs. Lincoln gave him thousands of documents and mementos. She saved whatever could be saved (including even the doodles JFK drew during meetings). Today, Robert White boasts the largest private collection of Kennedy memorabilia in the world, over 50,000 items. Receiving begins with the courage to ask.

The word "ask" appears five times in Matthew 7:7-11. Notice what happens if you take the three imperatives in verse 7 – ask, seek, and knock – and put them underneath each other:

Ask
Seek
Knock

Even the three words themselves cry out to us to ask. Ask! Seek! Find! These three words are all imperatives (or commands) and each word is a little more intense than the word preceding it. The last two words intensify the first. "Seeking" is more fervent than "asking" and "knocking" is still more intense than "seeking." The three words also encourage us to be persistent in our prayers. The person who keeps on asking, keeps on seeking, keeps on knocking, will eventually receive. James 4:2 says, "...You do not have because you do not ask." What does Jesus want us to do when it comes time to pray? Just ASK!

A LITTLE HUMOR: A boy asked his politician father, "What does the chaplain of Congress do?" The realistic dad replied, "He stands up, looks at the congressmen, and then prays for our country."

APRIL 23

THE BLESSINGS OF LONELINESS

"Jesus said, 'An hour is coming, and has already come, for you to be scattered, each to his own home, and to leave Me alone; and yet I am not alone, because the Father is with Me.'" (John 16:32, NASB)

Loneliness is a growing problem in our society. A study by the American Council of Life Insurance reported that the most lonely group in America are college students. That's surprising! Next on the lists are divorced people, welfare recipients, single mothers, rural students, housewives, and the elderly. To point out how lonely people can be, Chuck Swindoll mentioned an ad in a Kansas newspaper. It read, "I will listen to you talk for 30 minutes without comment for $5.00." Did anyone call? You bet. Swindoll says that it wasn't long before this individual was receiving 10 to 20 calls a day. The pain of loneliness was so sharp that some were willing to try anything for a half hour of companionship

Loneliness, however, can be a blessing. Men like Shakespeare, Leonardo da Vinci, Benjamin Franklin, and Abraham Lincoln never saw a movie, nor heard a radio, nor watched television. Imagine that! They still became men of gigantic achievement, emotionally stable, mentally balanced, and properly developed human beings. Almost incredible! How did those men become great? They learned the blessing of being alone; for when they were alone, the creative mood in them was let loose to do its magnificent work. A great amount of good can be accomplished when you're alone.

Many times Jesus went off to be alone to pray, to meditate, and to think. In His solitude, He found strength; and in quietness, He met with God. Jesus has promised never to leave us alone (Matthew 28:20; Hebrews 13:5). At one point, however, Jesus did feel the absence of the Father (Matthew 27:46). When He was made sin for us, He was separated from the Father. He was alone that we might never be alone. He was forsaken that we might never be forsaken. The greatest medicine for loneliness is God in you.

A LITTLE HUMOR: You know what's a real bummer? When you send your picture to the lonely hearts club, and they send it back with a note saying: "We're not that lonely!"

APRIL 24

NO WONDER IT'S CALLED AMAZING

". . . My grace is sufficient for you . . ." (2 Corinthians 12:9, NKJV)

Fiorello LaGuardia was the mayor of New York City during the days of the Great Depression. He was called by adoring New Yorkers "the Little Flower" because he was only five feet four and always wore a carnation in his lapel. He was a colorful character who used to ride the New York City fire trucks, raid speakeasies with the police department, take entire orphanages to baseball games, and whenever the New York newspapers were on strike, he would go on the radio and read the Sunday funnies to the kids. One bitterly cold night in January of 1935, the mayor turned up at a night court that served the poorest ward of the city. LaGuardia dismissed the judge for the evening and took over the bench himself.

Within a few minutes, a tattered old woman was brought before him, charged with stealing a loaf of bread. She told LaGuardia that her daughter's husband had deserted her, her daughter was sick, and her two grandchildren were starving. But the shopkeeper, from whom the bread was stolen, refused to drop the charges. "It's a real bad neighborhood, your Honor," the man told the mayor. "She's got to be punished to teach other people around here a lesson." LaGuardia sighted. He turned to the woman and said, "I've got to punish you. The law makes no exceptions – ten dollars or ten days in jail." But even as he pronounced sentenced, the mayor was already reaching into his pocket. He extracted a bill and tossed it into his famous sombrero saying,

"Here is the ten dollar fine which I now remit; and furthermore I am going to fine everyone in this courtroom fifty cents for living in a town where a person has to steal bread so that her grandchildren can eat. Mr. Baliff, collect the fines and give them to the defendant."

So the following day the New York City newspapers reported that $47.50 was turned over to a bewildered old lay who had stolen a loaf of bread to feed her starving grandchildren, fifty cents of that amount being contributed by the red-faced grocery store owner, while some seventy petty criminals, people with traffic violations, and New York City policemen, each of whom had just paid fifty cents for the privilege of doing so, gave the mayor a standing ovation.

That is the essence of grace! It recognizes our wretched condition; it pays our debt and it gives us more than we could ever have imagined. No wonder it's called amazing!

A LITTLE HUMOR: A man was driving down a dark road one evening and unfortunately ran over a cat that darted out in front of his car. Being concerned that he had run over the cat he decided he should tell the owner. "I really hate to tell you this, but I just ran over your cat with my car, so I'd like to replace him." "All right," said the lady, "there's a mouse in the kitchen."

APRIL 25

THE POWER OF FORGIVENESS

"Be kind to one another, tenderhearted, forgiving each other, just as God in Christ also has forgiven you." (Ephesians 4:32, NASB)

The eminent Swiss physician and author Dr. Paul Tournier in his book, *A Doctor's Case Book*, gave many examples from his own experience of people who were healed by the power of forgiveness. In one instance he told of a girl whom one of his friends had been treating for several months without much success for anemia. As a last resort his colleague sent her to the medical officer of the district in which she worked in order to get his permission to send her to a sanatorium. A week later the patient brought word back from the medical officer. He had granted the permit, but he added: "On analyzing the blood, however, I do not arrive at anything like the same figures as those you quote."

Tournier's friend, somewhat put out, at once took a fresh sample of the blood, and rushed to his laboratory. Sure enough, the blood count had suddenly changed. He returned to the patient and asked her, "Has anything out of the ordinary happened in your life since your last visit?"

"Yes, something has happened," she replied. "I have suddenly been able to forgive someone against whom I bore a nasty grudge; and all at once I felt as if I could at last say 'Yes' to life!"

Tournier comments, "Her mental attitude was changed and the very state of her blood changed along with it. When her mind was cured, her body was also on the way to being cured." Then Tournier quotes St. Thomas Aquinas: "Grace flows from the soul to the body."

No doctor can tell you how much effect the mind has over the body. Hospital rooms are filled with people who would not have been there if they had had the proper attitudes and habits. Where we are spiritually can affect our physical bodies. If we have let burdens like stress or resentment or despair to overwhelm us, it will be more difficult for the body to do its healing work. If we will work on our faith – trusting God, letting go of anxiety, practicing forgiveness, we will be healed.

A LITTLE HUMOR: Bubba walks in the doctor's office and the receptionist asked him what he had. Bubba said, "Shingles." So she wrote down his name, address, insurance info, and told him to have a seat. Fifteen minutes later a nurse's aide came out and asked Bubba what he had. Bubba said, "Shingles." So she recorded his weight, height, and assorted medical history and told him to wait in the examining room. A half hour later a nurse came and asked Bubba what he had. Bubba said, "Shingles." So the nurse gave Bubba a blood test, an electrocardiogram, and told Bubba to take off his clothes and wait for the doctor. An hour later the doctor came in and asked what he had. Bubba said, "Shingles." The doctor asked, "Where?" Bubba said, "Outside on the delivery truck. Where do you want me to put them?"

APRIL 26

LEARN TO MASTER YOUR ANGER

"Then the Lord said to Cain, 'Why are you angry? And why has your countenance fallen? If you do well, will not your countenance be lifted up? And if you do not well, sin is crouching at the door; and its desire is for you, but you must master it."
(Genesis 4:6-7, NASB)

The second human emotion mentioned in the Bible is anger. After being expelled from the garden Eve conceived and bore two sons, Cain and Abel. Cain became a tiller of the ground and Abel became a keeper of sheep. In their worship of God Cain brought the fruit of the field and Abel the fruit of the flock. Abel's sacrifice was accepted, Cain's was rejected.

Gently and mercifully the Lord dealt with Cain, seeking to cool his anger. God assured him if he would do right, he, too, would be accepted. But if not, the Lord warned, "sin is crouching at the door."

Anger is pictured as a ferocious beast crouching at Cain's door ready to spring on him and devour him. He was told he must master his anger, or it would devour him like a wild beast.

Anger was not just a problem for the first mortal man born on this earth but for every mortal man. It expresses itself in a myriad of ways: road rage, spousal abuse, security guards and metal detectors in schools, airports, at athletic events, courthouses, and almost every other public gathering place. It is not surprising that the Bible speaks often and candidly about anger. The Scriptures say, "Like a city that is broken into and without walls is a man who has no control over his spirit" (Proverbs 26:28).

In ancient times the walls of a city were its chief means of defense. A city with the walls broken down was vulnerable to every enemy. Uncontrolled anger is like that. Rather than being a strength, it is a sign of weakness. Either we master it or it masters us.

A LITTLE HUMOR: A Baptist pastor was inviting people in his neighborhood to visit his church. An elderly lady said, "No thank you, young man, I'm a Methodist." "If you don't mind," he asked, "tell me, why are you a Methodist?" "Well," she replied, "you see, my parents were Methodists, my grandparents were Methodists, and my great-grandparents were Methodists." The frustrated young Baptist pastor responded, "That's no reason, just because all your relatives are Methodists. What would you do if all your relatives were idiots?" "In that case," she smiled, "I'd probably be a Baptist!"

APRIL 27

HE IS ABLE TO DELIVER ME

"Who will set me free from the body of this death? Thanks be to God through Jesus Christ our Lord!" (Romans 7:24-25, NASB)

Some of you may be familiar with Jack London's classic story, *White Fang.* White Fang is half dog-half wolf. After living in the wild, he is domesticated and learns to live among people. White Fang was very fond of chickens. On one occasion he raided a chicken roost and killed fifty hens. His master, Weeden Scott, scolded him and took him into the chicken yard. When White Fang saw his favorite food walking around, he followed his natural impulse and lunged for a chicken. He was immediately checked by his master's voice. This continued until White Fang learned to ignored the chickens. Jack London said of White Fang: "He had learned the law."[39]

What law was that? Let's call it the law of obedience. White Fang moved from following the dictates of his own natural cravings to being obedient to the higher discipline of his master. Did you know that there are human beings who have done that?

There are people in this very city who were addicted to drink and drugs. Their only hope was to acknowledge that there is a higher power in this world, and to give their lives over to that power, and by the grace of God overcome their addiction. There are people whose marriages were endangered by their inability to deal with the lusts of their own bodies, but they made a commitment not only to their spouse but also to God, and by God's grace they have kept their vows and strengthened their unions.

Paul describers for us the war going on in his own mind and body. He describes

---

[39] *Dynamic Preaching.* July-September, 2002, page 20.

himself as a wretched man and he cries out, "Who will deliver me?" Then he answers his own question. He writes, "Thanks be to God through Jesus Christ our Lord!" (Romans 7:25). Jesus Christ delivered him, just as Christ can deliver you and me if we are willing to listen to His voice and obey.

A LITTLE HUMOR: A minister was preoccupied with thoughts of how he was going to ask the congregation to come up with more money than they were expecting for repairs to the church building. He talked with the church organist to see what kind of inspirational music she could play after the announcement about the finances to get the congregation in a giving mood. "Don't worry," she said, "I'll think of something." During the service, the minister paused and said, "Brothers and Sisters, we are in great difficulty; the roof repairs cost twice as much as we expected, and we need $4,000. Any of you who can pledge $100 or more, please stand up." Just at that moment, the organist started playing, "The Star Spangled Banner."

APRIL 28

WHY DOES GOD TEST OUR FAITH?

"My brethren, count it all joy when you fall into various trials, knowing that the testing of your faith produces patience." (James 1:2-3, NKJV)

Why does God test our faith? God has told us in His Word some reasons why He tests our faith.

First, God tries our faith **TO PROVE THE GENUINENESS OF IT.** Only when faith is tested is the reality of faith proved and demonstrated (cf. Genesis 22:1, 12).

Second, God tries our faith **TO INCREASE THE MEASURE OF IT.** Abraham's faith was stronger after he had trusted God for the gift of Isaac (cf. Romans 4:20); but it was even stronger after the experience of offering Isaac (cf. Genesis 22).

Third, God tries our faith **TO SECURE THE PRECIOUSNESS OF IT.** First Peter 1:7 is a great verse, and it should be read in conjunction with Malachi 3:3. The gold of our life is to His "praise and honor and glory" when it is separated from the dross, and the trial of our faith is so precious because it brings about this separation.

Fourth, God tries our faith **TO PRODUCE THE FRUIT OF IT.** This is what we learn from John 15:2. Our heavenly "Husbandman" is looking for "fruit" (v. 2); "more fruit" (v. 2) and "much fruit" (v. 5, 8). One method He employs for producing this increasing amount of fruit in the lives of His children is that of trials and testing.

Fifth, God tries our faith **TO USE THE TESTIMONY OF IT.** Read 2 Corinthians 11:23-28 and Philippians 1:12, and then compare Acts 16:22-25, and particularly notice the last six words in verse 25: "...the prisoners were listening to them."

God will always give back to us far more than He asks us to give up for Him.

A LITTLE HUMOR: A woman's husband had been slipping in and out of a coma for several months, yet she had stayed by his bedside every single day. One day, when he came to, he motioned for her to come nearer. As she sat by him, he whispered, eyes filled with tears, "Bessie, you know what? You have been with me all through the bad times. When I got fired, you were there to support me. When my business failed, you were there. When I got shot, you were by my side. When we lost the house, you stayed right here. You know what, Bessie?" "What dear?" she gently asked smiling as her heart began to be filled with warmth. "Bessie, I think you are bad luck!"

APRIL 29

PARTY CRASHERS OR INVITED GUESTS?

"Nothing impure will even enter it, nor will anyone who does what is shameful or deceitful, but only those whose names are written in the Lamb's book of life."
(Revelation 21:27, NIV)

The most infamous party crashers in the world, Tareq and Michaele Salahi, denied they finagled their way into a White House state dinner being held for the prime minister of India, and insisted they were invited by a Washington law firm with ties to a senior Pentagon official. White House press secretary Robert Gibbs said, "They were not on a list here at the White House. They'd been told on a number of occasions that they did not have tickets for that dinner."

Whether or not they were invited is yet to be seen at the time of my writing this article, but there is another event that will be taking place in the future and no one will be allowed but those whose names are on the list. I'm talking about one's entrance into heaven. But how do you get on heaven's list?

Well, just like any event, one is not allowed into heaven unless he or she is invited, and there must be a response (an RSVP). Thankfully, God issues an invitation to everyone as stated in Revelation 22:17." The Spirit and the bride say, 'Come!' And let him who hears say, 'Come!' Whoever is thirsty, let him come; and whoever wishes, let him take the free gift of the water of life." The invitation is extended but there must be an acceptance. One must pray to God and say, "Yes, I accept your Son, the Lord Jesus Christ, as my personal Savior."

God loves you. He wants you to spend eternity in heaven with Him. He invites you to accept His Son, the Lord Jesus Christ, as your Savior. If you will there will be a special place in heaven just for you. Have you accepted His invitation? There won't be any party crashers in heaven. It's by invitation only!

A LITTLE HUMOR: A husband said to his wife, "I'm not so sure you can't take your money with you when you die. I'm going to put a few thousand dollars in the attic, and when we go, we can pick it up on our way to heaven." When the husband later died, his wife went up to the attic to see how his plan had worked. The money was still there. As she went back downstairs she mused, "Maybe he should have put it in the basement."

APRIL 30

HOW TO FIND HAPPINESS

"He who heeds the word wisely will find good, and whoever trust in the Lord, happy is he." (Proverbs 16:20b, NKJV)

C. S. Lewis told the story about a child who was asked what he thought God was like. As far as the child could make out, God was always snooping around to see if anyone was enjoying himself, so He could put a stop to it!

Everyone in the world shares one basic desire: we all want to be happy. Different people define happiness different ways, but it boils down to the same basic desire: we all want to be happy. Have you ever noticed that no one ever says, "I wish I weren't so happy all the time!"?

However, most people are not happy. They often think happiness is just around the corner – just a few dollars more, or a new relationship away, or one career achievement away. Madonna has made a career of self-indulgent behavior and is one of the wealthiest people in show business. In an interview a couple of years ago, she was asked if she was happy and her response was: "I don't even know anybody who is happy!" An entire episode of *Frazier* was built around his brother Niles asking him the question, "Are you happy?" It took Frazier twenty-eight minutes and two commercial breaks before he could finally say, with reservations, "Yes, in the grand scheme of things, I guess you could say that I'm happy."

Our Scripture for today tells us two things we need to do in order to find happiness. First, we are to heed God's Word. The word *heed* means to pay attention. Paying attention to God's Word means that you read, understand it, and apply it to your life. Second, we are to trust the Lord. So, in order to be happy we must read the Bible, heed it; and trust the One who wrote it. The hymn writer, John H. Sammis put it this way: "Trust and obey, for there's no other way to be happy in Jesus, but to trust and obey."

A LITTLE HUMOR: At a wedding reception a woman and her friend watched the newly married couple cut their cake. As they watched, the woman remarked to her friend, "I never knew what true happiness was until I got married, but by then it was too late."

MAY 1

WATCH OUT FOR ENVY

"A sound heart is life to the body, but envy is rottenness to the bones."
(Proverbs 14:30, NKJV)

There is a Greek story about a man who killed himself through envy. His fellow citizens had erected a statue to one of their number who was a celebrated champion in the public games. But this man, a rival of the honored athlete, was so envious that he vowed that he would destroy that statue. Every night he went out into the darkness and chiseled at its base in an effort to undermine its foundation and make it fall. At last he succeeded. It did fall but it fell on him. He fell, a victim of his own envy.[40]

Envy is one of the most heinous sins of the flesh and one of the most uncalled for. Someone defined envy as "being sad about someone else's success or blessing and glad about someone else's failures or troubles." Leslie Flynn said, "Envy is among the darkest, vilest, and most devilish of sins, a vice which by itself proves the depravity of man." Donald Gray Barnhouse said, "Envy is a hive from which other sins swarm." Charles Swindoll says, "Envy is one of the great enemies of inner peace. It steals contentment from the heart." The Bible says "envy is rottenness to the bones."

The Latin word for envy is *invidia*, which paraphrased means staring into. A person who is envious of others probably spends a great deal of time "staring into" the status of others. A prime example of this is Joseph's brothers (Genesis 37). They spent a great deal of time "staring into" Joseph who was their father's favorite son (Genesis 37:3). Such envy gave birth to hatred (Genesis 37:4-5, 8).

There once was an envious merchant who was particularly envious of his number one competitor. One day as this man was walking along the beach he found a bottle with a genie inside. This genie said, "Sir, your wish is my command. However, whatever you wish for, I will give in double measure to the person you envy the most." This man thought for a second and then said, "I wish to be blind in one eye."

Envy is a tumor we dare not ignore. We must invite the Great Physician to remove it. If ignored, envy can become a terminal illness of the soul.

A LITTLE HUMOR: A man's wife bought a new line of expensive cosmetics guaranteed to make her look years younger. After a lengthy sitting before the mirror applying the "miracle" products she asked, "Darling, honestly what age would you say I am?" Looking her over carefully, he replied, "Judging from your skin, twenty; your hair, eighteen; and your figure, twenty-five." "Oh, you flatterer!" she gushed. "Hey, wait a minute!" he interrupted. "I haven't added them up yet!"

---

[40] Billy Graham, *Freedom from the Seven Deadly Sins* (Grand Rapids: Zondervan Publishing House, 1955), 41-42.

MAY 2

BEGIN YOUR DAY WITH GOD

"My voice You shall hear in the morning, O Lord; in the morning I will direct it to You, and I will look up." (Psalm 5:3, NKJV)

Remember the saying, "Breakfast is the most important meal of the day"? It's true. In fact, what you choose to eat for breakfast makes a big difference for your health. Studies show that people who successfully maintain a significant weight loss eat breakfast just about every day. After fasting all night, breakfast can kick-start your energy level for the rest of the day.

Likewise, as a Christian, it's important for us to start our day with a healthy spiritual diet of prayer. If we let prayer unlock the gates of the day, the ensuing hours are more likely to be filled with spiritual usefulness and blessing.

In the 1840's, a young man who was an earnest Christian found employment in a pawnshop. Although he disliked the work, he did it faithfully "as unto the Lord" until a more desirable opportunity opened for him. To prepare himself for a life of Christian service, he wrote on a scrap of paper the following resolution: "I do promise God that I will rise early every morning to have a few minutes – not less than five – in private prayer. I will endeavor to conduct myself as a humble, meek, and zealous follower of Jesus, and by serious witness and warning, I will try to lead others to think of the needs of their immortal souls. I hereby vow to read no less than four chapters in God's Word every day. I will cultivate a spirit of self-denial and will yield myself a prisoner of love to the Redeemer of the world."

That young man was William Booth, who later led thousands to Christ. The Salvation Army, which he founded, stands as a monument to his faithfulness in preparing himself each morning to serve the Lord.

There is much work to be done for the Lord. Each day has its own needs. People need the Lord. We need a good spiritual breakfast of prayer, Bible reading, and a willingness to be used of God to reach out to a world of people who need help and encouragement. Be sure to begin each day with the Lord.

A LITTLE HUMOR: A man who had been keeping company with a lady for a number of years took her out one night to a Chinese restaurant. They began studying the menu, and he inquired, "How would you like your rice, fried or boiled?" She looked up at him and said, very sharply, "Thrown!"

MAY 3

WHEN SATAN GOES FISHING

"But each one is tempted when he is carried away and enticed by his own lust."
(James 1:14, NASB)

The word *enticed* is a fishing term. A fisherman doesn't drop a bare hook into the water. He baits the hook to interest and entice a fish. Sometimes the bait is a colorful plastic worm. Sometimes it is a live wiggling minnow. Sometimes it is a tasty shrimp. He drops the bait into the water and keeps it dancing, jiggling up and down to attract the attention of the fish. The fisherman hopes the fish will pass nearby and will be unable to resist the bait and will be hooked before he knows it. Temptation always follows that same overall process. Notice how it works:

Step 1: The bait is dropped.
Step 2: The inner desire is attracted to the bait.
Step 3: We bite the bait; we yield to the temptation and sin.
Step 4: We end up hooked and cooked.
That's the tragic consequence of sin.

Satan appeals to our inner desires. Without that he would have little chance of leading us into sin. The thrust of temptation is always the same. The one who is below us (Satan) appeals to that which is within us (our desire) to draw us from the one who is above us (God).

God does not tempt us, but He does test us. God allows Satan to tempt people in order to refine their faith and to help them grow in their dependence on Christ. We can resist temptation to sin by turning to God for strength and choosing to obey His Word.

A LITTLE HUMOR: The late Grady Nutt used to be a regular on the television program "Hee Haw." On one of the programs he told of attending a small Christian college years before. He said that it was located five miles from any known sin. "The school had three rules," said Grady. "You won't smoke, you won't drink, and you won't want to." Grady said, "I was dismissed for wanting to."

MAY 4

ABUNDANT SUPPLIES

"And this same God who takes care of me will supply all your needs from the glorious riches, which have been given to us in Christ Jesus."
(Philippians 4:19, NLT)

On May 4, 1942, food was rationed in the United States. During the war, the federal government began the rationing system to ensure a fair division of essential items and to keep inflation from skyrocketing.

I was born in 1943 and although I was a baby at the time, I was issued a ration book, too. I still have it. Sugar was the first item to be rationed. Other items were quickly added: coffee, meat, gasoline, and canned goods. Everyone cooperated in the rationing system because we were at war and were willing to sacrifice for our soldiers.

Jesus promised that all who came to Him would never experience a spiritual "rationing." His promise is that those who receive Him as Savior will always have available to them all that pertains to life and godliness. He spoke of the "abundant life" (John 10:10), of "living water" (John 7:37-39) and "living bread" (John 6:51). Even the apostle Paul mentions God's sufficient grace (2 Corinthians 12:9) and the Lord supplying our every need (Philippians 4;19). All we need to live a godly life is supplied by our blessed Savior. We can come as often as we like and get all that we need or want.

There is no limit to heaven's resources.

A LITTLE HUMOR: A couple who had been married for over 50 years were sitting on the sofa. The wife said, "Dear, do you remember how you used to sit close to me?" He moved over and sat close to her. "Dear," she continued, "do you remember how you used to hold me tight?" He reached over and held her tight. "And," she went on, "do you remember how you used to hug me and kiss me and nibble on my ear?" With that, her husband got up and started to walk out of the room. "Where are you going?" she asked. "Well," he answered, "I have to go and get my teeth."

MAY 5

TO BE HUMAN IS TO BE TEMPTED

"If you think you are standing strong, be careful not to fall. The temptations in your life are no different from what others experience..." (1 Corinthians 10:12-13a, NLT)

At the zoo in Fort Worth, Texas, is a building where tropical birds are kept. The hallway where the people walk is dark; the birds are in lighted cases of glass. All along each side of the building is a long case that looks like a tropical rain forest. It has a miniature waterfall, a pool, trees, and all sorts of plants. Among the trees and rocky ledges the small, brightly colored birds fly. As people watch this, they eventually become aware that there is no glass between them and the birds. They could reach in and touch the birds if they chose. Why don't the birds fly out? A sign above the cage explains that the birds are afraid of darkness, and when it gets dark, they go to sleep. They love the light and will not deliberately fly from the light into the darkness.

There is a major difference between tropical birds and humans. Given the right circumstances we will wander into the darkness. There is a cartoon that has two characters saying: "How come opportunity knocks only once, but temptation beats down the door every day?" It's true.

No one is immune to temptation. Paul writes, "If you think you are standing strong, be careful not to fall. The temptations in your life are no different from what others experience..." (1 Corinthians 10:12a, NLT). Don't get the idea that just because you are a Christian that you are somehow immune to the temptations that vex the rest of humanity. Stay in the light of God's Word (Psalm 119:105) and in the light of God's Son (John 3:19-21).

A LITTLE HUMOR: Blondie and Dagwood, in the comic by the same name, are dining out. The waiter has brought the desserts over for all to choose. Dagwood looks at them individually and says, "No thanks." Blondie, with a smile on her face says, "Dagwood knows how to handle temptation." At that moment, the waiter holds up one more dessert and Dagwood, with a huge grin, says, "I'll take the Napoleon!" Still smiling, Blondie adds, "He yields to it."

MAY 6

TOO MUCH OF A GOOD THING CAN BE BAD FOR YOU

"The woman was convinced. She saw that the tree was beautiful and its fruit looked delicious, and she wanted the wisdom it would give her. So she took some of the fruit and ate it. Then she gave some to her husband who was with her, and he ate it, too."
(Genesis 3:6, NLT)

How would you like to live where candy bars grow on trees? That would be great, wouldn't it? If you could travel to South America to the hot, tropical lands falling 10 degrees on either side of the equator, you would find football-shaped pods hanging from trees. These pods are hacked from cacao trees and split open with machetes. The twenty to fifty ivory-colored beans nestled inside each pod are scooped out by hand. After drying, the cocoa beans are ready to be shipped to factories around the world – where they will be turned into candy bars. It makes me hungry just thinking about it.

What if we could have all the chocolate candy we wanted? Suppose we could go outside and pick candy bars off the trees. Would it be good for us to eat all that candy? No, it wouldn't. Too much candy could hurt our health.

There are many things in life like that. They tempt us. They appeal to us, but we really ought to leave them alone because they are not good for us. It is up to us to choose those things that build us up and to reject those things that tear us down.

A man asked his wife to help him shed some unwanted pounds. And so she stopped serving him TV snacks with fat and carbohydrates in them. Instead, she substituted celery. While he was unenthusiastically munching on a celery stalk one night, a commercial caught his attention. As he watched longingly, a woman spread gooey chocolate frosting over a freshly baked cake. When it was over, the man turned sadly to his wife. "Did you ever notice," he asked, "that they never advertise celery on television?"

Temptation is everywhere when you are weak. Remember, there are Seven

Deadly Sins . . . one for each day of the week, so . . . have a nice week!

A LITTLE HUMOR: A California scientist has computed that the average human being eats 16 times his or her own weight in an average year, while a horse eats only 8 times its weight. This all seems to prove that if you want to lose weight, you should eat like a horse.

MAY 7

SAFELY CONNECTED TO CHRIST

"For as in Adam all die, even so in Christ all shall be made alive."
(1 Corinthians 15:22, NKJV)

In his book, *Conquering the Fear of Death*, Spiros Zodhiates tells of a party of climbers, roped together, who were making their way along a snow ridge high up in the Alps when the leader slipped and fell over the edge of the precipice. The rope attached to him jerked the next man off his feet, and each of the party except the last man was in turn dragged over. The last man, an experienced climber, had time between the first slip until the rope tightened around his own body to plunge his ice-axe deeply into the snow, dig his heels into the snow, and brace himself for the coming strain; and when it reached him he held firm. For a short time all hung out in space, with a terrible death threatening them thousands of feet below. Then the first man swarmed up the rope and over the body of the next who followed after him. All of the climbers managed to climb to safety.

The first Adam slipped and fell over the precipice of eternal death, and in his fall he dragged all mankind after him (Genesis 3). As the God-man, Jesus Christ came to this earth for the purpose of saving fallen humanity. Through Him all mankind is enabled to climb to safety. Had those who were climbing the Alps not availed themselves of the rope, they could not have been saved. Likewise, if we fail to trust Christ as Savior, we will not be saved. The climbers made the decision to be connected. Confronted with the decision whether to remain "in Adam" or "in Christ," which will you choose?

A LITTLE HUMOR: A funeral procession was going up a hill and the coffin fell out. It went right down the hill, through a parking lot and a shopping center, and into a drug store where it stopped directly in front of the pharmacy. As it hit the counter, the coffin's lid popped open. The pharmacist looked down, and a lady looked up. The pharmacist didn't know what to do, so he asked, "May I help you?" She replied, "You have to give me something to stop this coffin."

MAY 8

PLEASE BE SEATED

"Tell everyone to sit down," Jesus said. (John 6:10, NLT)

Philip was greatly concerned. There were over five thousand people who had gathered to hear Jesus. It was lunch time. The people were hungry. Jesus asked, "Where can we buy bread to feed all these people?" (John 6:5, NLT). I can just see Philip running around, "What shall we do? What shall we do?" Jesus knew that panic never solved any problem. That's why Jesus said, "Tell everyone to sit down."

A lecturer on stress management raised a glass of water and asked his audience, "How heavy is this glass of water?" Various answers were called out. Then he replied, "The weight really doesn't matter. What matters is how long you try to hold it."

"If I hold it for a minute, that's not a problem," he said. "If I hold it for an hour, I'll have an ache in my arm. If I hold it for a day, you'll have to call an ambulance. In each case, it's the same weight, but the longer I hold it, the heavier it becomes."

"And that's the way it is with stress," he said. "If we carry our burdens all the time, sooner or later, as the burden becomes increasingly heavy, we won't be able to carry on. You have to put it down for a while and rest before holding it again. When we're refreshed, we can carry on with the burden.

That may be the best thing about worship. It's a time when we can sit still and reflect, and listen to the voice of God. Jesus knew it was important to settle the crowd down. And so He said to His disciples, "Tell everyone to sit down."

Whatever burdens you're carrying now, let them down for a moment if you can. Relax; pick them up latter after you've rested. Life is short. Enjoy it!" Please be seated!

A LITTLE HUMOR: A farmer was hauling a load of manure past a mental hospital. The patients were outside exercising, and one of them yelled at the farmer, "What are you going to do with that stuff?" "I'm taking it home to put on my strawberries," replied the farmer. The patient looked at another and said, "He should be in this place. He's more out of touch than we are. We put whipped cream on our strawberries."

MAY 9

WE OWE EVERYTHING TO HIM

"May it never be that I would boast, except in the cross of our Lord Jesus Christ..." (Galatians 6:14, NASB)

The cross was an instrument of death long before it was a symbol of eternal life. On it millions of victims were impaled in the most horrific form of torture known to humanity. No nation on earth allows crucifixion today. But the most famous death in history transformed its blood-stained wood into a gift of grace.

On March 15, 1985, Mr. Wayne Alderson appeared on *The Today Show.* Forty years earlier he was the first American to cross into Germany during World War II. An exploding grenade sent him face down and wounded into the mud. A German machine gun then began firing in his direction. But a fellow soldier turned him over so he could breathe and threw his own body over him. This friend died protecting him from certain death. With tears welling up in his eyes. Alderson said, "I can never forget the person who sacrificed his life to save me. I owe everything to him."

The Greek word for *boast* is a basic expression of praise, unlike the English word, which necessarily includes the aspect of pride. Paul gloried in the cross. Certainly this does not mean that he gloried in the brutality or suffering of the cross. He was not looking at the cross as a piece of wood on which a criminal died. He was looking at the cross of Christ and glorying in Him. Jesus Christ is mentioned at least forty-five times in the Galatian letter, which means that one third of the verses contain some reference to Him. The person of Jesus Christ captivated Paul, and it was Christ who made the cross glorious to him. We Christians feel the same about the cross of Calvary and the death of the Lord Jesus Christ. Our boast is not in ourselves but in our Savior. We can never forget the Person who sacrificed His life to save us. We owe everything to Him.

A LITTLE HUMOR: Once when the power went off at the elementary school, the cook couldn't serve a hot meal in the cafeteria. She had to feed the children something, so at the last minute she whipped up great stacks of peanut butter and jelly sandwiches. As one little boy filled his plate, he said, "It's about time. At last – a home cooked meal."

MAY 10

UNTIL THE LORD COMES, BE PATIENT

"Therefore, be patient, brethren, until the coming of the Lord...strengthen your heart, for the coming of the Lord is near." (James 5:7-8, NASB)

James, along with all the other writers of the New Testament, affirms his belief in the second coming of Christ. In view of the Lord's certain return, James encourages his readers to be patient (James 5:7-11). James uses three examples in urging us to have the right kind of patience until Jesus comes again.

The first example has to do with the farmer as he waits for his crops until the early and late rains have fallen (James 5:7). As the farmer needs patience to wait until nature does its work, so the Christian needs patience to wait until the Lord comes. Like the farmer he is busy getting everything ready for the harvest.

Next, James reminds us of the prophets (James 5:10). These men of God could never have done their work and borne their witness had they not patiently endured.

Then, James quotes the example of Job (James 5:11). We usually think of him in the context, "the patience of Job." The Greek word translated *patience* means anything but a passive patience. Instead, the word denotes a gallant perseverance. It is a very active and progressive concept. Such patience is revealed in some of Job's brave affirmations. "Though he slay me, yet will I trust him" (Job 13:15). "I know that my redeemer lives" (Job 19:25).

If we have the right kind of patience as we wait for the Lord, we will be faithfully serving and praising Him under all circumstances. The great theologian and preacher, Andrew Murray, declared, "Be assured that if God waits longer than you could wish, it is only to make the blessing doubly precious!" God waited four thousand years, till the fullness of time, before He sent His Son. Our times are in His hands. To believers of the first century and the twenty-first century alike, James' words ring out loud and clear: "Therefore, be patient, brethren, until the coming of the Lord…strengthen your heart, for the coming of the Lord is near." (James 5:7-8, NASB). The Lord keeps His word. Jesus will return! Be patient!

A LITTLE HUMOR: Don't give up. It took Noah six months to find a parking place.

MAY 11

PRESS ON

"I press on…" (Philippians 3:14a, NASB)

There are a lot of people in our churches today who have the attitude that they have arrived, when in reality, they are stopping traffic in the middle of the road. Our attitude needs to be, "I have not arrived. I am not what I ought to be." Our prayer ought to be, "Help me to grow, help me to mature, keep challenging me with circumstances of life that make me better and more like you."

Several years ago, *Forbes* magazine carried an article by David Glass who was at that time a symbol of Wal-Mart. They asked him who he most admired in life, and he mentioned without hesitation, Sam Walton. He said, "I have never known a day in the life of Same Walton to go by that he did not improve in some way." That's the way we ought to be as Christians. Always improving.

When Apple was a fledging computer company, Steven Jobs, the chairman, flew to New York City to meet with John Sculley, then president and chief executive officer of Pepsi. Jobs wanted Sculley to move to California to head up Apple Computer. They would come to an agreement, and then Sculley would back out. As this went on and on, it became more and more frustrating.

Finally, Sculley called Jobs and said, "I've got a final proposition. Let's bring this thing to a close. I want a million dollars bonus, and a million dollars severance, and I want all that just to stay here in New York City and be a consultant." Jobs responded by saying something that Sculley said changed his life: "Sculley, I want to ask you something. Do you want to spend your life selling sugared water, or do you want to change the world?" Sculley said that question changed his perspective on life.

There's nothing wrong with selling sugared water if that's what you are supposed to do, but there is more to be done. There are more hills to be climbed, more kingdoms to be conquered. Can we change the world? You bet we can, and that is Christ's calling to us.

A LITTLE HUMOR: A man and his wife were driving their recreational vehicle across the country and were nearing a town spelled Kissimee. They noted the strange spelling and tried to figure how to pronounce it – KISS-a-me; kis-A-me; kis-a-ME. They grew more perplexed as they drove into the town. Since they were hungry, they pulled into a place to get something to eat. At the counter, the man said to the waitress: "My wife and I can't seem to be able to figure out how to pronounce this place. Will you tell me where we are and say it very slowly so that I can understand. The waitress looked at him and said: "Buuurrrgerrr Kiiiinnnng."

MAY 12

JESUS IS OUR RESCUER

". . . But now, once for all time, he has appeared at the end of the age to remove sin by his own death as a sacrifice." (Hebrews 9:26, NLT)

On Wednesday, January 13, 1982, an Air Florida Boeing 737 jet left National Airport in Washington, D. C., during severely cold weather. Moments later it hit the 14th Street Bridge and crashed into the icy waters of the Potomac River. The tragic accident took seventy-eight lives.

Immediately after the crash six passengers held to a piece of the plane, trying to stay afloat in the icy Potomac. Helicopters from the Coast Guard and Park Police came to rescue these survivors. They lowered a lifesaving ring. One of the men caught the ring and handed it five times to his companions. All five made it to the helicopters.

As the helicopter returned for a final trip to rescue this man, he disappeared beneath the water. The survivors did not even know his name. He gave his life that they might live. His was an effective but deadly sacrifice.

Our rescuer has the name Jesus. He gave His life for our sins. His offering was effective because He has done away with sin by the sacrifice of Himself (Hebrews 9:26). His offering of himself needed no reputation. His offering was deadly because in doing God's will, He surrendered His own life. Jesus now holds out a lifesaving ring to us. By taking His offer we can receive eternal life.

A LITTLE HUMOR: A just-out-of-seminary pastor was about to conduct his first wedding and was worried sick. An elderly preacher gave him some advice, "If you lose your place in the ceremony book or you forget your lines, start quoting scriptures until you find your place." The wedding day came. And, sure enough, the young man forgot where he was in the ritual. Unfortunately, the only verse he could think of was, "Father, forgive them, for they know not what they do."

MAY 13

THIS IS THE DAY

"So teach us to number our days, that we may present to You a heart of wisdom."
(Psalm 90:12, NASB)

Warren Wiersbe writes, "We number our years, but it is wiser to number our days, for we live a day at a time." J. B. Fowler once wrote, "Because time flies, we ought to prize it highly, guard it carefully, enjoy it fully, use it wisely, pray over it faithfully, and give thanks for it continually." We must all learn to live "one day at a time." Here are five suggestions as to what we can do with each day God gives to us.

1. The Daily Code. The word "code" means a "systematic book of law." In Psalm 1 David refers to God's Word as "the Law of the Lord." In that sense we might refer to the Bible as a COD. We should have a daily appointment with the Bible (Acts 17:11).

2. The Daily Call. Psalm 88:9 reads, "…I have called upon You every day, O Lord; I have spread out my hands to You." We should reserve some time every day in which we can call (pray) upon the Lord.

3. The Daily Chore. Psalm 61:8 reads, "So I will sing praise to Your name forever, that I may pay my vows day by day." A chore is "a small or odd job." We should perform some little service for Jesus every day.

4. The Daily Cross. In Luke 9:23 we read, "And He was saying to them all, 'If anyone wishes to come after Me, he must deny himself, and take up his cross daily and follow Me'." Taking up one's cross did not simply mean carrying a heavy burden, but suffering a violent death by crucifixion. Believers must be completely willing to die to themselves and to live for God, even at the cost of their lives.

5. The Daily Care. Hebrews 3:13 states, "But encourage one another day after day, as long as it is still called 'Today,' so that none of you will be hardened by the deceitfulness of sin." Using the word "today" from Psalm 95:7, the author of Hebrews challenges us to warn each other every day against the deceptive and hardening power of sin.

Time has a way of slipping past us. Heeding the advice of Ephesians 5:16, we must make the most of our time. Live one day at a time.

A LITTLE HUMOR: Early one morning, a woman made a mad dash form her house when she heard the garbage truck pulling away. She was still in her bathrobe. Her hair was wrapped around big curlers. Her face was covered with sticky cream. She was wearing a chin-strap and a beat up old pair of slippers. In short, she was a frightful picture. When she reached the sidewalk, she called out, "Am I too late for the garbage?" The reply came back, "No, hop right in."

MAY 14

THANKS, MOM

"Honor your mother" (Exodus 20:12a, NKJV)

After an elementary teacher gave a science lesson on magnets, she gave her students a quiz to see how much they had learned. One of the questions read, "My name starts with 'M.' I have six letters and I pick up things. What am I?" Half the class answered with the six-letter word "Mother."

Thank goodness God made mothers because mothers not only pick up things, they pick us up. Who is the first person you think about when you fall down and go boom? Chances are it is your mother.

Moms don't have as much time to spend with their children as they use to. It starts early. They only get one night in a hospital to have a baby. Now they know what HMO stands for — "Hurry Mothers Out." Being a mother is tough. One kid said his mother said a prayer for him every night. She prayed, "Thank God he's in bed."

I heard about a mom who had finished a backbreaking job of stripping the kitchen floor and re-waxing it. She heard her husband say, "Kids, your mother has worked hard on this floor, see how nice and clean it looks? I want you to be careful because any of you who spills anything on the floor has to clean it up first, go to the spare room, close the door, and stay there by yourself for an hour." The mother heard this, spilt coffee on the floor, cleaned it up, ran to the room, and no one saw her for an hour.

Life isn't as scary with a mom around. Just ask the first grade boy who strutted in front of his classmates and proclaimed, "When I grow up, I'm going to be a lion tamer. I'll have lots of fierce lions, and when I walk in the cage, they will roar." He paused a moment and looked at his classmates' faces and then added, "Of course, I'll have my mother with me."

Abraham Lincoln was right, "No man is poor who has a godly mother."

A LITTLE HUMOR: A lady phoned her insurance company and said she wanted to change the beneficiaries of her insurance policy. "I've just had twins," she informed the agent. The agent had difficulty in hearing her, and asked: "Will you repeat that, please?" She shot back emphatically: "Not if I can help it!"

MAY 15

TOO GOOD TO BE CORNY

"As for me, I know that my Redeemer lives, and at the last He will take His stand on the earth." (Job 19:25, NASB)

Mr. Bill Cordova, Sr. is a friend of mine. I first met him at McDonalds on University Drive. A group of men met there every morning for their morning coffee and to visit for a while before going on to their daily activities.

Mr. Cordova is an avid reader of my weekly devotional and he would comment on them every week. Like many others, he especially likes the "A LITTLE HUMOR" joke that I add at the end of each devotional. The joke serves as an attention getter so people will read the devotional. People have said to me, "I read your devotional every week, especially the joke. In fact, I read the joke first, then I read the devotional." That's okay with me. The Bible says "A merry heart does good, like medicine" (Proverbs 17:22a, NKJV). That's why I started adding the humor. I believe God wants us to enjoy life and to laugh a lot. Mr. Cordova would laugh as he mentioned the joke and then say, "You have some of the corniest jokes I've ever read."

Woodworking is Mr. Cordova's hobby. He said to me one day, "I make ball point pens using wood for their housing. I have even made a housing for a ball point pen out of a corncob. I'm going to make one for you so you will have something corny to write with." We all had a good laugh. It wasn't too long after that that he gave me a ball point pen with a housing made out of a corncob. I couldn't believe it. A ball point pen with a corncob housing. I'm proud of it.

I'm always looking for an idea for a devotional and I started thinking how to write a devotional about a corncob ball point pen. Playing around with the word "corny," I finally came up with this acrostic: **C. O. R. N. Y.** – "**C**hrist the **O**nly **R**edeemer **N**ecessary for **Y**ou."

The Bible tells us that we are all sinners in need of a redeemer. Jesus Christ came into this world and died on the cross for our sins in order that we might be redeemed. First Peter 1:18-19 reads, "For you know that it was not with perishable things such as silver or gold that you were redeemed from the empty way of life handed down to you from your forefathers, but with the precious blood of Christ, a lamb without blemish or defect"(NIV).

In order to be redeemed one must admit that he is a sinner. He must repent of his sins, turn to Jesus Christ, and ask Him to save him. When one does this, the Holy Spirit enters his life (or heart), and he is redeemed from his sins and receives the gift of eternal life.

Have you been redeemed? If not, why don't you ask Jesus to be your redeemer today? "**C**hrist is the **O**nly **R**edeemer **N**ecessary for **Y**ou to be saved."

A LITTLE HUMOR: A man took his wife to a restaurant. The waiter, for some reason, took the man's order first. "I'll have the New York Strip steak, medium rare, please." The waiter said, "Aren't you worried about the mad cow?" "Nah," he said. "She can order for herself." And that's when the fight started.

MAY 16

CROWN HIM KING

"His eyes were like flames of fire, and on his head were many crowns..."
(Revelation 19:12a, NLT)

If you have ever played a game of checkers you know that the object of the game is to move your checkers to the last roll on the other side of the board. When you move your checker on to one of the squares you say, "Crown him!" The day is coming when Jesus Christ will return to this earth and when He comes, He will be wearing "many crowns." He will take His rightful place on His throne as King of kings and Lord of lords.

On August 22, 1485, King Richard III was defeated and killed at the battle of Bosworth Field. At dawn, on a field near the South Leicestershire town of Market Bosworth, King Richard III of the house of York and the Earl of Richmond, Henry Tudor of the house of Lancaster, faced each other in what would be the last battle in the thirty year War of Roses between the houses of York and Lancaster. Thirteen battles had been fought, and over 100,000 lives had been lost. The battle lasted only two hours, but during the course of fighting, King Richard was unhorsed and killed in a bog. A weary, but victorious Henry Tudor gathered his forces together and set his standard on a small rise now called Crown Hill. As he thanked and congratulated his men, Sir Reginald Bray appeared with the golden crown Richard had been wearing in battle. It had been found by a soldier in a thorn bush near the spot where he fell. The crown was handed to Lord Thomas Stanley who placed it on Tudor's head, declaring, "Henry VII King of England."

Many a king has risen only to lose his crown to another, but there is one King who will never lose His crown. John saw the Lord Jesus returning to earth with His heavenly armies, and on His head were many crowns. In the battle that followed, all the nations of the earth are gathered to make war against Him, yet when the battle is over the Lord Jesus emerges as the King of kings and Lord of lords still possessing His crowns.

It is our privilege today, to bow at the feet of the King who has never lost a battle and will never lose His crown. So, don't delay. Lift your hands in worship and declare, "The Lord Jesus Christ, the King of the Ages."

A LITTLE HUMOR: A man was sitting on the couch watching TV with the remote in his hand. His wife came in and sat down next to him. She asked, "What's on TV?" He said, "Dust!" And then the fight started.

MAY 17

IN A LITTLE WHILE

"For yet in a very little while, He who is coming will come, and will not delay."
(Hebrews 10:37, NASB)

It has been over two thousand years since Jesus returned to heaven. He promised He would return to this earth someday. Until He does return, what should we be doing?

We need to herald His coming. The second coming of Christ is one of the greatest themes of the Bible. It is the goal of every prophet of the Old Testament.

There's not one prophet from the first to the last whose eyes aren't set upon the return of the Lord Jesus Christ. In the New Testament, this theme is referred to no less than 300 times. In his final advice to young Timothy, the apostle Paul said, "I solemnly charge you in the presence of God and of Christ Jesus, who is to judge the living and the dead . . . preach the word . . ." (2 Timothy 4:1-2, NASB).

We need to hope for His coming. The Bible says, "Looking for the blessed hope and the appearing of the glory of our great God and Savior, Christ Jesus" (Titus 2:13, NASB). Dr. G. Campbell Morgan, the distinguished British clergyman, said, "I never begin my work in the morning without thinking that perhaps He may interrupt my work and begin His own. I am not looking for death, I am looking for Him."

We need to hunger for His coming. The flame of hope must be kept alive. The Bible says, "And the Lord direct your hearts into the love of God, and into the patient waiting for Christ" (2 Thessalonians 3:5, KJV). The word that's used for *"waiting"* in this verse signifies patient endurance. It's our hunger for the coming of Christ that enables us to endure the sorrows and trials of the waiting period.

We need to hasten His coming. The Bible says, "Looking for and hastening the coming of the day of God . . ." (2 Peter 3:12a, NASB). How can we hasten the coming of the Lord? We can hasten the coming of the Lord by praying for the salvation of the lost and by witnessing to them of the saving grace of God. Second Peter 3:9 (NLT) reads, "The Lord isn't really being slow about his promise, as some people think. No, he is being patient for your sake. He does not want anyone to be destroyed, but wants everyone to repent." Not too long ago I came across an acrostic for the word hope: H. O. P. E. = "Holding On Praying Expectantly."

A LITTLE HUMOR: Back in the days when the church janitor had to pump air into the pipe organ to make it work, Eloise, the new organist, dearly wanted to make an impression on the visiting preacher with her playing. She wrote a note to the old janitor who had been slack in pumping the organ air and handed it to him just before the service started. But, making a natural mistake, the janitor passed the note on to the visiting preacher, who opened it and read, "Keep blowing away until I give you the signal to stop."

MAY 18

OUT OF THE DEPTHS

"Out of the depths I have cried to Thee, O Lord." (Psalm 130:1, KJV)

Notice where the author of this verse is when he begins his prayer. He is in the depths. There are many kinds of depths a person can be in. We can be in the depths of poverty, stripped bare of all earthly possessions. We can be in the depths of sorrows, with plans all ripped to pieces by adversity. We can be in the depths of mental darkness, with nothing but surrounding sorrow and despair. We can be in the depths of sin, with nothing but guilt and shame. There is no doubt as to what has brought this man to the depths. It is his own perversity. He is in the depths to which there seems to be no bottom.

What can we do when in such depths? Cry! We can cry unto the Lord. Charles Spurgeon once said, “It little matters where we are if we pray; but prayer is never more real and acceptable than when it rises out of the worst places. Deep places beget deep devotion. Depths of earnestness are stirred by depths of tribulation. Diamonds sparkle most amid the darkness. He that cries out of the depths shall soon sing in the heights.”

In Genoa, Italy, after World War II, an artist was commissioned to create an eight-ton statue of Christ. Unlike other statues of Christ throughout the world, this one was not put on a high hill overlooking the city. Instead, it was lowered into the depths of the bay where the great battle had taken place—lowered into the depths, the depths where the sunken ships lay silent, where forgotten heroes rest in quiet memory. The statue is called *The Christ of the Deep.* It is a beautiful picture of the ministry of Christ reaching into the depths of the human heart to provide for us new levels of spirit and stability.

The psalmist who wrote Psalm 130:1 rose out of the depths of despair to the heights of assurance and hope. His spirit of expectancy is strongly emphasized by the repetition of the phrase, “I wait for the Lord” (vv. 5-6). He waits like a sentinel on the wall waits for the dawn. He affirms that the Lord is a God of mercy and forgiveness (v. 7).

The apostle John saw this same marvelous truth: “If we confess our sins, He is faithful and just to forgive us our sins, and to cleanse us from all unrighteousness” (1 John 1:9, KJV). When we come around to God’s point of view and acknowledge his righteousness and our sinfulness, then we open the door for God to forgive us and to cleanse us.

A LITTLE HUMOR: "I really loved my vacation in California," said the lady on the plane to the man sitting next to her. "Where did you stay?" he asked. "San Joe-Say." "Madam, in California we pronounce the ‘J’ as ‘H.’ We say, ‘San Hosay.’ How long were you there?" The woman thought for a moment, then responded carefully, "All of Hune and most of Huly."

MAY 19

RELYING ON THE LORD

"Who is among you that fears the Lord, that obeys the voice of His servant, that walks in darkness and has no light? Let him trust in the name of the Lord and rely on his God." (Isaiah 50:11, NASB)

Although it has been nine years since our nation was attacked by radical Islamic terrorists, it seems as though it were only yesterday. Our hearts are still sadden by the loss of lives and the suffering of so many people. In times such as these we must remember to rely on the Lord. The word *rely* means to lean upon the Lord as one does on a staff for support. Here are five inner qualities that are the results of relying on

Christ.

Lean on Christ for PEACE. Isaiah 26:3-4 reads, "You will keep in perfect PEACE him whose mind is steadfast, because he trusts in You. Trust in the Lord forever, for the Lord, the Lord, is the Rock eternal" (NIV). We cannot avoid strife in the world around us, but with God we can know perfect peace even in turmoil.

Lean on Christ for HOPE. Psalm 39:7 reads, "And now, Lord, for what do I wait? My hope is in You." We humans can live weeks without food, days without water, minutes without air, but we can't live one second without hope.

Lean on Christ for COURAGE. Deuteronomy 31:6 reads, "Be strong and of a good courage, fear not, nor be afraid of them: for the Lord thy God, he it is that doth go with thee; he will not fail thee, nor forsake thee" (KJV). Notice this verse encourages us to "fear not" because the Lord will "fail not" nor "forsake not."

Lean on Christ for WISDOM. James 1:5 reads, "But if any of you lacks wisdom, let him ask of God, who gives to all generously and without reproach, and it will be given to him" (NASB). Vance Havner once wrote, "If you lack knowledge, go to school. If you lack wisdom, get on your knees."

Lean on Christ for STRENGTH. Psalm 46:1 reads, "God is our refuge and strength, a very present help in trouble" (NASB). God is our refuge – He hides us. God is our strength – He helps us.

Pastor Martin Meimuller survived three years in a Nazi death camp. He once wrote, "You are much stronger than you think when God dwells in you." These five inner qualities will sustain you in any crisis.

A LITTLE HUMOR: Billy Graham told of a time early in his ministry when he arrived in a small town to preach a revival. Wanting to mail a letter, he asked a young boy where the post office was. When the boy had told him, Graham thanked him and said, "If you'll come to the church this evening, you can hear me give directions on how to get to heaven." "I don't think I'll be there," the boy replied. "You don't even know how to get to the post office."

MAY 20

DON'T LET THE BEDBUGS BITE

"Each one is tempted when he is carried away and enticed by his own lust. Then when lust has conceived, it gives birth to sin, and when sin is accomplished, it brings forth death." (James 1:14-15, NASB)

All of us can remember when we were going to bed at night being told, "Good Night. Sleep tight. Don't let the bedbugs bite." I always wondered what "bedbugs" were and why they would want to bite.

According to a recent news release a two-day event was held at a Chicago hotel to discuss the bedbug problem that has caught the attention of so many people. A few years ago, a "bedbug summit" would attract your local exterminator and his colleagues. More than 350 came to this one; the conference sold out five weeks in advance.

I have read that bedbugs have been feasting on sleeping humans for thousands of years, but DDT eradicated them. When the pesticide was banned, the bugs began making a comeback. They hide in mattresses and cracks and crevices of beds, waiting until we go to sleep. Then they go to dinner.

A website on bedbugs tells us that bedbugs crawl out just before dawn and bite us, sucking out blood for five minutes. We don't feel anything until they return to their hiding places. They are about the size of an apple seed, and leave a colorless welt with a burning or itching sensation. While they don't transmit disease, each bug can lay four or five eggs a day.

Dr. James Denison, whose devotional on this same subject stirred my interest, suggests that bedbugs have spiritual relatives hiding in the mattress of our souls. "Some temptations," he writes, "are easy to spot when they approach, but most are not. For instance, I've never met a man who set out to have an affair. A look turned into a thought which turned into a fantasy which turned into an action. James describes the process well: 'each one is tempted when he is carried away and enticed by his own lust. Then when lust has conceived, it gives birth to sin, and when sin is accomplished, it brings forth death'."

Be on your guard. Watch out for temptations. Spiritual bedbugs can cause a lot of problems.

A LITTLE HUMOR: A man at a motel had complained about several things he felt were wrong with his room, approached the desk clerk and said, "I have another complaint about the room you rented me." "Oh, what's eating you now?" asked the clerk. "That's exactly what I'd like to know," replied the man.

MAY 21

SOMETHING EVERYONE CAN DO

". . . I give myself to prayer." (Psalm 109:4b, NKJV)

It's Monday morning. I just got off the phone from talking to a very dear friend. His wife has breast cancer. It's very serious. They are seeking an appointment with doctors at the Mayo clinic for a second opinion. We had prayer over the phone with a promise to continue praying for them. I believe in prayer. I believe that is the best thing we can do for them right now.

One never knows from day-to-day what will happen. Each day brings its own blessings and problems. Both can be meet with prayer -- one, a prayer of thanksgiving for the blessings and the other, a prayer for healing or guidance or whatever the problem might be. God hears and receives both, especially when they are offered in His name, for His glory, and in fulfillment of His will. A few years ago I came across an acrostic for the word PRAYER:

P -- Personal
R – Retreat
A – Always
Y – Yields
E – Eternal
R – Rewards

Not everyone can preach, teach a Sunday school class, sing in the choir, or play a musical instrument. But there is one thing within the reach of every hand; one thing every person can do. We can pray! All of us! Any of us! We can reach out and touch the throne of grace through the hand of prayer. Hebrews 4:16 reads, "Let us therefore come boldly to the throne of grace, that we may obtain mercy and find grace to help in time of need."

In his book on prayer, Richard Foster writes, "If we truly love people, we will desire for them far more than it is within our power to give them, and this will lead us to prayer. Intercession is a way of loving others." Is there someone for whom you can pray?

A LITTLE HUMOR: Why did the cowboy buy a dachshund? He wanted to get a long little doggie!

MAY 22

HEAVEN'S RED CROSS

"So that there may be no division in the body, but that the members may have the same care for one another." (1 Corinthians 12:25, NASB)

On May 21, 1881, Clara Barton founded the American Red Cross. During the American Civil War, Barton worked with the Union armies "for the purpose of distributing comforts for the sick and wounded and nursing them."

After the war, she went to Europe to rest and while there heard about the International Committee of the Red Cross that had been formed in Switzerland. She worked closely with the committee and watched them in action during the Franco-Prussian War of 1870-71.

Upon returning to the United States, she began speaking out about the Red Cross and the need for such an organization in America to help people during the time of war or a natural disaster. At first the American State Department refused to be involved, but finally the Senate ratified the Red Cross Treaty. Barton served as the first president of the American Red Cross until her retirement in 1904.

The apostle Paul describes believers as being members of "Heaven's Red Cross." He speaks of the believer as being a member of a spiritual body that cares for others in times of suffering and need. The word "care" speaks of someone who is moved by the needs of others and reaches out to minister to them.

As we look upon the battlefield of life, we see those who are hurting and suffering. Today, seek to reach out to someone who could use a word of encouragement. Give them a call or send them a note. A visit may even be needed. Knowing that someone really cares may be just what someone needs today.

A LITTLE HUMOR: Abbie was listening to her father tell the story of Jonah as she lay in her bed. She loved bedtime stories so she was hanging on his every word. While telling of Jonah's disobedience, Abbie's father said, "God told Jonah to go preach to the Ninevites and Jonah disobeyed." He then stated, "We don't tell God 'no,' do we Abbie?" The little three-year-old replied, "Noooo, we say, 'No sir!'"

MAY 23

WHAT CANCER CAN'T DO

"And He has said to me, 'My grace is sufficient for you, for power is perfected in weakness.' Most gladly, therefore, I will rather boast about my weaknesses, so that the power of Christ may dwell in me." (2 Corinthians 12:9, NASB)

Nineteen ninety-eight was not a very good year for my wife and me as far as our physical health was concerned. That was the year that I had two heart attacks and by-pass surgery, and my wife, Linda, had breast cancer. When she first told me that she had been diagnosed with breast cancer I was stunned. It took me a few minutes to grasp the significance of what she was telling me. With the help of a fine surgeon and an oncologist here in Nacogdoches she received the best of medical care. Most of all, the Great Physician, The Lord Jesus Christ, gave both physical as well as spiritual healing. Linda has been cancer free for eleven years. Praise the Lord!

One of the most dreaded sentences a patient can hear is, "You have cancer!" These words bring a chill to the heart. Although great progress is being made in treating this disease, recovery can be long and painful, and many people do not survive. But even though the physical body may be damaged, the spirit can remain triumphant. I want to share a writing I found a few years ago that has been helpful to both of us and I trust for you too:

Cancer is limited . . .
It cannot cripple love,
It cannot shatter hope,
It cannot corrode faith,
It cannot eat away peace,
It cannot destroy confidence,
It cannot kill friendship,

It cannot shut our memories,
It cannot silence courage,
It cannot invade the soul,
It cannot reduce eternal life,
It cannot quench the Spirit,
It cannot lessen the power of the resurrection.

If a disease has invaded your life, refuse to let it touch your spirit. Your body can be severely afflicted, and you may have a great struggle, but if you keep trusting God's love, your spirit will remain strong. Our greatest enemy is not disease but despair. God's grace will be adequate no matter what the problem.

A LITTLE HUMOR: A Sunday school teacher asked a little boy in her class if they said a prayer before they ate their food. "No," he said, "my mom is a good cook."

MAY 24

DON'T WORRY, TRUST JESUS

"So do not worry about tomorrow; for tomorrow will care for itself. Each day has enough trouble of its own." (Matthew 6:34, NASB)

In the late 1980's, Bobby McFerrin's song, *Don't Worry, Be Happy*, rose to the top of the pop chart. The a cappella song with the light reggae beat invited listeners to chill out and put their worries aside.

Perhaps a remake of the song is in order. The current economic climate has heightened anxiety. In addition to financial uncertainty, 24-hour news programs thrive on doom-and-gloom reports from around the globe. Worry continues to grow like kudzu in the South, overtaking lives and imprisoning souls.

Actually, the Bible declares that worry is a sin. In the Sermon on the Mount, Jesus commands His followers not to worry (Matthew 6:25, 28, 31). It seems that Bobby McFerrin's cute, catchy song actually addresses a critical spiritual issue.

What do you worry about? What keeps you up at night? What causes your blood pressure to rise? Whether you worry about big things or small things, worry is futile. Ironically, worry robs us of life rather than adding to our lives. In teaching the "Parable of the Seeds" (Luke 8:14), Jesus described one seed that sprouted and grew but was "choked by life's worries." Not only will worry shorten your life, but it has the potential to kill you!

The cure for worry is to look beyond the ability of our human eyes and see the world from God's perspective. When we seek God's kingdom first, we can echo Paul's perspective in Philippians 4:12-13: "I know how to live on almost nothing or with everything. I have learned the secret of living in every situation, wither it is with a full stomach or empty, with plenty or little. For I can do everything through Christ who gives me strength." (NLT). To rephrase Bobby McFerrin's song, "Don't Worry, Trust Jesus!"

A LITTLE HUMOR: I used to worry about what people were thinking about me. Then I realized they weren't thinking about me at all. Instead, they were worrying about what other people were thinking of them.

MAY 25

THE CHEESEBURGER BILL

"Then the man said, 'The woman whom You gave to be with me, she gave me from the tree, and I ate'." (Genesis 3:12, NASB)

In late June 2002, Caesar Barber filed lawsuits against McDonald's, Wendy's, Burger King and Kentucky Fried Chicken. Barber claimed they sold him the food that made him obese and that they should be held accountable for "wrecking his life."

Gregory Rhymes and eight other overweight New York children filed suit against McDonald's Corp. According to a January 2003 article in *Capitalism Magazine,* "The lawyer acting on behalf of these outsized teens is Samuel Hirsch. He says people are too dumb to know what's good for them and that McDonald's has an obligation to make known their food is unhealthy, just like they should have warned Stella Liebeck it's not a good idea to get in a car and stick a cup of hot coffee between your legs while you're trying to get the lid off."

Because of such lawsuits, congressmen passed the "Cheeseburger Bill" through the House of Representatives in 2004 and 2005. It couldn't get past the Senate; but bill or no bill, the principle seems in order. People should take responsibility for their own actions. We cannot keep blaming others for the choices we make.

God expects people to take responsibility for their actions. When God confronted Adam for eating from the forbidden tree, Adam blamed Eve. Ever since then, people have tried to avoid taking responsibility for their actions by shifting the blame to others or to circumstances beyond their control. But God's Word teaches us that we will be held responsible for what we do! The apostle Paul says so in Romans 14:12: "So then each one of us will give an account of himself to God."

A LITTLE HUMOR: On the wharf in San Francisco a man walked into a restaurant and asked, "Do you serve crabs?" The waitress said quickly, "Sure, we serve anybody! Sit down!"

MAY 26

TRUSTING THE LORD

"Oh, taste and see that the Lord is good; blessed is the man who trusts in Him!"
(Psalm 34:8, NKJV)

When missionary John G. Paton was translating the Bible in the Outer Hebrides, he searched for the exact word to translate *believe.* Finally, he discovered it: the word meant lean your whole weight upon. That is what saving faith is – leaning your whole weight upon Jesus Christ.

Christians are people of faith. The Christian life begins with faith (Ephesians 2:8). Christians walk by faith (2 Cor. 5:7), work by faith (1 Thess. 1:3), live by faith (Romans 1:17), pray in faith (James 1:6), are protected from Satan's fiery darts by the shield of faith (Eph. 6:16), and live victoriously over the world by faith (1 John 5:4).

In Psalm 34 there are several burdens Christians can entrust to the Lord to receive blessings from Him. First, we should trust the Lord with our **FEARS.** Verse 4 reads, "I sought the Lord, and He heard me, and delivered me from all my fears. D. L. Moody's favorite verse was Isaiah 12:2: "I will trust and not be afraid." Moody said, "You can travel first-class or second-class to heaven. A second-class traveler says, 'What time I am afraid I will trust.' But the first-class way of traveling says, 'I will trust and not be afraid.'"

The second burden we Christians can cast on the Lord is our **FRUSTRATIONS.** Verse 17 reads, "The righteous cry out, and the Lord hears, and delivers them out of all their troubles." The word for *troubles* means to be in a bind or to be frustrated. When we have troubles, we need to pray for God's help.

Other concerns we can take to the Lord are our **FAILURES.** Verse 22 reads, "The Lord redeems the soul of His servants, and none of those who trust in Him shall be condemned." Nicolaus Copencius was the Polish astronomer who advanced the theory that the earth and other planets revolved around the sun. Even though he was a great intellect who told the number of the stars and pronounced the laws of the universe, in the presence of God, he saw himself, not as the scholar, or astronomer, but only as a sinner. On his grave stone at Frauenber, you can read the words he chose for his epitaph, "I do not seek a kindness equal to that given Paul; nor do I ask the grace granted Peter. But that forgiveness which thou didst grant to the robber – that, earnestly I crave." Yes, the forgiveness that Christ gave to the thief, that we all must seek.

A LITTLE HUMOR: A little girl complained to her mother that she had a stomach ache and didn't feel like going to church. Her mother said, "Your stomach hurts because it's empty. It will feel better when you put something in it." They went to church and as they were leaving, the pastor mentioned that he had a headache. The little girl told him, "Your head hurts because it's empty. It will feel better when you put something in it."

MAY 27

GOD'S GLORIOUS LOVE

"I have loved you," says the Lord. (Malachi 1:2, NKJV)

The Scottish preacher, George Matheson, was one of the most poetic and eloquent preachers of his time. It was at the age of 19 while he was studying for the ministry that he lost his eyesight. His heart was broken when his fiancée broke their engagement, returned his ring, and said to him, "I cannot see my way clear to go through life bound by the chains of marriage to a blind man." Matheson never married, but in 1882, at the age of 40, when one of his sisters married, her wedding brought back memories of his heartbreak and personal tragedy. From the depths of despair he reached out in faith and laid hold of the unchanging love of God. In that dark hour of his heart he penned the words of the great hymn:

O love that will not let me go,
I rest my weary soul in Thee;
I give Thee back the life I owe,
That in Thine ocean depths its flow
May richer, fuller be.

In the opening verses of Malachi, we are reminded that God's love is permanent, perpetual, and persistent. We are reminded that God's love will never let us go. There is no greater thought in all the Bible than that God loves us. There is only one word to describe God's love for us and that is the word "glorious!" "I have loved you." What a glorious statement. What a glorious announcement! What a glorious truth!

Notice carefully that God says, "I have loved you." The Hebrew words are in the perfect tense which means that God had loved them in the past, and He loves them in the present. God's love is not only an undeniable love, but also an unending love. In the words of Matheson, it is a "love that wilt not let me go." God will love us in spite of the length of our life, the depth of our sin, and the breadth of our misfortunes. There never has been a time when God did not love us. There will never be a time when God will not love us. What a glorious love!

A LITTLE HUMOR: A young executive was leaving the office at 6 PM when he found the CEO standing in front of a shredder with a piece of paper in his hand. "Listen, said the CEO, "this is a very sensitive and important document, and my secretary has left. Can you make this thing work?" "Certainly," said the young executive. He turned the machine on, inserted the paper, and pressed the start button. "Excellent, excellent!" said the CEO as his paper disappeared inside the machine. "I just need one copy."

MAY 28

LIVING WATER

"Behold, I will stand before you there on the rock at Horeb; and you shall strike the rock, and water will come out of it, that the people may drink." And Moses did so in the sight of the elders of Israel. (Exodus 17:6, NASB)

I read with interest the article in last Sunday's edition of the Nacogdoches, Texas newspaper, *The Daily Sentinel* about the marker that has been placed along LaNana Creek by Charles and Lois Marie Bright identifying "The Holy Springs of Father Margil." According to legend, Father Margil had spent the night in prayer and had a vision. The next morning he went to a specific place along the LaNana Creek, struck his staff against the rocky bank and two springs of life-saving water began to flow, thus saving the lives of those who were suffering from the drought of 1717-1718. I enjoy reading about the history and legends surrounding Nacogdoches. Mr. and Mrs. Bright are to be commended for their commitment in preserving our city's history.

Reading the article brought to my mind the story of Moses striking a rock that brought forth water (Exodus 17:1-7). Like the people of Father Margil's day, the people of Moses' day were also in need of water.

The situation has not changed over time. People of all ages have a thirst for water. But there is another kind of thirst that physical water cannot quench; it is a thirst for God and eternal life. Jesus mentioned this to the woman at the well (John 4:13-14). Later, as it is recorded in John 7:37-38, Jesus announced that He was that water that quenches the spiritual thirst of mankind, and it is freely offered to anyone who desires to drink. The apostle Paul said the rock Moses struck was Jesus Christ (1 Corinthians 10:4).

In Psalm 63 David talks about quenching one's thirst with the Living Water that comes from a deep and abiding relationship with God. He says his soul "thirsts" for God and his flesh "longs" to see God; he needed His life-giving refreshment.

You can avoid the life-threatening condition of spiritual dehydration by drinking deeply from God's fountain of life. Absorb the Word of God, bathe yourself regularly in prayer, and drink of God's goodness. In Him you will find no thirst.

A LITTLE HUMOR: A young and nervous bride planning her wedding was increasingly terrified about her upcoming marriage. To calm her nerves, she decided to have a Bible verse which had always brought her comfort (1 John 4:18, "There is no fear in love; for perfect love casts out fear") engraved on her wedding cake. So she called the caterer and all arrangements were made. About a week before the wedding, she received a call from the catering company. "Is this really the verse you want on your cake?" they asked. "Yes," she confirmed, it was the one she wanted. The wedding day came, and everything was beautiful . . . until the reception, when the bride walked in to find the cake emblazoned with John 4:18, "For you have had five husbands, and the one you now have is not your husband."

MAY 29

HONOR IS BETTER THAN HONORS

"For those who honor Me I will honor . . ." (1 Samuel 2:30, NASB)

Rosalie Elliott had made it to the fourth round of national spelling contest in Washington. The 11-year-old from South Carolina had been asked to spell the word "avowal." In her soft southern accent she spelled the word, but the judges were not able to determine if she had used an "a" or an "e" as the next to the last letter. They debated among themselves for several minutes as they listened to tape recording playbacks. Finally, the chief judge put the question to the only person who knew the answer.

"Was the letter an 'a' or was it an 'e'?" he asked Rosalie. By this time, being surrounded by whispering young spellers, Rosalie knew the correct spelling of the word. Still, without hesitation, she replied that she had misspelled the word, and she walked from the stage.

The entire audience stood and applauded, including some fifty newspaper reporters. The moment was a heartwarming and proud one for her parents. Even in defeat, she was a victor. Indeed, more has been written about Rosalie Elliott over the years than about the "unknown" winner of the event! Being honest will bring great honor.

A LITTLE HUMOR: Before their homecoming game, a group of college boys stole the school mascot of their opposing football team. It was a goat. Once they captured it they made intricate plans to smuggle the animal into their dormitory room. "But what about the smell?" someone asked. "The goat will just have to get used to it," the other replied.

MAY 30

GROWING SPIRITUALLY

"Therefore leaving the elementary teaching about the Christ, let us press on to maturity..." (Hebrews 6:1a, NASB)

In 1937, the spinach growers of Crystal City, Texas, erected a statue of Popeye. By the 1930's, the city had gained the reputation for being the "Spinach Capital of the World." In 1936 the first annual spinach festival was held, and the following year the statue of Popeye was erected across from the city hall in the city square. The cartoon sailor man, who gains his strength from eating spinach, was created by the Fleischer brothers in the 1930's.

Spiritual growth is an important part of our life in Christ. One of the complaints Paul had concerning the Corinthians was they had remained as babies in Christ (1 Corinthians 3:1). John spoke of believers as being "little children" (1 John 2:13) and then as "young men" with the believers ultimately becoming "fathers." He describes stages of physical growth to illustrate the place of spiritual growth.

One of the characteristics of spiritual growth is growing spiritually strong. Spiritual strength is needed to be able to stand against the attacks of the devil (Ephesians 6:11), to stand fast in the faith (1 Corinthians 16:13), and to stand fast in the will of God (Colossians 4;12). Believers do not have to eat spinach to become spiritually strong, but they do have to have an appetite for the Word of God. A daily diet of God's Word builds our spiritual muscles so that we are strong in the Lord.

Today, take the time to read and meditate in God's Word. You can't afford to skip one single "meal." If you want to be spiritually strong, it is essential.

A LITTLE HUMOR: The judge was baffled to see an 80-year-old woman in his court for shoplifting at a grocery store. When he asked about her offense, she confessed to stealing one can of peaches. Upon learning this was the full extent of her crime, the judge asked how many peaches were in the can. She replied, "Six." He then ordered her to spend one day in jail for each of the six peaches. When her husband heard the verdict, he jumped up and yelled, "Your Honor, she also stole two cans of peas!"

MAY 31

A SERVANT OF GOD

"As each one has received a gift, minister it to one another, as good stewards of the manifold grace of God." (1 Peter 4:10, NKJV)

An important responsibility of every Christian is service. God expects us to use the gifts, talents, and opportunities He gives us to benefit others and bring glory to Him. God intends for every believer to have a ministry. Attitude is important also. Here are four suggestions as to the kind of attitude we should have as we serve the Lord.

We should serve the Lord **GLADLY.** Psalm 100:2 reads, "Serve the Lord with gladness; Come before His presence with singing." A healthy sign of the grateful life is "serving with gladness." Who likes to be served by a gloomy or grouchy waitress? A young man doesn't consider it work to wash his car or to date the girl he's trying to impress. It's a matter of the heart more than the head. Serving God should be a love affair.

We should serve the Lord **FAITHFULLY.** In the parable of the talents (Matt. 25:14-30) the master commended the servant who had wisely used his talents by saying, "Well done, good and faithful servant" (vv. 21, 23). The Lord looks for dependable people who will take care of the things entrusted to them. Someone has said, "It is not success that God rewards but faithfulness in doing His will."

We should serve the Lord **HUMBLY.** Jesus once said, "A servant is not greater than his master" (John 15:20). Someone asked Leonard Bernstein, "What's the most difficult instrument to play?" Immediately he answered, "Second violin." John the Baptist was content being a "second violin" type person in his relationship to Jesus. In Matthew 3:11 he said, "He who is coming after me is mightier than I, whose sandals I am not worthy to carry." He humbly served the Lord. We should be willing to do the same.

We should serve the Lord **EAGERLY.** The word deacon is sometimes translated as servant. It's literal meaning, however, is "kicking up dust" and refers to a servant "kicking up dust" as he runs to carry out his master's orders. We should have the same eagerness as we serve the Lord. We serve the Lord when we serve one another. Every Christian has at least one talent or gift that can be used for the Lord. Don't waste your talent and your opportunity to do something for Jesus.

A LITTLE HUMOR: After preaching one Sunday morning, the pastor suddenly lost his balance as his blood pressure skyrocketed and he began perspiring profusely. He was rushed to the ER and his heart checked out fine, so they continued to run tests to determine the cause. He later received a get well card from one of the children in the church. It read, "Dear Pastor, I like to hear you preach. I hope your sermon doesn't make you sick next time."

JUNE 1

SIX WAYS GOD WILL BE YOUR HELPER

"God is our refuge and strength. A very present help in trouble."
(Psalm 46:1, NASB)

God is portrayed in Scripture as the Helper of the helpless. There are at least six ways God will be your helper.

H – God will HEAR YOUR PRAYERS.

Someone has said "when you bend your knees to pray, God bends His ear to listen." Psalm 18:6 reads, "In my distress I called upon the Lord, and cried to my God for help; He heard my voice out of His temple, and my cry for help before Him came into His ears."

E – God will ENCOURAGE YOUR HEART.

Isaiah 41:13 says, "For I am the Lord your God, who upholds your right hand, Who says to you, 'Do not fear, I will help you'." All three persons of the Godhead will encourage you. God the Father will encourage you (2 Cor. 1:3); God the Son will encourage you (2 Thess. 2:16-17); and God the Holy Spirit will encourage you (John 14:16).

L – God LOVES YOU UNCONDITIONALLY.

Every person has two basic needs: to be loved and to love. The most encouraging words a person can ever hear is that God loves them unconditionally. The story of the prodigal son verifies that (Luke 15:11-24).

P – God PROVIDES FOR YOUR EVERY NEED.

The apostle Paul wrote, "And my God will supply all your needs according to His riches in glory in Christ Jesus" (Philippians 4:19). If you were to break the word *provide* into two words you would have "pro" which can mean before and "vide" which means to see. *Provide* means that God sees beforehand what you need and has prepared in advance to meet your need.

E – God will ERASE YOUR SIN.

The psalmist wrote, "Hide Your face from my sin and blot out all my iniquities" (Psalm 51:9). Have you ever played with an Etch-a-Sketch? If so you know that you can erase all of your mistakes on the Etch-a-Sketch simply by shaking it. God will erase all of your sins.

R – God will REFRESH YOUR SPIRIT.

The word *refresh* means to restore strength; to revive; to freshen up. How are we refreshed? By prayer (1 Samuel 30:6, 8, 19b); by reading God's Word (I Kings 19:4-8; Jeremiah 15:16); and, by helping others (Philemon 7, 20).

Hebrews 13:5-6 summarizes this for us: "For He Himself has said, 'I WILL NEVER LEAVE YOU, NOR FORSAKE YOU,' So that we confidently say, 'The Lord is my helper; I will not fear'."

A LITTLE HUMOR: After the morning worship service, Alex turned to his mother and commented on his father's sermon. The teenager said, "Dad wasn't himself today." His mom then replied, "I know, and you could sure see the improvement."

JUNE 2

THE HUMAN HEART

"The heart is more deceitful than all else and is desperately sick; who can understand it?" (Jeremiah 17:9, NASB)

East Texas is known for its logging industry. If you were to cut down a tree and look at the end of it, you would see growth rings. While round, growth rings are not perfectly shaped. If the log was taken to a saw mill and cut into perfectly straight beams the rings would still be crooked. It is the nature of the tree.

Is man good or evil by nature? Is the human heart inclined toward righteousness or iniquity? Do we gravitate naturally toward holiness or rebellion? Are we innately sinners or saints? What does the Bible say about the condition of man's heart?

The Human Heart Is Deceptive. "The heart is more deceitful than all else." Deceitful means insidious. A good slang word would be sneaky. The human heart is not naturally good. Rather, it is subtle and sly, filled with trickery, fraud, and cunning guile. Our hearts deceive others and are more than capable of deceiving us as well.

The Human Heart Is Diseased. "The heart . . . is desperately sick." Our hearts are infected with sin. Jesus said, "From within, out of the heart of men, proceed the evil thoughts, fornications, thefts, murders, adulteries, deeds of coveting and wickedness, as well as deceit, sensuality, envy, slander, pride and foolishness. All these evil things proceed from within and defile the man" (Mark 7:21-23). Our hearts need to be healed.

The Human Heart Is Dumbfounding. "The heart . . . who can understand it?" Someone might say, "I know my heart," but the fact is only God knows a person's heart (Jeremiah 17:10). He knows us better than we know ourselves.

Man is a sinner by nature, prone to rebel against God. Our hearts are deceptive, diseased, and dumbfounding. Only God understands them, and only He can cleanse and change them by giving us a spiritual "heart transplant" through salvation (Ezekiel 36:26; John 3:3, 5). Guard and take care of you heart. Your life depends on it (Proverbs 4:23).

A LITTLE HUMOR: Frank and Gene began a discussion about marriage while waiting on the foursome in front of them at the golf course. Frank asserted that marriage required a lot of give and take. Gene quickly agreed. He said, "Yep, our marriage is built on give and take. Marge gives the orders and I take them!"

JUNE 3

OUR GOD IS ABLE

"Our God whom we serve is able to deliver us from the burning fiery furnace, and He will deliver us from your hand, O king." (Daniel 3:17, NKJV)

When Shadrach, Meshach, and Abednego said, "Our God is able" they were saying that God has the strength to act in a manner different from us and peculiar to Himself. Christians today may not face the ordeal of a fiery furnace, but they do face situations almost as demanding. It is easy to "cut corners" or "cross your fingers" instead of telling the truth, forgetting that you belong to the Lord. These three young men could have found all kinds of excuses for obeying the king's command, but they preferred to obey the Word of God.

"Our God whom we serve is able" (v. 17). This has been the testimony of believing saints down through the years. There are several ways that God is able to help us.

God is able to DELIVER US from temptation and sin (cf. 1 Corinthians 10:13; 2 Peter 2:9; Galatians 1:4). God does not promise to keep us out of difficulties, but rather to bring us out. He permitted the three men to go into the furnace – and then went in with them! He shares every trial you experience and enables you to come out a stronger and a better person, and through it all, to glorify Him.

God is able to KEEP US. "Unto Him that is able to keep you from falling" (Jude 24), or as others translate it, stumbling. The Good Shepherd cares for His sheep.

God is able to PROVIDE for us. Second Corinthians 9:8 reads, "And God is able to make all grace abound toward you, that you, always having all sufficiency in all things, may have an abundance for every good work."

The poet William A. Ogden puts it this way:

'Tis the grandest theme through the ages rung;
'Tis the grandest theme for a mortal tongue;
'Tis the grandest theme that the world e'er sung;
Our God is able to deliver thee.

Our God is able. Yes, but let's make it personal: MY GOD IS ABLE!

A LITTLE HUMOR: A young man asked an older gentleman how he made his money. "Well, son, it was 1932 and we were in the depth of the Great Depression," the older gentleman said. "I was down to my last nickel. I invested that nickel in an apple. I spent the entire day polishing the apple and at the end of the day, I sold it for ten cents. The next morning, I invested that ten cents in two apples. I spent the entire day polishing them and sold them for twenty cents. I continued this system for a month. Then, my wife's father died and left us two million dollars!"

JUNE 4

LIVING WITH NO REGRETS

"And He was saying to them all, 'If anyone wishes to come after Me, he must deny himself, and take up his cross daily and follow Me'." (Luke 9:23, NASB)

The words of Jesus as recorded in Luke 9:23 have always meant a great deal to me. I used that verse early in my ministry for a sermon. Being new at preaching I needed all the help I could get, and my pastor, Brother Ed Shirley, gave me an outline based on this verse that I still use to this day. He suggested four points from this verse: First, there is an invitation – "If anyone wishes to come after Me." Second, there is a challenge – "he must deny himself." Third, there is a command – "take up his cross daily." Fourth, there is a reward – "follow Me." I never think of that verse and outline that I don't think about Brother Ed and his influence on my life and my ministry.

Years later I came across the life story of William Borden, heir to the Borden Dairy estate. It is a great illustration of the truth of that verse. For his high school graduation present, Borden's parents gave him a trip around the world. As he traveled through Asia, the Middle East, and Europe, he felt a growing burden for the world's hurting people. He wrote home, "I'm going to give my life to prepare for the mission field." At the same time, he wrote two words in the back of his Bible: "No reserves."

Upon graduation from Yale, Borden wrote two more words in the back of his Bible: "No retreats." In keeping with that commitment, Borden turned down several high-paying job offers, enrolling in seminary instead. After graduation, he immediately went to Egypt to learn Arabic because of his intent to work with Muslims in China. While in Egypt, he contracted spinal meningitis. Within a month, twenty-five-year-old William Borden was dead.

Prior to his death, Borden had written two more words in his Bible. Underneath the words "No reserves" and "No retreats," he had written: "No regrets." Accepting the Lord's invitation to follow Him will be a great challenge for anyone, but it will be rewarding! And there will not be any regrets!

A LITTLE HUMOR: Here are a few signs that you might be in a Texas country church: The doors are never locked. The call to worship is "Ya'll come on in!" The preacher says, "I'd like to ask Bubba to help take up the offering," and five guys stand up. Opening day of deer hunting season is recognized as an official church holiday. A member requests to be buried in his four-wheel drive truck because, "I ain't ever been in a hole it couldn't get me out of." People wonder, when Jesus fed the 5,000 whether the two fish were bass or catfish. People think "rapture" is what happens when you lift something too heavy. The final words of the benediction are, "Ya'll come on back now, ya hear?"

JUNE 5

ON YOUR MARK

"No temptation has overtaken you except such as is common to man; but God is faithful, who will not allow you to be tempted beyond what you are able, but with the temptation will also make the way of escape, that you may be able to bear it." (1 Corinthians 10:13, NKJV)

Many ships used to be lost in accidents at sea due to overloading. After years and years of tragic losses, a man in England by the name of Samuel Plimsoll came up with the idea that a line should be painted on the side of merchant vessels, so that it would be easy to tell if they were overloaded. This later became known as the "Plimsoll Mark." It soon became illegal for any ship to be loaded more heavily than permitted by the "Plimsoll Mark" on its side.

In the same way, there is a mark on our lives. God will not allow Satan to tempt you any more than you are able to handle. In fact, God will show you the correct way to go, if you are willing.

Paul says to the Corinthian believers that temptation is common to man. The word *common* means mannish, that which is human, belonging to mankind. In other words, temptations are a part of life. No one is immune from temptation.

According to Spiros Zodhiates, the expression "way of escape" refers to what is to come out of a certain situation. It actually does not mean a way of escape, if by that we are to understand it as merely getting out of the situation, but rather it means that something is going to come out of it, that God in His faithful dependability is going to enrich our experience by any situation that tempts us. God never permits anything in our lives without a purposeful end (Romans 8:28). Knowing this makes every temptation involved in our humanity bearable as the last phrase states: "that you may be able to bear it."

Thank God for His protection over you, and ask Him to help you to be sensitive to His provision of a way out of the temptation.

A LITTLE HUMOR: A little boy came home from school, excitedly telling his father, "Daddy, Daddy! I'm going to be in the school play!" The father said, "That's great! What part are you going to play?" The son said, "I'm going to play a husband!" "A husband!", the father exclaimed. "Son, you march right back down to that school and tell them you want a speaking part!"

JUNE 6

LOOKING AT THE CAPTAIN

"Fearing that we would be dashed against the rocks, they dropped four anchors from the stern and prayed for daylight." (Acts 27:29, NIV)

Robert Louis Stevenson is one of the best known authors of English literature. His father was an engineer who built lighthouses on the coast of England and

Scotland. One day he took Robert with him on an inspection trip. Near Bell Rock, off the Irish coast, their ship was struck by a gale that lasted more than twenty-five hours and terrified young Robert. His father went on deck where only the captain stood. The captain had bound himself with a rope to the foremast to keep from being washed overboard. After approaching the captain, Stevenson returned to their cabin below. "Will the ship break up and sink, Father? And will we all drown?" asked young Stevenson. "No," said his father in calm assurance. "We will outride the storm. I looked into the captain's face and he smiled."

When the storms of life rage, if you will get close enough to Jesus, whom the writer of Hebrews calls "the captain of our salvation" (Hebrews 2:10), you will hear him say, "In the world you will have tribulation, but be of good cheer, I have overcome the world" (John 16:33, NKJV).

Put the helm of your life in Christ's hands, and He will make you an overcomer also – especially when the storms of life come.

A LITTLE HUMOR: A man was shipwrecked on a deserted island in the South Pacific. Despite his radio calls for help, it still took many months for rescuers to find him. When they did find him, they were surprised to see three huts on the beach. They said, "We thought this was a deserted island and you were all alone." The man said, "Oh, it is and I am." Then they pointed to the huts and asked, "Why are there three huts?" The man said, "The first one, there, that's where I live. The other hut, that's where I go to church. And the third one, that's where I used to go to church."

JUNE 7

BE FAITHFUL

"Moreover, it is required of stewards that one be found faithful."
(1 Corinthians 4:2, NKJV)

This past summer my wife and I were privileged to visit Greyfriars Kirk in Edinburgh, Scotland. Greyfriar's Kirk was the first church to be built in Edinburgh after the Reformation and was opened in 1620. It plays a significant role in Scottish history because it was here, in front of the pulpit, that the National Covenant was presented and signed on February 28, 1638. This was an extremely important document in Scottish history for it chose Presbyterianism over Anglicanism as the national religion. Those who signed the National Covenant paid with their lives.

Today if you visit Greyfriars Kirk, you would find that a large amount of attention is given to a dog that was named Greyfriars Bobby. Every day for 14 years, after the death of his master, this Skye terrier faithfully visited the grave of his master. The little dog was buried just inside the entrance to the churchyard and is memorialized for its fidelity to its master. Yet the real story of faithfulness is told in the lives of the 1,200 Covenanters who were imprisoned on the church grounds and martyred just outside the church grounds as result of the backlash of their signing the National Covenant. The Martyr's Memorial in one corner of the church graveyard tells the ultimate story of faithfulness. The real story of faithfulness is not to be found in a little dog that daily visited the grave of his master year after year, but in those who were willing to pay the ultimate price for their faith.

There are no greater examples of faithfulness than in those who were willing to give their lives rather than deny their faith. We may not be called upon to give our lives, but none-the-less, faithfulness is required of each of us. God always honors faithfulness. Ask God to help you to be faithful.

A LITTLE HUMOR: I felt like my body had gotten totally out of shape, so I decided to join a fitness club and start exercising. I decided to take an aerobics class for seniors. I bent, twisted, gyrated, jumped up and down, and perspired for an hour. But by the time I got my leotards on, the class was over.[41]

JUNE 8

LIVING WITH YOUR EYES OPEN

"See then that you walk circumspectly, not as fools but as wise., redeeming the time, because the days are evil." (Ephesians 5:15-16, NKJV)

Most of us have a fascination with time. The titles of many TV programs involve time: *60 Minutes, 48 Hours, Dateline, Prime Time, Good Morning America, Today, The Tonight Show.* The word time is in so many of our short sayings: "time marches on" . . . "pass the time of day". . . "race against time" . . . "time is up" . . . "taking time out" . . . "in the nick of time" . . . "spare time". . . "keeping up with the times"... "making up for lost time."

Would you consider yourself fortunate if every morning your bank credited your account in the amount of $86,400 but with the stipulation that it had to be spent that very day? No balance could be carried over to the next day. Every evening would cancel whatever sum you failed to spend during that day. Wouldn't you draw out and spend every cent every day?

Here's news for you. You do have such a bank. It's called the Celestial Bank of Time. Every morning this bank credits you with 86,400 seconds. But no balances are carried. Every night wipes off any time you failed to use. Failure to draw out this treasure is your loss. Time cannot be reclaimed.

There is an entire field of study called "time management." Stephen Covey said, "Time management is a misleading concept. You can't really manage time. You can't delay it, speed it up, save it or lose it. The challenge is not to manage time but to manage ourselves."

The Bible uses another word: "redeeming the time" (Ephesians 5:16). The phrase "walk circumspectly" means to be constantly looking around to make the most of

[41] Paul W. Powell, *Laugh and Live Longer* (Tyler, Texas, 2008). 60.

every opportunity. Emmet Smith was a great football running back, but he was not the biggest or the fastest, or the strongest. What he excelled at was running with his eyes open, and he was one of the best at seeing holes as they opened, then running through them. That's the way we should live, looking for every opportunity to invest time wisely, then darting through them.

A LITTLE HUMOR: For many years a minister had the reputation for his fine sermons which were not only inspirational, but unusually short. When asked about his unusual awareness of time, he told this story: "One Sunday I was delivering a sermon to my first congregation and I became so carried away by the sound of my words that I didn't realize how restless people were becoming until a small boy, who had been squirming and fidgeting in the front pew, caught my attention. I saw him tug at his mother's sleeve and then, in a voice that could be heard throughout the church, he said, "Mommy, are you sure this is the only way we get to heaven?"[42]

JUNE 9

DO YOU GET IT?

"And I pray that you . . . may . . . grasp how wide and long and high and deep is the love of Christ" (Ephesians 3:17-18, NIV)

According to a data collected by the Census Bureau's American Community Survey, Seattle, Washington, tops the list of America's most educated cities, with more than half its population twenty-five years and older holding at least a bachelor's degree. The article went on to say that more than half of America's twenty most educated cities also rank at the top of the list of the county's most prosperous cities, not surprising given that college graduates earn an average of nearly $2.1 million in their lifetimes. It pays to be educated!

In our text for today the apostle Paul prays that his readers would be educated in the knowledge of God's marvelous love. The word *grasp* is translated comprehend in the *New American Standard Bible*. If you were talking about a joke, we would ask, "Do you get it?" When Louis Armstrong was asked to explain jazz, he said, "Man, if I've got to explain it, you ain't got it." Paul prays that we "get it" when it comes to understanding the love of God.

What is the "width" of Christ's love? It's wide enough to encompass all mankind. What is the "length" of Christ's love? It's long enough to last for all eternity. What is the "depth" of Christ's love? It is deep enough to rescue the most despicable sinner. There is no heart in which the darkness of human sin is unreachable by the light of God's love. What is the "height" of Christ's love? It is high enough to take all His children to heaven!

After the Spanish inquisition, it is said that the bones of a Spanish prisoner were found in a dungeon with shackles still attached to his leg bones. Above where the

[42] Ted D. Bonham, Another Treasury of Clean Jokes (Nashville: Broadman Press, 1983), 140-141.

skeleton lay, the prisoner had scratched a cross into the face of the stone wall. At the top of the cross was the word "height," at the bottom the word "depth," at the end of one arm of the cross was the word "breadth," and at the end of the other arm of the cross was the word "length." That Spanish believer had died contemplating "the love of Christ which passes knowledge." The cross is a perfect symbol of the extreme of God's love for us.

A LITTLE HUMOR: A couple had been fighting over the purchase of a new car for weeks. He wanted a new truck. She wanted a fast sports car so she could zip through traffic around town. The discussion was getting very heated when finally the wife stated, "Look, I want something that goes from 0 to 180 in four seconds or less, and that's all there is to it! My birthday is coming up and you better surprise me, or it's gonna get mighty lonely for you around here, if you get my drift!" When her big day came, the wife went out to the garage, but there was no new car. Angry, she went back into the house looking for her husband, but he was not at home. Frustrated and upset, she went into the bathroom to get ready – there, sitting on the floor and wrapped in a red ribbon, was a brand new scale! Funeral services are pending.

JUNE 10

THE BIBLE: A VALUABLE SWORD

"And take . . . the sword of the Spirit, which is the word of God."
(Ephesians 6:17b, NASB)

A gold-encrusted sword Napoleon wore into battle in Italy two hundred years ago was sold Sunday, June 10, 2007, for more than $6.4 million. The intricately decorated blade is 32 inches long and curves gently, an inspiration Napoleon drew from his Egyptian campaign. Strong enough for battle, the sword is uncommonly ornate, with geometric designs in gold covering the hilt and most of the blade. "It's at the same time a weapon of war and a very beautiful work of art. It symbolizes more than anything else the power, the force, and the incontestable strength of the Emperor Napoleon," auctioneer Jean-Pierre Osenat explained. The sword was worn by Napoleon, who was not yet emperor at the time, into the battle of Marengo in June, 1800, where he launched a surprise attack to push the Austrian army from Italy and seal France's victory. After the battle, Napoleon gave the sword to his brother as a wedding present, and it was passed down through the generations, never leaving the family.

Of all the pieces of armor Paul listed in Ephesians 6:10-17, the sword of the Spirit is the only offensive piece of equipment that the Captain of our salvation provides for us in spiritual warfare. There are several qualities about the Bible, God's Word, that makes is a valuable sword.

First, God's Word is PERFECT. Psalm 19:7 says, "The law of the Lord is perfect...." The word *perfect* means complete, flawless, without error or defect.

Second, God's Word is PROFITABLE. Second Timothy 3:16 reads, "All

Scripture is inspired by God and profitable for teaching, for reproof, for correction, for training in righteousness; that the man of God may be adequate, equipped for every good work."

Third, God's Word is POWERFUL. Hebrews 4:12 says, "For the word of God is living and powerful..." (NKJV). The Greek word translated *powerful* means energizing, active. A metal sword pierces the body, but the Word of God pierces the heart.

Fourth, God's Word is PERMANENT. Psalm 119:89 says, "Forever, O Lord, Your word is settled in heaven." The Word of God has a built-in resilience, a power within itself to withstand attack.

Fifth, God's Word is PURIFYING. Psalm 119:9 reads, "How can a young man keep his way pure? By keeping it according to Your word." We like purity in our foods. We worry about additives. God desires the same thing from your heart. He wants a heart that is one hundred percent pure, with no additives. The Word of God cleanses our hearts (John 15:3).

A LITTLE HUMOR: Helping his wife wash the dishes, a minister protested, "This isn't a man's job." "Oh, yes it is," his wife retorted, quoting 2 Kings 21:13, "I will wipe Jerusalem as a man wipeth a dish, wiping it, and turning it upside down" (KJV).

JUNE 11

NO GOOD THING WILL HE WITHHOLD

"The Lord will give grace and glory; No good thing will He withhold from those who walk uprightly" (Psalm 84:11, NKJV)

God does not promise to give us everything we think is good, but He will not withhold what is permanently good. Satan tries to persuade us that God is withholding something good from us (see Genesis 3:4-5), but experience teaches us differently.

Billy Bray, the Cornish miner, whose rugged piety has been a blessing to many, said that one year his crop of potatoes turned out so poorly that, when he was digging them, Satan, at his elbow, said, "There, Billy, isn't that poor pay for serving your Father the way you have all the year? Just see those small potatoes!" He stopped digging and replied, "Ah, Satan, at it again; talking against my Father, bless His name! Why, when I served you I did not get any potatoes at all. What are you talking about?" And on he went digging and praising the Lord for small potatoes.

Thanking God for whatever He gives us is one sure way of resisting the devil. He cannot stand being around places where there is constant praise of God. He would rather be around where there is complaining and grumbling and praise of self.

In Matthew 7:7-11 Jesus talks about the generosity of our Heavenly Father. If earthly fathers give what their children need (vv. 9-10), will not God give to His children what they ask? Indeed He will: "If you then, being evil, know how to give good gifts to your children, how much more will your Father who is in heaven give good things to those who ask Him!" (v. 11, NKJV). God is good and everything He gives us is good (James 1:17). I enjoy singing the chorus "God is so good, God is so good, God is so good, He's so good to me."

A LITTLE HUMOR: The pastor of a church was sick one Sunday morning, so a substitute preacher was called. As the substitute preacher was greeting the congregation, he made the statement, "You know, a substitute preacher is like a piece of cardboard in a broken window. He fills up the space, but after all, he's not the real glass." He then proceeded with his sermon. After the service, a lady approached him trying to pay him a compliment by saying, "You weren't a replacement at all. You were a real pane."

JUNE 12

NINE FOR NINE

"I waited patiently for the Lord; and He inclined to me, and heard my cry. He brought me up out of the pit of destruction, out of the miry clay; and He set my feet upon a rock making my footsteps firm." (Psalm 40:1-2, NASB)

There were a lot of happy people in Somerset, Pennsylvania. The nine coal miners who were trapped for three days in the Quecreek Mine were rescued early Sunday morning July 28. The news account described the rescue as a desperate operation that included more than 150 workers, tons of heavy equipment, and 18 medical helicopters. All nine workers were pulled up a narrow shaft, one by one, in a yellow cylindrical capsule. "9 for 9" began appearing on signs all over town. It gives a person a wonderful feeling to know that we live in a country that believes human life is valuable. Rather than walking away and saying there was no use in trying, everything possible was done to save them. Seeing all nine of the men alive was worth it all.

I never think of a rescue such as this one that saved nine men without thinking about the rescue of my soul from the pit of sin that God performed for me through His Son, the Lord Jesus Christ.

The psalmist, David, made reference to such an experience in Psalm 40:1-2. It reads, "I waited patiently for the Lord; and He inclined to me, and heard my cry. He brought me up out of the pit of destruction, out of the miry clay; and He set my feet upon a rock making my footsteps firm" (NASB). Figuratively, David had been down in a horrible pit, but he waited on the Lord. God not only pulled him out, but He put him on a rock and established his footing.

Psalm 40:3 says, "And He put a new song in my mouth, a song of praise to our God." Warren W. Wiersbe has a devotional on these verses with the title, "From Mire to Choir." I like that. God does rescue us from sin. He does put a song in our mouths. There are a lot of happy people who sing about that greatest of all rescues. Praise the Lord! Has He rescued you?

A LITTLE HUMOR: A shy young man took his girlfriend for a ride into the country hoping to get her to be more affectionate toward him. He looked out the window and saw a cow licking her calf. He asked his girlfriend what she thought the cow was doing. She said the cow was licking her calf to show affection. She said, "I guess you could say the cow is kissing her calf." He asked, "Can I do that?" She said, "I don't care – it's not my calf."

JUNE 13

YOU ARE FORGIVEN

"Then He said to her, 'Your sins have been forgiven'." (Luke 7:48, NASB)

Several years ago Woody Allen was interviewed by a French television station. In the hour-long interview, one of the reporters asked him a most unusual question, "Do you believe in God?" Allen responded, "No, I am an atheist" (one who does not believe in God). But, Allen went on to say, "In my better moments I am an agnostic" (one who admits there may be a God, but if there is he does not know him).

Then the reporter asked him an even more unusual question, "If there were a God and he would say one thing to you, what would you like to hear him say?" And Woody Allen responded, "You are forgiven."

Only God knows how many people there are in the world today who would love to hear those words, "You are forgiven." If you are one of those people, I have good news for you. Christ can and will forgive your sins if you come to Him. The scriptures say, "If we confess our sins, He is faithful and righteous to forgive us our sins and to cleanse us from all unrighteousness" (1 John 1:9, NASB). ". . . and the blood of Jesus His Son cleanses us from all sin" (1 John 1:7, NASB).

Some skeptic may ask, "How can blood wash away sin?" And I answer, "I don't know." But I ask the skeptic, "How can water quench our thirst?" "I don't know that either. But I know that it does." And I'm not going to die of thirst trying to figure it out. I'm going to drink and live. Just so, I don't know how the blood of Jesus cleanses sin, but I know that it does. And I'm going to trust it and be cleansed. In Jesus Christ there is forgiveness and cleansing.

Hymn writer, Elisha A. Hoffman wrote, "Have you been to Jesus for the cleansing power? Are you washed in the blood of the Lamb?" How about you? Have you been forgiven? If not, call on the Lord Jesus today. If you will, you can hear the words, "You are forgiven."

A LITTLE HUMOR: During Sunday School, a teacher was telling the children that we all need God's forgiveness. After the Bible story, she asked one of the girls, "Lisa, when is a time you might need God's forgiveness?" Her blank stare prompted a response from another class mate. "It's okay, Lisa. You don't have to tell her." Then she turned to the teacher and said, "We don't have to tell you our problems. This isn't the Oprah Winfrey Show."

JUNE 14

TIM TEBOW AND JOHN 3:16

"For God so loved the world that He gave His only begotten Son, that whoever believes in Him shall not perish, but have eternal life." (John 3:16, NASB)

The Denver Broncos quarterback, Tim Tebow, threw an eighty-yard touchdown pass to receiver Demaryius Thomas on the first play of overtime against the Pittsburgh Steelers, winning the game for the Broncos and allowing them to advance in the NLF playoffs to determine if they would play in the 2012 Super Bowl.

Tebow is a devout Christian and is known for his witness as a believer in Christ. Among others things, he kneels on the sideline to pray and begins each postgame interview by expressing gratitude to Christ for giving him the ability to play football. Because of this, he has received an enormous amount of criticism and mockery by those who are opposed to such displays of religion.

Tebow's stat line in that game mirrored the numbering of the Biblical passage that Tebow at times had painted on to his black eye paint during his career at the University of Florida – John 3:16. In the game against the Steelers, Tebow threw for 316 yards. He set an NFL postseason single-game record with 31.6 yards per completion. And John 3:16 is His favorite Bible verse.

Why is Tebow so polarizing? Athletes like Kurt Warner or Josh Hamilton have proclaimed their Christianity without a hint of the hate that Tebow has endured. Other athletes in the past have stood up for their religion like Muhammad Ali and Sandy Koufax. Deion Sanders used to kneel in the end zone, and Reggie White was an ordained minister nicknamed the "Minister of Defense." So this is nothing new.

I don't know why people are so critical of Tebow's demonstration of his faith. For some reason it makes them feel uneasy. Some believe it's inappropriate. Some just oppose religion, especially Christianity. Jesus said, "If the world hates you, you know that it has hated Me before it hated you" (John 15:18, NASB). I admire Tebow's courage to let his "light" shine before others (Matthew 5:16). May we follow his example.

A LITTLE HUMOR: Noticing that prior to the football game, both teams gathered together and prayed briefly, a fan seated next to a preacher asked what he thought would happen if both teams prayed with equal faith and fervor. "In that event," replied the preacher, "I imagine the Lord would simply sit back and enjoy one fine game of football."

JUNE 15

THE GOD OF ALL COMFORT

"Blessed be the God and Father of our Lord Jesus Christ, the Father of mercies and God of all comfort; who comforts us in all our affliction . . ."
(2 Corinthians 1:3-4a, NASB)

God has given us many things just to comfort us and to strengthen us in times of trouble and trials. For example, God has given His Spirit for our comfort (John 14:16-18, 25). The word *comfort* comes from the Latin word *comfortis*. The prefix *com* means with and the root word *fortis* means strong. So a comforter is someone who not only gives solace after the battle, but gives strength for the battle. Real comfort is more than a pat on the back; it is strength for the soul. Jesus said the Holy Spirit would be our Helper. The word "Helper" comes from the same Greek word meaning comfort.

But God has also given us the Scripture for our comfort. The Bible says in Romans 15:4, "For whatever was written in earlier times was written for our instruction, that through perseverance and the encouragement of the Scriptures we might have hope," (NASB). The Psalmist said, "This is my comfort in my affliction, that Thy word has revived me," (NASB). God's word is a comfort for us during the times of trials and tribulations.

God has also given the Savior for our comfort. First John 2:1 tells us that Jesus is our "Advocate with the Father." The word "Advocate" is the same word for "comforter." Perhaps a modern concept of the term would be a defense attorney. Our Savior, the Lord Jesus Christ, stands up for us in the presence of our Heavenly Father. Christ's High-Priestly ministry guarantees not only sympathy but also acquittal.

So, God the Father, God the Son, and God the Holy Spirit are all involved in the comfort of the child of God. Andre Crouch captured the truth of God's comfort in his song, *Through it All*. The first stanza of his famous song includes these words: "In every situation, God gave blessed consolation that my trails come to only make me strong . . . Through it all, through it all, Oh, I've learned to trust in Jesus, I've learned to trust in God. Through it all, through it all, I've learned to depend upon His word."

A LITTLE HUMOR: A young preacher was to preach his first sermon for a church needing a pastor. An older preacher told him, "Every sermon should be moving, soothing, and satisfying." Weeks later, the older preacher asked the younger preacher how things turned out. "Well," he said, "I know my sermon was moving because half the congregation left. It must have been soothing, because the other half fell asleep. And apparently it was satisfying because they haven't asked me back."

JUNE 16

THE GREAT MAN'S WHISKERS

"But by the grace of God I am what I am . . ." (1 Corinthians 15:10, NASB)

In 1860 when Abraham Lincoln was seeking the nomination for President of the United States, he had less popular support than his opponent, William H. Seward. Mr. Seward was a favorite because of his just and kindly dealings with the people when he was an agent of the Holland Land Company. Lincoln also had many supporters, among them was Grace Bedell, a small girl who lived on Washington Street in Westfield, New York. Young Grace, having listened to the campaign talk among her elders, and having looked at pictures of the candidates, decided Mr. Lincoln would have a better chance if his appearance was improved. In her mind that could be accomplished by growing whiskers.

On October 15, 1860, she wrote a letter to Lincoln, telling him that she thought he would be more popular with the ladies, and thus influence more votes, if he would grow whiskers. Lincoln did grow a beard and during a campaign stop in Westfield he met Grace. As she was lifted up to meet the future president He said to her, "You see, my dear, I let these grow for you. Perhaps you made me President."

Lincoln's "whiskers" may have helped him to become President of the United States, but we as believers in the Lord Jesus Christ know that we are what we are because of God's grace. Like Paul, we know that the secret to the life we now live and enjoy is all because of God's amazing grace. We are saved by God's grace and are His "workmanship" (Ephesians 2:8-10). All that we do for God and anything that we become in His work, we have to say it is because of His grace. Today, give thanks for His grace. "Whiskers" or not, we are what we are by the grace of God.

A LITTLE HUMOR: A politician was approached by an irate voter. He insulted the man running for office. "I wouldn't vote for you if you were St. Peter himself." "If I were St. Peter," snapped back the candidate, "you couldn't vote for me. You wouldn't be in my district!"

JUNE 17

MAKING POP TOPS

"Honor your father . . ." (Exodus 20:12a, NKJV)

Father's Day is the one day when Pop gets to be tops! King for a day! It's a day for remembering "dear ole dad" in a special way. I remember reading about a bakery sign that suggested remembering dad in this way: "Remember Dad on Father's Day and buy a Devil's Food Cake."

Children are funny. One little boy entered an essay contest with the theme "My Pop's Tops." Among other things he wrote: "Pop never passed the seventh grade, yet he is as smart as if he was in the eighth." Another boy wrote a poem about his "Pop":

When Pop's down at the office
He's a mighty important guy.
He growls his orders, loud and fierce.
And makes his employees fly.
He's yessed by all, just like they think
Whatever Pop does is right.
When Pop's down at the office

He's a man of main and might.

But when Pop's home, he's different;
He hasn't much to say.
And does just what Mom tells him
And does it my Mom's way.
Mom contradicts him quite a bit,
And keeps Pop on the hop.
Pop's a "big shot" at the office,
But at home he's just a "pop."

Showering Pop with love is one way you can make this an extra special day for him. Fathers need love as much as anyone and there is nothing that thrills a father more than to hear his own children say, "Dad, we love you!" This is "Pop's Day." He deserves it. See what you can do to make Pop tops.

A LITTLE HUMOR: A woman was reporting her missing husband to the police – "He's short . . . bald-headed . . . wears false teeth . . . chews tobacco, and the juice is always running down his chin . . . on second thought, officer . . . just forget the whole thing!"

JUNE 18

MARRIAGE IS A WONDERFUL INSTITUTION

"Then the Lord God said, 'It is not good for the man to be alone. I will make a helper who is just right for him'." (Genesis 2:18, NLT)

Today is my wedding anniversary. It's my wife's, too. God has certainly blessed our marriage. We are still convinced beyond a shadow of a doubt that the Lord brought us together.

When God placed Adam in the Garden of Eden, the only thing that was not good in all of creation was Adam's aloneness. God soon fixed that. He made Eve — a helper, a partner, and an ideal friend (Genesis 2:18). Biblical scholar H. C. Leupold writes that God created her, as the Hebrew text indicates, "as agreeing to him" or as "his counterpart." Leupold says, "She's the kind of help man needs . . . mentally, physically, spiritually."

God knew what He was doing when He gave us men our wives. They are our full-time companions. Next to God, they know us best of all. To show our wives that we meant what we said when we declared our love and devotion to them we ought to follow the advice of the apostle Peter who wrote: "Husbands . . . be considerate as you live with your wives" (1 Peter 3:7, NIV). By *live with*, Peter meant more than reside at the same address. The word live, in this case, means to "be at home with someone." Husbands are to "be at home with" their wives in a considerate way; that is, having a proper understanding of their spouses. That a husband should be considerate implies more than just a kind attitude; it goes deeper, implying that his consideration of his wife is based on his knowledge of her needs, desires, gifts, and abilities.

Peter explained that a husband must also respect his wife as the weaker partner. The word for *weaker* refers to physical weakness, not to moral, spiritual, or intellectual inferiority. Men are not to bully their wives physically or sexually. A husband should not thunder and thump to get his way! While the woman may be "weaker," she is also a "partner," implying a side-by-side relationship of working together. A man who respects his wife will protect, honor, and help her. He will stay with her. He will respect her opinions, listen to her advice, be considerate of her needs, and relate to her both privately and publicly with love, courtesy, insight, and tact.

Yes, sir, marriage is a wonderful institution; if you like living in an institution. I do. I hope you who are married feel the same way, too.

A LITTLE HUMOR: A psychiatrist advised a henpecked husband to assert himself. "You don't have to let your wife bully you," he said. "Go home and show her you're the boss." The husband decided to take the doctor's advice. He went home, slammed the door, shook his fist in his wife's face, and growled, "From now on you're taking orders from me. I want my supper right now, and when you get it on the table, go upstairs and lay out my clothes. Tonight I am going out with the boys. You are going to stay at home where you belong. Another thing, you know who is going to tie my bow tie?" "I certainly do," said his wife calmly. "The undertaker."

JUNE 19

ON BEING A SPIRITUAL SWITCH-HITTER

"Therefore, submit to God. Resist the devil and he will flee from you."
(James 4:7, NKJV)

According to the *Beaumont Enterprise,* an unprecedented event unfolded during the ninth inning of a Minor League baseball game in New York on June 19, 2008. Pat Venditte was making his professional debut with the Class-A Staten Island Yankees just two weeks after being drafted by the New York Yankees in the 20th round. He was pitching to close out the game after striking out two batters and giving up a single. The Brooklyn Cyclones sent switch-hitter Ralph Henriquez to the plate and that's when it got interesting.

Since Venditte was pitching left-handed, Henriquez positioned himself to hit right-handed because a batter can see the ball better when a pitcher throws it from the opposite side. Venditte then put his specially made glove on his left hand and prepared to pitch right-handed since he is ambidextrous (his glove has six fingers and two webs so he can wear it on either hand). This confused Henriquez so he called for time and relocated to the other side of the plate. Venditte then switched his glove again. Henriquez then called for time and relocated to the other side of the place. Venditte countered. This continued again and again for five minutes until Venditte left the pitcher's mound and approached the home plate umpire. Both managers came out and discussed the matter with the entire umpiring staff. Since the Major League Baseball rulebook is unclear about such situations, it was agreed that both the pitcher and hitter could change sides one time per-at-bat, and the batter must declare first. Henriquez chose to bat right-handed so Venditte opted to pitch right-handed and struck him out on four pitches. Henriquez slammed his bat down in frustration and Venditte's Staten Island Yankees walked away with a 7-2 win.

As crazy as all of this sounds, it is similar to what takes place every day in the spiritual realm. Satan and his evil forces relentlessly seek the greatest advantage on every pitch so they can "steal, kill, and destroy" (John 10:10). For this reason it is imperative that we follow the admonition of James 4:7 to remain humble before God and resolute against the Devil. Otherwise we will strike out quickly and often.

A LITTLE HUMOR: A college student went home for the holidays. He had changed his dress style, haircut, etc. to be more like the styles at college. His dad said, "Son, you look like a fool!" Later, the grandfather saw the young man and said, "You look just like your father did twenty-five years ago when he came home from school!" The young man said, "Yes, that's what Dad was just telling me!"

JUNE 20

YOU CAN'T SHOUT A LIE

"Do not lie to one another, since you have put off the old man with his deeds."
(Colossians 3:9, NKJV)

Thomas Edison was one of the most productive inventors of his time. In spite of schooling that was limited to three months, at his death he held 1,300 U. S. and foreign patents. Among his major inventions were the phonograph, electric light bulb, microphone, fluoroscope and the telephone transmitter. Thomas Edison invented the phonograph at age thirty, yet he was almost totally deaf from childhood. He could only hear the loud noises and shouts. This kind of delighted him, for he said, "A man who has to shout can never tell a lie!"

A little boy was asked what a lie was and he replied, "A very present help in the time of trouble." We often excuse lies as an exaggeration of truth but in Proverbs we find that lying is one of the things God hates (Proverbs 6:16-19). With God there are no little white lies. They are all dark and hated by Him. Lying can take many forms. The exaggeration of who you are or what you have done is nothing more than a lie. Adding to a story and making it more than what it was is a lie. God's Word forbids lying in any form.

A Christian is to put away lying. If there is any person whose word should be reliable, it is the Christian. Today, ask God to give you a hatred for lying in any form. Ask God to search your heart for any lies you may have told. Oh, by the way, be honest with yourself.

A LITTLE HUMOR: By the time Jim arrived at the football game, the first half was almost over. "Why are you so late?" his friend asked. "I had to toss a coin to decide between going to church and coming to the game," he replied. "How long could that have taken you?" "Well, I had to toss it 14 times."

JUNE 21

WALKING IN HONESTY

"Let us walk honestly, as in the day. . ." (Romans 13:13a, KJV)

Bo Pilgrim, of the Pilgrim's Pride Corporation, made the largest deal in the history of the poultry industry in the acquisition of the ConAgra chicken division valued at more than $600 million. The deal caused Pilgrim's Pride to double its operations and the company jumped to $5.6 billion a year in annualized sales.

Bo Pilgrim said this about the business deal: "The deal came down to a single factor that I've come to recognize and value increasingly through the years: integrity… it's certainly at the root of all good financial decisions and business choices… What would a boy from Pine, Texas, – population less than one hundred people – know about business deals of that magnitude? In a word – nothing. But what would a boy from Pine, Texas, know about integrity – about being true to your word, standing on principle, and developing relationships that transcend the decades? Everything! Pine might have been small, but the principles I learned there were lasting and huge."[43]

While the Bible does not give definite guidelines and specific commands on every aspect of honesty, it does present general principles of conduct.

A person should be honest with himself. First Corinthians 3:18a reads, "Let no man deceive himself...". In order words, don't fool yourself into thinking that you are better than others. Be humble. Just as you would have an appraisal made of a piece of property you planned to purchase in order to pay a fair market price, likewise we are to make an honest appraisal of ourselves and thank the Lord that in spite of who and what we are, He loves us.

Second, a person should be honest with others. We should be honest in our speech (Psalm 15 and Proverbs 12:17-22). If you have to say, "I really shouldn't say this . . ." don't! Then, we must be honest in our business dealings (Proverbs 11:1; 20:10, 23; Luke 19:8-10).

Finally, a person should be honest with God. We dare not pretend with God. He knows us. We must be honest and agree with Him that we are sinners and are in need

---

[43] Bo Pilgrim, *One Pilgrim's Progress* (Nashville, Nelson Business, 2005), 3-4.

of redemption. If we are honest with God He will bless us (Psalm 24:3-5), strengthen us (Psalm 15), and preserve us (Psalm 41:12).

Why do we tend to be dishonest? It's because our hearts are "deceitful . . . and desperately wicked" (Jeremiah 17:9). God is the only one who can change our hardened, wicked hearts into living, honest hearts (Ezekiel 11:19; 36:26).

A LITTLE HUMOR: One Sunday a pastor asked the congregation to give a little extra to help catch up on the church's debt. He said that whoever gave the most would be able to pick out three hymns. After the offering plates were passed, the pastor glanced down and saw an $1,000 bill. He was so excited that he immediately shared it with the congregation. He then invited the person who gave the money to come forward. A very quiet, elderly, widow shyly raised her hand. The pastor asked her to come forward and told her to pick out three hymns. Her eyes brightened as she looked over the congregation, pointed to the three handsomest men in the building and said, "I'll take him and him and him!"

JUNE 22

STANDING SHOULDER-TO-SHOULDER

"But the Lord stood with me and strengthened me . . ." (2 Timothy 4:17a, NKJV)

Jackie Robinson, an African American, broke the color barrier in professional baseball by becoming the first black player to play. On April 15, 1947, Robinson played his first game for the Brooklyn Dodgers. When he stepped out onto the field in one particular game, the booing was so loud it became difficult for the game to proceed. He received a steady barrage of insults. Opponents spiked him, even crashed baseballs against his head when he stole second base. Shortstop Peewee Reece silenced the crowd as he left second base, walked to Jackie's side and stood-shoulder-to shoulder with him. Silence filled the air. Later Jackie said, "I would have quit baseball that very day if Peewee had not done what he did."

There are times in everyone's life when we could be encouraged by someone standing with us. The apostle Paul certainly felt that way. In verse fourteen Paul says that Alexander the coppersmith did him much harm. Then, in verse sixteen he says that "no one stood with me, but all forsook me." The words *stood with* were used to denote the function of a person who came into court to defend the accused. Paul had no legal counsel, no advocate, no one to counter the lies and distortions of men like Alexander. The word *forsook* means to desert.

However, Paul was comforted by the presence of the Lord. "The Lord stood with me," he said. Suddenly, Paul became aware that the Lord had come into that judgment hall. His heart no longer raced. His thoughts cleared. His resolve stiffened. Jesus had promised His disciples, "I am with you always, even unto the end of the world" (Matthew 28:20), and Paul proved, as never before, this promise to be true.

Whatever difficulties you may face, you can always count on the Lord to stand with you. He has promised to never leave us nor forsake us (Hebrews 13:5). Others may desert you, but the Lord never will. Claim that promise and receive His peace today.

A LITTLE HUMOR: Two elderly men were walking down the road one day and one said to the other, "It's windy isn't it?" The other replied, "No, it's Thursday." The first replied. "Me too, let's stop and get something to drink."

JUNE 23

HOW TO BEST SPEND YOUR TIME

"Teach us to number our days that we may gain a heart of wisdom."
(Psalm 90:12, NKJV)

Dr. Paul W. Powell, former Dean of the George W. Truett Theological Seminary, Waco, Texas, mailed "A Pastoral Letter" every month that was full of information a pastor might use in his ministry. One of the things he included was a sermon outline. I was looking at a copy of his newsletter and discovered an outline that he had found on the internet. I was impressed with the outline and added some "meat" to it. I want to share it with you. Based on Psalm 90:12 there are five statements of encouragement on "How to Best Spend Your Time."

First, **in happy moments, praise God.** There is no better time for us to praise the Lord than when things are going well and happiness is a constant experience. Don Hustad once said "Singing is for believers. The question is not, 'Do you have a voice?' but 'Do you have a song?'"

Second, **in difficult moments, seek God.** Everyone has his difficult moments and it is in such times that the wisest thing we could do is to seek the Lord. Horatius Bonar once wrote, "In the day of prosperity we have many refuges to resort to, in the day of adversity, only one." We know who that One is – the Lord Jesus Christ.

Third, **in quiet moments, worship God.** Jesus had his moments when He was alone with the Father. We need those moments as well; moments we can draw aside from the clamor of everyday living and spend some quiet moments worshiping the Lord. It was Vance Havner who quoted the words of Jesus, "Come ye yourselves apart . . . and rest awhile" (Mark 6:31) and then wrote, "This is a must for every Christian. If you don't come apart, you will come apart – you'll go to pieces!"

Fourth, **in painful moments, trust God.** All of us have our painful moments. It is in those times that we need to trust God. We may not understand why we are experiencing such moments, but God never makes a mistake. Vance Havner wrote, "Jesus does not say, 'There is no storm.' He says, 'I am here, do not toss but trust'."

Fifth, **in every moment, thank God.** Being able to thank God for every moment of every day is a sign of spiritual maturity. We are to give thanks to Him always (1Thessalonians 5:18). The whole Christian life is one great big "THANK YOU" to God for His goodness.

A LITTLE HUMOR: After finishing a chicken dinner, the visiting minister gazed out the window and noticed a rooster proudly strutting round the yard. "That's a mighty proud rooster you've got there," he remarked. The host replied, "He should be, one of his sons just entered the ministry."

JUNE 24

WHAT ARE YOU GRUMBLING ABOUT?

"Do all things without grumbling or disputing." (Philippians 2:14, NASB)

Many of us tend to be negative, and some are so negative they even have negative blood! One commentator said, "I've been around Christians long enough to know that telling us not to complain is like telling us not to breathe. It is so commonplace to grumble."

At a Women of Faith Conference a shortage of space tested everyone's patience. The floor had 150 fewer seats than needed. The arena staff tried to solve the problem by using narrow chairs. As a result, every woman had a place to sit, but everyone was crowded. Complaints contaminated the evening. Mary Graham, president of Women of Faith Conferences, asked Joni Eareckson Tada, a speaker for the evening, if she could calm the crowd. Joni was perfectly qualified to do so. A childhood diving accident has left her wheelchair-bound. The attendants rolled her onto the platform, and Joni addressed the unhappy crowd, "I understand some of you don't like the chair in which you are sitting. Neither do I. But I have about a thousand handicapped friends who would gladly trade places with you in an instant." The grumbling ceased.

Yours can too if you would learn to major on the grace of God. Who knows what you might discover?

A LITTLE HUMOR: A passenger in a taxi leaned over to ask the driver a question and tapped him on the shoulder. The driver screamed, lost control of the cab, nearly hit a bus, drove up over the curb, and stopped just inches from a large plate glass window. For a few moments everything was silent in the cab, when then the still shaking driver said, "I'm sorry, but you scared the daylights out of me." The frightened passenger apologized to the driver and said he didn't realize a mere tap on the should could frighten him so much. The driver replied, "No, no, I'm sorry; it's entirely my fault. You see, today is my first day driving a cab. I've been driving a hearse for the last 25 years."

JUNE 25

HOBSON'S CHOICE

"And if it seems evil to you to serve the Lord, choose for yourselves this day whom you will serve . . . but as for me and my house, we will serve the Lord."
(Joshua 24:15, NKJV)

In seventeenth century England there lived a man by the name of Thomas Hobson. Charitably, Mr. Hobson could be described as a strong-minded man, uncharitably, as a stubborn one.

He owned a livery stable. It was a conventional occupation for those times, but Mr. Hobson conducted his particular establishment in a rather unconventional fashion. When you wanted to rent a horse from him, you took whatever steed happened to be nearest the door. If you protested that you preferred some other animal, Mr. Hobson was likely to refer you to another stable.

Fate has a way of conferring fame on unlikely people at times, and she chose Mr. Hobson for immortality of a sort. It became the custom throughout the countryside to describe a situation in which a person had no alternative as a "Hobson's choice." Today you will find the phrase in almost every dictionary, defined as "a choice without an alternative . . . the thing offered or nothing at all."

In the sixth chapter of John's gospel, the disciples had to make a choice about following the Lord Jesus. After His discourse about His being the bread of life, many who had been following Jesus turned away: "Then Jesus said to the twelve, 'Do you also want to go away?' But Simon Peter answered Him, 'Lord, to whom shall we go? You have the words of eternal life. Also we have come to believe and know that You are the Christ, the Son of the living God.'" (John 6:67-68).

Do not all of us face a "Hobson's choice" in our decision as to whether we will accept Christ? Is it not true that the alternative is "nothing at all"? From the emptiness we see in the lives of those who try to live without Him, it would seem so.

A LITTLE HUMOR: A man was asked, "Do you have trouble making decisions?" He replied, "Well, yes and no."

JUNE 26

SEARCHING IN THE RIGHT PLACE

"And you will seek Me and find Me, when you search for Me with all your heart."
(Jeremiah 29:13, NASB)

A drunk was looking for something on the sidewalk one night under a street light. He groped along the ground, feeling the cement, occasionally grabbing the pole for support. A passerby asked what he was looking for. "Lost my wallet," the drunk replied. The passerby offered to help him look, but with no success.

"Are you sure you lost it here?" he asked the drunk.

"'Course I didn't!" The drunk replied. "It was a half block back there."

"Then why aren't you looking back there?"

"Because," answered the drunk with baffling logic, "there ain't no street lights back there."

Searching is important, but it doesn't do any good unless we search in the right places. Some people give up the pursuit of God in frustration, calling themselves atheists or agnostics, professing to be irreligious. Instead they find it necessary to fill the vacuum left within them with some other kind of deity. Therefore man makes his own "god" — money, work, success, fame, sex, alcohol, even food.

God has made a promise to us. If we sincerely seek Him, we will find Him. In Jeremiah 29:13 the Bible says, "And you will seek Me and find Me, when you search for Me with all your heart" (NASB). This verse says that God is accessible. If we seek Him, we will find Him when we want Him more than all else. The atheist or agnostic cannot find God for the same reason a thief cannot find a policeman — he's not looking for him!

Ultimately you must come to God by faith. Faith is the link between God and man. The Bible says: "Without faith it is impossible to please Him, for he who comes to God must believe that He is, and that He is a rewarder of those who seek Him" (Hebrews 11:6, NASB). God will reward the sincere seeker with forgiveness and righteousness.

A LITTLE HUMOR: A young Scotchman was admitted to a university. He moved into a dormitory. After a month passed, his mother called to check on him. "How are you doing, son?" asked his mother. "Oh Mother, there are strange and noisy people here. The one on this side bangs his head against the wall all night and won't stop. The one on the other side screams and curses until the sun comes up at dawn." "Oh how rude," said his mother. "How do you put up with such people?" "I ignore them, Mother. I just sit here quietly each night, playing my bagpipes."

JUNE 27

LEAVING BEHIND A WORTHY TESTIMONY

"So I will work hard to make sure you always remember these things after I am gone." (2 Peter 1:15, NLT)

On June 27, 1829, English scientist James Smithson died leaving a will that aroused attention on both sides of the Atlantic. His will stated that in the event that his only nephew died without any heirs, the whole of his estate would go to "the United States of America, to found at Washington under the name of the Smithsonian Institution, an establishment for the increase and diffusion of knowledge." Six years later when his nephew died without any children, President Andrew Jackson sent diplomat Richard Rush to England to negotiate the transfer of funds. Two years later,

Rush returned to the United States with 11 boxes containing a total of 104,960 gold sovereigns, 8 shillings, and 7 pence, as well as Smithson's mineral collection, library, scientific notes, and personal effects. After the gold was melted down, its worth amounted to over $500,000. On August 10, 1846, President James K. Polk, signed an act establishing the Smithsonian Institute into law. What was so surprising to many about Smithson's clause in his will is that he had never been to the United States. The Smithsonian Institute stands as a testimony to what one man left behind.

Peter knew that he was going to die, so he wanted to leave behind something that would never die – the written Word of God. If there were no dependable written revelation, we would have to depend on word-of-mouth tradition. If you have ever played the party game "Gossip," you know how a simple sentence can be radically changed when passed from one person to another. We do not depend on the tradition of dead men; we depend on the truth of the living Word. Men die, but the Word of God lives forever.

Have you ever thought about what you will leave behind and how you will be remembered? Ask God to help you to leave behind a testimony that will be a blessing to others and bring glory to God. You may not be able to bequeath thousands of dollars to a cause, but you can be remembered as one that pleased God (Heb11:5).

A LITTLE HUMOR: A guest preacher stood at the back door with the pastor to greet the people as they left church. A man stopped and said to him, "That sermon was terrible. The worst I have ever heard in my life." In just a few moments he came through the line again, and this time he said, "That sermon was so bad, your wife could have done better." Then he came back in line a third time. This time he said, "That sermon was so bad, I could have done better myself." The guest was astounded. He turned to the pastor and asked, "Do you have any idea what that man has been saying to me?" The pastor responded, "Don't pay any attention to him. He's the village idiot, and he just goes around repeating what other people are saying."

JUNE 28

THE REMEDY FOR EVERY TEMPTATION

". . . the Lord knows how to rescue the godly from temptation . . ."
(2 Peter 2:9, NASB)

What's the hardest thing in the world to control? Some 38.5 percent of us say the hardest thing in their lives to control is their weight. Another 32.3 percent say they wrestle most with their spending. Just 10.8 percent say the hardest thing to control is their anger, 16.9 percent pinpoint their fears, and 1.5 percent their smoking, drinking, or drug use. Everyone has their own TEMPTATION.

Did you know that over eight million children disappeared in the United States between 1987 and 1990? The year 1987 marked the first time the IRS required proof that children claimed as dependents actually existed. After that, many children started disappearing from income tax forms.

Nathan Horwitt, a mushroom expert, has said that a mushroom which is properly known as "Amanita Phalloides," is the deadliest of all mushrooms. It is also possibly the tastiest. Asked how he knows this, he explains that the poison is slow-acting and that often the first symptom of poisoning is communicated when the victim remarks, "Last night I ate the most delicious mushroom of my life." Just like TEMPTATION!

The remedy to temptation is not will power. It would be so easy if will power were the remedy. Just say, "No." Isn't that what they say? But some people have no will power. There is only One who will help: the Lord Jesus Christ. Fill your life so full of Christ, the Redeemer, that there simply is no room for the tempter to do his evil work.

A LITTLE HUMOR: An older minister was counseling a young youth leader. "You will discover," he said, "that in nearly every youth group there is one that is eager to argue. Your first impulse will be to silence him. I advise you to think carefully before doing so. He probably is the only one listening."[44]

JUNE 29

ONLY JESUS CAN HELP

"Then Jesus said to the twelve, 'Do you also want to go away?' But Simon Peter answered Him, 'Lord, to whom shall we go? You have the words of eternal life.'"
(John 6:67-68, NKJV)

When it comes to the crucial issues of life, to whom shall we turn? To whom shall we go with our broken hearts? With our broken lives? With our broken homes? There is ultimately only one Person to whom we can go: Jesus Christ.

Herman Melville's novel *Moby Dick* is a classic tale of Captain Ahab, who had a feud going with a great white whale of the deep. The captain had already lost his leg in an encounter with the great white whale and had become a brooding, unhappy, sullen, and terribly pessimistic man. Most of the time he kept himself closed up in his cabin.

On one of those rare occasions when he was walking around the deck of his ship, he came upon the ship's blacksmith, who was working on some metal. Captain Ahab said to him, "What are you doing, Smithy?" And he replied, "I am knocking the dents out of the harpoon, Captain." Captain Ahab stood there for a moment, then pointed to his heart and said, "Smithy, do you know anything that will take the dents out of here?"

Where do you go to take the dents out of your heart? Jesus is the only Person I know who can help. If your life has been broken by sin, the carpenter of Nazareth still mends broken men and women.

---

[44] Tal D. Bonham, *The Treasury of Clean Church Jokes* (Nashville: Broadman Press, 1986), 112.

A LITTLE HUMOR: A preacher was driving down a country road and looked out the window and saw a chicken running right along beside his car. He looked down at his speedometer and saw that he was clipping along about forty miles per hour and thought, "My soul, that's a fast chicken." So, he kicked the car up to fifty and the chicken stayed right with him. Then he kicked it up to sixty, and it kept right up with him. Then the chicken turned on the back burner, ran right past him, and cut up a trial toward a farmhouse.

The preacher slammed on the breaks and whipped up a country lane to that farmhouse himself. He got out and found the farmer standing by the chicken gate and asked, "Are those your chickens?" "Yep," replied the farmer. "They are fast, aren't they," said the preacher. "Yes, pretty fast," said the farmer.

"How did they get that way?" asked the preacher. "Well," said the farmer, "we like chickens around here. We especially like chicken legs. So we bred them and crossbred them until every one of those chickens now has three legs."

The preacher said, "Is that right? How do they taste?" The farmer replied, "Don't know, we never have caught one of them."[45]

JUNE 30

WATCH IT!

"From childhood you have known the sacred writings which are able to give you the wisdom that leads to salvation through faith which is in Christ Jesus."
(2 Timothy 3:16, NASB)

When the seventh and final book in the Harry Potter series was released it immediately sold in the millions. The first six Potter books have sold more than 325 million copies. People are just wild about Harry! People stood in line hours ahead of time just to be among the first to get a copy. People have even dressed like some of the characters in the Potter books. Without question, the Harry Potter books have influenced millions of people.

For many years the Bible has been the best-selling book in the world. Bibles can be found in millions of homes, but how many of those homes have been impacted and changed by the Scriptures? A Bible is great to own but you have to look at it if you want it to change your life. People wear a watch to keep them on track through the day. As Christians, we must allow the Bible to impact us daily to keep our spiritual lives on track. The most important habit you could develop is to read your Bible consistently. God's Word will equip you for every good work (2 Timothy 3:16-17).

A boy sat down next to a man on a park bench and started winding what obviously was a most-prized possession – his watch. "My, what a handsome watch," remarked the man. "Does it tell you the time?" "No, sir," replied the boy. "You've

---

[45] Paul W. Powell, *A Funny Thing Happened On the Way to Retirement* (Tyler, Texas, 2000), 46-47.

gotta look at it." Just like the little boy's watch, for the Bible to be of any use, you must look at it.

A LITTLE HUMOR: A preacher went to visit one of his parishioners, and as he stood by the bedside, the man began to gasp and motioned for the preacher to hand him a pencil and a piece of paper which is what he did. He assumed that the man wanted to write something important. Just as he finished, the man gave one last gasp and died. The preacher folded the note up, put it in his pocket, and assumed that it was something that he would want remembered as his last words. He decided to leave the note in his pocket until the funeral service and then take it out and read it to the congregation so that they could hear the man's last parting wish.

The time came for the service and the preacher walked out on the platform. Remembering the note, he reached in his pocket and pulled it out and read, "You are standing on my oxygen tube."[46]

[46] Paul W. Powell, *Laugh and Live Longer* (Tyler, Texas, 2008), 34-35.

JULY 1

LEARNING FROM THE BULLRING

"Consider it pure joy, my brothers, whenever you face trials of many kinds."
(James 1:2, NIV)

There is a Spanish proverb that says, "Talking bull is not the same as being in the bullring." There are things we learn in the bullring that could never be learned in a bull session. Experience is a great teacher. Adversity is the greatest teacher of all.

James is talking about "how we should take it" when he writes, "Consider it pure joy, my brothers, whenever you face trails of many kinds." Here James prescribes a most uncommon way of looking at the common problems of life. He admonishes, "Be happy when you find yourself in the middle of difficulty." In fact, four times in the first twelve verses of the first chapter of his book he either states or implies we should rejoice in time of adversity (vv. 2, 9-10, 12).

When troubles come, we always have two choices. We can sulk or we can sing. James does not tell us to rejoice about our adversities, but to rejoice in them. That's because adversities can teach us some of life's most enduring lessons, and these experiences can be instruments of spiritual growth and advancement for us.

A LITTLE HUMOR: A young man who had not had much schooling was being examined for a preaching license. One of the questions asked of him was, "What is the difference between the seraphim and cherubim?" He thought for a while and answered, "I knew there had been a little trouble between them, but I thought it had all been cleared up."

JULY 2

SHUT THE DOOR

". . . and when you have shut your door, pray to your Father . . ."
(Matthew 6:6, NKJV)

One evening a man who was visiting the United States wanted to make a telephone call. He entered a phone booth, but found it to be different from those in his own country. It was beginning to get dark, so he had difficulty finding the number in the directory. He noticed that there was a light in the ceiling, but he didn't know how to turn it on. As he tried again to find the number in the fading twilight, a passerby noted his plight and said, "Sir, if you want to turn the light on, you have to shut the door." To the visitor's amazement and satisfaction, when he closed the door, the booth was filled with light. He soon located the number and completed the call.

In a similar way, when we draw aside in a quiet place to pray, we must block out our busy world and open our hearts to the Father. The word *closet* refers to a private chamber or storeroom. The footnote for this verse in *The Criswell Study Bible* states that this is a reference to "a storeroom where treasures could be kept and may allude to treasures available to the Christian who prays regularly."

Our Lord often went to be alone with the Heavenly Father. We too can have the same experience. But we must remember that to "turn on the light," we must first "shut the door" by getting alone with God.

A LITTLE HUMOR: The pastor's morning prayer began, "O, Lord, give us clean hearts, give us pure hearts, give us sweet hearts," and every single girl in the congregation fervently responded, "Ah-men!"

JULY 3

A HEART PREPARED FOR PRAYER

"Let us therefore come boldly to the throne of grace, that we may obtain mercy and find grace to help in time of need." (Hebrews 4:16, NKJV)

The very thought of my being able to pray to God has always struck me as a wonderful privilege. It's a shame that more of us don't take advantage of it. It was F. B. Meyer who said, "The great tragedy of life is not unanswered prayer, but unoffered prayer." Here are some suggestions as to the kind of heart we should have as we approach God in prayer.

First, we should approach the throne of grace with **A CONFIDENT HEART.** That's what the word ***boldly*** means. Some Christians approach God meekly with heads hung low, afraid to ask Him to meet their needs. Others pray flippantly, giving little thought to what they say. We should come with reverence because He is our King, but also come with bold assurance because He is our Friend and Counselor.

Second, we should approach the throne of grace with **A CLEAN HEART.** The psalmist said, "If I had not confessed the sin in my heart, my Lord would not have listened" (Psalm 66:18, NLT). We cannot expect God to answer our prayers if there is unconfessed sin in our life. It's an old but true statement, "Cleanliness is next to Godliness."

Third, we should approach the throne of grace with **A FORGIVING HEART.** In the Gospel of Mark, chapter 11, Jesus said, "When you are praying, first forgive anyone you are holding a grudge against, so that your Father in heaven will forgive your sins too" (v. 25, NLT). John Blanchard has said, "The Christian can always afford to forgive – and can never afford not to!"

Fourth, we should approach the throne of grace with **A BELIEVING HEART.** In Matthew 21:22, Jesus said, "If you believe, you will receive whatever you ask for in prayer" (NLT). Yet few of us take these words seriously, and few dare to claim what God has so generously promised us.

Fifth, we should approach the throne of grace with **A HUMBLE HEART.** Peter wrote, "Humble yourselves under the mighty hand of God, that He may exalt you in due time" (1 Peter 5:8, NKJV). Someone has rightly said, "God is closest to those whose hearts are broken."

If we will follow these suggestions, we can be assured that God will hear and answer our prayers.

A LITTLE HUMOR: A little girl was in bed – scared of the dark. She went into her parent's room and told her mother she was afraid. Her mother said, "It's OK, sweetheart. There's nothing to be afraid of, God is in there with you." The little girl went back to her bed, and as she climbed into bed she said, "God, if you're in here, don't you say a word; you'll scare me to death."

JULY 4

IN GOD WE TRUST

"Some trusts in chariots, and some in horses; but we trust in the name of the Lord our God." (Psalm 20:7, NIV)

In the days of King David the most dreaded war-engine was the war-chariot, armed with scythes, which mowed down men like grass. But the people of God considered the name of Jehovah to be a far better defense.

In America it is easy to trust something or someone rather than the Lord. But to trust in our military strength alone spells failure (see Psalm 20:8). The name of the Lord is to be our watchword and our strength (Judges 7:18; 1Samuel 17:45; 2 Chronicles 16:8-9).

The familiar motto, "In God We Trust," which appears on most of our coins, is traced to a Maryland farmer who, in November, 1861, wrote to the then Secretary of the Treasury stating that since we claim to be a God-fearing, Christian people, we might at least make some recognition of that on our coinage.

Secretary of the Treasury, Salmon P. Chase, referred the letter to James Pollock, Director of the Mint, for serious consideration. Pollock enthusiastically endorsed the suggestion and immediately two mottoes, "Our Country, Our God," and "God Our Trust," were proposed.

Chase had the matter presented to the Congress at their next session, which was in 1862, but nothing was done about it. Again, the following year it was brought up, but still nothing was done.

Our country, at this time, was being racked by a civil war. The national spirit was slowly ebbing, a crisis was nearing. Realizing this, Chase made one last appeal in 1864. The motto, "God Our Trust" was offered as his chief argument. "It is taken from our national anthem, *The Star Spangled Banner,* he said, "and is familiar to every citizen of our country. It has thrilled millions of American freemen. The tune is propitious. Now in this time of national peril, our strength and salvation must be of God."

Secretary Chase won his plea. The Congress authorized the coining of a two-cent piece upon which was to be stamped the motto, "In God We Trust," in place of the old "E Pluribus Unum." The following year, on March 3, 1865, the Director of the Mint was further authorized to place the new motto on all gold and silver coins, thus fulfilling the words of Francis Scott Key in his poem, *The Star Spangled Banner:*

Then conquer we must
When our cause it is just,
And this be our motto,
"In God is our trust."

A LITTLE HUMOR: The reason some congressmen try so hard to get reelected is that they would hate to have to make a living under the laws they've passed.

JULY 5

YOU WERE RIGHT, MR. SKELTON, IT IS A PITY

"Blessed is the nation whose God is the Lord . . ." (Psalm 33:12a, NKJV)

It seems that every time we turn around someone is trying to remove any reference to God in any part of our government and country. Some time ago the ninth U. S. Circuit Court of Appeals ruled that reciting the Pledge of Allegiance is unconstitutional because it contains the words "under God." I am as outraged as everyone else that such a ridiculous ruling could be handed down by any court.

Such a ruling has reminded me of a newspaper article I read years ago; in fact, it was published in the March 1, 1969 edition of *The Dallas Morning News.* It was an article about an interpretation of the Pledge of Allegiance recorded by the late Red Skelton, a famous comedian. The recording by Columbia Records is a version of the pledge Skelton learned from a teacher while a schoolboy in Vincennes, Indiana. Here is the pledge as interpreted by Red Skelton:

"I remember this one teacher. To me, he was the greatest teacher, a real sage of my time. He had such wisdom. We were all reciting the Pledge of Allegiance, and he walked over. Mr. Lasswell was his name . . . He said:

'I've been listening to you boys and girls recite the Pledge of Allegiance all semester and it seems as though it is becoming monotonous to you. If I may, may I recite it and try to explain to you the meaning of each word:

'I, me, an individual, a committee of one.

'Pledge – dedicate all of my worldly goods to give without self-pity.

'Allegiance – my love and my devotion.

'To the flag – our standard, Old Glory, a symbol of freedom. Wherever she waves, there is respect because your loyalty has given her a dignity that shouts freedom is everybody's job.

'Of the United – that means that we have all come together.

'States – individual communities that have united into 48 great states. Forty-eight individual communities with pride and dignity and purpose, all divided with imaginary boundaries, yet united to a common purpose, and that's love for country.

'Of America.

'And to the Republic – a state in which sovereign power is invested in representatives chosen by the people to govern. And government is the people and it's from the people to the leaders, not from the leaders to the people.

'For which it stands.

'One nation – meaning, so blessed by God.

'Indivisible – incapable of being divided.

'With liberty – which is freedom and the right of power to live one's own life without threats or fear or some sort of retaliation.

'And justice – the principle or quality of dealing fairly with others.

'For all' – which means it's as much your country as it is mine.'"

Skelton continued, "Since I was a small boy, two states have been added to our country and two words have been added to the Pledge of Allegiance – 'under God.'

"Wouldn't it be a pity if someone said, 'That's a prayer' – and that would be eliminated from schools too?"

Every American citizen ought to be enraged because of this ruling. It's time to stand up and say, "Enough is enough!" Our country was founded upon Judeo-Christian beliefs whether we like it or not. To tamper with that is to destroy the very roots upon which our country was founded. If this doesn't stop now the next thing you know we will not be able to sing our National Anthem because it contains the words "Praise the Power that hath made and preserved us a nation!" (a reference to God) and the words "In God is our trust!" And then there are the words "In God We Trust" that are printed on our coins. It seems to me that certain judges ought to be ruled unconstitutional and removed!

A Little Humor: A man took his Social Security check down to the bank to deposit it. As he stood and waited in the long line, he inadvertently began to nervously fold and unfold his check. It finally came his turn at the teller's window. As he handed the teller a ruffled government check she said, "Sir, can't you read this check? It says, 'Do not fold, spindle, or mutilate'." "So?" replied the customer. "Well," said the teller, "you shouldn't do that. The government doesn't like it." Looking her straight in the eye he replied, "Well, the government does a lot of things I don't like, too."

JULY 6

THE STRENGTH OF A NATION

"Righteousness exalts a nation, but sin is a disgrace to any people."
(Proverbs 14:34, NASB)

During his visit to China, President Bill Clinton and his family visited the Great Wall of China in Mutianyu, outside Beijing. The President told reporters that the

Great Wall of China was "even more magnificent than I imagined." He wrote that message in an official guest book and underlined the word *magnificent.*

The Great Wall of China is indeed one of the great wonders of the world. Built of stone and bricks, it was begun in 221 B. C. and snakes itself 2,000 miles across the northern borders of China. The walls are twenty-five feet wide at the base, twenty-five feet high, and have thirty foot towers every two hundred to three hundred yards. Our American astronauts told us that it was the only man-made structure they could see from space.

When the Great Wall of China was completed, the people settled down behind it with a sense of safety and security. The walls were too high for an enemy to scale, and they were too strong to be battered down. But, in the first few years after the wall was completed, it was breached three times by the enemy. Was it because the enemy was able to scale the wall? No, it was too high for that. Was it because some foes battered it down? No, it was too thick for that. It happened because three times the enemy bribed a gatekeeper.

The people of China learned what we need to learn – the strength of a nation is not found in the height or thickness of its walls or the size and strength of its armies, but in the character of its gatekeepers. As Confucius said, "The strength of the nation is not in its square acres, but its square men."

Wherein lies the strength of America? The answer is found in the Bible. The writer of Proverbs 14:34 says, "Righteousness exalts a nation, but sin is a disgrace to any people." The word *righteousness* comes from the root word meaning to be right. It suggests the idea of moral uprightness and social justice. The word *reproach* means to bend low in shame, in disgrace, or in an ultimate downfall.

The strength of our nation, then, is in our people walking in uprightness, standing for truth and justice, reaching out in mercy, bowing in reverence, and kneeling in submission before God. And sin, selfish and shameful living, will ultimately bring us to disgrace and downfall. If we are to remain strong as a nation, we must pay attention to our moral fiber.

A LITTLE HUMOR: Will Rogers said that all he needed for his humor was the Congressional Record. He said, "There's no trick to being humorous when you have the whole United States government working for you."

JULY 7

SINCERE AND BLAMELESS

". . . that you may . . . be sincere and blameless until the day of Christ."
(Philippians 1:10, NASB)

There are few things that are more needed in the world today than Christians who exhibit sincerity. In the Scripture verse for today Paul prayed that the Philippian Christians would be *sincere and blameless.* The word *sincere* (also translated *pure* in some translations) actually comes from a Latin word meaning without wax. The Greek term means sun-tested.

Some ancient potters made a very fine porcelain which was greatly valued and therefore expensive. When fired in the potter's kiln, tiny cracks would often appear. Dishonest merchants would smear pearly-white wax over these cracks, which would allow their pottery to pass for true porcelain – unless held up to the light of the sun. In contrast, honest dealers marked their flawless ware *sine-cere* – which means literally, without wax, or able to withstand the test of the sun.

The word *blameless* refers to that part of a trap to which the bait was attached. It was a snare which caused an animal to fall into a trap. To be blameless means not to be a stumbling block or a snare which caused someone else to fall.

In these two words, *sincere* and *blameless,* Paul was referring to the inward and the outward parts of our character. Concerning ourselves, we are to be pure. Concerning others, we are to be blameless.

Hypocrisy, lying to other people about your relationship with the Lord, is a common way Christians try to cover up cracks in their lives. Are you willing to hold your life up before the sunlight of God's Word and His Spirit until every last crack and flaw have been revealed? When the light of Christ shines through and tests your life, only the absence of cracks will guarantee the presence of truth.

A LITTLE HUMOR: A wino boarded a bus and sat next to a nun. His hair was mussed up, his clothes were wrinkled, and his breath reeked of alcohol. He opened the newspaper and proceeded to read. Presently he turned to the nun and asked, "Sister, what causes arthritis?" The sister thought, this is a good opportunity to witness so she replied, "Sin. Pure and simple. Drinking whiskey, smoking big, long, black cigars and carousing. Why do you ask?" The man replied, "I just read here in the paper that the Pope has arthritis."

JULY 8

WHERE ARE THE NINE?

"Were there not ten cleansed? But where are the nine?" (Luke 17:17, NKJV)

Many years ago a boat was wrecked in a storm on one of the Great Lakes. Rescue teams were sent to help, including a team of Northwestern University students. Edward Spencer, one of those young men, rescued at least sixteen people from the sinking ship. When he was carried exhausted from the scene, he could only ask, "Did I do my best? Do you think I did my best?"

Years later, at a class reunion, one of the speakers recalled this act of heroism. Someone called out that Edward Spencer was present in the audience. He was invited to come forward. He made his way to the podium as the assembly cheered and applauded. The speaker asked him if there was anything particular he remembered about that day. "Only this," he replied, "of all those people I saved, not one of them thanked me."

A similar event happened to Jesus as recorded in Luke 17:11-19. Ten lepers were healed by Jesus but only one of the ten expressed gratitude to Him. Why were the other nine ungrateful? Several reasons have been suggested:

1. Maybe they thought, "He knows I'm grateful."
2. They may have become so absorbed in the gift they forgot the giver.
3. They may have forgotten both the gift and the giver.
4. Maybe they thought they deserved to be healed.
5. They may have been conceited; selfish.

We sometimes scold the nine for not expressing gratitude to the Lord but fail to pause and ask if we would have raised the ratio. There are two classes of people in the world: those who take things with gratitude and those who take things for granted.

The people on the sinking ship would likely have drowned had it not been for Edward Spencer. The ten lepers were suffering from a horrible disease. Without Christ they would not have been healed. Likewise, without Jesus Christ we are doomed to spend eternity in hell. When we have called on Jesus to save us from sin, we should have tremendous gratitude, just as the one leper. Have you ever thanked God for all He has done to save you? Why not take a few minutes to do so now.

A LITTLE HUMOR: A doctor wondered why his practice was decreasing. He consulted a physician friend who agreed to spend a few days in the office and observe his methods. After an hour, his friend had the answer, "Wilbur, you'll have to stop humming 'Nearing My God to Thee' when writing out a prescription."

JULY 9

POUR YOUR HEART OUT TO GOD

"Trust in Him at all times, you people; pour out your heart before Him; God is a refuge for us." (Psalm 62:8)

On July 9, 1982, Michael Fagan, a thirty-one-year old unemployed painter and decorator, managed to climb a ten-foot wall topped by spikes and barbed wire; he shinnied up a drainpipe, and climbed through a window to roam thc vast palace corridors of Buckingham Palace in London, England. For fifteen minutes he evaded guardsmen, bobbies, servants, surveillance cameras, and electronic devices to reach the royal bedroom. Abruptly awakened by the intruder, the Queen spent an eerie ten minutes conversing with him. The Queen managed to press an alarm bell, which failed to get a response. Twice she used her bedside phone to call security, but no one came. Fagan sat on her bed and told her all of his family problems. The Queen responded with small talk. "Do you have a cigarette?" he asked. "No, I do not, but I'll find one for you," the Queen responded. As she left her bedroom she found a chambermaid. "There is an intruder in my bedroom. Call palace security immediately," she commanded. Security guards finally arrived and took Fagan away. It was later learned that Fagan had penetrated the palace five weeks earlier during a state visit by President and Mrs. Reagan.

As believers, we have the privilege of telling the King of Kings about our troubles, and we don't even have to climb a fence or shinny up a drainpipe to do so. All we have to do is to cry out to Him and He will be there. Psalm 62:8 speaks of pouring our hearts out to God.

Are you experiencing a time of difficulty in your life? Are the burdens of life pressing and distressing you? Do you need someone to tell your troubles to? If so, today pour out your heart to the Lord. You need not worry that someone will escort you away. He will listen as long as you need to talk. The door to His palace is open, and you are always welcome.

A LITTLE HUMOR: A military officer who had been overseas on an extended tour received a letter from his wife, telling about a prayer that their four-year-old daughter made: "Dear Lord, please send me a baby brother so we will have something to surprise Daddy with when he get home."

JULY 10

PUT ME IN, COACH

"Also I heard the voice of the Lord, saying: 'Whom shall I send, and who will go for us?'" (Isaiah 6:8, NKJV)

A college football coach liked to give his players mental workouts by quizzing them on what they would do during hypothetical situations.

One day, walking the sidelines he stopped where a player named Johnson was sitting. "Johnson!" the coach barked out, "if it were 3rd and 25, and we were at midfield, what would you do?"

The player thought for a moment and then said, "I would move down to the next bench to get a better view of the play."

God doesn't ask anyone to sit on the bench. In fact, we are instructed not to. You can't win if you are on the sidelines. Get in the game and play.

Do you remember the John Fogerty song, *Centerfield?* The chorus went, "Put me in coach, I'm ready to play!" Our attitude needs to be the same as Isaiah's. When God said, "Whom shall I send, and who will go for Us?" Isaiah responded, "Here am I! Send me." (Isaiah 6:8). He was saying, "Put me in coach." I challenge you to say the same thing today.

A LITTLE HUMOR: A winning football coach became enraged at a referee whom he thought had made a number of bad calls during a game. The coach yelled at him, "You stink!" The referee picked up the football, marked off another penalty of ten yards, turned toward his abuser, and yelled, "How do I smell from here?"

JULY 11

THE BEST GUIDE BOOK

"All Scripture is given by inspiration of God, and is profitable for doctrine, for reproof, for correction, for instruction in righteousness." (2 Timothy 3:16, NKJV)

During Super Bowl XXXVII, FedEx ran a commercial that spoofed the movie *Castaway,* in which Tom Hanks played a FedEx worker whose company plane went down, stranding him on a desert island for years. Looking like the bedraggled Hanks in the movie, the FedEx employee in the commercial goes up to the door of a suburban home, package in hand. When the lady comes to the door, he explains that he survived five years on a deserted island and during that whole time he kept this package in order to deliver it to her.

She gives a simple "Thank you." He is curious about what is in the package that he has been protecting for years. He says, "If I may ask, what was in that package after all?" She opens it and shows him the contents saying, "Oh, nothing really. Just a satellite telephone, a global positioning device, a compass, a water purifier, and some seeds."

Like the contents in this package, the resources for growth and strength are available for every Christian who will take advantage of them. The Bible is our guide and manual for life.

A LITTLE HUMOR: The local Baptist church burned down and the congregation contracted with a local tavern to hold services in their facilities until a new church building could be erected. On Saturday night, after the festivities, church members would clean up the tavern, rearrange the furniture, and prepare for Sunday morning. The tavern had a talking parrot to entertain its guests.

One Saturday night the cleanup crew failed to remove the parrot. The next morning the choir came in and the parrot said, "I see we have a new chorus line." The preacher came in and the parrot said, "I see we have a new bartender." Then the congregation came in, and the parrot said, "Yeah, but it's the same old crowd!"

JULY 12

REMEMBERING WHERE WE'RE FROM

"For our citizenship is in heaven, from which we also eagerly wait for the Savior, the Lord Jesus Christ." (Philippians 3:20, NKJV)

Many years ago, a British military officer stationed in an African jungle was visited by a longtime friend. One day when the friend entered the officer's hut, he was startled to see him dressed in formal attire and seated at a table beautifully set with silverware and fine china. The visitor, thinking his friend might have lost his mind, asked why he was all dressed up and seated at a table so sumptuously arrayed out in the middle of nowhere. The officer explained, "Once a week I follow this routine. I do so simply to remind myself of who I am – a British citizen. I want to maintain the customs of my real home and live according to the codes of British conduct, no matter how those around me live. I want to avoid substituting a foreign culture for that of my homeland."

We Christians should have a similar concern. Because our citizenship is in heaven, it's of the utmost importance that we avoid substituting the foreign culture of the world for that of our real homeland.

E. Taylor Cassel wrote the hymn *The King's Business* which is the theme song for The Royal Ambassadors' mission organization for young boys in our church. The first stanza reads:

I am a stranger here, within a foreign land;
My home is far away, upon a golden strand;
Ambassador to be of realms beyond the sea,
I'm here on business for my King.

A LITTLE HUMOR: Mistakes can sometimes happen that result in embarrassing blunders in church bulletins. One that should have used the word *life,* printed the sermon topic: "How to Change Your Wife Through Prayer." When the error was shown to the pastor, he said, "Let it alone. Someone might need it."

JULY 13

THE PURPOSE OF TRIALS

"Consider it all joy, my brethren, when you encounter various trials, knowing that the testing of your faith produces endurance. And let endurance have its perfect result, so that you may be perfect and complete, lacking in nothing." (James 1:2-4, NASB)

An anonymous person has written, "The gem cannot be polished without friction, nor man perfected without trials." In our Scripture for today James doesn't say "if" we face trials, but whenever we face them. He assumes that we will have trials and that it is possible to profit from them. God has a purpose for trials.

We Can Display Joy in Times of Trial. We are to greet trials with "all joy." We can have "joy inexpressible" (1 Peter 1;8), like the early apostles did when they suffered for preaching the Gospel (Acts 5:40-41). Whenever we are squeezed by trouble, the joy of Jesus should come out.

We Can Develop Endurance in Times of Trial. Times of testing produce "endurance." Endurance not only stubbornly withstands a trial but also conquers it. Weight lifters break down the cells in their muscles. With rest, the muscles rebuild and grow back stronger and larger. Likewise, our trials build muscles of spiritual fortitude.

We Can Demonstrate Maturity in Times of Trials. The word *perfect* refers to maturity. Trials help us grow in grace and in Christ-likeness. When a believer is tested, it gives him the opportunity to respond maturely in faith and obedience.

Becoming a Christian does not exempt us from facing difficulties. We will have trials in this world (John 16:33). Yet, Jesus is able to make us victorious. Are you discouraged by circumstances? Do not be. Count every difficulty as a glorious stepping-stone that will lead to joy, endurance, and maturity. God has a purpose in your trials.

A LITTLE HUMOR: A young mother was quite alarmed when her young son swallowed a coin. "Hurry, send for the doctor," she urged her husband. "No, I think we should send for the preacher," replied the father. "The preacher? Why, you don't think he is going to die, do you?" exclaimed the mother. "Oh, no," the husband replied. "But you know our preacher – he can get money out of anybody!"

JULY 14

WHAT SHALL I DO WITH JESUS?

"Pilate said to them, 'Then what shall I do with Jesus who is called Christ?' They all said, 'Crucify Him!'" (Matthew 27:22, NASB)

Pilate, the Roman Governor of Judea, was all that stood between Jesus and the cross. At that critical moment, Pilate asked a very important question that each of us much answer: "What shall I do with Jesus?"

Some Condemn Jesus as a Liar. Atheists, infidels, and other liberals often say that Jesus was deceitful. They refer to Him as an overzealous rabbi at best, or a cunning deceiver at worst. They doubt the validity of His miracles and deny His teachings. In their opinion, He was certainly not who He claimed to be – the almighty Son of God.

Some Classify Jesus as a Lunatic. Still others believe that Jesus was simply some sort of religious extremist who manipulated crowds. They consider Jesus to have been a madman who attracted weak, gullible people.

Some Crown Jesus as Lord. To those who believe the Bible, and have met Jesus personally in salvation, He is Lord. His miracles and teachings are not only real and true, but they are also available and applicable today.

What will you do with Jesus? Your answer to that question is most important. Read the Bible and weigh the evidence. Jesus is no liar or lunatic. He is Lord. Crown Him as your Lord today.

A LITTLE HUMOR: And then there was the undertaker who signed all his correspondence, "Eventually Yours."

JULY 15

REACHING OUT TO GOD

"Draw near to God and He will draw near to you." (James 4:8, NASB)

The little girl's eyes were wide open as she drank in the wonders of the popular vacation attraction called Disney World. The lights, the colors, the costumed characters, and the rides made quite an impression on the young child. But another attraction also captivated her attention. She could not stop talking about the bathroom sinks. Whenever she would hold her little hands over the sink, the water would automatically turn on. When she removed her hands from the sink, the water would automatically turn off. Unknown to her, an electronic sensor turned the water flow on and off. Marveling to her mother, the little girl exclaimed, "Mom, now I know why they call it the Magic Kingdom!"

The simplest things are sometimes the most amazing. All we have to do is go to God in prayer, and the God of the Universe, the Creator of all mankind, hears and answers our prayers. God is not the One who cuts Himself off from us. He is constant; He is always there. It is when we withdraw from Him that the power is cut off, when the Spirit no longer guides and directs us. As long as we are standing in the right place, in Christ, with our hands reaching up to God, God will supply our every need.

A LITTLE HUMOR: A pastor said to a six-year-old boy: "So your mother says a prayer for you each night. Very commendable. What does she say?" The little boy replied, "Thank God, he's in bed!"

JULY 16

PREACHING THE GOOD NEWS

"...my preaching was very plain. I did not use wise and persuasive speeches, but the Holy Spirit was powerful among you." (1 Corinthians 2:4b, NLT)

There's an old story about a small church out in a rural area that needed a pastor to fill in for a time. So they contacted a nearby seminary. The seminary sent a student who had never been outside of the city. When he arrived at the church, the student preacher was shocked to see a hound dog seated on the second row next to the church's lay leader, a crotchety old man who was known to run off young student pastors.

In a heat of righteous indignation the young preacher headed straight toward the dog. He screamed at it and drove it out of the church. The startled congregation held its breath, to see what the lay leader would do, but nothing happened.

After the sermon everyone quickly scooted out the side door and waited for the older man to come out. When he graciously greeted the young pastor at the front door, everyone was taken aback. They had never seen him be that courteous to a student pastor before. The old lay leader extended his hand and said, "I want to thank you for kicking my dog out of church."

The pastor was also shocked, "You want to thank me?"

"Yep," said the older man, "I wouldn't had my dog hear that sermon for nothin'."

Sometimes when a sermon is not presented in an effective manner, it can be rather bad. However, it's not the message, but the messenger that's the problem. A preacher has the privilege of preaching the greatest news the world has ever heard – the good news of Jesus Christ. One would hope that any preacher would do his best in presenting the gospel.

Once when Lord Tennyson was on vacation in a country village he asked an old cleaning woman, "Is there any news?"

"Well," she replied, "there is only one piece of news that I know, and that is that Christ died for my sins."

Tennyson responded, "That is old news, good news, and new news."

The presentation may be good or bad, but the good news of Jesus Christ is still the best news the world has or ever will hear.

A LITTLE HUMOR: A man came out of church, stopped in front of the preacher and said, "Pastor, you are smarter than Albert Einstein." The pastor blushed and said, "Smarter than Einstein? Einstein was the smartest man who ever lived. What makes you think I'm smarter than him?" The man replied, "Einstein was so smart when he spoke people could only understand 5% of what he said. When you speak, people can't understand anything you say."

JULY 17

MAKING A NAME FOR YOURSELF

"A good name is more desirable than great riches; to be esteemed is better than silver or gold." (Proverbs 22:1, NIV)

The name of Mario Mendoza will live forever in the annals of Major League Baseball. Mendoza was an infielder whose last season was 1982. By all rights, his name should be forgotten. But it so happened he was inept with the bat. When the Rangers finally cut him, Mendoza's average was an awful .118. Weekly statistics inevitably had him bringing up the rear among the hitters in his league. If your numbers were below those of Mendoza, you were in big trouble.

The Royal's George Brett, later a Hall of Famer, said, "The first thing I look for in the Sunday papers is to see who's below the Mendoza line." The phrase stuck – and now "The Mendoza Line" is a solid baseball term signifying the dubious feat of hitting below .200.

You're only passing through this world for a short while, but your name lives on. You've got those years to make of it what you will. Your name could become the equivalent of Stradivarius – the ultimate in violins; or Benedict Arnold – a synonym for traitors. Your work is one way to establish your name. Will it mean excellence, perseverance, and integrity? Do more than live up to your name – make it a stamp of quality.

A LITTLE HUMOR: A local pastor joined a community service club and the members thought they would have some fun with him. Under his name on the badge they printed "Hog Caller" as his occupation. Everyone made a big fanfare as the badge was presented. The pastor responded by saying: "I usually am called the 'Shepherd of the Sheep' . . . but you know your people better than I do."

JULY 18

AMERICA'S FAVORITE BOOK

"Heaven and earth will pass away, but My words will not pass away."
(Matthew 24:35, NASB)

According to a new Harris Poll survey, America's number one favorite book is the Bible. Behind the Bible, the classic Margaret Mitchell novel, *Gone With the Wind*, comes in second and J. R. R. Tolkien's *Lord of the Rings* series, J. K. Rowling's *Harry Potter* books and Stephen King's *The Stand* come in third, fourth and fifth respectively.

The Bible is indeed a highly treasured book. Here are four suggestions regarding our response to God's Word – the Bible:

First, **WE MUST CRAVE THE WORD OF GOD (**1 Peter 2:2). The word *desire* does not mean merely to want something, but rather to long for something with all of one's being. The purpose of studying God's Word is to grow spiritually.

Second, **WE MUST RECEIVE THE WORD OF GOD** (1 Thess. 2:13). The word *receive* is found twice in this verse. The first word means to hear and refers to an objective receiving of information. The second word means to welcome, to receive with delight and joy. The people in Thessalonica heard the Word of God with their ears and responded with their hearts.

Third, **WE MUST LIVE BY THE WORD OF GOD** (Luke 4:4). Jesus responded to Satan's temptation by quoting Deuteronomy 8:3. Jesus refused to operate independently of God and His Word.

Fourth, **WE MUST BE DOERS OF THE WORD OF GOD** (James 1:22). It's important to listen to what God's Word says, but it is much more important to obey it.

Melvin Worthington has written, "Christians need to peruse, ponder, and pray over the Scriptures. This takes time, thought, toil, and tenacity. We need to pray – 'Father, help me hear, heed, hold, honor, and herald the Word of God'."

The Bible is America's favorite book. Are you included in that group who puts God's Word at the top of their list of favorite books?

A LITTLE HUMOR: Did you ever notice when you put the two words "The" and "IRS" together it spells "Theirs"?

JULY 19

ME, MYSELF, AND I

"For the love of Christ controls us . . . and He died for all, so that they who live might no longer live for themselves, but for Him who died and rose again on their behalf." (2 Corinthians 5:14-15, NASB)

Warren Wiersbe has written, "When the enemy fails in his attacks from the outside, he then begins to attack from within; and one of his favorite weapons is selfishness. If he can get us thinking about ourselves and what we want, then he will win the victory before we realize that he is even at work."[47] Selfishness is something that comes naturally from all of us. Children often show us just how selfish we can be at times. I found this "Property Laws of a Toddler" and pass it on to you:

1. If I like it, it's mine.
2. If it's in my hand, it's mine.
3. If I can take if from you, it's mine.
4. If I had it a little while ago, it's mine.
5. If it's mine, it must never appear to be yours in any way.
6. If I'm doing or building something, all the pieces are mine.
7. If it looks just like mine, it's mine.
8. If I saw it first, it's mine.
9. If you are playing with something and you put it down, it automatically becomes mine.
10. If it's broken, it's yours.

Selfishness has been referred to as "the sin that bleeds," and like a leech, it does bleed the saint of likeness to Christ, who pleased not Himself but emptied Himself to save others. A selfish Christian is a "Dead-Sea" person – always receiving but never giving or sharing. May each of us be preserved from becoming like the man Cicero described, "A lover of himself without rival."

A LITTLE HUMOR: Many people live on the cafeteria plan – self-service only.

JULY 20

IQ OR FQ?

"Unless you turn from your sins and become as little children, you will never get into the Kingdom of Heaven." (Matthew 18:3, NLT)

---

[47] James R. Adair, Editor. *Be Quoted: From A to Z with Warren W. Wiersbe* (Grand Rapids: Baker Books, 2000, 148.

"Einstein" is synonymous with brilliance, yet a recently auctioned letter by the famed physicist reveals his lack of understanding about God. In a letter written one year before his death, Einstein shared his views about God and the Bible with philosopher Eric Gutkind. The handwritten letter in German stated, "The word God is for me nothing more than the expression and product of human weaknesses, the Bible a collection of honorable but still primitive legends which are nevertheless pretty childish." Einstein further wrote, "For me, the Jewish religion like all other religions is an incarnation of the most childish superstitions." The January, 1954 letter, which was expected to sell for about $15,000, went for $400,000 at a London auction on May 15, 2008. The manuscript holds the musing of a man who changed the face of physics, paved the way for nuclear power, and wrestled with the mysteries of our universe, but could not believe the eternal words of Christ: "unless you turn from your sins and become as little children, you will never get into the Kingdom of Heaven" (Matthew 18:3, NLT). Right standing with God comes through childlike faith. It's FQ (Faith Quotient) not IQ (Intelligence Quotient).

A LITTLE HUMOR: A preacher who suffered extremely strained relations with his congregation was finally appointed chaplain at the state prison. Elated to be rid of him so easily, the people came in great numbers to hear his farewell discourse. The pastor chose as his text, "I go to prepare a place for you . . . that where I am, there you may be also." (John 14:3).

JULY 21

THE ALMOST FORGOTTEN BEATITUDE

"...remember the words of the Lord Jesus, that He said, 'It is more blessed to give than to receive.'" (Acts 20:35, NKJV)

In many Bibles, the words of Jesus are in red. Most of them are found in the four Gospels, but there is one sentence from the lips of Christ that appears in Acts 20:35. We could call it "the almost-forgotten beatitude." There are many Beatitudes in the Bible but only once in the Bible does the phrase "more blessed" occur.

Why is it more blessed to give than to receive? When we receive, we are acting like ourselves; but when we give, we are acting like God. Receiving is us-like. Giving is Christ-like.

As a young man, John D. Rockefeller was strong and husky. When he entered business he drove himself like a slave. He was a millionaire by age 33. By 43, he controlled the largest business in the world. At 53, he was the world's richest man. But he developed a disease called alopecia. His hair fell out and his digestion was so bad he could only eat crackers and milk. One night, unable to sleep, Rockefeller realized he couldn't take a thin dime into the next world. Everything was sand castles, doomed by the inevitable tide. Money was not a commodity to be hoarded, but something to be shared. The next morning, he lost no time transforming his money into blessings for others. He established the Rockefeller Foundation to channel his fortune to needed areas. He gave hundreds of millions to universities, hospitals, mission work, and underprivileged people. The focus of his life changed from "getting" to "giving." The result is that he did not die at age 53. He lived to be 98. Whether or not Rockefeller was a born-again believer, he did discover one of the moral laws of God placed in the universe: Giving is good for us. It enriches our lives.

A LITTLE HUMOR: One Sunday a father gave his son a fifty-cent piece and a dollar. "Put the dollar in the offering," the father said. "Then you can have the fifty cents for ice cream." When the boy came home he still had the dollar. "Why didn't you put the dollar in the offering?" his father asked. "Well, it was like this," the boy answered. "The preacher said God loves a cheerful giver. I could give the fifty-cent piece a lot more cheerfully than I could the dollar."

JULY 22

ENCOURAGE ONE ANOTHER

"Therefore encourage one another, and build up one another, just as you also are doing." (1 Thessalonians 5:11, NASB)

When geese migrate, they can be seen flying in a V-shaped formation. To us on the ground, it is a thing of beauty; but to the geese it is essential for survival. If you watch them, you will observe that at certain intervals relative to the strength of the wind, the lead bird, who is doing the most work by breaking the force of the wind against him, will drop off and fly at the end of the formation. It's been discovered that the flapping wings create an uplift of air, and the effect is greater at the rear of the formation. So the geese take turns uplifting one another. By cooperating and working together, the geese achieve long migrations that otherwise would be exceedingly difficult for even the strongest.

It is in a similar manner that God has called us as His people. As believers in Christ, we are to lift one another up through prayer. We are to share material means and heart to heart friendship in caring. And we can go further into godliness than we ever would be able to if we attempt our pilgrimage all alone.

William Barclay has written, "One of the highest of human duties is the duty of encouragement...The world is full of discouragers. We have a Christian duty to encourage one another."

A LITTLE HUMOR: A brilliant magician was performing on an ocean liner. But every time he did a trick, a talking parrot on stage would say, "It's a trick. He's a phony. That's not magic." Then one evening during a storm, the ship sank while the magician was performing. The parrot and the magician ended up in the same lifeboat. For several days they just glared at each other, neither saying a word to the other. Finally the parrot said, "All right, smarty, you and your stupid tricks. What did you do with the ship?"

JULY 23

A WORD OF ENCOURAGEMENT

"And when he wanted to go across to Achaia, the brethren encouraged him and wrote to the disciples to welcome him; and when he had arrived, he greatly helped those who had believed through grace." (Acts 18:27, NASB)

Several months before Linda and I were married she received a letter from a pastor's wife, a longtime family friend of her parents, who wanted to encourage her as she was about to become a pastor's wife. She wrote, "There is no life more interesting and rewarding than to be married to a Baptist preacher. It isn't always the easiest life, but it will be a happy life. God has called your husband to be a pastor – God's messenger. This is the most important call God can extend to a man, and He has allowed you to share in this." My wife has kept this letter and from time to time she has taken it out and reread it. Each time she is encouraged and reassured that what this dear lady wrote to her is true.

Words of encouragement are always helpful for those to whom they are spoken or written. William Barclay has written: "One of the highest of human duties is the duty of encouragement . . . Many a time a word of praise or thanks or appreciation or cheer has kept a man on his feet. Blessed is the man who speaks such a word."[48]

In his book, *Strengthening Your Grip,* Charles Swindoll defines encouragement as "the art of inspiring others with renewed courage, spirit, or hope. When we encourage others we spur them on, we stimulate and affirm them."[49]

You don't have to be a pastor's wife to need encouragement. We all have vulnerable moments, moments where we need to be reminded of God's love and the adequacy of His provisions. All of us can use a good word of encouragement from time to time. Mark Twain once said, "I can live for two weeks on a good compliment."

But what if there is no one around to encourage you? If that's your predicament, it's not a lost cause because you can follow the example of Paul who stated there was a time when he really needed someone to encourage him, but all had deserted him (2 Timothy 4:16). At such a time he said, "But the Lord stood with me and strengthened me" (2 Timothy 4:17). The Lord has promised to never leave us nor desert us (Hebrews 13:5). Take courage from words of encouragement spoken by either others or the Lord.

---

[48] William Barclay, "The Letter to the Hebrews" in *The Daily Study Bible* (Philadelphia: The Westminster Press, 1957), 137-138.
[49] Charles R. Swindoll, *Strengthening Your Grip* (Waco, Texas; Word Books Publisher, 1982), 44.

A LITTLE HUMOR: A man went into a restaurant to order breakfast. A rough looking waitress came out to take his order. "What do you want?" "Some eggs and a few kind words," he replied. She just stared at him and walked toward the kitchen. After a while she returned and flopped the plate of eggs in front of him. The man looked at the eggs and then looked at her and asked, "What about the kind words?" She said, "Don't eat them eggs!"

JULY 24

DON'T PLAY AROUND WITH SIN

"When the woman saw that the tree was good for food, and that it was a delight to the eyes, and that the tree was desirable to make one wise, she took from its fruit and ate: and she gave also to her husband with her, and he ate." (Genesis 3:6, NASB)

In 1939, a coast guard vessel was cruising the Canadian Arctic when the men spotted a polar bear stranded on an ice floe. It was quite a novelty for the seamen, who threw the bear salami, peanut butter, and chocolate bars. Then they ran out of food. Unfortunately, the polar bear hadn't run out of appetite, so he proceeded to board their vessel. The men on ship were terrified and opened the fire hoses on the bear. The polar bear loved it and raised his paws in the air to get the water under his armpits. We don't know how they did it, but eventually they forced the polar bear to return to his ice pad — but not before teaching these seamen a horrifying lesson about feeding polar bears.[50]

Some people make the same mistake with sin that these sailors nearly made with the polar bear. They begin feeding it — a little at a time without thinking through the consequences. It is so easy to be lured into the betrayal of sin. It seems such a trifling thing at first -- a mild flirtation, a few dollars taken from the till, or a small misrepresentation on our income tax form. But families have been lost, reputations have been lost, fortunes have been lost, because someone stepped across a line that should never have been crossed.

Eve flirted with temptation. The devil deceived her. The Bible says she "saw that the tree was good for food, and that it was pleasant to the eyes, and a tree to be desired to make one wise." (Genesis 3:6). Her act of disobedience led to the disobedience of Adam and both of their actions brought sin into the world (Romans 5:12). Adam and Eve never gave a second thought about the consequences of their sin.

Temptation must be avoided at all cost. If you are in the presence of evil, get out of there. If you are being tempted, flee! You can cozy up to temptation for only so long. Before you know it, it will have you in its snare. That which you think is of

---

[50] Erma Bombeck, *All I Know About Animal Behavior* (New York: Harper Collins, 1995).

little consequence will have an enormous impact. As someone said, "If you dance with the devil, you always end up with burn marks on your suit." Avoid sin.

A LITTLE HUMOR: A Sunday school teacher was teaching her class about the difference between right and wrong. "Okay children, let's take an example. If I were to get into a man's pocket and take his billfold with all his money, what would I be?" A little boy raised his hand, and with a confident smile, he blurted out, "You'd be his wife!"

JULY 25

A WARM HAND IN THE DARK

"Then he gave her his hand and lifted her up..." (Acts 9:41a, NKJV)

When Helen Keller was a little girl, her parents took her to the home of Alexander Graham Bell, the inventor of the telephone. Bell was greatly moved by the plight of this child who could neither see nor hear. He took her in his arms and she felt the tenderness of his concern. It was partly by the methods introduced by Bell that Helen was taught to communicate. One day, she wrote a letter to the inventor in which she said, "Dear Mr. Bell, I love you." More than 30 years later when Bell was 71, Helen again wrote him, "Even before my teacher came, you held out a warm hand to me in the dark."

Who among us doesn't need a warm hand in the dark occasionally? More than that, there are those around us who are going through some dark times that could use the encouragement that comes from a warm hand being extended to them. Look around you. Stretch out your hand to someone who may be in the dark.

A LITTLE HUMOR: A man's wife wasn't feeling well one Sunday so he went to church by himself. When he got home, she asked him how he liked it. He said, "I didn't." She asked, "Why? What didn't you like?" He said, "We sang choruses instead of hymns." She said, "Paw, what's the difference in a chorus and a hymn?" He said, "If I came home and said, 'Mama, I'm home', that would be a hymn. But if I came home and said, 'Mama, dear Mama, sweet Mama, precious Mama, loving Mama, good Mama, I'm home, I'm home, I'm home. I'm home.' That would be a chorus."

JULY 26

MADAME CURIE

"Your word I have hidden in my heart, that I might not sin against You."
(Psalm 119:11, NKJV)

Madame Marie Curie holds her place in history as a pioneer in the study of radioactivity. In 1903, she was the first woman to win the Nobel Prize, capturing the honor in physics. Then, in 1911, she received a second Nobel Prize, this one in chemistry.

Such a wonderful contribution did not come without tremendous sacrifice. Madame Curie died of leukemia caused by prolonged exposure to radioactive materials. Even today, scholars who wish to read her handwritten journals and lab papers must wear protective clothing because these archives are still radioactive.

No one today would approach radioactive material without protection. But many seem unconcerned about exposure to the dangers of sin. The Bible warns us against sinful attitudes, speech, and behavior.

Obedience to God's law is a spiritual safeguard from sin and its deadly consequences. The psalmist also wrote, "Your word I have hidden in my heart, that I might not sin against You" (Psalm 119:11, NKJV).

Madame Curie didn't know about the serious health dangers of exposure to radioactivity. But God has given us ample warning about the dangers of sin. Let's apply daily what we read in His life-giving Book.

A LITTLE HUMOR: Planning is an important part of life. However, it can be overdone. I heard about a woman who married four men in this order: a banker, an actor, a preacher, and a mortician. She said that one was for the money, two for the show, three to get ready, and four to go.

JULY 27

MAN, THAT'S LIVING!

"Your gold and your silver have rusted; and their rust will be a witness against you and will consume your flesh like fire. It is in the last days that you have stored up your treasure!" (James 5:3, NASB)

A wealthy man many years ago was somewhat of a free spirit and requested a very special burial congruent to his lifestyle. After his death the burial took place as he had directed: donned in a sports jacket and hat, with his cigar in his mouth, he was placed in a sitting position at the steering wheel of his brand new red Cadillac convertible, with the speedometer set at 80 mph – then he was lowered into the tomb. A friend nearby looked through his tears and said, "Man, that's living!"

The truth is that is not living at all. Those niceties of life may be put in the grave, but that is exactly where they stay. In the East there were three main sources of wealth. There was food (James 5:2a): corn and grain, that is , the kind of wealth that can rot. There were clothes (James 5:2b): garments. Even gold and silver would corrode (James 5:3). To concentrate on material things is not only to concentrate on a decaying delusion, it is to concentrate on a self-produced destruction. Someone has written:

Out of this life I never shall take,
Things of silver and gold I make.

All that I cherish and hoard away,
After I leave, on the earth will stay.
Though I have toiled for a painting rare,
To hang on the wall I must leave it there.
Tho I call it mine and boast its worth,
I must give it up when I quit the earth.
All that I gather and all that I keep,
I must leave behind when I fall asleep.

A LITTLE HUMOR: A new pastor came to the church and everyone was excited. The first Sunday he stood to deliver his sermon and said, "If I'm gonna be pastor of this church, it's gonna walk." And the people replied with an enthusiastic, "Amen, let her walk, brother, let her walk."

He said, "And, furthermore, if I'm gonna be pastor of this church, she is gonna run." And the people replied, "Amen, let her run, brother, let her run."

He said, "More than that, if I'm gonna be the pastor of this church it's gonna fly." They replied, "Amen, brother, let her fly, let her fly."

Then he said, "If this church is gonna fly, then it is gonna to take money." They replied, "Let her walk, brother, let her walk!"

JULY 28

WHAT IS A FRIEND?

"I have called you friends." (John 15:15, NKJV)

Socrates once asked a simple old man what he was most thankful for. The man replied, "That being such as I am, I have had the friends I have had."

Some friends are fickle. In the book of Proverbs we read, "Wealth makes many friends, but the poor is separated from his friend" (Proverbs 19:4). A true friend, however, "loves at all times" (Proverbs 17:17) and "sticks closer than a brother" (Proverbs 18:24).

Our English word *friend* comes from the same root as the word *freedom.* A genuine friend sets us free to be who and what we are. We can pour out our doubts and talk freely without reservations.

A friend also affirms our worth. Queen Victoria said of William Gladstone, "When I am with him, I feel I am with one of the most important leaders in the world." But of Benjamin Disraeli she said, "He makes me feel as if I am one of the most important leaders of the world."

Christians have an inside track on making and being friends because we are a part of one family. Haven't you felt that family tie while talking with a stranger – only to discover that you had Christ in common? And no wonder – He is the truest Friend anyone can have.

A LITTLE HUMOR: A pastor was accustomed to ending his sermons with a question and answer time. A bright-eyed young lady sat on the front row listening eagerly. When he asked for questions, her hand shot up like a roman candle. "How did Jonah survive three days and three nights in the belly of the whale?" she asked. The pastor responded, "I don't know. But, when I get to heaven I will ask him." She responded, "But, suppose he's not in heaven?" The pastor then replied, "In that case, you ask him."

JULY 29

THE SWEETEST THING YOU'LL EVER TASTE

"How sweet are Your words to my taste, sweeter than honey to my mouth."

(Psalm 119:103, NKJV)

In 1928, William Dreyer, ice cream maker, and Joseph Edy, candy maker, shook hands on a partnership to make the highest quality ice cream possible. Dreyer's ice cream expertise and Edy's skill in making candy proved to be a winning combination. They opened a small ice cream factory at 3315 Grand Avenue in Oakland, California, and their ice cream factory quickly became a gathering place for people to eat a sundae, pick up a five-layer ice cream cake, and other ice cream products. One night, Dreyer was whipping up a batch of chocolate ice cream and decided to add nuts and marshmallows. It was 1929; the stock market had crashed and tough times we beginning to face people. Dreyer and Edy picked a name for the ice cream creation that would give folks something to smile about. "Rocky Road" became a blockbuster flavor and remains one of the best sellers of all time.

Before you rush off to the refrigerator, let me tell you about something that is better than a bowl of "Rocky Road" ice cream. It is sweet as honey to the mouth. I am speaking of God's wonderful Word. The Psalmist found that the sweetest thing he had ever "tasted" was God's blessed Words. He declares in Psalm 19:10, "More to be desired are they than gold; yes, than much fine gold; sweeter also than honey and the honeycomb" (NKJV). Today, taste the wonderful Word of God. There is no sweeter taste! Taste all you want, for it is good for you.

A LITTLE HUMOR: Here is a love-letter lament: "Dearest Jimmy, No words could ever express the great unhappiness I've felt since breaking our engagement. Please say you'll take me back. No one could ever take your place in my heart, so please forgive me. I love you, I love you, I love you! Yours forever, Marie. P. S. And congratulations on winning the lottery."

JULY 30

BAD BREATH --- FOUL MOUTH

"Keep your tongue from evil and your lips from speaking deceit."
(Psalm 34:13, NASB)

According to the health section of the September, 2008 *Reader's Digest*, bad breath (also called halitosis) is caused not by smelly foods, but by bacteria that is trapped by crevices on the tongue, producing the smelly compounds. Bacteria thrives on the tongue, not just on teeth and gums. The article goes on to suggest the use of a tongue scraper twice a day to help get rid of the odor. "Think of your tongue as a carpet. Some people have shags that are harder to keep clean," says Anthony Dailley, DDS, of the Center for Breath Treatment near San Francisco. Dailley also states that one should not use alcohol-based mouthwashes; they dry out the mouth making the problem worse. Drink lots of water to flush the bacteria away.

The tongue can give off a foul odor in another way too. James 3:10 states, "Out of the same mouth proceed blessing and cursing. My brethren, these things ought not to be so" (NKJV). Swearing is neither smart, sensible, nor worthwhile. A salesman who was known for using profanity quite often was asked if he were paid anything for swearing. The salesman replied, "No." "Well," came the answer, "you certainly work cheap. You lay aside your character as a gentleman, inflict pain on your friends, break one of the Ten Commandments, lose your own soul, and all for nothing!" A person who uses the name of the Lord in vain will not easily run to the One he profaned in the hour of need. Proverbs 18:10 says, "The name of the Lord is a strong tower; the righteous runs into it and is safe."

One might excuse his use of profanity by saying, "It's just a bad habit." But a criminal arraigned before a judge for stealing could never hope to gain acquittal by pleading that stealing was just a bad habit with him. No, a foul tongue needs a good tongue scraper.

A LITTLE HUMOR: For the benefit of people taking flash pictures, a sign was placed near the speaker's platform. It read, "Do not photograph the speaker while he is addressing the audience. Shoot him as he leaves the platform"

JULY 31

"PRAY-ERS" AND "DO-ERS"

"Then Hezekiah took the letter from the hand of the messengers and read it, and he went up to the house of the lord and spread it out before the Lord. Hezekiah prayed before the Lord . . ." (2 Kings 19:14-15a, NASB)

Although prayer is the most important thing we can do, it is rarely the only thing we can do. If reading the account of Hezekiah's response to the threat of an attack by Sennacherib of Assyria (2 Kings 18:13-37) gives us the impression that all he did was pray, we misread it.

Aware that Assyria would attack, Hezekiah prepared his city and his people, as 2 Chronicles 12:2-8 indicates. He had a long tunnel dug through the rock form the Gihon Spring to the Pool of Siloam to protect the water supply (2 Kings 20:20). He also rebuilt the existing city walls, added exterior walls, reorganized his military, and rearmed the people. But in the midst of these preparations, his message to his people was "be strong and courageous, do not fear or be dismayed because of the king of Assyria nor because of all the horde that is with him, for the one with us is greater than the one with him. With him is only an arm of flesh, but with us is the Lord our God to help us and to fight our battles. (2 Chronicles 32:7-8).

Hezekiah knew the need for preparation, but he also knew that plans have limits. Deliverance would have to come from the Lord.

Writing about Hezekiah's preparation and prayer, Gary Inrig said, "We need to pray first, and we need to pray last. Sometimes all we can do is pray. But more often, we can also plan, and prepare. Christians tend to fall into two opposing camps – the "do-ers" and the "pray-ers." Hezekiah shows us we need to be both.[51]

Are you under an attack today? Is it your health? Is it a financial need? Is it a ruptured relationship? Is it a temptation? We need to follow Hezekiah's example and Inrig's advice, make what preparations we can and then pray. Do both and leave the rest to God.

A LITTLE HUMOR: An elderly preacher is reported to have prayed the following prayer each day: "O Lord, give me a backbone as big as a saw log and ribs like the large timbers under the church floor. Put iron shoes on my feet and galvanized breeches on my body. Give me a rhinoceros hide for skin, and hang up a wagonload of determination in the gable-end of my soul. Help me to sign the contract to fight the devil as long as I've got a tooth – and then gum him until I die."

---

[51] Gary Inrig, *Holman OT Commentary: 1 & 2 Kings* (Nashville: Broadman & Holman Publishers, 2003), 321.

AUGUST 1

THE GOD WHO SEES

"Oh that I knew where I might find Him . . . I go forward but He is not there, and backward, but I cannot perceive Him; when He acts on the left, I cannot behold Him; He turns on the right, I cannot see Him. But He knows the way I take . . ."
(Job 23:3, 8-10a, NASB)

Have you ever been in a difficult situation and needed the Lord's help but it seemed as hard as you tried you couldn't find Him? You wonder where God is when you are walking through the pain of divorce, or the heartbreak of watching a loved one die.

It's not wrong to feel that God has abandoned you in such a time. Job said, "I've got a case to present to the Lord if only I could find Him. I've looked high and low for God but I can't find Him anywhere. I've looked north, south, east and west. I've looked on my right hand and on my left, but He's not to be found." Then Job rose to a higher level of faith and declared, "I can't see Him, but it doesn't matter because I know He sees me."

You may recall the story of Hagar who fled from the household of Abraham and Sarah. Pregnant and alone, she wandered in the barren desert. The Lord found her near a spring and told her to go back to Abraham and Sarah. He also told her to name her son Ishmael, which means "God hears," because the Lord had heard of her misery. She replied with one of the wonderful statements of the Old Testament, "You are the God who sees me." (Genesis 16:13). She actually gave God a name – El Roi – which means in Hebrew – "the God who sees."

Here is a name of God for those of us who are going through trials – El Roi – "the God who sees." You may not see Him but He sees you. He knows what you are going through. To quote Job, "He knows the way I take."

Ethel Waters made popular the song "His Eye Is on the Sparrow." The refrain to that song reads, "His eye is on the sparrow, and I know He watches me." Yes, there may be times when you cannot see Him, but He can see you.

A LITTLE HUMOR: A kindly parson who had just married a young couple had a parting word for the groom: "Son, God bless you. You're at the end of all your troubles." A year later, the groom returned to the scene and moaned. "What a year I've gone through! And you're the man who told me I was at the end of my troubles." "So I did, son," replied the parson. "I just didn't tell you which end."[52]

---

[52] Bob Phillips, *The Awesome Book of Heavenly Humor* (Eugene, Oregon: Harvest House Publishers, 2003), 188.

AUGUST 2

A QUESTION WE ALL ASK

"Good Teacher, what must I do to get to heaven?" (Mark 10:17, LB)

An eminent psychologist was called to testify in court. A severe no-nonsense professional, she sat down in the witness chair unaware that its rear legs were set precariously on the back of the raised platform. "Will you please state your name?" asked the district attorney. Tilting back in her chair, the psychologist opened her mouth to answer, but instead catapulted head-over-heels backward and landed in a stack of exhibits and recording equipment. Everyone watched in stunned silence as she extricated herself, rearranged her disheveled dress and hair and was reseated on the witness stand. The glare she directed at onlookers dared anyone to so much as smirk. "Well, doctor," continued the district attorney without changing expression, "perhaps we could start with an easier question."

A young man came to Jesus with what he thought was a deep and challenging question: "Good Teacher, what must I do to get to heaven?" (Mark 10:17, LB). That's what we all want to know, isn't it? What must we do to get to heaven? Entry into heaven is determined not by what we do, but what Christ has done for us. All we can do is receive it. If you think you earned Frequent Flyer points for heaven by being in worship services, you are mistaken. If you think that putting a fat check in the offering plate will get you through the pearly gates, you are in for a surprise. Heaven is a matter of being, not of doing. If you have received Christ into your life, there is nothing more you need do. It's already done.

Jesus said to this young man, "You lack only one thing." Ah, this is what this man had come expecting. He only needed one thing. Get out the check book. Whatever the Master asked of him, he knew he could afford, if not in money, at least in time. Support the building program? Work with the youth? Teach a Sunday School class? Knock on doors? "Go and sell all you have and give the money to the poor — and you shall have treasure in heaven — and come, follow me" is what Jesus said in response to his question. And like the lady psychologist, he catapulted head-over-heels backward. Well, that's not exactly how Mark tells it. He says, "Then the man's face fell and he went sadly away, for he was very rich." What he needed was simply to receive the grace that God was ready to pour out upon him. Author Max Lucado put it this way: "You don't need a system, you need a Savior. You don't need a resume, you need a Redeemer."

"How do we get to heaven?" is a question we all have. Jesus gives the same answer to everyone: "Follow Me."

A LITTLE HUMOR: A young preacher had just gone to his new pastorate. His picture had been in the newspaper, in the church mail-outs, and he was on television. So he thought everyone in town should know him. He went to the nursing home to visit an elderly member of his congregation. As he walked down the hall she was sitting in a wheelchair outside her room. He walked up to her with a smile on his face, stuck out his hand, and said, "Do you know who I am?" She replied, "No, but if you'll ask the lady at the nurse's station, she may be able to tell you.

AUGUST 3

TEMPER! TEMPER!

"He who is slow to anger is better than the mighty, and he who rules his spirit than he who takes a city." (Proverbs 16:32, NKJV)

Former heavyweight-boxing champion Mike Tyson is just as scary out of the ring as he is inside of it. Tyson was accused of battery by ex-wife Robin Givens during their brief marriage in the late '80s. But Tyson's anger issues really came to a head during a 1997 boxing match with Evander-Holyfield. During the fight, Tyson stopped throwing punches and started biting Holyfield on the ear. Holyfield lost part of his ear, and Tyson lost his boxing license for more than a year.

We may not like to admit it, but all of us have a temper. I know I do, and sometimes it's hard to control. Now, before you straighten up your halo, why don't you be honest and admit that every once in a while you "fly off the handle" and express your temper, too.

Perhaps the author of Proverbs 16:32 saw a conquering hero returning from a battle only to see him lose his temper over some trivial matter. The story is told about a friend of Alexander the Great who became intoxicated and began to ridicule the emperor in front of his men. Blinded by anger and quick as lightning, Alexander snatched a spear from the hand of a soldier and hurled it at his friend, killing him. Overcome with guilt, Alexander attempted to take his own life. Alexander the Great conquered many cities but failed to control his own spirit.

Ben Franklin called anger the most expensive luxury in life. Someone else has said that "anger" is only one letter short of "danger." A woman came to Billy Sunday and asked him to pray for her bad temper. Then, embarrassed, she added, "But it's over in a minute." "So is a shotgun blast," answered Sunday, "but it blows everything to bits."

You can lose so many things because of your anger: your friends, your job, your family, your health. It must be brought under control. Jesus was despised and rejected of men, yet He cried from the cross, "Father, forgive them." We must learn to love like Jesus, pray like Jesus, and act like Jesus. We must surrender to Jesus and let His beauty be seen in us.

A LITTLE HUMOR: When a golfer was asked why he bought a new putter, he said, "The old one didn't float."

AUGUST 4

CHRIST IS OUR PEACE

"For He Himself is our peace, who made both groups into one and broke down the barrier of the dividing wall." (Ephesians 2:14, NASB)

"Christ the Redeemer of the Andes" is a statue of Christ commemorating a series of peace and boundary treaties between Argentina and Chile. The twenty-six foot statue holds out its right hand in blessing over the disputed nations that for years have quarreled about boundaries. The left hand clings to a cross, and under the feet is the western hemisphere. Sitting on a base of granite and fashioned from the very cannons that once were used to strike terror into the hearts of the Chileans, it stands at the point where the two countries meet, a symbol of peace. One plaque at its base reads, "He is our peace, Who hath made us one." At the dedication ceremony, the statue was presented to the world as a sign of the victory of good will.

If there is any one thing our world needs today more than anything else, it is peace. Not just any peace and certainly not the kind of peace the world has to offer. The world's peace never lasts. Just think of all the peace treaties that have been made and then broken. The peace we need is the peace that only God can give through His Son, the Lord Jesus Christ.

The One who said to the waves "peace, be still" (Mark 4:39), said to the woman with the issue of blood, "go in peace" (Mark 5:34). The One who stood in the midst of the troubled disciples and said, "Peace be unto you" (Luke 24:36) is the "Prince of Peace" (Isaiah 9:6). Real peace can be found in Christ alone.

Christ is more than a statue commemorating peace; He is a blessed person living in our hearts who says, "My peace I give unto you" (John 14:27).

A LITTLE HUMOR: Three little boys were bragging about who had the fastest father. The first boy said, "My dad can run a mile in only five minutes." The second boy countered, "My dad can mow the whole lawn in only ten minutes." The third boy jumped in," My dad's the fastest of all. His job ends at 5 p.m. and he's always home by 3 p.m."

AUGUST 5

WHEN PEOPLE RUB YOU THE WRONG WAY

"Be gentle and ready to forgive; never hold grudges. Remember, the Lord forgave you, so you must forgive others." (Colossians 3:13, LB)

Do you remember when Jimmy Johnson took over as coach of the Dallas Cowboys? The Cowboys had been on a downward spiral, but within a few years he rebuilt the organization and took them to the Super Bowl – and won! The next year he did it again. After winning his second Super Bowl, what did owner Jerry Jones do? Give Jimmy Johnson a raise? No, he fired him! Together they had rebuilt the Cowboy dynasty and had accomplished the seemingly impossible, but they couldn't get along. Winning wasn't compensation enough, and Texas just wasn't big enough for both men's massive egos, so they parted company. This serves to remind us that even when things are going well, it's hard to maintain unity.

As you go through life you're going to find some people simply rub you the wrong way. Maybe they don't do anything specific – but there's something about them that gets under your skin. Also, there will be times when you find that you rub someone else the wrong way. You might not have anything against this person, but they've got something against you. No matter how hard you try, they've decided in advance not to like you.

The key to forgiving others is remembering how much God has forgiven you. Is it difficult for you to forgive someone who has rubbed you the wrong way when God has forgiven you so much? Realizing God's infinite love and forgiveness can help you love and forgive others.

A LITTLE HUMOR: In a domestic-relations court, the judge listened intently to both sides in a case against an elderly man who was charged by his wife with non-support. After all the evidence was in, the judge told the defendant: "You haven't taken proper care of this good woman and I'm going to give her $100 a month." The defendant beamed with pleasure. "That's mighty nice of you, Judge," he said, "and I'll give her a few dollars from time to time myself."

AUGUST 6

IT'S YOUR MOVE

"Draw near to God and He will draw near to you . . ." (James 4:8a, NASB)

A married couple was driving down the road. The wife turned to her husband and said, "What's happened with us?"

"What do you mean?" the husband asked.

She said, "We're not like we used to be."

"How did we use to be?" the husband asked.

"We were closer. More connected. We held hands all the time. In fact, here's a perfect example right now. Remember when we'd get in the car, and we'd sit right next to each other?"

The husband turned to her and said, "Who moved?"

This story illustrates an important Biblical principle that we must always remember. If you're not as close to God as you used to be, you're the one who moved. God didn't move. If you want to get back to where you used to be, you need to move in His direction. In drawing near to God, I recommend three things.

First, **draw near early.** Make it a habit to begin each day in prayer. C.S. Lewis once wrote, "The real problem of the Christian life comes where people do not usually look for it. It comes the very moment you wake up each morning." Psalm 5:3 reads, "In the morning, O Lord, You will hear my voice; in the morning I will order my prayer to You and eagerly watch."

Second, **draw near often.** Luke 5:16 reads, "But Jesus Himself would often slip away to the wilderness and pray." Look for every opportunity to grab a few minutes of solitude to spend in prayer.

Third, **draw near now.** Don't wait until you're better, because you never will be. Most goals take a long time to accomplish. But there's one goal you can accomplish immediately. You can be closer to God . . . right now!

There is a song we sometimes sing. We would sing, "Draw me nearer, nearer, nearer blessed Lord, to thy precious bleeding side." It's a beautiful hymn and I'm not suggesting we stop singing it. What I am saying is: God has already done all He can for you through His Son Jesus Christ. Now, it's your time to draw near to Him. Here is a rock solid promise on which you can build your spiritual life. If you draw near to God, He will draw near to you. It's your move.

A LITTLE HUMOR: "So far today, God, I've done all right. I haven't gossiped, I haven't lost my temper. I haven't been selfish, grumpy, nasty, or overindulgent. I'm really glad about that. But in a few minutes, God, I'm going to get out of bed, and from then on I'm probably going to need a lot more help. Thank you. In Jesus' name, amen."

AUGUST 7

WHAT HAPPENS IN VEGAS STAYS IN VEGAS

"Each of us shall give account of himself to God." (Romans 14:12, NKJV)

There is a cartoon of two men sitting in hell and one said to the other, "I was under the impression that what happened in Vegas stayed in Vegas." The fact is, it won't stay there. It's going all the way to the throne of God because you will have to tell it yourself.

The Greek word for account is *logos.* It means to speak something. One day we shall stand before the Lord and we shall have to make a defense for ourselves. In the American judicial system, a person cannot be compelled to testify against himself/herself. He or she can plead the Fifth Amendment. But in the court of eternity there is no provision for the Fifth Amendment. We must all give an account of ourselves to God.

Duke McCall, former president of Southern Seminary, former executive director of the Southern Baptist Convention, former president of the Baptist World Alliance, tells that his father served as city judge in Memphis, Tennessee. When Duke was about sixteen years old he was arrested for speeding. He was going thirty mph in a twenty mph speed zone. His father's policy was to charge $2 a mile or two days in jail for every mile over the speed limit. He was going 10 mph over the speed limit, so his fine would be $20 or twenty days in jail.

When he was taken before his father, Duke said, "Dad gave no indication that he recognized me when I appeared in his courtroom – just another case: "Guilty or not guilty?" 'Guilty,' I answered. I just stood there on one foot and then the other because there wasn't anything for me to do but go to jail. Finally he said, "Come to the bench.' Then he gave me twenty dollars and said, 'Go pay your fine.'"

That's a beautiful picture of how it will be for us on the judgment day. The scriptures say, "My little children, these things I write to you, so that you may not sin. And if anyone sins, we have an Advocate with the Father, Jesus Christ the righteous. And He Himself is the propitiation for our sins, and not for us only but also for the whole world" (1 John 2:1-2, NKJV)

On that solemn day when we stand before God, Jesus will be with us and He will say, "Father, I represent the accused. He is guilty by his own admission, but I paid the price for him on Calvary and he should go free." And in the court of eternity, God will rap on His desk and say, "Penalty paid, you are free to go."

We are ultimately accountable to God. Our accountability is as sure as God is. It is as broad as humanity is. It is as personal as the individual is. But redemption has been provided through the blood of Jesus Christ.

A LITTLE HUMOR: A Texan was in New York City and needed to make a phone call. When He got the operator she said, "That will be $1.75, please." He exclaimed, "$1.75! Why in Texas, we can call hell and back for less than that." She replied, "Yes, but in Texas that would be a local call."

AUGUST 8

WALKING IN GENTLENESS

"I . . . implore you to walk in a manner worthy of the calling with which you have been called, with all . . . gentleness . . ." (Ephesians 4:1-2)

What does the word gentleness suggest to you? Someone who is weak? Does it bring to mind a picture of a Caspar Milquetoast or a Barney Fife? Many people have trouble thinking of themselves in terms of gentleness. But gentleness that is referred to in the Bible might best be illustrated by a quote by Carl Sandburg when he described Abraham Lincoln as a man of "velvet steel." Someone has well said, "Nothing is so strong as gentleness; nothing so gentle as real strength." As Christians we are to walk in gentleness. Ephesians 4:1-2 reads, "I...implore you to walk in a manner worthy of the calling with which you have been called, with all humility and gentleness, with patience, showing tolerance for one another in love." I suggest four ways we are to show gentleness.

First, **we should be gentle in what we say.** Proverbs 15:1 reads, "A gentle answer turns away wrath, but a harsh word stirs up anger." Do you argue at home? At work? At school? Often it is not so much what we say but the way we say it.

Second, **we should be gentle in what we hear.** In Job 12:11 we read, "Does not the ear test words, as the palate tastes its food?" Have you ever wished when unkind words were being spoken that you could close your ears and not have to listen? Woodchucks can do just that. The woodchuck spends a great deal of time digging tunnels. The Lord has provided him with muscles he can operate to close his ears tightly so dirt won't get in them. Wouldn't it be wonderful if we had this same ability?

Third, **we should be gentle in what we think.** First Corinthians 4:5 says, "So be careful not to jump to conclusions before the Lord returns as to whether or not someone is faithful. When the Lord comes, he will bring our deepest secrets to light and will reveal our private motives." Someone has said, "Keep your thoughts in line, or they'll lead you astray."

Fourth, we should be gentle in what we do. In Bud Blake's comic strip, "Tiger," a little boy stands and watches a girl carry a football past him. When his teammates criticize him for not tackling her, he says, "I was afraid I'd hurt her." The last frame of the strip shows this little boy walking home with head down and shoulders slumped saying, "I got thrown out of the game for unnecessary gentleness." Titus 2:7 reads, "In all things show yourself to be an example of good deeds."

Christ emerges from the pages of the New Testament as our eternal contemporary. His gentleness inspires us to imitate Him. Gentleness truly is the most powerful of weaknesses.

A LITTLE HUMOR: After a hard-preached sermon on gossip, a lady came crying to the preacher. "I want to lay my tongue on the altar." The preacher replied, "We may have to do this in two meetings, our altar is only 14 feet long."

AUGUST 9

SAIL ON

"He guides me in the paths of righteousness for His name's sake." (Psalm 23:3b)

The word "paths" is a symbol, not of rest, but of progress. What would you think of a sheep that persistently sat down and refused to go on? And what would you think of a Christian who acts very much in the same manner?

In his book, A Shepherd Looks at Psalm 23, Phillip Keller writes: "Sheep are notorious creatures of habit. If left to themselves they will follow the same trails until they become ruts; graze the same hills until they turn to desert wastes; pollute their own ground until it is corrupt with disease and parasites. The greatest single safeguard which a shepherd has in handling his flock is to keep them on the move."[53]

You will notice in the New Testament that the Christian life is depicted as a journey of forward progress:

"Walk" – Colossians 2:6, "Therefore as you have received Christ Jesus the Lord, so walk in Him."

"Run" -- Hebrews 12:1, "Therefore, since we have so great a cloud of witnesses surrounding us, let us also lay aside every encumbrance and the sin which so easily entangles us, and let us run with endurance the race that is set before us."

"Step" – 1 Peter 2:21, "For you have been called for this purpose, since Christ also suffered for you, leaving you an example for you to follow in His steps."

"Paths" – Psalm 23:3, "He guides me in the paths of righteousness for His name's sake."

---

[53] Phillip Keller, *A Shepherd Looks at Psalm 23* (Grand Rapids: Zondervan Publishing House, 1970), 70.

"The Way" – Acts 9:1-2, "Now Saul, still breathing threats and murder against" the disciples of the Lord, went to the high priest and asked for letters from him to the synagogues at Damascus, so that if he found any belonging to the Way, both men and women, he might bring them bound to Jerusalem."

We are not meant to be today where we were yesterday, but always farther on.

When Christopher Columbus was on his voyage which ended in the discovery of the New Word, the log-book of his ship contained entries of exciting events of both good or evil omens; but day after day there was nothing to record, and so page after page of that sea diary contained the same, almost monotonous sentence: "Today we sailed on!" Over and over and over again it was the same; nothing happened – except the best thing that would have happened: they sailed on. Something very like it is to be seen in Hebrews 6:1, "Let us go on." In your spiritual journey do what Christopher Columbus and his crew members did: "Today, we sailed on!"

A LITTLE HUMOR: A man who obviously thought he was a Romeo sat next to an attractive lady on a plane. To break the ice he said, "I'm doing a survey and would like to know, 'What kind of men interest you?"

She replied, "I really like native Americans. They are so in touch with nature. But, I also like Jewish men. They hold women in such regard. And, then, I also like Southern men. They are so gracious and thoughtful."

The man then said, "Permit me to introduce myself. My name is Running Bear Goldstein, but my friends call me Bubba."

AUGUST 10

H. O. P. E.

"Blessed be the God and Father of our Lord Jesus Christ, who according to His abundant mercy has begotten us again to a living hope through the resurrection of Jesus Christ from the dead." (1 Peter 1:5, NKJV)

Dr. Ralph Bowlin served as a missionary in Africa for thirty-four years. During that time he spent twenty-eight years as president and professor in the Zimbabwe Seminary. Upon retirement he was offered a teaching position in one of our Southern Baptist Seminaries but turned it down in order to live near his elderly mother-in-law.

Dr. Bowlin lived near Nacogdoches, Texas, during his retirement and served as pastor in one of the small rural churches. That's when I met Dr. Bowlin and grew to love him as a brother in Christ and dear friend. Dr. Bowlin was what I would call a master at creating acrostics and alliterations out of words. I still cherish a folder full of his creations that he gave to me.

One day I was preparing a sermon for a funeral I was scheduled to conduct. Dr. Bowling stopped by to visit and while we were together I shared with him that I was preparing a funeral message. I asked him, "Dr. Bowlin, can you give me an acrostic for the word 'hope'?" Immediately he said, "Heavenly Optimism Permeating Everything." My eyes lit up and my heart jumped with excitement. I not only used that acrostic for that funeral but have often used it in others. It has been an inspiration to me as well as to others. Hope does permeate everything with heavenly optimism.

I often remind our people that when the Bible uses the word *hope,* it is not used in the way we refer to it today. When we use the word hope, it is used with the meaning of doubt or uncertainty. We're not quite sure that something is true, but we hope it is. However, when the word hope is found in the Bible, it is always with the meaning of confidence. We know beyond a shadow of a doubt that what we are referring to is true. Peter wrote that our God, our Heavenly Father, has "begotten us to a living hope through the resurrection of Jesus Christ our Lord from the dead" (1 Peter 1:3). Hope is alive. The believer need never be distressed by fears if Christ is his "living hope." The writer of Hebrews speaks of this "hope" as an "anchor of the soul, both sure and steadfast" (Hebrews 6:19). The Christian's hope is the Lord Jesus Christ who is "the same yesterday, and today, and forever" (Hebrews 13:8).

A LITTLE HUMOR: A preacher's son was talking to his friend and learned that he liked the sermons of the assistant pastor better than his father's. "But why?" he asked his friend. "Well, you see," the boy said, "when the assistant comes to the end of his sermon he usually says, 'And now, in conclusion,' and he concludes. But when your Dad comes toward the end, he says, 'And now, lastly,' and he really lasts."

AUGUST 11

IF YOU THINK IT'S HOT NOW!

"Do not fear those who kill the body but are unable to kill the soul; but rather fear Him who is able to destroy both soul and body in hell." (Matthew 10:28, NASB)

During this time of year it's always hot in Texas. I mean hot, hot, hot! It's not unusual to have many days of over one hundred degree temperature with the heat index even hotter. Grass and trees die, the ground becomes parched -- even the air is hot. It almost takes your breath away.

All of this hot weather reminds me of the terrible place the Bible calls hell. Hell is a real place. Our sophisticated age would like to erase the thought of hell's torment from the mind of modern man. Hell is described in the Bible as a place of death (Rev. 2:11); a place of destruction (2 Thess. 2:7-9); a place of punishment (Luke 12:47-48); a place of outer darkness(Matt. 25:30; and, a place of eternal fire (Rev. 20:14-15). Hell is for real.

Who will be in hell? The devil and his demons will be there. Contrary to what many think, the devil is not in charge of hell. The devil will be tormented in hell just like everyone else who will be there (Rev. 20:10). We often hear that heaven is a prepared place (John 14:2-3), but so is hell. In Matthew 25:41 Jesus said, "Depart from Me, accursed ones, into the eternal fire which has been prepared for the devil and his angels." All unbelievers whose names are not in the Book of Life will be in hell (Rev. 20:12-15; 21:8, 27; 22:15)

It is God's desire that no one should go to hell. Second Peter 3:9 says that God “is patient toward you, not wishing for any to perish but for all to come to repentance.” Any person who is willing to admit that he or she is a sinner and is willing to repent of sin and place their faith in Christ as Lord and Savior will not only receive eternal life, but will escape the flames of hell also (John 3:16).

An old Scottish preacher had to go past a glass factory each day on his way to the church. On one occasion, he had a little extra time, and since the factory door was open, he decided to look inside. There before him was a large blazing furnace. The preacher gazed into the white, blue, and purple mass of liquid flame, and the intense heat almost seared his face. As he turned to leave, a workman, standing in the shadow nearby, overhead him exclaim, “Ho, mon, what shall Hell be like!” Several days later the man came to the preacher and said, “You don’t know me but the other night when you stepped into the furnace door I heard what you said. Now every time I open that hot door to stoke the fire those words ring in my mind, ‘What shall Hell be like!’ I have come to you, sir, to find out how to be saved. I don’t ever what to know the reality of that place.”

It is enough that our Lord tells about hell and its torments. A loving Savior speaks no idle words. We must heed His warning. Plead His mercy. Receive the Savior who took our penalty and paid the price for our salvation at Calvary. Christ’s death and resurrection guarantee that those who trust Him will never perish (John 10:28).

A LITTLE HUMOR: The late Vance Havner said, "Whether the weather be cold, or whether the weather be hot, whether the weather be good or whether the weather be not. Whatever the weather, we'll weather the weather, whether we like it or not."

AUGUST 12

JUST PRETENDING

“Therefore, putting aside . . . hypocrisy . . .” (1 Peter 2:1, NASB)

In his youth John Philip Sousa, the grandson of America’s great composer and conductor by the same name, received large sums of money as a guest bandleader. Soon, however, his conscience began to trouble him. He knew that he was asked to conduct because of his famous grandfather, not due to his own ability. In fact, the younger Sousa couldn’t read a note of music. So he decided to give up his lucrative charade and start earning a real living.

Have you ever pretended to be someone you’re not? Could you be masquerading as a devoted disciple of Jesus when in fact you’re a spiritual sham?

The sin that Jesus most often denounced was the hypocrisy of the Pharisees (cf. Matthew 23:23-28). They were playing the role of God fearers but not living in holy and grateful obedience to His will.

Are you pretending? That question compels prayerful self-examination. It should motivate us to make the needed changes in our attitudes and in the way we live.

A LITTLE HUMOR: Church finances were a little tight, so the pastor took extra time one particular Sunday to emphasize the importance of everyone giving their tithes and offerings. He went on to challenge the people to give enthusiastically because 2 Corinthians 9:7 says, "God loves a cheerful giver."

As the plate was passed, a little boy in the second pew slipped off his necktie and placed it in the offering plate. His mother, absolutely mortified, asked him what in the world he thought he was doing. The boy replied, "The pastor said put your ties in the offering plate and do it joyfully."

AUGUST 13

SHARING THE LOAD

"Take My yoke upon you . . . for My yoke is easy and My burden is light."
(Matthew 11:29-30, NASB)

A yoke is most commonly associated with oxen and other animals that are harnessed together so they can help farmers plow. To be yoked with Christ is to allow Him to share the burden of our daily lives, to allow Him to take off our shoulders the weight of trying to solve our problems alone. Being yoked with Christ is one of the secrets of a productive life.

Dr. Herb True tells about a conversation he had with a trainer of Clydesdale horses. According to this trainer the average Clydesdale is able to pull about 7,000 pounds. Put two Clydesdales together, however, and their combined pull should equal 18,000 pounds. However, working as a team, with proper training the same two Clydesdales are capable of pulling 25,000 pounds – more than three times as much as one Clydesdale. In business this is called synergy. Get two people complementing one another to work in tandem, and much more can be produced than by either one working alone. Imagine then how effective our lives could be if we worked in tandem with the One who is the source of all ideas, the source of all energy, the source of all that has ever been created.[54]

Jesus stands today with the yoke upon His shoulder. He calls to each one of us and says, "Come and share my yoke, and let us plow together the long furrow of your life. I will be a true yokefellow to you. The burden shall be on Me."

How about you? Are you tired of being sick and tired? Are you ready to trust Him with your worries and emotional conflicts? "Take My yoke upon you and learn from Me," says the Master, "for I am gentle and humble in heart, and you will find rest for your souls."

---

[54] *Dynamic Preaching*, July, Aug., Sept., 2011, Vol. XXVII, No. 3, 7.

A LITTLE HUMOR: Sometimes I worry at night and can't go to sleep. Somebody told me to put a wastebasket beside the bed, and when I have trouble sleeping just pretend I'm throwing my worries in it. But it didn't work. Just about the time I was falling asleep the basket would overflow and I'd have to get up and empty it!

AUGUST 14

KEEPING YOUR PROMISE

"When you make a promise to God, don't delay in following through, for God takes no pleasure in fools. Keep all the promises you make to Him. It is better to say nothing than to make a promise and not keep it. Don't let your mouth make you sin."
(Ecclesiastes 5:4-6, NLT)

According to legend, the Pied Piper of Hamelin charmed the children and led them out of the city never to be seen again. The story is told of a strange and wondrous figure attired in a coat of many colors who arrived in the town of Hamelin, Germany. He pretended to be a rat catcher and promised to rid the town of rats and mice for a fixed sum of money which the citizens promised to pay. The stranger produced a pipe and began to play. Soon all the rats and mice came running out of their homes. The Pied Piper led them to the River Weser where they drowned. The people of Hamelin went back on their word and refused to pay the Pied Pier. According to the legend, the Piper returned and once again played his pipe. Only this time, it was not rats and mice that came out but children. He led them through the Ostertor gate into the very heart of a hill, where they all disappeared.

Although this is only a legend, this story reminds us that promises (or vows) are not to be broken. The wise man Solomon states very plainly that if we make a promise, God expects us to keep that promise. In fact, we are told that it is better not to make a promise than to make a promise to God and break it.

The Psalmist echoes the same thought when he says, "Make thankfulness your sacrifice to God, and keep the vows you made to the Most High." (Psalm 50:14, NLT).

Have you made any promises to God? God keeps His promises and He expects us to keep ours.

A LITTLE HUMOR: "I'm careful of the words I say, I keep them soft and sweet. I never know from day to day which ones I'll have to eat."

AUGUST 15

THE SEVEN DEADLY SINS

"For the wages of sin is death, but the free gift of God is eternal life in Christ Jesus our Lord." (Romans 6:23, NASB)

Pope Gregory the Great, at the end of the 6th century, divided all sins under seven heads. He said that every sin that a man commits can be classified by seven words. He named the sins: pride, anger, envy, impurity, gluttony, slothfulness and avarice. They have been called down through the centuries "the 7 deadly sins." These sins are nowhere collectively mentioned in a single passage in the Bible, and yet they are all condemned separately in many places. Thomas Aquinas and most of the great theologians have agreed with Pope Gregory, and these seven deadly sins have become a recognized part of moral theology.

What the medieval church fathers knew then, social scientists are now admitting: we are defeated today by the same sins. The seven deadly sins are just as prevalent today as they were in the past. If left unchecked they will not only defeat us, they will destroy us.

Sin is serious business and has serious repercussions. Sin contaminates every human being. Every person on God's green earth is infected with it. "For all have sinned and fall short of the glory of God" (Romans 3:23, NASB). No one is immune. No one includes me – and you. Make no mistake about it: sin is real. It is just as real as the air we breathe.

Sin not only contaminates every human being but also contaminates every part of being human. It is like a drop of dye placed in a clean glass of water; the dye's color permeates every molecule of water. It is like a rotten apple in a bushel basket; the toxins of the rotting apple eventually infect the whole bunch.

Sin leads to death; it is a fatal disease. It sentences us to a slow, painful death. Sin does to life what shears do to flowers. A cut of the stem separates flowers from the source of life. Over time the leaves will wilt, and the petals will drop. No matter what you do, the flowers will never live again.

How do we remove sin from our lives? Honestly, we can't. We must rely on another person, and that other person is none other than Jesus Christ. Jesus died on the cross, bearing the sins of all humans so that our sins would be removed permanently from our record. The Bible says, "If we confess our sins, He is faithful and righteous to forgive us our sins and to cleanse us from all unrighteousness." (1 John 1:9, NASB). Have you trusted Christ for the forgiveness of your sins? If not, why not do it now!

A LITTLE HUMOR: A Sunday school teacher asked a little girl, "What are the sins of omission?" After some thought, she answered, "They're the sins we ought to have committed but haven't."

AUGUST 16

A GREAT GAIN BUT A GREATER LOSS!

"For what profit is it to a man if he gains the whole world, and loses his own soul? Or what will a man give in exchange for his soul?" (Matthew 16:26, NKJV)

In the 1950's, the European wrestling champion, Yussif, the Turk, came to America to fight Strangler Lewis for the "world championship" and $5,000. Yussif weighed 350 pounds and Strangler weighed just a shade over 200 pounds.

Although he wasn't very big, Strangler had a simple plan for defeating his opponents and it had never failed. Strangler would put his arm around the neck of his opponent and cut off the oxygen. Many an opponent had passed out in the ring with Strangler Lewis.

The problem when he fought Yussif, the Turk, was that Yussif didn't have a neck. His body went from his head to his massive shoulders. Lewis could never get his hold, and it wasn't long before the Turk flipped Lewis to the mat and pinned him. After winning the championship, the Turk demanded all $5,000 in gold. After he wrapped the championship belt around his vast waist, he stuffed the gold into the belt and boarded the next ship back to Europe. He was a success! He had captured America's glory and her gold!

He set sail on the SS Bourgogne. Halfway across the Atlantic, a storm struck and the ship began to sink. In a panic, Yussif jumped for a lifeboat, missed, and went straight to the bottom like an anvil before they could get him into a lifeboat. He was never seen again. His golden belt had become a golden anchor, a vivid illustration of the deadliness of greed.[55]

Success promises a view from the top, but, without God in the picture, success will drag you down just as it did Yussif, the Turk. The term "fool" in biblical language is not a description of mental ability but of spiritual discernment. It is an individual who makes choices as if God doesn't exist and who lives as if God hasn't spoken.

If that description fits us, then we are choked by the grip of greed. And it's no laughing matter. We need to be released from the terror of its stronghold. The satisfaction that greed promises can be met only in an ongoing walk with Jesus Christ.

A LITTLE HUMOR: After church one Sunday morning, a mother commented, "The choir was awful this morning." The father commented, "The sermon was too long." Their seven-year-old daughter added, "But, you've got to admit it was a pretty good show for just a dollar."

---

[55] Rick Ezell, *The 7 Sins of Highly Defective People Rick Ezell* (Grand Rapids: Kregel Publications, 2003), 94.

AUGUST 17

WHAT CAN I DO FOR YOU?

"Whoever desires to become great among you, let him be your servant."
(Matthew 20:26, NKJV)

Debbie Fields, founder of Mrs. Fields' Cookies, said that her best public relations approach was a good cookie. When she was twenty years old and newly married, she wanted to sell the soft, chewy cookies that she'd been baking at home. She opened her first cookie store, and the first day nobody bought any. So, she filled a tray, stepped out onto the sidewalk, and began giving cookies away. People followed her back to the store to buy more. Even today, with over 700 stores, she uses the same technique. At every location, passersby are invited in to sample free cookies.

Sounds like an odd way to build a business, doesn't it? Getting people to buy your product by giving it away? It worked because Mrs. Fields realized that her primary objective wasn't really making money; it was serving customers.

In the same way, our best "public relations" approach is to focus on what we can do for others, rather than what they can do for us. This applies to employees, employers, spouses, family members, co-workers, customers, churches — anyone.

Danny Thomas said, "Success has nothing to do with what you gain or accomplish for yourself. It's what you do for others." This is why Thomas will be remembered for establishing St. Jude's Children's Hospital in Memphis long after people have forgotten "Make Room For Daddy."

Jesus taught us to live by this principle of "What Can I Do For You?" He said, ("Whoever desires to become great among you, let him be your servant" (Matthew 20:26, NKJV). Whatever secondary roles we may fill in our lives, we must keep in mind that the primary role for all believers is that of a servant. Every day offers a new opportunity to invest our lives in others.

Einstein said, "Only a life lived for others is worthwhile." The University of Michigan Research Center performed a study that found that people who are involved in service to others dramatically increase their life expectancy and vitality. In other words, being a servant adds years to your life and life to your years. This is because God created us to serve.

When Mother Teresa received the Nobel Peace Prize in 1979, she said, "What we are doing is just a drop in the ocean. But if that drop was not in the ocean, I think the ocean would be less because of that missing drop."

Today you can add another drop to the ocean by looking for an opportunity to serve someone in the name of Christ.

A LITTLE HUMOR: Think you're having a bad day? A woman came home to find her husband in the kitchen shaking frantically, almost in a dancing frenzy, with some kind of wire running from his wrist towards the electric kettle. Intending to jolt him from the deadly current, she whacked him with a handy plank of wood, breaking his arm in two places. Up to that moment, he had been happily listening to his Walkman.

AUGUST 18

PURITY IS MORE PRECIOUS THAN LIFE

"You are already clean because of the word which I have spoken to you."
(John 15:3, NKJV)

In the forest of northern Europe and Asia lives a little animal called the ermine, known for his snow-white fur. He instinctively protects his white coat against anything that would soil it.

Hunger takes advantage of this unusual trait by smearing the entrance and interior of the ermine's home. The hunters set their dogs loose to find and chase the ermine. The frightened animal flees toward home but doesn't enter because of the filth. Rather than soil his white coat, he is trapped by the dogs and captured while preserving his purity. For the ermine, purity is more precious than life.[56]

A pure heart is the work of Christ, and only in His power can we remain clean. In the midst of His imagery of the vine and the branches, Jesus said: "You are already clean because of the word which I have spoken to you" (John 15:3, NKJV). Bible scholar W. E. Vine says that the Greek word for *clean* means free from impure admixture, spotless. Jesus has made us clean through His sacrifice and His Word. The results of this purity is demonstrated in several ways.

To be pure results in having **pure thoughts.** In Philippians 4:8 Paul challenges us to think on things that are pure: "Finally, brethren, whatever things are . . . pure . . . meditate on these things" (NKJV). What we put into our minds determines what comes out in our words and actions. We should program our minds with thoughts that are pure.

To be pure results in having **pure speech.** In the NLT version of the Bible, Proverbs 15:26 reads, "The Lord . . . delights in pure words."

To be pure results in having pure eyes. The psalmist declared, "I will refuse to look at anything vile and vulgar . . ." (Psalm 101:3a, NLT). Matthew 5:28 records the words of Jesus: "I say, anyone who looks at a woman with lust has already committed adultery with her in his heart" (NLT).

To be pure results in have **pure religion:** "Pure and genuine religion in the sight of God the Father," James writes, "means caring for orphans and widows in their distress and refusing to let the world corrupt you" (James 1:27, NLT).

The Lord wants His people to keep themselves separated from the filth of this world at all costs. Purity, to the Christian, is more precious than life.

A LITTLE HUMOR: "My wife doesn't understand me," he complained. Turning to his closest friend, again he cried, "My wife doesn't understand me! Does yours?" "I don't' know," his friend replied, "she never mentions you."[57]

---

[56] *Our Daily Bread* (Grand Rapids: RBC Ministries, April 21, 1997)

[57] Tal D. Bonham, *Another Treasury of Clean Jokes* (Nashville: Broadman Press, 1983), 37.

AUGUST 19

DO YOU GRUMBLE?

"I have learned in whatsoever state I am, therewith to be content."
(Philippians 4:11, KJV)

There's an old spiritual song called *The Grumbler Song.* Some of the words go like this: "In country, town or city, some people can be found who spend their lives in grumbling at everything around; O yes, they always grumble, no matter what we say, for these are chronic grumblers and they grumble night and day."

Grumbling is serious in God's eyes because it is indicative of that which lurks deep in the heart. Like the hands of the clock out of order which had a sign, "Don't blame me; the trouble lies deeper," so a grumbling tongue indicates trouble deeper in a person's heart. Here are a few suggestions that can help you overcome a grumbling spirit.

First, **learn to be content.** The apostle Paul wrote, "I have learned in whatsoever state I am, therewith to be content" (Philippians 4:11, KJV). The words "I have learned" imply that there was a time when he was not content. He had to learn to be content. Someone has said we live in one of two tents: content or discontent. The word *content* meant that Paul was dependent upon Christ for his happiness and not circumstances or conditions.

Second, **learn to give thanks.** Paul also wrote, "In everything give thanks: for this is the will of God in Christ Jesus concerning you" (1 Thessalonians 5:18, KJV). A Swedish proverb says, "Those who wish to sing always find a song." We always can find something to be thankful for. A newspaper published a whole page ad showing nothing but black dots. "Try counting them," said the advertiser. Then he added, "It would take 17,296 pages with 57,816 dots on each page to total a billion." Though actually reaching even a million in counting our blessings one by one may be unlikely, our reasons for gratitude are countless.

Third, **learn to trust in God.** Job exercised masterful faith when tragedy struck. Although children, possessions and health went, he said, "The Lord gave, and the Lord hath taken away; blessed be the name of the Lord" (Job 1:21-22, KJV).

Those who use the tongue to grumble disobey God's Word: "Do all things without murmuring" (Philippians 2:14, KJV). May we find things for which we are grateful and may a grumbling spirit never be found in our hearts.

A LITTLE HUMOR: A woman was standing at the front door of her parents' house after Thanksgiving dinner, ready to go home. Her four little children stood at her side, and her arms were full of coats. Her husband, coming down the stairs, asked why she was standing there. She replied, handing him the coats, "This time, you put the children's coats on and I'll go honk the horn."

AUGUST 20

LIFE UNDER THE JUNIPER TREE

"It is enough! Now, Lord, take my life, for I am no better than my fathers."
(1 Kings 19:4, NKJV)

Depression is the common cold of our emotions. Eventually it touches everyone. A classic example of a depressed person in the Bible is the prophet Elijah. He became so discouraged at one point in his life that he ran away, sat down under a juniper tree and asked God to let him die. "I've had it, Lord," he said. "Take my life for I am no better than my ancestors" (1 Kings 19:4). Elijah was having a pity party.

Elijah's depression wasn't bound up in any one cause. Rather, it stemmed from a number of things. There were at least four causes of his depression as revealed in 1 Kings 19: fear (v. 3), failure (v. 4), fatigue (v. 5), and futility (v. 10).

Fortunately, we are not the helpless victims of our emotions. We can bounce back from depression to live useful lives. In his book, *Feet of Clay,* Paul W. Powell offers four suggestions taken from the experience of Elijah for our consideration in dealing with depression.[58]

Take Time Off. Elijah took some time off so he could get physically and emotionally rejuvenated. He had been so busy taking care of others he had neglected his own needs. No one can run full throttle all the time. We need to slow down to an idle occasionally.

Let It All Out. Elijah talked through his frustrations with God. Talking is one of the best ways to rid ourselves of harmful emotions. When we talk, it is like pulling the plug out of the bathtub. All sorts of bad feelings are drained from us. You can talk to others, but don't forget to talk to God. Say what you want to God; God can take it. God will not condemn you as you pour out your hurts.

Get Life Back in Perspective. Depressed people often feel alone. They often focus on the negative. Many times, they arrive at the wrong conclusions. Elijah thought he was more important than he really was. He thought everything depended on him. If God's work depends solely on you and me, God is in serious trouble.

Get Back in the Mainstream. The time for complaints and self-pity came to end. Elijah needed to get back to work. With us, as it was with Elijah, the best way to quit feeling sorry for ourselves is to start feeling sorry for someone else.

Psychiatrist Karl Menninger was once asked by a newspaper reporter, "Suppose you think you're heading for a nervous breakdown. What should you do?" Most thought he would say, "See a psychiatrist." But he didn't. Instead his reply was, "Go straight to the front door, turn the knob, cross the tracks, and find somebody who needs you."

Elijah whipped his depression and went on to a lifetime of useful service. And so can you.

---

[58] Paul W. Powell, *Feet of Clay* (Macon, Georgia: Smyth and Helwys Publishing, Inc., 1999), 1-9.

A LITTLE HUMOR: Still thinking you're having a bad day? The average cost of rehabilitating a seal after the 1989 Exxon Valdez oil spill in Alaska was $80,000. At a special ceremony, two of the most expensively saved animals were being released back into the wild amid cheers and applause from onlookers. A minute later, in full view, a killer whale ate them both.

AUGUST 21

KNOCKED DOWN BUT NOT KNOCKED OUT

"We get knocked down, but we are not destroyed." (2 Corinthians 4:9b, NLT)

I like the story of C. D. "Bigboy" Blalock, a boxer back in the 1930s. Blalock once fought against an unnamed boxer from Mississippi. The only reason we remember Bigboy is because of a dubious distinction that he earned in that fight.

Bigboy was a powerful man with a devastating roundhouse swing. He decided to try this move against this boxer from Mississippi. Unfortunately, when Bigboy swung his famous roundhouse blow, at that very moment his opponent stepped too close. Bigboy's arm swung all the way around the man's head and Bigboy ended up hitting himself in the face instead of his opponent. Bigboy fell back and was down for the count. He is the only boxer in the history of boxing known to have knocked himself out.[59]

The word for *knocked down* in 2 Corinthians 4:9b means "to be smitten down or flung down to the ground." Thrown over and again to the ground is one way of putting it. In prison at Jerusalem (Acts 22:24-26) – in prison at Philippi (Acts 16:23-24) -- in prison in Caesarea (Acts 23:31-35) – in prison at Rome (Acts 28:16) -- in prison at Rome again (2 Timothy 1:17). Paul knew what it was to be flung to the ground. "But not destroyed!" He cries triumphantly, "I may be knocked down and knocked down and knocked down – but I'm never knocked out!" Nobody could knock Paul out. His enemies could mob him and malign him and mock him and maul him. They could even murder him – but even then they could not win. In the end, all they could do is martyr him!

Thankfully, most of us are not like Bigboy. Hopefully we are more like the apostle Paul. The Lord spared his life so that he could continue to preach the Good News of Jesus Christ and testify to God's deliverance. May the same be said of us.

A LITTLE HUMOR: An ancient myth teaches that at creation, the dog, the horse, the monkey, and human beings were given forty years each to live on this earth. The dog, the horse, and the monkey, said, "We don't need all that time to live." So, they each gave man ten years of their allotted forty years. Now you know why man leads a dog's life between forty and fifty, works like a horse between fifty and sixty, and after, that he just monkeys around.

---

[59] *Dynamic Preaching,* Oct.-Dec, 2011, 5.

AUGUST 22

WHAT'S YOUR PURPOSE IN LIFE?

"For to me, to live is Christ..." (Philippians 1:21a, NASB)

The apostle Paul wrote this verse from a prison cell. He knew his life was coming to an end. He sums up his life by stating his main purpose in living: "For to me, to live is Christ." What a wonderful way to sum up one's life.

Josh McDowell tells about the time he was visiting with a "head-hunter" – an executive recruiter who seeks new corporate executives for companies. The man told McDowell about a recent experience he had with a man he interviewed. "When I get an executive that I'm trying to hire for someone else," said the head-hunter, "I like to disarm him. I offer him a drink, take my coat off, then my vest, undo my tie, throw up my feet and talk about baseball, football, family, whatever, until he's all relaxed. Then, when I think I've got him relaxed, I lean over, look him square in the eye and ask, 'What's your purpose in life?' It's amazing how top executives fall apart at that question.

"Well," he continued, "I was interviewing this fellow the other day, had him all disarmed, with my feet up on his desk, talking about football. Then I leaned up and asked, "'What's your purpose in life?' And he said, without blinking an eye, 'To go to heaven and take as many people with me as I can.' For the first time in my career," said this corporate head-hunter, "I was speechless."[60]

You and I would probably use different language, but could we state our life purpose that succinctly and would our life purpose contain a reference to Christ? For example we might say, "To leave this world a better place." Or we might say, "To live a life of love following the example of Jesus Christ." The question is, is our faith the pre-eminent decider in choosing our life purpose?

If you were to sum up your life in a six or eight-word memoir, how would it read?

A LITTLE HUMOR: This little grandmother was surprised by her seven-year-old grandson one morning. He had made her coffee. She drank what was the worst cup of coffee in her life. When she got to the bottom, there were three of those little green army men, and she asked him why they were there. Her grandson replied, "On television, they say, 'The best part of waking up is soldiers in your cup!'"

---

[60] *Dynamic Preaching,* July-September, 2011, 70.

AUGUST 23

THE RIGHT WAY TO LIVE AND DIE

". . . Let me die the death of the righteous, and let my last end be like his!"
(Numbers 23:10b, KJV)

Today is August 23. On this day in 1977, Elvis Presley was buried at his Graceland Mansion in Memphis, Tennessee. Best known as the king of rock and roll, Presley was found dead at his home August 16. His funeral sparked off scenes of fanatical hero-worship as more than 80,000 fans arrived to pay their last respects. Crash barriers had to be erected around his mansion to keep the crowds back. Dozens fainted from either the heat or the pressure of the crowd. Two fans were killed when a drunken driver ran his car into the crowd. More than 30,000 filed into the house to see the singer lying in state. Thousands more lined Elvis Presley Boulevard to watch the funeral procession of white Cadillacs. The grave was decked out with wreaths in the shape of hound dogs and guitars. His death was officially blamed on an irregular heartbeat which many speculate was drug related.

When death comes, and it will come to us all, what will matter is not the size of our funeral or if it should draw national attention. What is important is not even how we die. What will be important is whether or not we are saved. All the fame and wealth of the world will mean nothing. What will matter is our relationship to God. John Wesley once said of the Methodists, "Our people die well." The last words spoken by Wesley himself were, THE BEST IS GOD WITH US.

If we know Christ as our Lord and Savior, we are righteous in Him and because we are righteous in Him we should live a righteous life. Today, ask God to help you live the way you want to die. Since we know that death is certain, why not make plans to die as the righteous man. That's the only way to live and die.

A LITTLE HUMOR: As with many funerals, it was a cloudy, rainy day. The deceased was a little old lady who had devoted her entire married life to nagging her poor husband. When the graveside service had no more than ended, there was a tremendous lightning bolt accompanied by a burst of thunder and more rumbling thunder. The little old man looked at the pastor and calmly said, "Well, she's there."

AUGUST 24

IT'S A QUESTION OF PRIORITIES

"If anyone wants to be first, he must be the very last, and the servant of all."
(Mark 9:35, NIV)

In the late 1980's and early 1990's, Chris Spielman was an awesome linebacker for the Detroit Lions and the Buffalo Bills. Football was his passion, or so everyone thought. But in 1994, Chris Spielman gladly gave up football when his wife, Stefanie, was diagnosed with cancer. He moved into his wife's hospital room and waited on her hand and foot. He only ate what she ate, only slept when she slept. When Stefanie lost her hair to chemotherapy, Chris shaved his head. He became the primary caretaker for their two children. Today, Stefanie is in remission and feeling good. And Chris has no regrets about giving up his career. As he says, "This is my family. This is my responsibility. This is my duty."[61]

Jesus and his disciples had just arrived in Capernaum. When they were settled in, Jesus asked them, "What were you arguing about on the road?" Suddenly it got very quiet. Why? Because the disciples were embarrassed. They had been arguing about who was the greatest. They were arguing over who was number one. How is it that this argument seemed perfectly reasonable and important to the disciples until they had to lay it before Jesus? Suddenly, they saw it for what it was: sinful, petty pride. No wonder they were embarrassed. No wonder they didn't want to tell Jesus what they were arguing about.

Chris Spielman probably thought at one time in his life that winning at football was the most important thing in life. How his priorities changed when someone he loved had her life threatened by disease.

Jesus called the twelve and said to them, "If anyone wants to be first, he must be the very last, and the servant of all" (Mark 9:35, NIV).

All of us are under pressure to succeed in life. All of us want to be the best we can be. We are all juggling balls in the air. There is nothing wrong with that — as long as we remember which of the balls is rubber and which are glass. If you drop one of the rubber balls, it will bounce back. But if you drop one of the glass balls — like family, health, friends, or faith — they will be irrevocably scuffed, marked, nicked, damaged, or even shattered. When asked why he had been so successful, the late Tom Landry responded, "In 1958, I did something everyone who has been successful must do, I determined my priorities for my life: God, family, and then football." What's important to you?

A LITTLE HUMOR: A large fire was consuming building after building in a small town with a volunteer fire department. Onlookers wondered how the fire department would get close enough to the fire to put it out. Suddenly, the fire truck came racing down the street and ran right into the middle of the inferno. The volunteers immediately jumped out of their fire truck and extinguished the fire. The citizens were so proud of them that they took up a collection. The mayor presented the check and asked the chief what they would buy with the funds. He said, "The first thing we will do is fix the brakes on the fire truck."

---

[61] *Dynamic Preaching.* July-September, 2000, Vol. 15, No. 3, 71.

AUGUST 25

SAY NO TO DISCOURAGEMENT

"Let us not lose heart in doing good, for in due time we will reap if we do not grow weary." (Galatians 6:9, NASB)

Do you ever get discouraged? Discouragement is unique to human beings, and it's universal –eventually everyone gets it. I have no doubt you've experienced discouragement at times, maybe many times. You might even be discouraged at this very moment. Here are four suggestions that will help you to say no to discouragement.

Return to the Lord. When discouraged, many Christians drift away from the Lord, neglecting prayer, reading their Bibles, and stop going to church. Malachi 3:7 reads, "Return to Me, and I will return to you," says the Lord. No matter how difficult the situation may be, you can receive help from the Lord. If you have drifted away from Him, the best thing you can do now is to return to Him.

Radiate for the Lord. Our Lord admonishes us to "Let your light shine before men in such a way that they may see your good works, and glorify your Father who is in heaven" (Matthew 5:16). Often times when we are discouraged we spread gloom and doom. We only see the bad in our situation. We should replace negative thoughts with positive ones and radiate for the Lord.

Rely on the Lord. Some Christians rely on temporal possessions more than on God. Others rely too much on people. The psalmist wrote, "Commit your way to the Lord, trust also in Him, and He will do it" (Psalm 37:5). Depend on the Lord. He never disappoints or fails.

Rejoice in the Lord. Many Christians fall into discouragement because they fail to offer enough praise to God. They are too involved with selfish pursuits. It is difficult, if not impossible, to rejoice in the Lord and be discouraged at the same time. The psalmist said, "I will bless the Lord at all times" (Psalm 34:1).

Fight back! Discouragement is a choice. If you feel discouraged, it's because you've chosen to feel that way. No one is forcing you to feel bad. Hang on! Do what's right in spite of your feelings.

A LITTLE HUMOR: Poor Charlie Brown is leaning against the wall looking like he just lost his best friend. Lucy stops in front of him and remarks, "Discouraged again, eh, Charlie Brown?" Charlie Brown is too lost in his melancholy thoughts to reply. Lucy continues, "You know what your trouble is? The whole trouble with you is that you are you." With a look of despair, he asks her, "Well, what in the world can I do about that?" Now Lucy walks off, unconcerned, "I don't pretend to be able to give advice...I merely point out the trouble!"

AUGUST 26

MAKE UP YOUR MIND

"I am the door. If anyone enters by Me, he will be saved, and will go in and out and find pasture." (John 10:9, NKJV)

An Arab chief tells the story of a spy captured and sentenced to death by a general in the Persian army. This general had the strange custom of giving condemned criminals a choice between the firing squad and "the big black door."

The moment for execution drew near, and guards brought the spy to the Persian general. "What will it be," the general would ask, "the firing squad or the big black door?" The spy hesitated, debating the choice. Finally he said, "the firing squad."

A few minutes later, hearing the shots ring out confirming the spy's execution, the general turned to an aide and said, "They always prefer the known to the unknown. People fear what they don't know. Yet, we gave him a choice." "What lies beyond the big black door?" asked the aide. "Freedom," replied the general.[62]

We have all sinned and are condemned to eternal death, yet God gives all of us the same choice. He does not hide the choices. We can continue on to death and hell or walk into His freedom. He clearly states this in Romans 6:23, "For the wages of sin is death, but the gift of God is eternal life in Christ Jesus our Lord."

Have you accepted His gift? Do you know Jesus Christ as your Savior and Lord? If not, why not decide today. The Bible says, "For whoever calls on the name of the Lord shall be saved" (Romans 10:13). Our Scripture for today records the statement of Jesus: "I am the door." The door is open right now. All you have to do is to enter in through faith.

A LITTLE HUMOR: Two flies were buzzing around a messy kitchen table that had the remains of a recently prepared bologna sandwich. The knife used to slice the bologna was covered with little particles of meat. The two flies started at the tip of the knife and ate their way to the end of the handle. Then they flew away, only to become dizzy and fall to the floor – dead! The moral of the story is: "Don't fly off the handle when you're full of bologna."[63]

AUGUST 27

HIS GREATEST PURCHASE

"The laws of the Lord are true; each one is fair. They are more desirable than gold, even the finest gold . . ." (Psalm 19:9b-10a, NLT)

John Wanamaker (1838-1922) one of the country's greatest merchants, religious

---

[62] *My Quiet Time* printed by Student Discipleship Ministries, Series 1, 11.
[63] Charles Lowery, "Thanksgiving Melody," *SBC LIFE,* November, 2007, 16.

leaders, civic and political figures, was considered by some to be the father of modern advertising and a "pioneer in marketing." Have you ever purchased an item and had the clerk say to you, "If for any reason you need to return this product there is a money-back guarantee"? If so, you need to thank John Wanamaker. Although he did not invent the fixed-price system, he popularized it into what became the industry standard, and did create the money-back guarantee that is now standard business practice.

In 1889 Wanamaker was appointed United States Postmaster General by President Benjamin Harrison. Until his death, Wanamaker had been the last surviving member of Harrison's Cabinet. From 1908 to 1914, he financed Anna Jarvis' successful campaign to have a national Mother's Day holiday officially recognized. His fame was considerable around the world in his heyday. In the original play Pygmalion (1912) by George Bernard Shaw, Alfred Doolittle is left a legacy by an American philanthropist millionaire name "Ezra Wanafeller", a combining of Wanamaker's name with John D. Rockefeller, Sr. Wanamaker was a wealthy man.

At a meeting in one of his buildings he said to his guests: "I have, of course, made large purchases of property in my lifetime . . . and the buildings and grounds in which we are now meeting represent a value of approximately twenty million dollars. But it was as a boy in the country, at eleven years of age, that I made my biggest purchase. In a little mission Sunday school, I bought from my teacher a small, red leather Bible. The Bible cost me $2.75 – which I paid in small installments as I saved. That was my greatest purchase, for that Bible made me what I am today."

Isn't that amazing! Wanamaker had made a lot of money in his lifetime. He was a successful business man. He had purchased a lot of property. Yet, his "biggest purchase" was a $2.75 Bible that he paid for by making "small installments as I saved." Reading and obeying God's Word made him what he had become.

Do you own a Bible? Do you read it? Do you practice what it teaches? The psalmist said that "the laws (a synonym for the Word of God) of the Lord . . . are more desirable than gold, even the finest gold." Of all our earthly possessions the Bible is the greatest item we could ever own. Don't neglect it. Treasure it! Practice it! It makes you a person with whom God will be pleased.

A LITTLE HUMOR: An elderly Christian man who attended prayer meeting faithfully always confessed the same things during prayer and testimony time. His prayer always went something like this: "O Lord, since we last gathered together, the cobwebs have come between me and Thee. Clear away the cobwebs, that I may again see Thy face." One night, after the old man had prayed this prayer for the umpteenth time, another church member whispered to the person next to him, "Why doesn't he ask the Lord to kill the spider?"

AUGUST 28

CHEERING FOR THE UNDERDOG

"The stone which the builders rejected, this became the chief corner stone." (Matthew 21:42, NASB)

Football teams have been practicing for several days and the first game for all of the area teams will be soon. Football is a wonderful sport. What is interesting about all sports is that there are some people who always cheer for the underdog. In every game there is an underdog, a team that is overmatched, or a team not expected to win. And many of us can't help cheering for that underdog.

Our text for today suggests that Jesus knew what it was to be an underdog. "The stone which the builders rejected" is a clear reference to Christ. Jesus was rejected by His own people. Jesus knows what it is to battle overwhelming odds. He knows what it is to be disrespected, to be in great pain, and ultimately, to confront death.

Remember that the next time you are in a tight spot. Remember that when you are rejected, when you lose the big contract, when you get bad news from the doctor, even when the final door – the door of death – is closing in your face – Jesus has faced it all, too. He knows what it is to be on the losing end.

The Christian faith is a positive faith, a hopeful faith. It is a faith of overcoming obstacles, a faith of believing that no mountain is too high, no valley is too deep. As Rocky Balboa said in one of the Rocky movies, "You, me, or nobody is gonna hit as hard as life. But it ain't about how hard you hit; it's about how hard you can get hit and keep moving forward." That's who we want to be – people who, by the grace of God, keep moving forward regardless of what life may send.

Remember also that it's not in our strength that we conquer. Our verse for today goes on: "This came about from the Lord, and it is marvelous in our eyes." It is the Lord who is our strength. It is God who gives us the victory. Here is the good news for the day – if you trust in God, you will ultimately win with God.

A LITTLE HUMOR: Did you hear about the place kicker who was so angry with himself after missing a field goal that when he got to the sidelines, he literally kicked himself. Yep, he missed there, too.

AUGUST 29

WHEN LIFE MAKES YOU WEARY

"My soul is weary of my life; I will leave my complaint upon myself; I will speak in the bitterness of my soul." (Job 10:1, KJV)

On June 22, 1969, Judy Garland was found dead in her bathroom from what doctors described as "an incautious self-over dosage of sleeping pills." At the age of seventeen, her role in *The Wizard of Oz* made her a superstar. By 1948, she was the leading musical actress. Yet by the age of eighteen, she was seeing a psychiatrist, attempted suicide at twenty-eight, had four failed marriages and had been addicted to uppers to perform and downers to sleep since her early years as an actress. Living with her fifth husband in London, she was found locked in her bathroom, sitting with her head slumped over in her lap. Doctors said it was not suicide but that she had taken her usual dose of Seconal to sleep, then awakened and, confused, swallowed more pills. Her daughter, Liza Minnelli said in a statement soon after, "It wasn't suicide, it wasn't sleeping pills, it wasn't cirrhosis. I think she was just tired, like a flower that blooms and gives joy and beauty to the world and then wilts away."

It may surprise you to know that certain great Bible characters were tired of living. Job is one such example. He confessed to being weary of life. All the things Job found himself going through made him tired of living. Maybe you have been there. The problems of life have a way of making us weary of life. Isaiah states, "Even the youths shall faint and be weary" (Isaiah 40:30), but then gives us the antidote for such weariness: "But they that wait upon the Lord shall renew their strength; they shall mount up with wings as eagle" (Isaiah 40:31). Today, if things have left you tired of life, God has just what you need to make your life worth living.

A LITTLE HUMOR: Little Harold was practicing the violin in the living room while his father was trying to read in the den. The family dog was lying in the den; and as the screeching sounds of little Harold's violin reached his ears, the dog began to howl loudly. The father listened to the dog and the violin as long as he could. Then he jumped up, slammed his paper to the floor, and yelled above the noise, "For Pity's sake, can't you play something the dog doesn't know?"

AUGUST 30

WHAT CAN WASH AWAY MY SIN?

"You are stained red with sin, but I will wash you as clean as snow. Although your stains are deep red, you will be as white as wool." (Isaiah 1:18, TEV)

I keep looking at my hands. There are stains on both of them – ugly, dark stains that will not come off. I've tried everything I can think of: soap and water, goop, a buffing compound, lemons – all to no avail. I have two pecan trees in my yard. I found a good crop of pecans on them the other day and notice that some of them were ready for picking. So I removed them and in the process I had to tear off some of the pecan's outside skin. That's where the stains came from. I didn't notice the stains until I went into the house to show the pecans to my wife. I'm sure there's a remedy for such a stain, but until I find it I'll just have to live with the stains.

The Bible says that there is another stain that is difficult to remove, but not impossible. It's the stain of sin and it mars the human heart. As our text for today says, "You are stained red with sin; your stains are deep red." The words *stained red with sin* come from one Hebrew word that is translated in the King James Version of the Bible as scarlet. The word *scarlet* really means double-dyed or twice-dyed. The scarlet color in ancient times was the result of two dippings. This word teaches the permanency of sin. It has been said that there is no power in chemistry that can take the scarlet color out without destroying the fabric. But what is impossible in chemistry is possible in grace. The red blood of the Lord Jesus Christ obliterates our scarlet sins, and the white robe of the spotless righteousness of God is thrown over the penitent one. Praise God for that word of hope: "Although your stains are deep red, you will be as white as snow."

The hymn writer, Robert Lowry, wrote of the only remedy for the stain of sin: "What can wash away my sins? Nothing but the blood of Jesus." John, the beloved apostle, also wrote of sin's only remedy: "If we confess our sins, He is faithful and just to forgive us our sins, and to cleanse us from all unrighteousness" (1 John 1:9). May it be so, dear reader, in your experience.

A LITTLE HUMOR: While attending a marriage seminar on communication, Delbert and his wife Betty listened to the instructor declare, "It is essential that husbands know the things that are important to their partners." He then addressed the men, "Can you describe your wife's favorite flower?" Delbert leaned over, touched his wife's arm gently and whispered, "Pillsbury All-purpose, isn't it?" The rest of the story is not pleasant.

AUGUST 31

THE VANITY OF PROFANITY

"You shall not take the name of the Lord your God in vain." (Exodus 20:7, NASB)

We're not to take the name of the Lord "in vain." What does that mean? Well, the Hebrew word means meaningless, empty of content. It has its root in the idea of a tempest or storm. The Hebrews used the word to describe a storm because it seemed so random, with no rhyme or reason. It was erratic, just a worthless and nonproductive thing.

One of the most ignorant things a person could ever do is profane the name of God. When you use God's name in profanity, it shows two things: an empty head and a wicked heart. Jesus said, "Out of the abundance of the heart the mouth speaks" (Matthew 12:34).

The Federal Communication Commission (FCC) upset millions of Americans when it ruled in October, 2003 that certain profanities are okay on television as long as they are not used to describe sexual actions. As if the airwaves are not already filled with enough filthy words, now the green light has been given to go ahead and use what every profane words they can belch out of the sewer of filth.

Michael Powell, chairman of the FCC is seeking help from Congress to crack down on violations of the agency's broadcast decency standards. I say more power to him!

Changing the channel is not the answer. Decency is. Being responsible is. Knowing that someday each of us will be held accountable for every word we speak should wake us up to the seriousness of being profane.

A LITTLE HUMOR: A preacher visited an elderly woman from his congregation. As he sat on the couch he noticed a bowl of peanuts on the coffee table. "Mind if I have a few?" he asked. "No, not at all," the old woman replied. They chatted for an hour, and as the preacher stood to leave, he realized he had emptied most of the bowl. "I'm so sorry for eating all your peanuts," he said. I really just meant to eat a few." "Oh, that's all right," replied the old woman. "Ever since I lost my teeth, all I can do is suck the chocolate off them."

SEPTEMBER 1

HUNKER DOWN

"Humble yourselves in the sight of the Lord, and He will lift you up."
(James 4:10, NKJV)

The headline for the Friday, September 12, 2008 issue of *The Daily Sentinel* read: "HUNKER DOWN." Hurricane Ike was on its way to East Texas and we were warned to take cover and stay put until the storm passed. The expression "HUNKER DOWN" got my curiosity going, so I looked up the word in the dictionary. The dictionary defines "HUNKER" as meaning "to squat" or "to get as close to the ground as one possibly can in order to hide out or take shelter."

The Bible doesn't use the words "HUNKER DOWN," but it does use the word *humility.* The Greek word for humility is *humas,* and it literally means the ground, which signifies a lowly state of mind. Humility, or "HUNKERING DOWN" before the Lord is the proper attitude one should have. Such an attitude is a good way to find shelter and to hide out. Micah 6:8 reads, "He has shown you, O man, what is good; and what does the Lord require of you but to do justly, to love mercy, and to walk humbly with your God?"

Robert J. Hastings wrote, "Humility is not the frosting on the cake; rather it is the basic ingredient in the batter. Humility is not the flagpole atop the building, it is the unseen foundation beneath the surface. Humility is not a desirable 'extra' in the Christian life; it is the basic virtue on which all others rest."[64]

A LITTLE HUMOR: A preacher was deathly sick in the hospital. Following the regular meeting of his deacons, they sent him this message, "Your deacons have voted to pray for your recovery by a vote of 15 to 5."

SEPTEMBER 2

AN INVITATION TO TIRED SOULS

"Come to me, all of you who are weary and carry heavy burdens, and I will give your rest." (Matthew 11:28, NLT)

One of the greatest missionaries of the twentieth century was a man named E. Stanley Jones. Jones was a man of amazing energy who wrote several best-selling books. It is hard to imagine that his career was once threatened and nearly cut short by chronic worry.

When he first arrived in India, Jones wore himself out, working and worrying. He suffered from brain fatigue and nervous exhaustion. He was forced to return to America. After a year's rest, he attempted to return to India, but became a bundle of

[64] Robert J. Hastings, *Take Heaven Now!* (Nashville: Broadman Press, 1968), 22.

nerves on the return trip and arrived in Bombay a broken man. His colleagues warned him that any attempt to continue ministering in such a state of anxious care could be fatal.

While praying one night, groping in emotional darkness, Jones seemed to hear a Voice saying, "If you will turn that over to Me and not worry about it, I will take care of it." Jones answered, "Lord, I close the bargain right here."

A great sense of peace closed in over Jones. He felt a rush of abundant life that seemed to sweep him off his feet. His energy returned, his enthusiasm bubbled over, and he plunged back into his work with a vitality he had never had known before.[65]

Maybe you and I need to close a bargain with God. Do you have that sense of peace that Jones found in his encounter with God? So many of us are tired because of mental and emotional conflicts that are draining us of our energy. We need to turn our worries, our concerns, our doubts and fears over to God.

A LITTLE HUMOR: A nurse at a hospital received a call from an anxious woman. "I'm diabetic and I'm afraid I've had too much sugar today," she said. "Are you light-headed?" asked the nurse. "No," she said, "I'm a brunette."[66]

SEPTEMBER 3

THOUGHTS ABOUT LABOR

"Six days you shall labor and do all your work." (Exodus 20:9 NASB)

Because this is Labor Day weekend our attention naturally turns to the work ethic. Abraham Lincoln once said, "If this country is ever demoralized, it will come from trying to live without work." The concept that work is a privilege and the attitude that I am accomplishing something worthwhile as I work is what has helped to build American into such a great nation. Several thoughts might be considered as we celebrate Labor Day.

First, I believe we should be thankful for our jobs. Many people in America are unemployed and therefore have no steady income for the support of their families. If you have a job, be thankful. Many don't.

Second, we should always give our best while working. When a person goes home after a day's work with the knowledge that he has done his best and accomplished something worthwhile, he does so with a sense of personal satisfaction. He feels good about himself for giving "an honest day's work for an honest day's pay." Sir Christopher Wren used to tell of a stranger who came to three workmen, all employed on the same job. He asked each worker what he was doing. Growled the first man, "I'm breaking rocks." Said the second, "I'm earning a living." But the third man replied with a smile, "I'm building a cathedral."

---

[65] *Dynamic Preaching,* July-September, 2011, Vol. 27, No. 3, 6.
[66] *Turning Points*, August, 2011, 50.

Third, if one does not have a steady job he should still be busy doing something, rather than being lazy or idle. Proverbs 14:23 reads, “In all labor there is profit, but mere talk leads only to poverty.” The person who wrote that was not anti-talk; he was pro-work. Talking about work is fine, and planning must be done, but plans and talk must grow arms and legs if there is to be a profit.

Having a job can be hard work. Even for those who truly enjoy their jobs, it’s nice to have a Labor Day breather. But until the day comes when our work is over, our task is to make our labor a testimony to God’s glory.

A LITTLE HUMOR: One man said that he had tried farming and gave it up because there were too many ups and downs. He had to wake up, then get up, wash up, chow down, and hitch up. Then when he checked up, he didn’t have enough to pay down, so he just gave up.

SEPTEMBER 4

THE VOICE OF THE LORD

“The voice of the Lord is powerful, the voice of the Lord is majestic.” (Psalm 29:4, NASB)

Do you recognize the name Elwood Edwards? Many of you hear his voice every day, and yet you don’t know his name. Actually, Elwood’s voice is heard more than 27 million times a day. This equals more than 18,000 times each minute of the day. Elwood Edwards is the man behind those three special words, “You’ve got mail!”

In 1989, Edward’s wife Karen was working in customer service for a little-known outfit in Vienna, Virginia called Quantum Computer Services. She overheard the company’s CEO describe how he wanted to add a voice to its user interface. She said, “Hey, you should try Elwood.” Her husband’s entire career had been in radio and TV. Edwards agreed to record his voice saying “You’ve got mail!” and the rest, as they say, is history.[67]

The individual who wrote Psalm 29 wrote of another voice that can also be heard and recognized as that of the voice of the Lord. He described the voice of the Lord as being “powerful” and “majestic.”

It is still possible to hear the Lord’s voice today. Billy Graham was once asked what had been the best experience of his entire ministry. He replied, “By far the greatest joy of my life has been my fellowship with Jesus. Hearing Him speak to me, having Him guide me, sensing His presence with me and His power through me. This has been the highest pleasure of my life!”

It can be for us too. We should draw near to God in prayer, but don’t just talk. Listen quietly. Listen closely. Hear God speak your name today.

---

[67] *Dynamic Preaching.* January-March, 2004, Vol. 19, No. 1,17.

A LITTLE HUMOR: A surgeon, an architect, and a politician found themselves in a friendly debate about which of their honored professions happened to be the oldest. "The Lord removed a rib from Adam's side," said the surgeon, "in order to create Eve. That was obviously a surgical procedure." "Yes," replied the architect, "but the world was formless and void before the Spirit of the Lord moved upon it. The precision of the universe had to be the result of a masterful, architectural design." The politician, taking a long puff from his cigar, smiled and said, "And who do you think created the chaos in the first place?"

SEPTEMBER 5

GOING BACKWARD

"Demas has forsaken me, having loved this present world, and has departed." (2 Timothy 4:10, NKJV)

Demas had been one of Paul's closest associates, yet there came a time when he forsook Paul. The word "forsaken" means "to utterly abandon," with the idea of leaving someone in a dire situation. Demas was a fair-weather disciple who had never counted the cost of genuine commitment to Christ.

On November 16, 1811, an unusual thing happened to the Mississippi River. The name "Mississippi" comes from an Indian word that means "big river." The river flows some 2,348 miles from its source in northwestern Minnesota to the Gulf of Mexico. What happened in 1811 was unprecedented for the river. An earthquake hit the state of Missouri and had a strange effect on the river. For a short period of time the river's direction was interrupted and it flowed backward.

There have been many that found themselves going backward in their Christian life. We find several examples in the Bible. In addition to Demas there were Peter (Mark 14:71), Mark (Acts 15:38), and the classic example of Jonah (Jonah 1:2-3).

Instead of cleaving to the Lord, there is often a leaving of the Lord. Many could describe their spiritual condition in the words of Kirkpatrick's hymn, "I've wandered far away from God." If that be the case with you, may I suggest you say, "Lord, I'm coming home. The paths of sin too long I've trod, Lord, I'm coming home."

A LITTLE HUMOR: A community orchestra was plagued by attendance problems. Several musicians were absent at each rehearsal. As a matter of fact, every player in the orchestra had missed several rehearsals, except for one very faithful oboe player. Finally, as the dress rehearsal drew to a close, the conductor took a moment to thank the oboist for her faithful attendance. She, of course, humbly responded, "It's the least I could do, since I won't be at the performance."

SEPTEMBER 6

THE GRACIOUS HAND OF GOD

"The gracious hand of our God is on everyone who looks to him." (Ezra 8:22, NIV)

This verse tells us three things. First, that God is a gracious God. Second, that God is gracious to everyone who looks to Him. Third, that we must look to God if we are to receive blessings from His gracious hand. The Bible has a lot to say about the hands of God. I mention only four blessings that come from God's gracious hand.

First, God's hand is **A Guiding Hand** – "Your hand will guide me" (Psalm 139:10, NIV). All of us need guidance every day of our lives. Joseph Gilmore wrote a hymn about the guidance of the Lord. The firsts stanza reads, "He leadeth me! O blessed thought! O words with heavenly comfort fraught! Whatever I do, wherever I be, Still 'tis God's hand that leadeth me!"

Then, we discover that God's hand is **A Generous Hand** – "God, who gives generously to all" (James 1:5, NIV). The word "generously" means "to spread out." God's hands are spread out. He is not a greedy God. He loves to give and give and give. According to the legend of an ancient kingdom whose sovereign died, ambassadors were sent to choose a successor from twin infants. They found the infants asleep, and looking at them observed one had his tiny fist closed tight, the other had his wide open. They chose the infant with the open hand. He even came to known as "The king with the open hand." We could say the same about God. His hand is always open to give.

Furthermore, God's hand is **A Supportive Hand** – "The Lord upholds him with his hand" (Psalm 37:24, NIV). The word "upholds" means "to prop upon" or "to lean upon." We who believe in the Lord and who love Him dearly find Him to be One on whom we can lean on. God will hold us up. I like what H. W. Webb-Peploe wrote, "Don't try to hold God's hand: let Him hold yours. Let Him to the holding, and you do the trusting."

Finally, God's hand is **A Secure Hand** – "No one can snatch them out of My Father's hand" (John 10:28-29). There is great comfort in knowing that we are safe in the Lord's hands. Neither man nor Satan can snatch us away from the strong hands of God! The Father's hand is more powerful than that of any enemy. He keeps His people safe.

Whatever difficulty you may be facing today, remember: "The gracious hand of our God is on everyone who looks to him."

A LITTLE HUMOR: A father was at the beach with his children when the four-year-old son ran up to him, grabbed his hand, and led him to the shore where a seagull lay dead in the sand.

"Daddy, what happened to him?" the son asked.

"He died and went to heaven," the dad replied.

The boy thought a moment and then said, "Did God throw him back down?"

SEPTEMBER 7

THE VOICE OF CONSCIENCE

"How much more will the blood of Christ . . . cleanse your conscience from dead works to serve the living God." (Hebrews 9:14, NASB)

Billy Graham has said, "I believe there is no greater argument for the existence of God in the world today than conscience. There is no greater proof of the existence of a moral law and Lawgiver in the universe than this little light of the soul. It is God's voice to the inner man."[68]

Animals do not have a conscience. Man is the only creature who has a conscience. The conscience has three functions: (1) to aid us in distinguishing between right and wrong, (2) to urge us to do right and reject wrong, (3) to approve us when we do right and to condemn us when we do wrong.

Having a good conscience should be the goal of every person (1 Peter 3:16). Having a good conscience involves at least five things: First, receive Jesus Christ as your Savior and Lord. Hebrews 9:14 speaks of Christ's blood cleansing our conscience. Second, confess any known sin. Proverbs 28:13 says if we hide our sins we will not prosper, but 1 John 1:9 assures us if we confess our sins God will forgive and cleanse us of all our sins. Third, make restitution if it is due. Luke 19:2-9 speaks of Zaccheus who promised to make things right with anyone he had defrauded. Fourth, concentrate on what is good. Philippians 4:8-9 speaks of concentrating on all that is true, honorable, right, pure, lovely and of a good report. Fifth, meditate on the Word of God. Psalm 1:2 speaks of that person whose delight comes from meditating on God's law.

In ancient times men spoke of a magic ring that could be worn, and whenever an evil thought passed through the mind of the wearer, or he was tempted to do an evil deed, the ring pressed painfully upon his finger. Each of us wears a ring – the ring of conscience. When we set out to do wrong, it presses painfully upon our soul. When we do right, it gives us peace within our heart.

A LITTLE HUMOR: A minister decided that a visual demonstration would add emphasis to his Sunday sermon. Four worms were placed into four separate jars. The first worm was put into a container of alcohol. The second worm was put into a container of cigarette smoke. The third worm was put into a container of chocolate syrup. The fourth worm was put into a container of good clean soil. At the conclusion of the sermon, the minister reported the following results: The first worm in alcohol – dead. The second worm in cigarette smoke – dead. The third worm in chocolate syrup – dead. The fourth worm in good clean soil – alive. So the minister asked the congregation, "What can you learn from this demonstration?" A little old woman in the back raised her hand and said, "As long as you drink, smoke and eat chocolate, you won't have worms!"

---

[68] *Decision*, March, 1971, 12.

SEPTEMBER 8

LEARNING FROM OUR FAILURES

"Be strong and of good courage, do not fear nor be afraid; for the Lord thy God ... will not leave you nor forsake you." (Deuteronomy 31:6, NKJV)

Mary Lou Retton, America's Golden Girl gymnast at the Summer Olympics in 1984, said that, to succeed, one has to set her goal and be willing to pay the price to achieve it. "Achieving that goal is a good feeling, but to get there you have to also get through the failures. You've got to be able to pick yourself up and continue."

Failure. It's not a dirty word — and yet we sometimes act as if it is. Every great person fails at some time in his or her life. Everyone falls, but not everyone fails. It depends on whether you fail backward or you fail forward. In his *One Hour With God* prayer guide, John Maxwell shows us the difference between failing backward or failing forward:

We fail backward when . . .
1. Failure keeps us from trying again.
2. We become negative about life.
3. We make excuses and blame others.

We fail forward when . . .
1. We learn from our failures.
2. We discover our own true self.
3. We turn everything over to God.[69]

Carl Walenda was a well-known tightrope walker and circus performer. He said, "My whole life is high-wire walking." But one day as he was on the wire, something snapped in his brain and he fell to his death. His wife said, "All he thought about for three months before was falling." He had concentrated on failure, on falling, rather than on walking.

The apostle Paul failed; Peter failed; every one of the twelve apostles failed. David, Israel's greatest king, failed; Moses, the great Law giver, failed. Who hasn't failed? It is not failing that is the problem; it is what one does after he has failed. R. H. Macy failed seven times before his store in New York caught on. Babe Ruth struck out 1,330 times, but he also hit 714 home runs. So, don't let failure get you down or keep you down. If you fall down, get up. If you stop, start over. Remember, it's always too early to quit. Take encouragement from knowing that God does not fail: "Be strong and of good courage, fear not, for the Lord thy God ... will not fail nor forsake you" (Deuteronomy 31:6).

---

[69] John C. Maxwell, *One Hour With God* (El Cajon, California: INJOY, 1994).

A LITTLE HUMOR: A chemist concocted a soft-drink formula and called it one-up. But it didn't sell. He tried to improve it, and changed the name to two-up. Still it didn't sell. Again he revised the formula and the name to three-up. Still, it was a failure. He kept trying till he called his product six-up. Still no success. Then he quit.[70]

SEPTEMBER 9

UNSEEN DANGER!

"The human heart is the most deceitful of all things, and desperately wicked. Who really knows how bad it is?" (Jeremiah 17:9, NLT)

In 1987, workers were drilling deep into the banks of the Thames River in London. The work seemed to progress normally, and the day appeared to be quite routine. But that was about to change quickly! As they reached the 21-foot level they struck what appeared to be a large cast-iron pipe. Their curiosity soon turned to horror. They crept away softly to report the finding of a 2,200-pound, unexploded Nazi bomb, one of the largest bombs the Luftwaffe ever dropped on an enemy!

Immediately the police cordoned off the streets and evacuated nearby residents and office workers. For thirty long hours, frightened people waited anxiously while a ten man army team skillfully defused the huge bomb. Then, just as quickly as the whole thing started, it ended. The work was done![71]

In a like manner, in the human heart lies something far more deadly than any bomb. God calls it sin. Bombs can blow away an arm or a leg or blast away life. In a similar way sin destroys and mutilates, but it also brings shame and terrible judgment. Unless it is carefully removed from our lives, sin can bring us to dreadful ruin. It cannot be defused and left where it is. Sin must be utterly removed and destroyed. How is that done?

First, accept God's description of your present condition. "For all have sinned and fall short of the glory of God" (Romans 3:23, NASB).

Second, repent of your sin and admit your need to be saved. "If we confess our sins, He is faithful and righteous to forgive us our sins and to cleanse us from all unrighteousness" (1 John 1:9, NASB).

Third, receive Jesus Christ by faith. "But as many as received Him, to them He gave the right to become children of God, even to those who believe in His name" (John 1:12, NASB).

Satan, the cunning enemy of our souls, tries to tell us it is impossible to remove the deadly bomb of sin from our hearts. But there is One who can overthrow sin and its consequences. Those in London knew the right people to call for their dangerous job. In like manner we must call on the only One who can effectively deal with sin. He alone can remove it and make our lives completely whole and free. His name is Jesus.

---

[70] Leslie Flynn, *A Source Book of Humorous Stories* (Grand Rapids: Baker Book House, 1973), 7.

[71] *Have A Good Day!,* July, 1994.

A LITTLE HUMOR: The wealthy elderly lady asked her minister if her recently deceased beloved pet dog could be buried in the church's cemetery with a religious service. "I'm sorry," the minister answered, "but we Baptist don't perform religious burial services for dogs." "That's too bad," the lady said, "I was prepared to donate ten thousand dollars for such a ceremony in the dog's name." "Wait a minute," the minister answered. "You didn't tell me the dog was a Baptist."

SEPTEMBER 10

LONELY, BUT NEVER ALONE

"I will ask the Father, and he will give you another Counselor, who will never leave you." (John 14:16, NLT)

If you were to compile a list of great literary classics, it would have to include Daniel Defoe's immortal *Robinson Crusoe.* It was not only the first English novel, but it deals dramatically with something to which all flesh is heir — loneliness. A great book is one with which we can identify, and this is surely the case in the loneliness and isolation, which haunted the shipwrecked Crusoe. For twenty-four years, he devised methods by which to survive and remain sane. Each morning he climbed a tree, shaded his eyes and scanned the horizon for the sight of a sail.

After several years, he noticed a footprint on the beach. He looked, he longed, he prayed, and then found the man whom he called Friday. Life changed for Robinson Crusoe. He gained the man's confidence, taught him English, and became his friend. The whole story underscores man's desperate need for friendship and fellowship. It is this theme that gives Robinson Crusoe a timeless, ageless quality.

AT&T, the nation's largest long-distance telephone company, spent sixty million dollars to find just the right phrase to move people to make long-distance calls. The result of all this expensive research, testing, and creative development was a simple five-word slogan: "Reach Out And Touch Someone!" All the commercials are effective because they touch a real longing in each of us to be reached, to be touched, to be known.

Billy Graham offers his own experience for dealing with loneliness. He writes, "I will give you a little recipe I have found for conquering loneliness. First, I am never lonely when I am praying, for this brings me into companionship with the greatest friend of all — Jesus Christ. Then, I am never lonely when I am reading the Bible. I read it every day — whole chapters of it. Nothing dissolves loneliness like a session with God's Word. Then, I am never lonely when I am sharing Him with others. There is a great exhilaration in talking to others about Christ. This is something we can all do."[72]

---

[72] *The Billy Graham Christian Worker's Handbook,* Edited by Charles G. Ward (Minneapolis: World Wide Publications, 1984, 1986), 191.

Loneliness has its way of winning victory. No one is ever completely immune to its touch. If we exercise the right disciplines, however, we can gain an upper hand on the problem. Jesus promises that He will never leave us or desert us (John 14:8; Hebrews 13:5). In the barrenness of life, He assures us: “You are never alone.” He can fill the vacuum and help us bear the burdens of life.

A LITTLE HUMOR: I don't understand why so many “so called” chocolate lovers complain about the calories in chocolate when all true chocoholics know that it is a vegetable. It comes from the cocoa bean; beans are veggies – 'nuff said.

SEPTEMBER 11

NEVER FORGET

“You have heard that it was said, 'You shall love your neighbor and hate your enemy.' But I say to you, love your enemies, bless those who curse you, do good to those who hate you, and pray for those who spitefully use you and persecute you.”
(Matthew 5:43-44, NKJV)

On September 11, 2001 nineteen members of the terrorist group al-Qaeda hijacked four commercial passenger jet airplanes. The hijackers intentionally crashed two of the airliners into the Twin Towers of the World Trade Center in New York City. A third plane was crashed into the Pentagon in Arlington, Virginia, just outside Washington, D. C. The fourth plane crashed into a field near Shanksville in rural Pennsylvania after some of its passengers and flight crew attempted to retake control of the plane. There were no survivors from any of the flights. Thousands of innocent people were killed and wounded. Many family members and friends continue to grief over their loss.

Nine-eleven is a day we must never forget. We must never forget those who lost their lives that day. We must never forget the first responders, firefighters and police personnel, who went to rescue people from the terrorist attacks. The overwhelming majority of casualties in all four attacks were civilians, including nationals of over seventy countries. We must never forget to pray for family members of those whosc loved ones died. They continue to grieve over their losses. We must never forget the members of our armed forces who are serving in Iraq and Afghanistan. We must never forget those who have lost their lives or have been wounded serving our country. The list is endless of those we must never forget.

But on this special day of remembrance we must go back two thousand years to another day that lives in infamy. It was the day that Jesus Christ died on the cross of Calvary for our sins. When He was on the cross, the first prayer Jesus prayed was: “Father, forgive them, for they do not know what they do.” (Luke 23:34). He set the example for us as to how we should treat our enemies. It was Charles H. Spurgeon who said, “Let us go to Calvary to learn how we may be forgiven. And let us linger there to learn how to forgive.” We must never forget to love and forgive our enemies.

This is perhaps the most difficult thing of all that must be done. Jesus commanded, "You have heard that it was said, 'You shall love your neighbor and hate your enemy.' But I say to you, love your enemies, bless those who curse you, do good to those who hate you, and pray for those who spitefully use you and persecute you." (Matthew 5:43-44, NKJV).

In the September, 2011 edition of *Decision* magazine, Franklin Graham writes: "As we remember 9/11 – all that we lost that day and all the troubles we face today – let's never forget that Jesus has overcome the world. We may not be able to see it yet, but we will soon."

The day is coming "that at the name of Jesus every knee should bow, in heaven and on earth and under the earth, and every tongue confess that Jesus Christ is Lord, to the glory of God the Father" (Philippians 2:10-11).

In Jesus – and in Him alone – we have victory and peace.

A LITTLE HUMOR: A preacher was trying to patch up a difference between two friends. "You must not cherish enmity against your neighbor," he said to the one who was complaining. "If you neighbor does you harm you must forget it." "I do forget it, but I have such a bad memory that I keep forgetting that I forgot."

SEPTEMBER 12

GOD'S ANCHORS FOR LIFE'S STORMS

"They cast four anchors out of the stern, and wished for the day." (Acts 27:29, KJV)

The *USS Dwight D. Eisenhower* is one of the largest ships in the world. This gigantic aircraft carrier is, from keel to mast, the size of a twenty-two-story building. It has a flight deck that comprises four and one-half acres. It weighs 95,000 tons. It carries over 6,000 sailors and serves those sailors 18,000 meals every day. The *USS Eisenhower* also has two anchors. Each anchor weighs 60,000 pounds. Each anchor is attached to a chain that weighs 665,000 pounds and stretches to a full length of 1,082 feet. Just one solitary link in that huge chain weighs 365 pounds. The anchors keep the ship from drifting. It's the anchors that keep the ship exactly where it needs to be.

In the Book of Acts, chapter 27, the Bible describes a storm in which the Apostle Paul and his traveling companions encountered on their way to Rome. For fourteen days and nights, without light of sun or star, they were beaten and driven by the storm until hope of safety was gone. It was then that "they cast four anchors out of the stern, and wished for the day" (Acts 27:29). God has given the Christian four anchors that never drag, and that hold no matter how rough the sea. Let me name them for you.

The first anchor is the promise that He will always be with us. Hebrews 13:5 reads, "I will never leave thee, nor forsake thee" (KJV). For the Christian, no danger can come so near that God is not nearer.

The second anchor is the promise that He will work out all things for our good. Romans 8:28 reminds us of this fact: "For we know that all things work together for good to them that love God, to them who are the called according to his purpose" (KJV).

The third anchor is the promise of His peace. Philippians 4:6-7 reads, "Don't worry about anything; instead, pray about everything . . . If you do this, you will experience God's peace . . . His peace will keep your thoughts and your hearts quiet and at rest as you trust in Christ Jesus" (LB).

The fourth anchor is the promise of His love. In Romans 8:35 the Apostle asked a question: "Who shall separate us from the love of Christ? Shall trouble or hardship…? (NIV). His answer was "nothing will ever be able to separate us from the love of God demonstrated by our Lord Jesus Christ when he died for us" (LB).

These four anchors safely hold us in the midst of any storm in this life. Are they yours? Then let your soul rest in sweet confidence. Storms will give way to calm. Priscilla J. Owens wrote a hymn in which she asked the question, "Will your anchor hold in the storms of life, when the clouds unfold their wings of strife? When the strong tides lift, and the cables strain, will your anchor drift, or firm remain?" She then answered her own question in the refrain: "We have an anchor that keeps the soul steadfast and sure while the billows roll, fastened to the Rock which cannot move, grounded firm and deep in the Saviour's love."

A LITTLE HUMOR: When a sudden storm blew up at sea, a young woman, leaning against the ship's rail, lost her balance and was thrown overboard. Immediately another figure plunged into the waves beside her and held her up until a lifeboat rescued them. To everyone's astonishment, the hero was the oldest man on the voyage. That evening he was given a party in honor of his bravery. "Speech! Speech! the other passengers cried. The old gentleman rose slowly and looked around at the enthusiastic gathering. "There's just one thing I'd like to know," he said testily. "Who pushed me?"

SEPTEMBER 13

THE BIBLE -- GOD'S WONDERFUL BOOK

"For the word of God is living and powerful, and sharper than any two-edged sword, piercing even to the division of soul and spirit, and of joints and marrow, and is a discerner of the thoughts and intents of the heart." (Hebrews 4:12, NKJV)

This verse perfectly and accurately describes the written Word of God, and in this verse we are told several important things about God's wonderful Word -- the Bible.

The Bible Is Living In Its Nature. The Bible is spoken of as being *quick* or *living*, or "full of life." As God breathed into man the breath of life and man became a living soul (Genesis 1:26), so God has breathed into the Bible so that it has become a living book. The word *inspiration* in 2 Timothy 3:16 literally means God-breathed. C. H. Spurgeon said of the Bible, "If you cut it into a thousand pieces, every piece would grow and live." The late J. B. Phillips testified that when he first began translating the

New Testament he did not believe that all of the Bible was divinely inspired, but in the process of translating it he received so many "shocks" that he changed his mind. He wrote, "Translating the Bible was like trying to rewire a house without pulling the main switch. God's word is alive."

The Bible Is Powerful In Its Operation. The word *powerful* means energetic. The Bible is powerful. It is so powerful that it can literally change a person's life. It is like a two-edged sword that penetrates the inward parts of our human nature. The word *discerner* means critic. A critic is one who passes judgment upon a subject or person, and God's Word passes judgment upon man. Sometime ago a man took his worn New Testament to a bookbinder to have it bound with a fine Morocco leather cover and to have the words The New Testament printed on the edge in gold leaf letters. At the appointed time he returned to find his New Testament beautifully bound. The bookbinder had one apology, however: "I did not have small enough type in my shop to print out fully the words on the edge so I abbreviated them." Looking on the edge of his New Testament, the man saw the letters – T. N. T. How true. God's Word is powerful. The Bible says, "The Gospel is the *power* of God unto salvation" (Romans 1:16).

The Bible Is Clear In Its Demands. Notice the first word in our key-verse – "For the word of God . . ." This links us with the previous verses and indicates the two-fold demand that this Word makes upon us: faith (as indicated by verse 2), and obedience as indicated by verse 11. The way to be happy, holy, and useful to God is to read His Word, believe it and obey it! God's Word exposes our hearts; and then, if we trust God, the Word enables our hearts to obey God and claim His promises. John H. Sammis wrote: "When we walk with the Lord, in the light of His Word, what a glory He sheds on our way; while we do His good will He abides with us still, and with all who will trust and obey. Trust and obey, for there's no other way to be happy in Jesus, but to trust and obey."

Gypsy Smith told of a man who said he had received no inspiration from the Bible although he had "gone through it several times." "Let it go through you once," replied Smith, "then you will tell a different story!" Yes, God's Word is wonderful and when the Bible becomes a part of you, you'll be less likely to come apart.

A LITTLE HUMOR: A young man just out of seminary was being interviewed by a pulpit committee. One of the members of the pulpit committee was an English teacher in the local high school. She asked him, "Young man, when you speak in public it's important to use good English. Bad grammar might drive people away. Which would you say was proper – to speak of a hen as sitting or setting on eggs?" The young preacher thought a moment, then responded. "It's like back on the farm. When the hen did some cackling, we would have to decide whether she was laying or lying!"[73]

[73] Leslie Flynn, *A Source Book of Humorous Stories* (Grand Rapids: Baker Book House, 1973), 18-19.

SEPTEMBER 14

I CAN HEAR YOU!

"Then Hezekiah took the letter from the messengers, read it, and went over to the Temple and spread it out before the Lord . . . 'O Lord our God, I pray, deliver us from his hand that all the kingdoms of the earth may know that You alone, O Lord, are God'." (2 Kings 19:14, 19, NASB)

On Friday, September 14, President George W. Bush went to where the World Trade Center buildings once stood to visit rescue workers who were trying to find any possible survivors from the terrible attack of the terrorists. You may have watched and listened as President Bush put his arm around Bob Beckworth, a retired fire-fighter from Queens, and with a bullhorn in his other hand, told the crowd that the nation honored their efforts and mourned those killed in Tuesday morning's terrorist attack.

At one point someone in the crowd called out, "We can't hear you!" President Bush responded, "I can hear you. The rest of the world hears you, and the people who knocked these buildings down will hear all of us soon." Mr. Bush went on to say, "America is on bended knee in prayer for the people whose lives were lost here, for the workers who work here, for the families who mourn."

In the Old Testament book of 2 Kings, chapter 19, one may find the story of the time when the people of Israel were under attack by the Assyrians. The Assyrian king sent a letter to King Hezekiah demanding that they surrender. Hezekiah did a wise thing. Verse 14 says he "took the letter from the messengers, read it, and went over to the Temple and spread it out before the Lord." He then prayed to God, "O Lord our God, we plead with you to save us from his power; then all the kingdoms of the earth will know that you alone are God" (2 Kings 19:14, 19). Verse 20 says that the prophet Isaiah sent a message to Hezekiah: "The Lord God of Israel says, "I have heard you!"

At this critical time in America we must be people who are on bended knee in prayer as President Bush said. If we will humble ourselves before God and in a spirit of repentance, ask for His forgiveness of our sins, I believe the Lord will hear our prayers and will comfort us in our time of sorrow and bring about a healing that our nation needs (Read 2 Chronicles 7:14).

Hezekiah received an encouraging word from the Lord as recorded in verse 34: "I will defend and save this city for the sake of my own name..." We need the Lord's protection. The psalmist wrote, "Unless the Lord protects a city, sentries do no good" (Psalm 127:1, LB). Safety and victory for America will come, not because we deserve it but for the sake of God's own name. May our attitude and response to this tragedy be one that will bring honor and glory to His name. If we will stay on bended knee God will hear us!

A LITTLE HUMOR: A man was worried that his wife was losing her hearing. He decided to try an experiment to see if she really was losing her hearing. He got a chair and set it several feet behind the couch where she was seated. He whispered, "Can you hear me?" She said nothing. He moved his chair up a little closer and asked again, "Can you hear me?" She said nothing. He moved his chair up even closer and asked a third time, "Can you hear me?" Again, she said nothing. He moved his chair right up behind her and asked a fourth time, "Can you hear me?" His wife stood up, turned around and said, "For the fourth time, YES!"

SEPTEMBER 15

WEIGHTS OR WINGS

"I warned you when you felt secure, but you said, 'I will not listen!' This has been your way from your youth; you have not obeyed me." (Jeremiah 22:21, NIV)

In a book now out of print entitled *Counsels to the Young,* one may find this excellent quotation: "We act from habit nine times for every time we act from purposeful deliberation. Little do we comprehend the momentous consequences of our frequently repeated actions, for habits can add wings or weights to our feet."

When the western United States was being settled, roads were often just wagon tracks. These rough trails posed serious problems for those who journeyed on them. on one of these winding paths was posted a sign which read: "Avoid this rut or you'll be in it for the next twenty-five miles."

In a similar way, we must be careful to steer clear of sinful attitudes and deeds, because once we get into these "ruts" we may be trapped by them for many years. Negative thoughts may seem harmless, but if we do not check them daily and replace them with forgiveness and loving acts, we soon become critical in our whole outlook on life. Nurturing godly habits takes work especially if old patterns of behavior must be uprooted.

A wise father was strolling through a forest with his curious son by his side. The father suddenly stopped and pointed to four plants. The first was a tiny sprout coming out of the earth. Another had rooted itself quite firmly in the fertile soil. The third was a small shrub, and the fourth had grown into a well-developed tree.

The father said to his son, "Pull up the first plant." He pulled it up easily with his fingers. "Now pull up the second." The boy obeyed, and with slight effort the plant came up -- roots and all. "And now the third." He pulled with one hand, then the other, but it would not come. Then he used both hands and with all his strength pulled the plant out of the ground. "And now," said the father, "try the fourth." He grasped the trunk, pulling and tugging, but hardly a leaf shook. "I cannot move it," he exclaimed. "So it is, my son," said the father, "with all our bad habits. When they are young and small, we can cast them out; but when they are full grown, they cannot be uprooted."

Jeremiah 22:21 reads, "I warned you when you felt secure, but you said, 'I will not listen!' This has been your way from your youth; you have not obeyed me" (NIV). All of us form habits. Some are good and some are bad. If we are to form good habits we must yield to the Holy Spirit's control. We must fill our minds with the truths of Scripture. We must choose to obey them. We must avoid whatever causes us to lose our self-respect. We must keep forming good character traits, believing that God is working in us to reinforce our good habits. They will become for us wings that will help us make our way successfully through the wilderness of this world.

A LITTLE HUMOR: Don't let people drive you crazy when you know insanity is within walking distance.

SEPTEMBER 16

A BUILT IN WARNING SYSTEM

"I also do my best to maintain always a blameless conscience both before God and before men." (Acts 24:16, NASB)

Atop Central Fire Station in downtown Nacogdoches, Texas is an almost forgotten symbol of an era in our town's history. The emergency siren on the roof of Central Fire Station was at one time used to "call out the volunteers" when our town depended solely on volunteers to fight fires. The siren was first installed on the building in November, 1927. When the siren went off it could be heard all over the city. Today, the siren is not operable. It has been disconnected.

Every person has a built-in "warning system" called the conscience. The conscience has at least three functions. The first function is to aid us in distinguishing between right and wrong. The second function is to urge us to do right and to reject wrong. The third function is to approve us when we do right and to condemn us when we do wrong. The conscience serves as a sentinel which guards the soul. It is God's voice in the soul. Unfortunately some people "disconnect" their conscience when it comes to doing something they know is wrong. They don't want the siren of conscience to sound a warning. An American Indian once gave the following definition of the conscience: "Conscience is a little three-cornered thing inside me. When I do wrong it turns around and hurts me very much, but if I keep on doing wrong it turns so much that the corners come right off and it doesn't hurt me anymore."

The Bible lists several different kinds of consciences. It speaks of an evil conscience (Hebrews 10:22); a seared conscience (1 Timothy 4:1-2); a defiled conscience (Titus 1:15); a weak conscience (1 Corinthians 8:7); and a good conscience (1 Peter 3:16). Our goal should be to possess a good conscience. A good conscience is a conscience that has been cleansed and enlightened by God's grace to know what is right and wrong and to obey its dictates. Billy Graham has said, "If we put a stopper in our conscience; if we go against the wooing of the Spirit of God when He speaks to us about coming to the cross for the forgiveness of our sins; if we reject Christ and neglect Him: I warn you that after awhile there will be no ability even to call on God. We will call, but He says, 'I will not hear you.' What a tragedy!"

Adam Clark was a clerk in a store selling fine silk to well-to-do people in London. One day his employer showed Adam how to increase profits by subtly stretching the silk as he measured it out. Young Clark looked the man straight in the eye and said, "Sir, your silk may stretch but my conscience won't." Throughout the Apostle Paul's letters he mentions the importance of having a clear conscience. One such Scripture is Acts 24:16, "I also do my best to maintain always a blameless conscience both before God and before men" (NASB).

People today are more and more ignoring their conscience. They have "disconnected" it so they will not be bothered. Following the examples of Adam Clark and the Apostle Paul will help us to honor Christ and be a witness to those around us. Confessing our sins to God and asking for His forgiveness, as well as confessing to others when we have hurt or let them down will keep our conscience clear.

A LITTLE HUMOR: The IRS once received a letter from an anonymous taxpayer. It read, "I have cheated on my income tax for the pasts seven years, and tonight my conscience is troubling me to the point that I cannot sleep. I have enclosed a $100 bill as my way of saying 'I'm sorry.' If I find that I still can't sleep, I will send the rest of what I owe."

SEPTEMBER 17

WHIPS AND TONGUES

"Blessed are you when people insult you, persecute you and falsely say all kinds of evil against you because of me. Rejoice and be glad, because great is your reward in heaven for in the same way they persecuted the prophets who were before you."
(Matthew 5:11-12, NIV)

"The blow of a whip raises a welt, but a blow of the tongue crushes bones." That statement from the Apocrypha (Ecclesiasticus 28:17) may not be inspired in the same manner as the Holy Bible, but it is certainly true. Cutting and crushing words of criticism can make a person wonder, "Is it worth it all?"

I've made an amazing discovery. I have found a way to avoid criticism. In order to avoid criticism do the following: "Believe nothing! Do nothing! Dream nothing! Expect nothing! Plan nothing! Say nothing! Support nothing! Think nothing!" This approach to life may work, but honestly, is that the way we want to live? Sitting still and doing nothing will bring criticism, too. If you want to think tall, believe big, plan powerfully, dream dynamically and roll up your sleeves and be somebody with your life, then prepare yourself for criticism.

Basically, there are two kinds of people: the Carpenters and the Criticizers. The Criticizer is a captive imprisoned by his own faults. The Criticizer is a casualty of his own inadequacies. And the Criticizer makes for himself a cesspool of filth in which he has to wade. It would not be such a bad idea for the Criticizer to hide himself permanently, for these times demand Carpenters, not Criticizers. A man who had only one talent was asked, "And what is that one talent?" "The talent of criticism," he replied. "Well," suggested the questioner, "maybe you'd better do the same thing with your talent that the man of one talent in the parable did — go and bury it. Anybody whose only ability is to criticize might as well bury it, and himself with it."

When it comes to criticism, the first rule is to *Expect it.* Even Jesus Christ, the Master Carpenter by trade and spirit, wasn't a stranger to criticism! Who among all men is better qualified than He to advise, "Blessed are you when people insult you, persecute you and falsely say all kinds of evil against you because of me. Rejoice and be glad, because great is your reward in heaven for in the same way they persecuted the prophets who were before you" (Matthew 5:11-12, NIV)

Another suggestion in responding to criticism is to *Evaluate it.* Not all criticism is bad. "Never fear criticism," A.W. Tozer said, "if the critic is right, he has helped you. If he is wrong, you can help him. Either way, somebody gets helped." If we feel that the criticism is unjust, we want to fight back. But that may be just what the enemy wants us to do! Someone has said, "Never kick a skunk. You may manufacture a worse problem than you started with." Wise advice indeed!

Our immediate response to severe criticism may be to phone our friends and gather our forces. But our first task is to quiet our own hearts. A chat with a friend might help us calm down, but the peace we really need can come only from God. (If you need some "medicine," try Isaiah 54:16-17, Psalms 34 and 37, Philippians 2:1-18 and Romans 12:9-21). It does us good to face criticism from time to time, even though we may not enjoy it. Satan may want to use criticism as a weapon to batter us; but if we let Him, God can use it as a tool to build us.

A LITTLE HUMOR: A preacher said to a friend of his, "I'm going to take a survey in my church to find out what my members think I could do to make our church better." His friend said, "Hey, that sounds like a good idea. Let me know how it turns out." A few weeks later, the two met again and his friend said to him, "How did that survey turn out?" He said, "Not so good. Their response was too vague. They didn't specify which lake . . . or what kind of kite."[74]

SEPTEMBER 18

WHAT WOULD IT TAKE?

"I consider everything a loss compared to the surpassing greatness of knowing Christ Jesus my Lord, for whose sake I have lost all things." (Philippians 3:8, NIV)

An old man looks out from prison bars. This is a view he's seen before. He's

[74] Paul W. Powell, *Laugh and Live Longer* (Tyler, Texas), 31.

been arrested many times. He has suffered numerous beatings. Funny how life turns out. He was once a man of prominence. His family name carried influence. He was well educated — well respected. He had the right name, the right job, the right social connections. But he lost it all – kicked out of the cushy job – hated by his own family, and his friends wanted him dead. How do these things happen? He had been somebody. Now he was nobody, all because of one decision he would never second guess.

The old man sits down and grasps a pen in his arthritic fingers. Who knows how much time he's got left to tell his story? For all he knows, this could be his last letter. There's been talk of his upcoming execution. Powerful people want him dead. Strangely, the old man is not afraid. He squints down at his paper and begins to write: "I consider everything a loss compared to the surpassing greatness of knowing Christ Jesus my Lord, for whose sake I have lost all things" (Philippians 3:8, NIV). You recognize those words don't you? The apostle Paul wrote them almost 2,000 years ago to the believers in the city of Philippi. How could a man who had lost everything write words filled with so much hope?

A few years ago, Carolyn Johnson, a 73-year-old widow, lost her house and all her possessions in a flood. When asked how she was handling the loss, Mrs. Johnson remarked, "I've never been in a situation like this. Everything I had in the world is in that house. I don't have anything now," she said, "but Jesus." That's the situation Paul found himself in after his conversion. He lost everything. Like Carolyn Johnson, Paul could say, "I don't have anything now, but Jesus." Maybe that's not such a bad trade. Maybe it takes losing everything to discover the one thing that is truly important.

Joe DiMaggio, commenting on the suicide of his former wife, Marilyn Monroe, said, "She had everything to live with but nothing to live for." What a sad epitaph. Paul's situation is the exact opposite. At this stage in his life he had nothing to live with, but he had everything to live for. The salvation he found in Jesus was worth more than any possession or title ever could be.

A LITTLE HUMOR: One fellow was bragging to another about his grandfather: "My grandfather," he said, "knew the exact day of the exact year when he was going to die. Not only that, he knew the time he would die that day as well." His friend said, "Wow, that's incredible. How did he know all of that?" The first fellow said: "Because the judge told him."

SEPTEMBER 19

TRASH TALK

"If we say that we have no sin, we are deceiving ourselves, and the truth is not in us. If we confess our sins, He is faithful and righteous to forgive us our sins and to cleanse us from all unrighteousness. If we say that we have not sinned, we make Him a liar, and His word is not in us." (1 John 1:9-10, NASB)

Trash is a growing problem in our world. Americans throw out about 160 million tons of garbage a year, 3.5 pounds apiece each day. We are hearing more and more about recycling, because landfills are becoming a constant source of trouble for cities all across the country. When garbage is placed in a landfill, bulldozers cover it over with dirt, simply hiding the trash. Some companies burn their trash in an incinerator, but of course, the smoke generated then causes air pollution. Whatever the method of trash disposal, it is a serious problem. We are up to our ears in garbage, and it is rising fast.

Getting rid of our sin is also a constant struggle. Some of us may let it pile up like garbage in a landfill, until it hinders both us and others. If we try to hide sin, it is still a problem — we have just buried it. We need to understand the importance of allowing God to "incinerate" our sin.

A city cannot pretend that it has no garbage and deny the problem. If they do, a greater problem will soon arise. Our lives are much the same, nevertheless, Jesus has promised to be faithful to take care of our personal landfills, ridding us of the garbage we keep inside. We just have to confess, plead guilty, then give it to Him. The word *confess* means to agree with. True confession includes an agreement with God concerning the seriousness of sin. Confession is our part; forgiving and cleansing is God's part.

Notice the words "all unrighteousness." There are no sins that God will not cleanse. Every stain, every spot, every blur, every blot, every blemish in your life may be washed whiter than snow. "Forgive" means that God takes away our guilt; "cleanse" means that He removes the pollution of sin. To deny that we have sins to confess is to practice self-deception. The word "deceive" means "we lead ourselves astray."

A college freshman went to the dorm laundry room with his dirty clothes bundled into an old sweatshirt. But he was so embarrassed by how dirty his clothes were that he never opened the bundle. He merely pushed it into a washing machine and when the machine stopped he pushed the bundle into a dryer and finally took the still-unopened bundle back to his room. He discovered, of course, that the clothes had gotten wet and then dry, but not clean.

God says, "Don't keep your sins in a safe little bundle. Don't deceive yourself by covering up the sin in your life. I want to do a thorough cleansing in your life. If you will confess your sins, I will forgive you of them."

A LITTLE HUMOR: During his first day in school, a little boy was caught saying an inappropriate word. The teacher quickly scolded him and asked where he had heard such a word. The little boy said, "My daddy says it all the time." "Well, that doesn't matter. You shouldn't use that word. Besides, you don't even know what it means," said the teacher. "I do so," said the little boy. "It means the car won't start."

SEPTEMBER 20

CHECK THE GAUGE

"A new commandment I give to you, that you love one another, even as I have loved you, that you also love one another. By this all men will know that you are My disciples, if you have love for one another." (John 13:34-35, NASB)

For over thirty years my father was the production manager for the Coca-Cola Bottling Company of my home town, Pittsburg, Texas. Part of his responsibility was to light the boiler that heated the water to be used in sterilizing the bottles used in the bottling process. There was no timer on the boiler so my dad had to get up early — and I mean early — to go to the plant and light the boiler so the water would be heated by the time the men came to work. As a child I would often go to the plant during the day. The boiler room was rather large to accommodate the size of the boiler. It was hot in the boiler room, too. I remember asking my dad how he knew there was water in the boiler since there was no apparent way of looking inside. He pointed to a tiny glass tube mounted on the side of the boiler. The glass tube served as a gauge. He told me as the water stood in the little glass tube, so it stood in the great boiler. When the tube was half full, the boiler was half full; if empty, so was the boiler.

How does a person know if he loves God? Look at the gauge. Your love for others is the measure of your love for God. Jesus made the statement: "A new commandment I give to you, that you love one another, even as I have loved you, that you also love one another. By this all men will know that you are My disciples, if you have love for one another" (John 13:34-35, NASB). The word "new" does not mean "new in time," because love has been important to God's people even from Old Testament times (see Lev. 19:18). It means "new in experience, fresh." It is the opposite of "worn out." Love would take on a new meaning and power because of the death of Christ on the cross (John 15:13). With the coming of the Holy Spirit, love would have a new power in their lives. The true evidence, the gauge that shows we belong to the Lord, is the love we have for others. The church leader, Tertullian, (A.D. 155-220) quoted the pagans as saying of the Christians, "See how they love one another?"

When Wycliffe translator Doug Meland and his wife moved into a village of Brazil's Fulnio Indians, he was referred to simply as "the white man." The term was by no means complimentary, since other white men had exploited them, burned their homes, and robbed them of their lands. But after the Melands learned the Fulnio language and began to help the people with medicine and in other ways, they began calling Doug "the respectable white man." When the Melands began adapting the customs of the people, the Fulnio Indians gave them greater acceptance and spoke of Doug as "the white Indian." Then one day, as Doug was washing the dirty, blood-caked foot of an injured Fulnio boy, he overheard a by-stander say to another: "Whoever heard of a white man washing an Indian's foot before? Certainly this man is from God!" From that day on, whenever Doug would go into an Indian home, it would be announced: "Here comes the man God sent us."[75] How do you know the love of God dwells in you? Check the gauge. Love for others is an indication that the love of God dwells in you. "By this all men will know that you are My disciples, if you have love for one another."

A LITTLE HUMOR: Years ago a little girl rode a train with her family. At night they slept in the sleeping car with the little girl on the top bunk by herself. Mom assured her they would be right below her, and God would look after her. As the darkness became quiet, the little girl got scared. She called out, "Mommy, are you there?" Her mother replied, "Yes, dear." A few minutes passed and she asked her father the same question. Dad let it be known he was right below her. Several minutes later the questions were repeated and she also asked about her brother and sister. After everybody answered, "Yes," she was quiet – for a while. Later she began asking the same questions again, and another passenger lost his patience. In a deep voice he said, "We're all here! Your father, your mother, your brother, and your sister. Now GO TO SLEEP!" Complete silence followed his pronouncement. Then the little girl whispered, "Mommy, was that God?"[76]

SEPTEMBER 21

STRESS WITHOUT DISTRESS

"Do not fret . . ." (Psalm 37:1, NASB)

The phrase "all shook up" was made popular by the late Elvis Presley. Shortly before his death he said he would pay a million dollars for one week of a normal life of peace, to be able to move up and down the streets of his city without harassment. He discovered that money won't alleviate stress. This forty-two-year-old man, whose funeral brought over five tons of flowers from people all over the world, lived his life all shook up. That very theme became his personal trademark.[77]

Three times in Psalm 37 we are told: "Do not fret" (vv. 1, 7, 8). The word *fret* means to burn; to become heated up; incensed. The word for stress in Latin is *strictus* which means "to be drawn tight." There are some things a stress-ridden person can do in order to bring his stress under control.

First, realize that some stress is good for you. The psalmist wrote, "The punishment you gave me was the best thing that could have happened to me, for it taught me to pay attention to your laws. They are more valuable to me than millions in silver and gold" (Psalm 119:72-73, LB).

Second, keep putting your trust in the Lord. Psalm 37:3 reads, "Trust in the

---

[75] James C. Hefley, *Encyclopedia of 7700 Illustrations* (Rockville, Md., 1979), 757.

[76] *Bits and Pieces,* March 5, 1992, pages 21-22.

[77] Charles R. Swindoll, *Three Steps Forward, Two Steps Back* (Nashville: Thomas Nelson Publishers, 1980), 41-42.

Lord, and do good; dwell in the land and cultivate faithfulness" (NASB).

Third, seek your happiness in the Lord. Psalm 37:4 reads, "Delight yourself in the Lord; And He will give you the desires of your heart" (NASB).

Fourth, learn to rest in the Lord. "Rest in the Lord and wait patiently for Him; do not fret . . ." (Psalm 37:7, NASB). What you do while you wait on the Lord is important. Perhaps the acrostic below will help:

W – Whisper a prayer (Luke 18:1)
A – Anticipate the best (Romans 8:28)
I – Invest your time wisely (Ephesians 5:16)
T – Trust in the Lord (Proverbs 3:5-6)

Charles R. Swindoll has written: "Those threatening storms are designed to slow us down, to make us climb up into His arms, to force us to depend on Him. Maybe it's time to say, 'Lord, through your strength I will not be moved. I will stop running, stop striving. I will hold on to You.'"[78]

A LITTLE HUMOR: Can it be an accident that "STRESSED" is "DESSERTS" spelled backward?

SEPTEMBER 22

GET RID OF YOUR GUILT

"My guilt has overwhelmed me like a burden too heavy to bear." (Psalm 38:4, NIV)

The late baseball legend Gil Hodges told this story. Once, when he was managing the Washington Senators, he discovered four of his players had broken curfew the previous night. Immediately, he called a team meeting and said, "I know who you are, but I do not wish to embarrass you. You know the rules; you will each be fined $100. I have placed a cigar box on my desk. I expect the four of you who broke curfew to put your money in the box by 3:00 p. m." At the end of the day, Hodges found $700 in his cigar box!

What Gil Hodges discovered is that a lot more people are struggling with guilt than he imagined. Guilt plagues everyone to some degree, for we all have to lay our head on our pillow at night and accept the fact that we have not done as well as we could have.

Guilt has been a problem since the beginning of time. It was guilt that caused Adam and Eve to hide when God came walking in the cool of the day (Genesis 3:8). It was guilt over his adulterous affair that caused David to cry, "My iniquities are gone over my head; as a heavy burden they weigh too much for me" (Psalm 38:4). It was guilt that caused Isaiah to cry out, "Woe is me . . . for I am a man with unclean

---

[78] Ibid, 46.

lips" (Isaiah 6:5) when he came into the presence of the Living God. When the Pharisees brought the woman caught in adultery, Jesus looked at the angry mob and said, "He who is without sin among you, let him be the first to throw a stone at her" (John 8:7). It was guilt that caused the men to drop their stones, one by one, and walk away. It was guilt that caused Judas Iscariot to take his own life after he betrayed Jesus in the Garden of Gethsemane (Matthew 27:5).

Guilt continues to haunt the human race. The IRS once received a letter from an anonymous taxpayer. It read, "I have cheated on my income tax for the past seven years, and tonight my conscience is troubling me to the point that I cannot sleep. I have enclosed a $100 bill as my way of saying 'I am sorry.' If I find that I still can't sleep, I will send the rest of what I owe." Guilt has been a companion of mankind from the beginning.

When Jesus died on the cross He paid the price for your sins, once and for all. Your guilt, your shame, your sin was laid upon Him, and nailed to the cross. The punishment you deserved, He received. If you are willing to confess and forsake your sins and seek forgiveness, you are assured that He is willing to forgive and cleanse (1 John 1:9). Jesus doesn't lay guilt on anyone. He removes it. He takes it away.

A LITTLE HUMOR: A husband and wife were sitting at the breakfast table on his day off. She said to him, "Please don't think of playing golf this morning." He replied, "It's the farthest thing from my mind. Please pass the putter."

SEPTEMBER 23

NEVER UNDERESTIMATE THE POWER OF TEARS

"Those who sow in tears will reap with songs of joy." (Psalm 126:5, NIV)

Have you ever wondered what it takes to earn a starting position on a National Championship college football team? Strength? Endurance? Speed? How about the ability to cry? Sounds crazy, but it happened.

In Lou Holtz' second season as head coach of the Notre Dame Fighting Irish, his team experienced a humiliating loss against Texas A & M in the Cotton Bowl. Holtz said he was absolutely dejected when he walked into the locker room after the game. He couldn't help but notice that most of the Notre Dame players didn't seem to be bothered at all by the loss, with one exception, a second-string sub named Chris Zorich who sat in front of his locker crying deep, gut-heaving sobs. He was thoroughly crushed by the defeat. Holtz decided at that moment the next year's team would be composed of players who loved football as much as Chris. The next season this young man went from sub to starter to team captain, and helped lead the Irish to a National Championship. Chris Zorich won a starting position at Notre Dame because he was the only player on the team who cared enough to cry.

Some things are worth caring about. Certain areas of your life — maybe your job, your family, a person you're trying to disciple or lead to Christ — sometimes require more emotional involvement than an "ordinary" person would be willing to give. It may be tempting to tell yourself that it's not worth crying over. But remember, caring is the key to making a difference.

It is interesting to notice that before Jesus raised Lazarus from the dead, He wept for his friend (John 11:35-36). As He approached Jerusalem toward the end of His ministry, Jesus wept over the city saying, "If you had only known what would bring you peace" (Luke 19:41, NIV). He cared enough to cry. Caring comes with a price, but it also comes with a reward. The Psalmist wrote, "Those who sow in tears will reap with songs of joy" (Psalm 126:5, NIV).

Never underestimate the power of tears, or what those tears represent. It isn't until you are willing to become emotionally involved — until you care enough to cry — that you are able to change people's lives or your own.

A LITTLE HUMOR: A man rushed into the doctor's office and shouted, "Doctor! I think I'm shrinking!" The doctor calmly responded, "Now, settle down. You'll just have to be a little patient."

SEPTEMBER 24

AS A CHILD TO HIS FATHER

"One of his disciples said to him, 'Lord, teach us to pray'. . . He (Jesus) said to them, 'When you pray, say, 'Father . . .'" (Luke 11:1-2, NIV)

What's the first thing we are to say when we pray? "Father!" The God to whom we pray is a very loving, special, personal God who wants us to call him "Father." He wants us to talk to Him as a child does with his father. He doesn't want us to be afraid to approach Him or to share with Him what is on our hearts.

Some years back, Joe Creason described a farmer not accustomed to praying in public who was called on to lead the benediction at a rural church in Cumberland County, Kentucky. Creason told what happened in the *Louisville Courier-Journal.* He made a stab at leading the benediction, but rambled on and on, unable to find a place to stop. Creason said, "Suddenly, in the middle of a sentence, the farmer turned to his wife. 'Sara, you wind this up,' he said in a loud whisper. 'Danged if I ain't got her in a terrible twist!'"

This Kentucky farmer made a mistake lots of us make — and that is too much concern over the mechanics of prayer. There is no reason why we must talk to God in formal, stained-glass language. Imagine your teenager walking up to you with this request, "O great and wise father, knower of all things, provider of my shelter and daily food, author of family order and peace, generous and benevolent ruler of the house, would you please lend me the car?" Not only would you think he was crazy, you would suspect he was up to something questionable. When we speak to our heavenly Father in prayer, it should be as a child speaks to his earthly father. It takes no special language, no specific formula, no certain place or posture. No topic is off limits. The child of God can pray anywhere, any place, any time, about anything.

Sam W. Foss wrote a little poem which is not great poetry from a literary standpoint. But as common sense, Foss hits the nail on the head. In the opening stanzas, he described "Deacon Lemuel Keyes" who says one must pray on his knees. "No," replied Reverend Doctor Wise, who insisted one must stand up straight with outstretched hands. In the closing stanza, Fosss quotes from Cryus Brown, who settled the issue once and for all:

"Last year I fell in Hidgin's well
  Head first," said Cyrus Brown.
"With both my heels a stickin' up,
  My head a-pointin' down;
An' I made a prayer right then an' there --
  Best prayer I ever said,
The prayingest prayer I ever prayed,
  Was a-standing on my head!"[79]

A LITTLE HUMOR: A little boy prayed, "Lord, if you can't make me a better boy, don't worry about it. I'm having a real good time like I am!"

SEPTEMBER 25

OUR GOD IS AN AWESOME GOD

"How awesome is the Lord Most High, the great King over all the earth."
(Psalm 47:2, NIV)

In 1962 John Glenn became the first American to orbit the earth and in 1998, at the age of 77, he became the world's oldest astronaut to ever go into space. A newspaper article stated that for John Glenn, life in orbit is almost a religious experience. John Glenn, who is a Presbyterian, said, "Looking at the Earth from this vantage point, looking at this kind of creation and to not believe in God, to me, is impossible. To see (Earth) laid out like that only strengthens my beliefs. I know 'awesome' is an overused word, but if anything is really awesome, it's looking out and seeing that."

John Glenn not only has the "right stuff" when it comes to being an astronaut, he also has the right stuff when it comes to his opinion of God. Our God is an awesome God. God created a universe so large that it would take a person between 200 and 500 billion years to travel around the universe at the speed of light (186,000 miles per second). He created the world out of atoms so small that it would take the whole population of the world 180 million years to count the atoms in a cup of water, counting at one per second. If it cost one cent to ride 1000 miles, a trip around the

[79] Curtis C. Mitchell, *Praying Jesus' Way* (New Jersey: Fleming H. Revell Company, 1977), 142.

world would cost 25 cents. A trip to the moon would cost $240, and a trip to the sun, $930. But a trip to Alpha Centauri, the nearest star system, would cost $260 million. When it comes to creation, our God is an awesome God!

The psalmist agrees. He wrote, "How awesome is the Lord Most High, the great King over all the earth" (Psalm 47:2, NIV). In most cases, the word translated "awesome" means "to be afraid," "to fear," or "to revere." The awe felt by God's people is an appropriate response to who God is. But awe does not drive us from God. We know that this majestic God whose being and glory are immense and awe-inspiring has chosen to love us and to invite us into the most intimate of relationships with Him.

As awesome as creation is, there is something that is even greater. It is the salvation of a soul from sin. The Bible says, "If anyone is in Christ, he is a new creation; the old has gone, the new has come!" (2 Corinthians 5:17, NIV). John W. Peterson wrote a song about the miracle of creation and of the recreation of the human soul in salvation: "It took a miracle to put the stars in place/ It took a miracle to hang the world in space; but when He saved my soul, Cleansed and made me whole, It took a miracle of love and grace!"

Collins, the *Freethinker*, once met a plain countryman going to church. He asked him where he was going. "To church to worship God." "Is your God a great or little God?" "He is both, Sir." "How can He be both?" "He is so great, Sir, that the heaven of heavens cannot contain Him; and so little that He dwells in my heart." Thanks, John Glenn, for reminding us that our God is an awesome God!

A LITTLE HUMOR: A grandmother and her five-year-old grandson were taking a walk in the country just after the first heavy frost of the season had dyed the foliage and given it a brilliantly colored, crazy-quilt appearance. "Just think," the grandmother marveled, gazing at a scarlet and gold-tinted hillside, "God painted all that." "Yes," the grandson agreed, "and He even did it with His left hand." "What do you mean 'He did it with His left hand?'" she asked, somewhat puzzled by the remark. "Well," the boy replied reasonably, "at Sunday School, they told us that Jesus is sitting on the right hand of God!"

SEPTEMBER 26

HEAD OR HEART?

"The word is near you, in your mouth and in your heart — that if you confess with your mouth Jesus as Lord, and believe in your heart that God raised Him from the dead, you shall be saved." (Romans 10:8-9, NASB)

I have just returned from a tour of the Holy Land with several of our church members. What an experience! To actually be in the land where our Lord and Savior, Jesus Christ, was born, lived, died, rose again and will return some day was a life-time dream come true.

Our tour guide was a remarkable young man. He was a commander in Israel's army. He won our hearts. Each day he greeted us with his winning smile, clever sense of humor, and incredible knowledge of Israel. From the story of Abraham and Isaac to the account of Jesus' resurrection, our guide had it all down. He carried a Hebrew/English Bible and read from it frequently.

Once during the week I had the opportunity to speak to him about Jesus. "Was he a believer? Did he know Jesus? Was Jesus his Savior?" Sadly, the answer was no. He knew the Bible better than most of us. He daily walked where Jesus had. He had been giving tours to Christians for several years. But he didn't know his Messiah. In fact, he said he had never even heard of Jesus until he went to the special school where he was taught to be a tour guide. Here was a man who was born in Jerusalem and lived in Jerusalem all his life, yet he had never heard of Jesus until trained to be a tour guide.

Could that be your situation? I'm not talking about your being a tour guide. I'm talking about your relationship with Jesus Christ. Could you have a knowledge of God and His Son Jesus in your head but not in your heart? It's not all that unusual. Knowing about Jesus is not the same as knowing Him. We must acknowledge Jesus as "the Christ, the Son of the living God" (Matthew 16:16). We must accept His forgiveness for our sins and enter into a personal relationship with Him.

Have you trusted Jesus? Is your knowledge of Him in your head but not in your heart?

A LITTLE HUMOR: Two evangelists sit beside the road to the old bridge. Each is holding a sign saying, "Beware, the end is coming." Every time a car goes by, they hold up their signs. After hearing several loud crashes, one says to the other, "Do you think we should have said, 'Because the bridge is out'?"

SEPTEMBER 27

WHEN WORRY DIES

"So do not worry about tomorrow; for tomorrow will care for itself. Each day has enough trouble of its own." (Matthew 6:34, NASB)

The New Testament word for worry is translated "take thought" and "be careful" in the *Authorized Version*. The word *worry* comes from the Greek word *merimnao* which is a combination of two words: *merizo* which means "to divide," and *nous* which means "mind." So to worry is to have a mind divided between legitimate thoughts and destructive thoughts. No wonder James says that a double-minded man is "unstable in all his ways" (James 1:8).

The word "anxious" that Paul uses is a synonym for our word "worry." It is the same word that Jesus used when He told Martha that she was "worried and troubled about many things" (Luke 10:41). Our Lord also used this word in talking with His disciples when he told them that they were to "take no thought" about food, drink, clothing, or shelter (Matthew 6:25-34). Obviously, He was not suggesting that they should never think about such things; rather, He was reminding them that they should not worry about them.

When worry takes over in our lives, it chokes out the Word of God (Matthew 13:7, 22). It causes us to abandon our trust in the Lord who tells us to cast all of our care upon Him (1 Peter 5:7). How can we rid ourselves of worry?

There once was an airplane pilot in the pioneer days of aviation who was making a flight around the world. After he was two hours out of his last landing field, he heard a noise in his plane, which he recognized as the gnawing of a rat. He realized that while his plane had been on the ground a rat had gotten in. For all he knew the rat could be gnawing through a vital cable or control of the plane. It was a very serious situation. He was both concerned and anxious. At first he did not know what to do. It was two hours back to the landing field from which he had taken off and more than two hours to the next field ahead. Then he remembered that the rat is a rodent.. It is not made for heights; it is made to live on the ground and under the ground. Therefore the pilot began to climb. He went up a thousand feet, then another thousand and another until he was more than twenty thousand feet up. The gnawing ceased. The rat was dead. He could not survive in the atmosphere of those heights. More than two hours later the pilot brought the plane safely to the next landing field and found the dead rat.[80]

Worry is a rodent. It cannot live in the secret place of the Most High (Psalm 91:1). It cannot breathe in the atmosphere made vital through prayer and familiarity with the Scripture. Worry dies when we ascend to the Lord through prayer and His word.

A LITTLE HUMOR: "Now, Jim," said the doctor, "as I have repeatedly told you after many thorough examinations, there is absolutely nothing wrong with your heart, so please stop worrying about it. If it will make you feel any better, I will personally guarantee you that your heart will last as long as you live!"

SEPTEMBER 28

GENUINELY ARTIFICIAL

"But Jesus perceived their malice, and said, 'Why are you testing Me, you hypocrites?'" (Matthew 22:18, NASB)

If you see someone in January with a deep bronze tan, it may not mean that they recently went to Jamaica — it could mean they've spent a few hours in a tanning booth. People have proven they'll pay good money to look tan, but are they really suntanned? No. These people have subjected themselves to an artificial experience so it will look like they have undergone the real thing. The only way to get a real tan is to spend time under the sun.

---

[80] David Jeremiah, *Turning Toward Joy* (Wheaton: Victor Books, 1992), 184-185.

For you to be a godly person, you must spend time in the presence of the "Son" — the Lord Jesus Christ. Many Christians today do their best to appear godly, but there is only one way to actually be like Jesus — spend time with Him. There is no substitute. Some people may make Christianity sound easy and effortless, but the truth is, there are no shortcuts.

Peter and John spent time in the presence of Jesus, and their lives reflected that reality. Those who observed them "were astonished and took note that these men had been with Jesus" (Acts 4:13, NIV). How can people tell you have been in the presence of the Lord?

For one thing, it will be evident by your **countenance.** There will be something about your physical appearance that will indicate that you have been in the presence of the Lord. That was true of Moses. When Moses came down from Mount Sinai, the Bible says his face was radiant because he had spoken with the Lord (Exodus 34:29). It was true of Stephen who had "the face of an angel" (Acts 6:15).

It will be evident also by your **conduct**. A person who has spent time with Jesus will conduct himself in a manner worthy of his calling (Ephesians 4:1) and will allow his "light" to shine before men that they may glorify their Heavenly Father (Matthew 5:16). The early followers of Christ were called "Christians" because they behaved like Christ (Acts 11:26).

Furthermore, it will be evident in your **conversation.** Jesus said that the words which came from a person's mouth actually came from within his inner self (Matthew 12:34-37). Peter tried to deny he had been with Jesus, but his accuser said, "You certainly are one of them, you know; it's obvious from your accent" (Matthew 26:73, Phi).

Finally, it will be evident by your **courage.** The Bible says "they saw the courage of Peter and John" and were convinced they had been with Jesus. These disciples were filled with holy boldness as they were filled with the Holy Spirit. They gave a powerful witness for the Lord.

Is this true of your life? Have you been spending time with the "Son"? Be sure today that your Christianity is the real thing and not an artificial look-alike. People will know the difference sooner or later.

A LITTLE HUMOR: A railroad clerk was being pestered with questions by a traveler while people in a long line waited impatiently. The clerk decided to teach the difficult man a lesson. "Upper or lower berth?" he asked. "What's the difference?" "Well, the difference is twenty dollars. The lower berth is higher than the upper one. The higher price is for the lower. If you want it lower you have to go higher. We sell the upper lower than the lower. Most people don't like the lower upper, although it's low on account of being higher. When you occupy an upper you have to go up to bed and get down to get up.[81]

[81] Tal D. Bonham, *The Treasury of Clean Jokes* (Nashville: Broadman Press, 1981), 154.

SEPTEMBER 29

SO, WHAT'S THE CATCH?

"Do not be deceived: God is not mocked. A man reaps what he sows. The one who sows to please his sinful nature, from that nature will reap destruction; the one who sows to please the Spirit, from the Spirit will reap eternal life. Let us not become weary in doing good, for at the proper time we will reap a harvest if we do not give up." (Galatians 6:6-9, NIV)

What would you be willing to do in order to spend the next seven years of your life with every material pleasure and comfort you desired? How much would you be willing to sacrifice in order to experience such a life?

In Africa there is a tribe that is willing to offer that kind of promise. This particular group has a custom in which they elect a new king every seven years. During the seven years of a king's reign, he has absolute rule and enjoys every possible pleasure and abundance that life has to offer. There is only one negative point; at the end of his reign, he is killed on the same day that the new ruler is installed. The one thing the king cannot do is change that tradition. That is quite a price to pay for seven years of pleasure. Do you think it's worth it? Whatever your opinion may be, there are many people in Africa who are willing to die just so they can experience that kind of life style, even if it is only for a short time.

Though we may be surprised at such a custom, we, too, sometimes try to live our lives that way — seeking our own immediate pleasure and comfort, regardless of future effects. We need to understand that actions always bring results, even when the effects aren't quite as obvious as they are for these African kings. Our daily pursuits always take us somewhere. The Bible promises that: "Do not be deceived: God is not mocked. A man reaps what he sows. The one who sows to please his sinful nature, from that nature will reap destruction; the one who sows to please the Spirit, from the Spirit will reap eternal life. Let us not become weary in doing good, for at the proper time we will real a harvest if we do not give up" (Galatians 6:6-9, NIV).

When God says, "Be not deceived," He means, "Don't kid yourself, no one ever breaks God's rules and gets away with it." In Latin, there is an ancient phrase: *lex talionus.* It refers to the law of retaliation, of punishment or reward, in kind. When we sow evil, we reap evil. When we sow goodness, we reap goodness. These verses are warning each of us that every act, is really a seed. Our daily deeds, once planted, do not end. Like a seed, they may lie dormant for a time, but then they sprout and bear some kind of fruit.

Are you sowing seeds of destruction or eternal life? Either way, you will one day reap the results of your daily actions. Even if the results are delayed, never be misled into thinking they won't come. Sooner or later, they will. In the words of Dr. R. G. Lee, you can always count on a "payday someday." Robert Louis Stevenson once said, "Sooner or later we must all sit down to a banquet of consequences." What will you be reaping on that day?

A LITTLE HUMOR: A little five-year-old was watching his older brother get disciplined by their father. After a thorough lecture, the dad reminded his elder son that he would now have to live with the consequences of his actions. A few minutes later the little brother spoke with his dad and made a special request, "Dad, if David has to go live with the consequences, can I have his room?"

SEPTEMBER 30

THE HEART OF THE MATTER

"Blessed are the pure in heart, for they will see God." (Matthew 5:8, NIV)

Ivory soap is a special kind of soap. It's not like all the other brands of soap. It's almost completely pure. Most soaps have lots of different ingredients and extra stuff in them. The chief ingredients of soap are fats and chemicals called alkalis. Manufacturers may use animal fats or such vegetable oils as coconut oil and olive oil. But not Ivory soap. It's just pure soap and air. That's all. Actually, Ivory soap was made by accident. You see, soap is made by mixing all sorts of ingredients together, and then putting the mixture into a giant machine that stirs and stirs and stirs it all up. One day, the man at a certain soap factory forgot to turn off the stirring machine. It just kept stirring and stirring the soap for a much longer time than usual. When the man came in the next morning, he discovered that he had made a new type of soap. It was completely pure, with nothing yucky in it. In fact, this new soap was so pure that it floated on top of water. Today, manufacturers make floating soaps by mixing the warm soap solution with air in a machine equipped with cooling coils.[82]

Now I'm sure that a pure soap like Ivory soap is a good thing to have. But having a pure heart is even greater. On one occasion Jesus went up on a mountain and preached to large crowds of people. He talked about what kind of people are the happiest people, what kind of people make God happy. Jesus said, "Blessed are the pure in heart, for they will see God" (Matthew 5:8, NIV) When you have a pure heart, it means you keep your heart focused on God. You love God more than anything else. In fact, a pure heart is so full of God's love that there's hardly any room for sin in there.

The Greek word for "pure" is *katharos* from which we receive our words, *catharsis* or *cathartic*. *Katharos* means to make pure by cleansing from dirt, filth, or contamination. A pure heart has been purged, cleansed, refined, and purified. A pure heart refers to one that has no hypocrisy, inward sham, deceit, or moral filth. A pure heart is a single heart with no selfish interest. A heart that is *katharos* is one that is honest with no hidden motive.

A pastor was offered some theater tickets to a rather famous play that had a few questionable immoral scenes in it. The godly pastor kindly refused the offer

---

[82] *Dynamic Preaching,* January - March, 1999, 78.

prompting the person to inquire why he could not go. The pastor explained: “It’s this way. Before a doctor operates on someone, he scrubs his hands until they are absolutely germ free. He wouldn’t dare operate with dirty hands. I am a servant of Christ and deal with precious human souls. I wouldn’t dare to do my service with a dirty life.”

“A person who lets the light shine through” is the way a small boy defined a saint. He got this idea from watching the sun shine through prophets and other men of God in the stained-glass windows of his church. Saintliness is purity and single-mindedness. Membership is open to anyone with courage to clean the cobwebs of hypocrisy from his heart.

A LITTLE HUMOR: A little boy of a Baptist minister was in church when he saw for the first time someone being baptized by immersion. He was greatly interested in it, and the next morning proceeded to baptize his three cats in the bathtub. The first kitten bore it well, and so did the second one, but the old family cat rebelled. It struggled with him, clawed and tore him, and got away. With considerable effort he caught it again and proceeded with the ceremony one more time. But the cat acted worse than ever, clawed at him, spit, and scratched his hands and face. Finally, after barely getting her splattered with water, he dropped her on the floor in disgust and said, "Fine, be an atheist!"

OCTOBER 1

WHEN GOD CALLS

"I am the Lord, I have called you..." (Isaiah 42:6a, NASB)

There was an interesting article in the newspapers sometime back about a "Husband-Calling" contest that is held each year at the Illinois State Fair. One winner of that distinguished prize was a woman named Tish Dixon. To accomplish her prize-winning call Tish shoves two fingers into her mouth, whistles sharply and wails, "Scott-eeeee!" Dixon declares that her husband does respond — that's why they have such a good marriage. Husband-calling was combined with the fair's hog-calling contest, a practical skill for the farmers who enter the competition. "I really do call my pigs twice a day to feed them," said one participant. "And they do respond," he said. "They're very smart." I don't know whose idea it was to combine husband-calling and hog-calling. I would not dare to comment on the relative merits of these pastimes."[83]

Some of us can remember when as children we would be out playing when suddenly over the din of things our mothers would call our name. "It's time to come home," she would insist. "It's supper time." Strangers rarely call out our name. Only people to whom we are important call our names. So, what a magnificent idea it is that, according to Isaiah, the Creator of the universe would call our name. We are known. We are loved. Let no one say his or her life does not matter. The Lord of creation has called our name.

We are not simply called; we are called to a purpose. When God calls us it is a call to eternal life (1 Timothy 6:12), to righteousness (Isaiah 42:6), to fellowship with Christ (1 Corinthians 1:9), to liberty (Galatians 5:13), to peace (1 Corinthians 7:15), and to mercy (Mark 10:49).

Jesus said He calls His own sheep by name (John 10:3) and they follow Him because "they know His voice" (John 10:41). To this day the voice of Jesus can be heard calling us unto Himself. Those who want to hear and respond to His call are blessed beyond measure.

Listen! Is that your name He's calling?

A LITTLE HUMOR: A man was admiring the tropical fish in a pet shop. When he was offered assistance, he mentioned that his new wife was a fish fancier. After being shown around, he shouted, "There she is! That's the one. I'll take it." As the large, sluggish goldfish with a gray splotch at the top of its head was being scooped out, the man exclaimed, "My bride will love this! She's always wanted to know what my first wife looked life!"

---

[83] *Dynamic Preaching.* January-March, 2002, Vol. 17, No. 1, 17.

OCTOBER 2

STILL ON THE PHONE

"Then you will call, and the Lord will answer; you will cry for help, and he will say: 'Here am I'." (Isaiah 58:9, NIV)

Sometimes children are confused about prayer. One little girl said prayer is messages sent up at night and on Sunday when the rates are low. We adults sometimes make prayers too formal, especially at church. When the pastor steps up to the pulpit, he suddenly has a holy tone and talks with a stained glass voice. What if I came home one day and my daughter said to me, "Hail, thou illustrious Senior Pastor of First Baptist Church. I welcome thee home from thy sojourn down North Street. Wouldst thou grant to your daughter, Carrie, funds that I may sojourn to yonder apothecary and procure for myself some cosmetics with which to adorn myself, oh gracious Father?" I'd accuse her of snorting Sweet and Low. She doesn't talk like that. She would say something like, "Hi, Daddy. Love you. Missed you. I would like to buy some things I need, got any money? Thanks Dad."

Prayer is not trying to persuade God to do what you want. A professor in a college English class was trying to impress upon his students the value of a rich vocabulary. He said to them, "If you will take a new word and use it ten times it will be yours forever." A young woman in the class looked dreamily out the window and started saying, "George, George, George, George . . ."

That's the way some people pray, looking for the right password to get the "George" of their dreams. Prayer is telling God you want to be a partner in what He wants to do. You can't find a better partner.

Does God answer prayer? Sure He does. The Bible says, "Then you will call, and the Lord will answer; you will cry for help, and he will say: 'Here am I'" (Isaiah 58:9, NIV). Sometimes he doesn't answer the way we want Him to. Even Garth Brooks understands that. He sang *Thank God for Unanswered Prayers.* Sometimes God says, "No," because you don't need what you want. Sometimes He says, "No," because you have the wrong motive. Sometimes the timing is wrong and He says "Not now." Sometimes He says, "Yes."

One little girl heard the church choir singing "God is Still on the Throne." On the way home from church she told her mom, "I really like that song 'God is still on the phone'." God is still on the phone. Why don't you give Him a call — local, direct, and free of charge?

A LITTLE HUMOR: Corrie ten Boom wrote of a little boy whose mother heard his reciting the alphabet while sitting in the corner of his room. His mother asked, "What are you doing?" He replied, "Mom, you told me to pray, but I have never prayed in my life and I don't know how. So I gave God the alphabet and asked him to make a good prayer of it."[84]

---

[84] Corrie ten Boom, *Clippings From My Notebook,* 1982, 16.

OCTOBER 3

GOOD FORGETTERS

"Then Peter came to Him and said, 'Lord, how often shall my brother sin against me and I forgive him? Up to seven time?" Jesus said to him, "I do not say to you, up to seven times, but up to seventy times seven." (Matthew 18:21-22, NKJV)

Forgiveness is crucial to our happiness. This is especially true when family members practice annoying habits.

A man told about his wife who he believed had never changed the toilet tissue roll since they had been married. He got so mad that he started writing the date and time on every cardboard cylinder he changed. One day he had had enough, and in his frustration, he went to the closet and grabbed two large plastic bags full of cardboard cylinders with the date and time on each one. As he was dumping the cardboard cylinders all over the room he declared, "I have proof you have never changed the toilet tissue roll!" She looked at the cylinders all over the room and said, "You're sick!"

"I'll show you who's sick," He said. "We're going to see the psychiatrist!" He made an appointment, and they went, with him carrying the two plastic bags full of cardboard cylinders. The psychiatrist asked, "What seems to be the problem?" The man said, "The problem is that my wife has never changed the toilet tissue roll, and I have proof." He started dumping the cardboard cylinders all over the psychiatrist's desk and the psychiatrist looked at him and said, "You're sick!"[85]

We are all sick and defective and our Maker has recalled every one of us. No one will measure up to your expectations — even you don't measure up to your own expectations. So forgive yourself and forgive others for not being perfect. Be more like children.

I heard about a little boy who was mad at his best friend, Andrew. They got into a fight and he told his mother, "I hate Andrew, I never want to see him again — and I hope his dog dies!" The next day he was going out to play and his mother said, Where are you going?" He said, "I'm going to play with Andrew." She said, "I thought you never wanted to see him again and hoped his dog died." He said, "Yeah, I said that about Andrew, but me and Andrew are good forgetters."[86]

So chill out! Let's be good forgetters and what you can't forget, forgive. We all carry around our plastic bags full of something, waiting to dump it on one who has wronged us. You need to realize that carrying it around does more damage to you than it will do to the person you dump on. Remember the words of Jesus when Peter asked how many times he should forgive someone who had sin against him. Thinking he was being rather generous he asked Jesus, "Up to seven times?" Jesus said to him, "I do not say to you, up to seven times, but up to seventy times seven" (Matthew 18:21-22, NKJV). The point is not to keep count at all, but to always be willing to forgive. Let's be good forgetters!

---

[85] Charles Lowery, "Good Forgetters," *SBC LIFE*, September, 1998, 16.

[86] Ibid, 16.

A LITTLE HUMOR: "I want to go from Chicago to Hippopotamus, New York." The agent was at a loss for words. Finally, the agent asked, "Are you sure that's the name of the town?"
"Yes, what flights do you have?" replied the customer.
After some searching, the agent came back with, "I'm sorry, ma'am. I've looked up every airport code in the country and can't find a Hippopotamus anywhere."
The customer retorted, "Oh, don't be silly. Everyone knows where it is. Check your map!"
The agent scoured a map of the state of New York and finally offered, "You don't mean Buffalo, do you?"
"That's it! I knew it was a big animal!"

OCTOBER 4

TRUE RICHES

"Lay up for yourselves treasures in heaven, where neither moth nor rust destroys and where thieves do not break in and steal." (Matthew 6:20, NKJV)

A young man asked an old rich man how he made his money. The old guy fingered his worsted wool vest and said, "Well, son, it was 1932, and we were in the depth of the Great Depression. I was down to my last nickel. I invested that nickel in an apple. I spent the entire day polishing the apple and, at the end of the day, I sold the apple for ten cents. The next morning, I invested those ten cents in two apples. I spent the entire day polishing them and sold them at 5:00 p. m. for 20 cents. I continued this system for a month. Then my wife's father died and left us two million dollars!"

How about you? Are you rich?" According to Pastor T. D. Jakes you are. He writes: "...riches are what you have, but wealth is what you are. You are wealthy in opportunities, wealthy in creativity, and wealthy in the chance to prioritize your life, maximize your potential, and reassess your strengths. You are wealthy because God loves you."

A stroll through the New Testament will reveal to you how really rich you are. Romans 2:4 says we are rich because of God's "kindness and forbearance and patience." Romans 9:23 and Ephesians 1:18 and 3:16 talk about the riches of God's glory, and Romans 11:13 tells us of the riches of His wisdom. In Ephesians 1:7 and 2:7, we learn of the riches of His grace, and Ephesians 2:4 promises us the riches of God's mercy. Ephesians 3:8 declares that the Lord "richly blesses all who call upon Him."

Next time the numbers in your bankbook get you down, remind yourself that your true riches, the only wealth that really matters, are in God's love for you. True riches do not come from chasing "The American Dream." It comes from seeking the kingdom of God.

A LITTLE HUMOR: The minister asked, "Is there anybody in the congregation who wants a prayer said for their shortcomings?" "Yes," was the answer from a man in the front pew. "I'm a spendthrift. I throw money around like it is growing on trees!" "Very well," said the minister. "We will join in prayer for our brother — just as soon as the collection plates have been passed."

OCTOBER 5

THE WAY OF THE PILGRIM

"Blessed is the man whose strength is in You, whose heart is set on pilgrimage."
(Psalm 84:5, NKJV)

Christians in earlier days often referred to life as a pilgrimage. The word "pilgrim" is made up of two Latin words. The prefix, *Pil* is a Latin preposition meaning through. The root word for *grim* is from an old Latin word meaning land. A pilgrim is someone traveling through a foreign land, a wayfarer. John Bunyan, writing from his prison cell in Bedford, England, devoted an entire book to the pilgrim lifestyle – *Pilgrim's Progress*. Many of our old hymns speak of the Christian life as a pilgrimage.

While we walk the pilgrim pathway,
Clouds will overspread the sky;
But when traveling days are over,
Not a shadow, not a sigh.

At the time Psalm 84 was written, every Jewish man was required to go to Jerusalem to celebrate the feast three times a year. Whole villages would make their pilgrimage together, singing along the way. This psalm tells us four things about the way of the pilgrim.[87]

The Pilgrim's Pathway is Happy. The word *blessed* means happy, fortunate, to be congratulated. Although we have our ups and downs, trials and tribulations, we also have our times of joy. Paul said, "Rejoice in the Lord always. Again I will say, rejoice!" (Philippians 4:4, NKJV).

The Pilgrim's Strength is in God. Psalm 84:5 tells us that a pilgrim's strength is in God, and verse 7 tells us that a pilgrim will "go from strength to strength." Like the writer of Psalm 46, he says, "God is our refuge and strength, a very present help in trouble."

The Pilgrim's Route is Difficult. Psalm 84:6 says that the pilgrim's route winds through the "Valley of Baca." The Hebrew word *Baca* means weeping. But read on:

---

[87] Robert J. Morgan, *Nelson's Annual Preacher's Sourcebook*, 2002 Edition (Nashville: Thomas Nelson Publishers, 2002), 408-410.

"As they pass through the Valley of Baca, they make it to a spring." Their pathway is both appointed and anointed, and they have a transforming effect as they pass through this world.

The Pilgrim's Destination is Glorious. Look again at verse 7: "They go from strength to strength; each one appears before God in Zion." Every one of the pilgrims reaches his destination – heaven. There's an old song that says:

I am a poor wayfaring stranger
While traveling through this world below.
Yet there's no sickness, toil or danger
In that bright world to which I go.
I'm going there to see my father;
I'm going there no more to roam.
I am just going over Jordan;
I am just going over home.

The purpose of the pilgrimage as described in this psalm was to allow the person to go to the temple to worship God. We can worship God anywhere, at any time, but we know, too, that going to a place of worship can help us to withdraw from the world for a time of meditation and prayer. Life is a pilgrimage, and along the way there are times and places for us to pause and fellowship with Him.

A LITTLE HUMOR: A lady had lost three husbands and found herself married to the fourth man. She had been married to a banker, a man in show business, a preacher, and finally an undertaker. Someone asked her why she had married in that order. She answered, "I wanted one for the money, two for the show, three to get ready, and four to go."

OCTOBER 6

NOBODY CAN BE YOU BUT YOU!

"I will give thanks to You, for I am fearfully and wonderfully made; wonderful are Your works, and my soul knows it very well." (Psalm 139:14, NASB)

Every person at one time or another has struggled with low self-esteem. One of the reasons we do is because we compare ourselves with others, or we may have been ridiculed by someone who caused us to look down on ourselves as being of no intrinsic value.

In his book of illustrations, *The Tale of the Tardy Oxcart,* Chuck Swindoll tells the story of the time when his children were smaller, and they were going on a long trip. Trying to break the boredom, they decided to play a game called "What if?" The question was "What if you could be anybody on earth – who would you like to be?"

One of the daughters said, "I would like to be the bionic woman." The other children followed suit and thought of someone famous they would like to be. But his youngest child, Chuck, Jr., never said a word. As they pulled up to a stop sign, Chuck, Sr. looked at his son and asked, "Chucky, who would you like to be?" His son said, "I'd like to be me." His dad said, "Why do you want to be you?" Chucky replied, "Because I like me better than anybody I know."[88]

Chucky had it right. A good self-esteem comes from an acceptance of ourselves. Nobody can be you but you. You are the most unique person in the world. There is not another person like you. God formed you the way He wanted you to be, and when you begin to accept yourself for who you are and realize that God loves you as though you were the only person in the world, bingo! A good, healthy self-esteem is born.

Someone might be thinking, "Well, look at me; look at my shortcomings. How can I feel good about myself when I look the way I do?" Until we can thank God for our shortcomings, for the scars in our lives, we will never conquer the problem of inferiority. Why not confess your struggles with inferiority feelings to the Lord right now. Ask the Lord to deliver you from your preoccupation with yourself and give you a fresh touch of His Holy Spirit that will allow you to see yourself as He sees you.

It really boils down to what you choose to think about yourself. No one can make you feel inferior without your consent. Only you can ultimately stop the plague of self-doubt. You are valuable. You are unique. You are greatly loved by the Lord.

A LITTLE HUMOR: A man who was obsessed with feelings of inferiority went to a psychiatrist over a period of months at the cost of thousands of dollars. At long last the psychiatrist shocked the client when he said, "Mr. Jones," the doctor intoned in a professional air, "I have discovered the root of your problem. You're just plain inferior!"

OCTOBER 7

HAPPINESS IS HAVING A FRIEND

"The greatest love is shown when a person lays down his life for his friends."
(John 15:13)

"I don't have a friend in the world." If true, that has to be one of life's most tragic statements. No matter how independent we imagine ourselves to be, each of us needs a friend, not someone who is only a friend in words, but a friend in deed — someone who'll stick by us through thick and thin.

In Charles Shultz's book entitled, *I Need All the Friends I Can Get,* Charlie Brown says to Lucy, "I don't have any friends. I don't have one single person I can call a friend." Lucy says, "Define 'friend'!" Then a number of striking definitions of friend are given:

---

[88] Charles R. Swindoll, *The Tale of the Tardy Oxcart* (Nashville: Word Publishing, 1998), 511.

"A friend is someone who will take the side with the sun in his eyes." (He has a tennis racket in his hand and is looking across the net.)

"A friend is someone who can't stand the same sort of music you can't stand."

"A friend is someone who's willing to watch the program you want to watch" (on TV).

"A friend is someone who sticks up for you when you're not there."

"A friend is someone who accepts you for what you are."

At that point Lucy says, "I think you try too hard, Charlie Brown. Be like me. I don't need any friends. I'm self-sufficient!" "Not me," he says, "I need all the friends I can get! I'd even settle for a 'fair-weather' friend."

Jesus Christ said, "The greatest love is shown when a person lays down his life for his friends" (John 15:13), a life given to save a life! That's friendship tested and proven. Jesus Himself is the best example of the truth of his own words. Is that a new thought for you — Jesus Christ as your *friend?* Maybe you've pictured Him as someone remote, austere, and inaccessible. If so, you're depriving yourself of one who wants to be your best friend.

If Jesus is not your friend, don't blame Him. The Bible gives a graphic picture of His wanting to come into your life. Jesus says: "I have been standing at the door and I am constantly knocking. If anyone hears me calling him and opens the door, I will come in and fellowship with him and he with me" (Revelation 3:20).

Is that Friend who died for your sins outside your life? He wants to come in and bring you a peace and happiness you've never known before — a peace and happiness that comes only from the knowledge that your sins are forgiven, and because of that you have the assurance of eternal life. When Jesus Christ comes into your life, an eternal friendship has begun! Has this great event happened to you? It can!

A LITTLE HUMOR: After a disastrous season, a football coach said, "I had only one friend – my dog. Even my wife was mad at me, and I told her a man ought to have at least two friends. She agreed, and bought me another dog."

OCTOBER 8

KEEP FOCUSED

"One thing I do: forgetting what is behind and straining toward what is ahead, I press on toward the goal to win the prize for which God has called me heavenward in Christ Jesus." (Philippians 3:13-14, NIV)

The New York City Marathon is considered the ultimate race, with runners coming from all over the world to compete in it. While much prestige is given to the winner of the race, much respect is also given to those who simply qualify to participate and then actually finish the race. The course covers a distance of twenty-six miles, and the record finish is two hours and seventeen minutes.

In 1986, Bob Weiland entered the New York City Marathon along with 50,000 other runners. He and 19,800 of the other runners finished. But while the average runner finished in approximately four hours, Bob Weiland finished in four days, seventeen hours, and seven minutes. Why? What took him so long to complete the race? Bob Weiland has no legs! He ran the race by sitting on the ground and swinging himself forward step by step with his arms!

Could any runner without legs face a greater problem than a twenty-six mile marathon? And not only face it but participate and actually finish? But rather than be depressed Bob Weiland overcame the greatness of his problems by keeping his eyes, not on each immediate, painful step, but on the big picture of finishing the race. He focused on his goal.[89]

What problems are you facing that seem greater than you can bear? What situation in your life seems impossible? Amy Carmichael, the great missionary to India, wrote, "When we are facing the impossible, we can count upon the God of the impossible!"

The Apostle Paul knew how to run a race to win. In Philippians 3:13-14 he wrote, "One thing I do: forgetting what is behind and straining toward what is ahead, I press on toward the goal to win the prize for which God has called me heavenward in Christ Jesus" (NIV).

Too many Christians are too involved in "many things," when the secret of progress is to concentrate on one thing. It was this decision that was a turning point in D. L. Moody's life. Before the tragedy of the Chicago fire in 1871, Mr. Moody was involved in Sunday School promotion, Y. M. C. A. work, evangelistic meetings, and many other activities; but after the fire, he determined to devote himself exclusively to evangelism. "This one thing I do!" became a reality to him. As a result, millions of people heard the Gospel.[90]

No athlete succeeds by doing everything; he succeeds by specializing. There are those few athletes who seem proficient in many sports, but they are the exception. The winners are those who concentrate, who keep their eyes on the goal and let nothing distract them. The writer of the book of Hebrews had it right: "Let us run with perseverance the race marked out for us. Let us fix our eyes on Jesus" (Hebrews 12:1-2, NIV).

A LITTLE HUMOR: A local health club owner installed an indoor coin-operated jogging machine. When asked why, the owner replied, "I want to give people a run for their money."

---

[89] Anne Graham Lotz, *The Vision of His Glory* (Dallas: Word Publishing, 1996), 19-20.

[90] Warren W. Wiersbe, *The Bible Exposition Commentary, Vol. 2* (Wheaton, Illinois: Victor Books, 1989), 89.

OCTOBER 9

LOOK AT WHAT JESUS HAS DONE FOR YOU

"Go home to your friends, and tell them what great things the Lord has done for you, and how He has had compassion on you." (Mark 5:19, NKJV)

There was a mother – a teetotaler – who was very vocal from time to time about her theory that only grape juice – not wine – should be served at the Lord's Supper. During one of these discussions her daughter said: "But mother, don't you remember at Cana Jesus turned water into wine?" The mother, eyes blazing, said, "Yes! And He NEVER should have done it either!"

When I think of all the Lord has done, I am mindful that He never did anything He should not have done. There are three places in the Bible where Jesus used the words "for you." Each of them describes something he has done for you or is doing for you. Let's notice them.

First, there is THE PRICE HE HAS PAID FOR YOU. In 1 Corinthians 11:24, Paul looks back to the night of the Lord's last meal with His disciples. He said Jesus took the bread, blessed it, broke it, and then said, "This is my body, which is broken for you" (KJV). Jesus was speaking of His death and telling His disciples that He would die for them. Jesus died for you.

Second, there is THE PLACE HE IS PREPARING FOR YOU. Before He left this earth to return to heaven Jesus announced, "I go to prepare a place for you." One of the things Jesus is doing right now in heaven is getting a place ready for you. He is building a mansion for you.

Third, there are THE PRAYERS HE IS PRAYING FOR YOU. Jesus told Peter, "I have prayed for you" (Luke 22:32). Lest you think the Lord's prayers are limited to Peter, Hebrews 7:25 declares that Jesus "always lives to make intercession for them" (NKJV). This is one of the most thrilling and encouraging thoughts in the Bible. Jesus is praying for me and for you.

Just look at what Jesus has done for you. Oh how blessed we are!

A LITTLE HUMOR: In the Garden of Eden, Adam asked God one day, "Why did you make Eve so beautiful?" "To attract your attention," God replied. "Why did you give her such a sweet personality?", Adam asked. "So you would love her," God replied. "Just one more question, God," Adam said." Why did you make her so dumb?" God smiled and answered, "So that she would love you!"

OCTOBER 10

A MOTHER'S INFLUENCE

"Honor your . . . mother . . ." (Exodus 20:12, NKJV)

As a lawyer, as a congressman, as Governor of Ohio, and as President of the United States of America, William McKinley had a close relationship with his mother. He either visited her or sent a message to her every day. When she became seriously ill, he arranged to have a special train standing by, ready to take him to her bedside. Mrs. McKinley died December 12, 1897, in the arms of her 54-year-old son. Her gentle, Christian virtues helped mold the President's character, for when he was gunned down in Buffalo, New York, about four years later, he showed no bitterness toward his assassin. With Christian courage he said, "God's will be done." Before he died, he asked to hear once again the hymn, *Nearer, My God, To Thee*, which his mother had taught him.

We set aside one day a year to honor mothers, and I'm glad we do. The majority of them deserve it, and they truly are VIPs. Abraham Lincoln declared, "No man is poor who has had a godly mother. Someone else has said, "The instruction received at Mother's knee, together with the pious and sweet souvenirs of the fireside, are never effaced entirely from the soul."

A little boy in the Easter play was fortunate enough to have the part of Jesus. One of his lines was, "I am the light of the world," but when he got to that part, he forgot it. All of a sudden, here comes Mom to the rescue. You know how mothers are — she got up out of her seat and went to the front so she could prompt him. He looked at his mother and she mouthed the words, "I am the light of the world." He smiled at his mother, turned to the audience and said, "My mother is the light of the world."

Mothers may not be the light of the world but they definitely brighten it up — probably because they reflect so much of God's love.

A LITTLE HUMOR: Chad and his little sister Emily grew up with their mother regularly complaining about the relentless work around the house and her desire for "just a little peace and quiet." Since Chad got his driver's license a few weeks before Mother's Day, he asked his father if he could take Emily and the car to get their mom a gift. They drove for hours shopping endlessly and finally ended up at the local florist. They had no sooner walked through the door when they found the perfect gift. Hanging above the counter was a large wreath they immediately purchased. It read. "Rest in Peace."

OCTOBER 11

IT'S A PERSONAL THING

"The thief comes only to steal and kill and destroy; I have come that they may have life, and have it to the full." (John 10:10, NIV)

Ernest Hemingway, the literary genius, said of his life, "I live in a vacuum that is as lonely as a radio tube when the batteries are dead, and there is no current to plug into."

This is a startling statement, given the fact that Hemingway's life would be the envy of anyone who had bought the values of our modern society. Hemingway was known for his tough-guy image and globe-trotting pilgrimages to exotic places. He was a big-game hunter, a bullfighter, a man who could drink the best of them under the table. He was married four times and lived his life seemingly without moral restraint or conscience. But on a sunny Sunday morning in Idaho, he pulverized his head with a shotgun blast.

There was another side to Hemingway's life, one that few people know about. He grew up in an evangelical Christian home. His grandparents were missionaries, and his father was a devoted churchman and friend of D. L. Moody. Hemingway's family conformed to the strictest codes of Christianity, and as a boy and young man he was active in his church.

Then came World War I. As a war correspondent, Hemingway saw death and despair firsthand. His youthful enthusiasm for Christianity soured, and Hemingway eventually rejected the faith he had once claimed.

While we don't know all that transpired in Hemingway's heart, it seems he never developed a truly personal relationship with Jesus Christ. Genuine Christianity means more than living in a Christian environment, going through catechism, conforming to the codes, and affirming the truths of Scripture. True Christians are non-negotiated followers of Christ, those who are progressively moving toward Him and who understand all of life in the context of His teaching.

The point is not Hemingway's life. It's my life and your life. If we aren't cultivating a living, vital relationship with Jesus Christ, then we, too, may respond as Hemingway did when life's questions are agonizingly unanswerable or when our inner impulses are too seductive for us to resist. An allegiance based on systems, rituals, and rules is never enough to keep us loyal.

Jesus said, "The thief comes only to steal and kill and destroy; I have come that they may have life, and have it to the full" (John 10:10, NIV). In contrast to the thief who takes life, Jesus gives life. The life He gives right now is abundantly richer and fuller. Life in Christ is lived on a higher plane because of His overflowing forgiveness, love, and guidance. Have you taken Christ's offer of life? It's a personal thing!

A LITTLE HUMOR: It has been said that the seven stages of a person's life are spills, drills, thrills, bills, ills, pills, and wills.

OCTOBER 12

THE ONE SURE FOUNDATION

"He is like a man building a house, who dug deep and laid the foundation on the rock." (Luke 6:48a, NKJV)

The Leaning Tower of Pisa has to be seen to be believed! A visitor must wonder whether the sight is an optical illusion, or if the towering structure actually is defying the law of gravity?

The answer is that it does indeed lean . . . and it leans a bit more each year. This bell tower of the Cathedral of Pisa, built in 1274, leaned slightly from the outset — a problem the builders did not consider to be serious at the time.

Slowly and almost imperceptibly over the past seven centuries it has leaned farther and farther. Today it deviates more than seventeen feet from the vertical, and it is only a matter of time until the tower collapses. In a nearby building, equipment for an emergency operation is at hand for use if the tower should register a sudden worsening of the tilt. The equipment includes huge iron rings to grip the tower and connect it to ground-pylons by steel cables.

The problem exists because not enough attention was given to planning and building a proper foundation. The flaw, noticed early in construction, could have been rectified by altering and strengthening the foundation. But the lack of an adequate foundation makes its eventual collapse certain.

The same is true for us in life. There is a basic a question that we too often neglect: On what is my life built?

Jesus Christ contended that careful attention to life's foundations is critical. "All who listen to my instructions and follow them are wise, like a man who builds his house on solid rock," he stated. "Though the rain comes in torrents, and the floods rise and the storm winds beat against his house, it won't collapse, for it is built on a rock" (Matthew 7:24-25, LB). He then added, "But those who hear my instructions and ignore them are foolish, like a man who builds his house on sand. For when the rains and floods come, and storm winds beat against his house, it will fall with a mighty crash" (Matthew 7:26-27, LB).

Do you feel that your own life lacks focus and direction? Or does it seem as though life is tumbling in around you? Is it a foundation problem?

Jesus Christ is the one sure foundation in life: "And no one can ever lay any other real foundation than that one we already have — Jesus Christ" (1 Corinthians 3:11, LB). He loves you so much that he died for your sins (John 3:16). When you put your faith in Him, he becomes your Savior and Lord and your life's sure foundation.

A LITTLE HUMOR: The young executive had been complaining of aches and pains to his wife. They could not account for his trouble. Arriving home from work one night, he informed her, "I finally discovered why I've been feeling so miserable. We got some new ultramodern office furniture two weeks ago, and I just learned today that I've been sitting in the wastebasket.

OCTOBER 13

HAPPY BIRTHDAY!

"To everything there is a season, a time for every purpose under heaven. A time to be born, and a time to die." (Ecclesiastes 3:1-2, NKJV)

Today is my birthday. I was not born in a hospital but in a house. I was born at night during a rain storm. My mother said when I was born I had a respiratory problem. A lady friend who was present when I was born bathed me first in warm water and then in cool water to stimulate my breathing. I don't know the technical term for such a problem or technique used by her, but my mother often said I was blue in color and she used the term, “a blue baby.” Whatever the problem or technique, I’m glad my mother chose to give birth to me.

In his sermon titled “Every Man’s Life a Plan of God,” Horace Bushnell said that (a) there is a divine purpose in every life that comes into the world, (b) God has a task for every man and woman to perform, (c) there is a blueprint for every life, and it is ours to find the blueprint and follow the specifications.[91]

Part of God’s plan for my life included my salvation at the age of seven and my response to God’s call for ministry at the age of seventeen. Those decisions have made all the difference in my life. My education, my family, and my career as a minister have all been a part of God’s purpose for me.

His Way . . . Mine! is one of the most widely recognized gospel songs written by Dick and Bo Baker. It was the first song that the brothers wrote together. In 1954, they had taken their Birchman Avenue Baptist Church young people to youth camp in Glen Rose, Texas. They were impressed by the Lord that the young people needed encouragement to follow the Lord’s leading in their lives. The words that Bo wrote were put to Dick’s melody, and this song became a theme for that camp week and went on to make an impact on many in the 50’s and 60’s. Today, people still remember how God used this song in their lives.

His Way . . . Mine!

God has a place for every planned creation,
A path for every star to go.
He drew the course for every river’s journey,
Now I know he has a way for me.
Chorus:
I place my life in the hands of God.
Those hands so scarred now outstretched for me.
Wherever it may be, over land, over sea,
May thy will sublime, O Thou God divine, be mine.

Now in His will my soul finds life worth living,
Each day new blessings from above.
Tho shadows come and valleys seem unending,
Still I know He makes a way for me.[92]

God’s plan and purpose is unique for each individual. To know God’s will for your life is the greatest knowledge you will ever have. To do God’s will is the greatest act of obedience.

---

[91] Charles L. Allen and Mildred F. Parker, *The Happy Birthday Book.* (Dallas: Word Publishing, 1988), 43.
[92] http://hiswaymin.com

A LITTLE HUMOR: A wife asked her husband, "Dear, could I have some spend money?" He replied, "Money, money, money. If you ask me, I think you need brains more than you need money." She responded, "I was just asking you for what I thought you had the most of."

OCTOBER 14

THE ULTIMATE DEADLINE

"It is appointed unto men once to die, but after this, the judgment." (Hebrews 9:27)

Deadlines! We deal with them constantly, day in and day out. You may be a student rushing to turn in an important assignment; a business person that must make a decision before five o'clock; a newspaper editor trying to get all the articles ready before the paper goes to press; a mother trying to get her child to the doctor at an appointed hour; or a pastor trying to get his sermon ready before Sunday morning. For most Americans, April 15 is always what might be called in the parlance of the day "the mother of all deadlines."

The term deadline actually came out of the Civil War. At the infamous prison camp at Andersonville, the Confederate guards would draw a line in the sand outside the fence. Any Union prisoner of war outside that line would be shot on sight. Instead of saying we need to "meet" a deadline, we should really talk about not "crossing" a deadline.[93]

Scripture makes it clear that the one "deadline" no person should dare to cross is our individual deadline for accepting Christ as Lord and Savior. Isaiah 55:6 reads, "Seek ye the Lord while he may be found" (KJV), implying there would come a time when He could not be found. 2 Corinthians 6:2 says that "now is the accepted time; behold, now is the day of salvation" (KJV). God Himself has said that His Spirit would not always strive with man (Genesis 6:3), and that while we had the opportunity, we must not harden our hearts but hear the Lord when He speaks to us and respond to Him in a positive manner (Hebrews 3:12-15).

The ultimate deadline is death and judgment. Hebrews 9:27 says, "It is appointed unto men once to die, but after this, the judgment." The word *appointed* could be translated reserved. Every person has an appointment, a reservation — a deadline — with death. We would like to pass it by and avoid it. We like to assume it will not happen to us. But it will (Ecclesiastes 8:8).

Sarah Winchester's husband had acquired a fortune by manufacturing and selling rifles. After he died of influenza in 1918, she moved to San Jose, California. Because of her grief and her long time interest in spiritism, Sarah sought out a medium to contact her dead husband. The medium told her, "As long as you keep building your home, you will never face death."

Sarah believed the spiritist, so she bought an unfinished 17-room mansion and

---

[93] Dennis Cone, Editor of current *Thoughts and Trends,* Vol. 9, No. 4, April, 1993, page 2.

started to expand it. The project continued until she died at the age of 85. It cost five million dollars at a time when workmen earned fifty cents a day. The mansion had 150 rooms, 13 bathrooms, 2,000 doors, 47 fireplaces, and 10,000 windows. And Mrs. Winchester left enough materials so that they could have continued building for another eighty years. Today that house stands as more than a tourist attraction. It is a silent witness to the dread of death that holds millions of people in bondage (Hebrews 2:15).[94]

We need not fear crossing the deadline of death. Jesus Christ said, "Because I live, you shall live also" (John 14:19, KJV). Jesus met the deadline for us!

A LITTLE HUMOR: A minister and city manager had a falling out. One day the preacher phoned a complaint to the city manager. A donkey had died on the church parking lot and the minister wanted it removed. The city manager said sarcastically, "Reverend, I thought it was your duty to bury the dead." The minister said sweetly, "It is, sir! But my first duty is to notify the next of kin."

OCTOBER 15

REST FOR THE RESTLESS

"Come to me, all you who are weary and burdened, and I will give you rest."
(Matthew 11:28, NIV)

Have you ever stood around so long that your legs got tired? Maybe you were waiting in line somewhere, and it seemed like you were standing there forever, and you thought your legs were going to break, they were so tired. That's no fun, is it?

But did you know that horses can stand for hours and hours at a time without getting tired? Horses even sleep standing up, and their legs never get tired. Isn't that amazing? You see, horses' legs and bodies were made differently from humans' legs and bodies. When we stand up, our bodies are resting on the muscles and bones in our legs. But muscles get tired after a while. That's when our legs start to hurt. But when a horse stands up, all its weight is resting on the bones and tendons. And bones don't get tired. So a horse never gets tired of standing up for hours on end.

Our bodies were made so that sometimes we can work and play and do many things, and sometimes we need to stop and rest. And just like our bodies need rest, sometimes our hearts and minds need rest, too. Maybe we are sad, or scared, or worried about something. Being sad or scared or worried can make our heart and mind feel tired too. We feel like we're just not strong enough to overcome our problems on our own. But Jesus says to us, "Come to me, all you who are weary and burdened, and I will give you rest" (Matthew 11:28, NIV). Jesus wants us to rest our hearts and minds as well as our bodies. Jesus is here to help us; to take all our tiredness and our worry and our sadness and our fear away.

---

[94] *Our Daily Bread* (Grand Rapids: RBC, April 2, 1994)

I like the writings of the late Vance Havner. Commenting on the words spoken by Jesus as recorded in Mark 6:31, "Come ye yourselves apart . . . and rest a while," he said: "This is a must for every Christian. If you don't come apart and rest, you will come apart — you'll go to pieces! We cannot *rest* in God until we *nest* in God. To nest is to settle, to abide." He also said, "If we cannot go away for a vacation, we can take an 'inside vacation' and find grace to help in time of need."

Horatius Bonar wrote a hymn entitled *I Heard the Voice of Jesus Say.* The first stanza reads like this:

I heard the voice of Jesus say,
"Come unto Me and rest;
Lay down, thou weary one,
Lay down Thy head upon My Breast."
I came to Jesus as I was,
Weary, and worn, and sad;
I found in Him a resting place,
And He has made me glad.

A LITTLE HUMOR: A doctor went to a party one night and he saw one of his patents out on the dance floor with a beautiful girl. They were dancing like mad and having a great time. The doctor walked up to the man and said, "Fellow, what in the world are you doing?" And the fellow said, "Well, doctor, I'm following your advice." The doctor said, "Following my advice? What do you mean?" He said, "Well, you told me to get me a hot mama, and be cheerful." The doctor said, "Oh, no, no! I said, 'You've got a heart murmur, be careful! "

OCTOBER 16

HOW GULLIBLE ARE YOU?

"Beloved, do not believe every spirit, but test the spirits to see whether they are from God; because many false prophets have gone out into the world." (1 John 4:1, NASB)

A country boy was invited to a fancy dinner. He was surrounded at the table by well-mannered aristocrats. In the course of the meal he got a large hot piece of potato in his mouth. He spit it out in the palm of his hand and put it on his plate. This shocked the genteel company. They cleared their throats and tried to divert their eyes, but he looked right at them and said, "You know, a fool would have swallowed that." Well, a lot of people are swallowing foolish things these days. It is amazing sometimes how gullible people can be.

John warned that in the last days there would be many false prophets and much false teaching going on in the name of God with a lot of gullible people believing them. Believers are not to be gullible when it comes to believing everything they hear just because it may be coming from a so-called prophet or someone who claims to have a special word from God. John said to test the spirit for authenticity. The word *test* was used in ancient times of the testing of metals for genuineness. In Luke 14:19 it is employed by the man who said, "I have bought five yoke of oxen, and I go to prove them." In other places it is used as in proving the will of God (Rom. 12:2), of the testing of every man's work by fire (1 Cor. 3:13), of God trying the heart (1Thess. 2:4), and so forth. It is the word used by Paul in 1 Thessalonians 5:21, "Prove all things; hold fast that which is good."

One way to "test the spirit" is to check to see if it matches God's Word, the Bible. The most important test of all is what they believe about Christ (1 John 4:2). Do they teach that Jesus is fully God and fully man? A true teacher must believe that Jesus Christ is God's unique Son who came in a human body. He did not merely appear to be a man; he actually became a man with a human body.

Think about it: If Jesus Christ was not and is not the God-man depicted in the New Testament, then it follows that all of Scripture is suspect, and our sins are not, in fact, forgiven. Believers have a responsibility to call into question any church or teaching that rejects a historic, orthodox belief about the person of Jesus Christ.

A LITTLE HUMOR: A gentle Quaker was milking his cow, when all of a sudden the cow swished her tail and knocked the gentle Quaker from his milking stool. He got up, brushed himself off and proceeded with his milking. Then the cow picked her foot up and put it in his milk bucket. He picked the bucket up and started milking again. Then the cow, swished her tail and knocked him off the stool and put her foot in the bucket of milk. He got up, brushed himself off and set the bucket upright again, and said to the cow, "O, cow, thou knowest that I cannot smite thee; and thou knowest that I cannot curse thee; but what thou doest not know is that I can sell thee to a Baptist."

OCTOBER 17

HANGING IN THERE

"Let us not become weary in doing good, for at the proper time we will reap a harvest if we do not give up." (Galatians 6:9, NIV)

Charles Goodyear could not stop thinking about India rubber. He'd come across a bit of the stuff. He was told that if only India rubber withstood temperature changes, the substance would be highly useful. Over a period of years, he spent every last dollar he had on experiments and research. Somehow, some way, he'd discover how to make the rubber hold up to cold and heat. Goodyear's friends began to ridicule him. His upset family failed to understand his obsession. In February, 1839, he found the answer: adding sulfur to the rubber. A huge business was built on Goodyear's stubborn perseverance.[95]

Success always requires perseverance. Detroit Lions running back Barry Sanders

---

[95] *Stand Firm* (Nashville: LifeWay Press, June 23, 1999).

has become only the third player in the NFL to rush for 2,000 yards. No one denies his ability. But when we realize he made that yardage with 300-pound linebackers trying to stop him every step of the way, we realize the place of perseverance.[96]

Do you want to be the best bass fisherman in the state? You will need perseverance. Do you want to be the top accountant in the firm? You will need perseverance. Do you want to have a successful marriage? You will need perseverance. Do you want to be a good teacher? You will need perseverance. Do you want to overcome temptations? You will need perseverance. In Galatians 6:9 the apostle Paul wrote: "Let us not become weary in doing good, for at the proper time we will reap a harvest if we do not give up" (NIV).

In 1979, Larry Singleton attacked and raped Mary Vincent, chopped off her forearms and left her for dead. She walked three miles and was rescued by motorists. Her physical and emotional recovery has been difficult. She said, "I wanted to totally give up, but whenever I said, 'I don't want to, I won't do it and I don't want to,' a very stubborn hospital therapist would say, 'You can, you will and you must.'"[97]

Arnold Palmer is one of the greatest golfers to ever play the game. This great golfer never flaunted his success. Although he has won hundreds of trophies and awards, the only trophy in his office is a battered little cup that he got for his first professional win at the Canadian Open in 1955. In addition to the cup, he has a lone framed plaque on the wall. The plague tells you why he has been successful on and off the gold course. It reads:

If you think you are beaten you are.
If you think you dare not, you don't.
If you'd like to win but think you can't,
It's almost certain you won't.
Life's battles don't always go
To the stronger or faster man,
But sooner or later, the man who wins
Is the man who thinks he can.[98]

A LITTLE HUMOR: Two church members were discussing a sermon just delivered by a visiting preacher. "I thought it was divine," said the first member. "It reminded me of the peace of God. It passed all understanding." "Funny, I thought it was divine, too," said the second member, "only it reminded me of the mercies of God. I thought it would endure forever."

---

[96] Ibid.
[97] *The Houston Post,* Monday, April 18, 1988.
[98] John Maxwell, *Developing the Leader Within You* (Nashville: Thomas Nelson Publishers, 1993), 91.

OCTOBER 18

WATCH WHERE YOU ARE GOING

"I am still not all I should be, but I am bringing all my energies to bear on this one thing: Forgetting the past and looking forward to what lies ahead, I strain to reach the end of the race and receive the prize for which God is calling us up to heaven because of what Christ Jesus did for us." (Philippians 3:13-14, LB)

Some people seem to drift aimlessly through life, headed in no specific direction. Without clearly defined objectives, it is not surprising that many adopt a lifestyle that lacks definition and purpose.

Thomas Huxley, a famous nineteenth-century scientist and lecturer, had completed a series of lectures in Dublin and was in a rush to catch a train to his next engagement. He hailed a horse-drawn coach and shouted to the driver, "Hurry! I'm late. Drive fast!" Then, assuming that the cab was headed for the railway station, he settled back for the ride. The horses galloped off at full speed.

After a few moments, Huxley realized that the coach was going in the wrong direction. Do you know where you're going?" he snapped at the driver. Without a backward glance, the coachman replied, "No, your honor. But I'm driving very fast!" There was lots of motion, but no sense of direction.

That can be true of our lives. Psychologist Rollo May observed, "It is an old and ironic habit of human beings to run faster when we have lost our way." Motion and activity are not substitutes for direction and purpose, but many people seem to be traveling at a great clip to no particular destination. "When the pilot does not know what port he is heading for," says a Roman proverb, "no wind is the right wind."

As he neared the end of his full life, the apostle Paul shared the secret of his single-minded life purpose and direction: "Everything else is worthless when compared with the priceless gain of knowing Christ Jesus my Lord. I have put aside all else, counting it worth less than nothing, in order that I can have Christ, and become one with Him, no longer counting on being saved by being good enough or by obeying God's laws, but by trusting Christ to save me; for God's way of making us right with himself depends on faith — counting on Christ alone" (Philippians 3:8-9, LB). That resolute purpose provided direction and meaning — and it will for us.

Have you settled your relationship with God by trusting Jesus Christ alone as your Savior? Or are you going around in circles — at a feverish speed? In that same passage of Scripture, Paul puts it all in focus: "I am still not all I should be, but I am bringing all my energies to bear on this one thing: Forgetting the past and looking forward to what lies ahead, I strain to reach the end of the race and receive the prize for which God is calling us up to heaven because of what Christ Jesus did for us." (Philippians 3:13-14, LB)

Are you dabbling in life? Or do you have that unshakable sense of direction, meaning, purpose, and destination that comes when you admit your sin and wandering and receive Christ by faith? That can happen right now if you will open your life to Him.

A LITTLE HUMOR: On a overseas flight, a jetliner ran into some very rough weather. It was extremely foggy and turbulent. The pilot made the following announcement over the plane's intercom: "Ladies and gentlemen, I have two announcements to make. One is good news and the other is bad news. First, I'll give you the bad news. We're lost! Now I'll give you the good news. We're making very good time."

OCTOBER 19

THE ELDER BROTHER SYNDROME

"And he said to him, 'My child, you have always been with me, and all that is mine is yours'." (Luke 15:31, NASB)

The parable of the Prodigal Son is one of the best-known of our Lord's stories, but we often neglect the plight of the elder son who complained that though his father had made a feast for the prodigal, he himself had never received so much as a kid that he might make merry with his friends. The father's answer was, "My child, you have always been with me, and all that is mine is yours." If we're honest, many of us are suffering from the "Elder Brother Syndrome."

In west Texas there is a famous oil field known as the Yates pool. During the depression this field was a sheep ranch, owned by a man named Yates. Mr. Yates was not able to make enough money on his ranching operation to pay the principal and interest on the mortgage, so he was in danger of losing his ranch.

One day a seismographic crew from an oil company came into the area and told Mr. Yates that there might be oil on his land. They asked permission to drill a wildcat well. At 1,115 feet they stuck a huge oil reserve, giving 80,000 barrels a day. In fact, thirty years after the discovery, a government test of one of the wells showed that it still could flow 125,000 barrels of oil a day. And Mr. Yates owned it all. The day he purchased the land he received the oil and mineral rights. Yet, he was living on relief. He was a multimillionaire living in poverty. What was the problem? He did not know the oil was there. He owned it, but he did not possess it.

That is like many Christians today who don't realize how rich they are in Christ. The Bible says "we are children of God: and if children, heirs also, heirs of God and fellow heirs with Christ" (Romans 8:16-17).

A LITTLE HUMOR: An efficiency expert concluded his lecture with a note of caution. "You don't want to try these techniques at home." "Why not?" asked somebody from the audience. "I watched my wife's routine at breakfast for years," the expert explained. "She made lots of trips between the refrigerator, stove, table, and cabinets, often carrying a single item at a time. One day I told her, 'Hon, why don't you try carrying several things at once?'" "Did it save time?' the guy in the audience asked. "Actually, yes," replied the expert. "It used to take her 20 minutes to make breakfast. Now I do it in seven."

OCTOBER 20

DON'T GET ALL CHOKED UP

"Therefore do not worry about tomorrow, for tomorrow will worry about its own things. Sufficient for the day is its own trouble." (Matthew 6:34, NKJV)

In a "Blondie" newspaper carton Dagwood and his friend Herb are sitting on the back steps of Dagwood's home eating watermelon. Dagwood turns to Herb and says, "Ya know, Herb . . . life is kinda like a watermelon." Herb asks, "How's that?" Dagwood says, "Well, it's hard to get thru it without swallowing a few seeds." The last frame of the carton shows Dagwood spitting out watermelon seeds and Herb looking at the reader and saying, "That one would've choked up Socrates!"

Sometimes life can be full of "seeds" making it hard and confusing and even frustrating. We never know from day to day what will happen. That's why it is so important that we put our trust in the Lord. As the song says, we may not know what the day may hold, but we know who holds the day. Here are three suggestions for you to practice each day.

FRET NOT — Three times in Psalm 37 we are told to not fret (vv. 1, 7, 8). The word fret means to get heated up or to become incensed. In other words, keep your cool! Fretting only heats the bearings; it does not generate the steam. It is no help to a train for the axles to get hot; their heat is only a hindrance. When the axles get heated, it is because of unnecessary friction; dry surfaces are grinding together, which ought to be kept in smooth cooperation by a delicate cushion of oil. Fretfulness is closely akin to the word friction, and is an indication of the absence of the anointing oil of the grace of God.

FAINT NOT — Jesus said we ought to pray always and not faint (Luke 18:1). The word faint means to lose heart or to give up. When things don't go our way, it's easy to become discouraged and give up. Remember: "Be cheerful. The kettle keeps singing though it is up to its neck in hot water."

FEAR NOT — Isaiah 41:10 says, "Fear thou not." We live in a world plagued by fear. People worry about illness, poverty, family, war, famine, and the future. A pastor preached a sermon on the scarecrows of life. He said a scarecrow is simply an advertisement that announces that some very juicy and delicious fruit is to be had for the picking. He concluded that "faith is a bird which loves to perch on scarecrows. All our fears are groundless." Someone has said that "fear is the dark room where negatives are developed." But perfect love casts out fear (1 John 4:18).

Remember: In life we may have to swallow some "seeds," but we need to learn to keep our cool, pray about everything, and don't let fear get a grip on us.

A LITTLE HUMOR: While checking his bags at the airport, a man became indignant with the employee who handled luggage. For several minutes he belittled the young man and criticized his every move. Surprisingly, the curbside porter didn't seem troubled by this man's verbal abuse. After the angry man entered the airport, a woman approached the luggage handler and asked, "How do you put up with such injustice?" The young man said, "It's easy. That guy's going to New York, but I'm sending his bags to Brazil."

OCTOBER 21

GOOD INTENTIONS

"Enter by the narrow gate; for wide is the gate and broad is the way that leads to destruction, and there are many who go in by it." (Matthew 7:13, NKJV)

According to a report in the *Evangelical Press* sometime back, it may be a little harder to go Hell this year. A bridge on the main road leading to Hell, Michigan, is badly in need of repair — a project that could close the road for three months. Business owners in the town fear that the disruption in traffic could force some stores into bankruptcy. "It'll close the whole town," complained Jim Ley, president of the Hell Chamber of Commerce. Officials acknowledge that the repair work will cause some disruption, but insist that plans to fix the road to Hell spring from good intentions. The road suffers damage each year when Hell freezes over.

I don't know where the phrase originated that the road to Hell is paved with good intentions. It's not biblical, but certainly, it is accurate. Many who are in Hell never intended to go there. They intended to "get prepared" someday but "someday" never came around.

Jesus told about some very foolish people who waited until it was too late to get ready for a wedding. The story is found in Matthew 25:1-13.There were ten young women, five were wise and five were foolish. The wise women were considered wise because they had made adequate preparation for the arrival of the bridegroom. The foolish women were considered foolish because they had not made the necessary arrangements. Not being ready when the hour came, the foolish women were shut out. Verse 10 says of the wise women, "They that were ready went in."

There once lived a king who gave to his royal clown, the court jester, a crude stick as a mock scepter and declared him to be "The King of Fools." "If you ever meet a greater fool than yourself, give him your scepter and dub him 'a royal fool'." Years passed. The jester kept his stick. One day the king was dying. He called for his court jester and said, "I am going on a long journey. I must bid you a last farewell." "But where are you going and when will you return and what provisions have you made for the journey into that far country?" asked the jester. With a deep pathos in his voice, the king replied, "I do not know, and I have made no provisions. None whatsoever. None whatsoever." "Then," said the court jester, "You had better take the fool's scepter, for with all my folly, I am not as great a fool as you."

I don't know what kind of condition the road is in that leads to Hell. I do know this: Good intentions are not enough. A tourist driving down a country road came face to face with a sign that read, "Road closed — Do not enter." The road ahead look pretty good to him, and having had great experiences as a traveler, he ignored the sign and pressed on. Five miles down the road he came to a bridge that was out, and he had to turn around and retrace his route. As he reached the point where the warning sign stood, he read the words printed on his side of it: "Welcome Back, Stupid!"

Jesus has put up a road block on the road to Hell. It is a cross. Anyone who is willing to repent of his sins and put his trust in Jesus Christ as his only Savior doesn't have to go to Hell.

A LITTLE HUMOR: A businessman was scheduled for a very important meeting that required him to take a late-night train to his destination. Knowing he would most certainly be asleep when the train came to his stop, he spoke with one of the attendants and requested his help. He said, "I have the most important meeting of my life in the morning, and I cannot afford to miss it. When the train pulls into Chattanooga at 2:00 A. M. wake me up and help me off the train. I will be grumpy and beg for sleep, but do whatever it takes to get me off this train." The next morning when the man awoke he was still on the train and had missed his stop. Livid, he raged all over the porter who was supposed to have assisted him off the train. When the irate man stormed away, a passenger who had witnessed the whole thing commented, "In all my life I have never seen anybody get so upset." The porter replied, "That's nothing,' you should have seen the guy I threw off the train at 2:00 AM in Chattanooga."

OCTOBER 22

GRATITUDE FOR A GIVING GOD

"But if any of you lacks wisdom, let him ask of God, who gives to all men generously and without reproach, and it will be given to him." (James 1:5, NASB)

No holiday is comparable to Thanksgiving. At Thanksgiving we do not celebrate anyone's birthday, a political revolution, or a battle. Thanksgiving is simply a time to remember that God has not failed in providing another harvest for man's needs. James 1:5 provides five ways in which God gives to us.

First, God's gifts are generous. The word *generously* means to spread out; to stretch out; to have an open hand. God is not stingy. He gives and gives and gives. It is God's nature to give.

Second, God's gifts are good. James 1:17 reads, "Every good thing bestowed...is from above..." There are no degrees of goodness with God. He is good. The word *good* means gentle and noble. Exodus 34:6 says that God is "abundant in goodness" (KJV).

Third, God's gifts are perfect. James 1:17 also says, "...every perfect gift is from above..." The word *perfect* means complete; fully developed; faultless; mature. The word suggests that God has a purpose, a goal for us to reach, and each gift aids us in the reaching of that goal which is perfection.

Fourth, God's gifts are constant. The word *give* suggests that it is God's habit to give. The words "coming down" (v. 17) speak of an ongoing, continuous stream of blessings coming from God. His mercies are new every morning.

Fifth, God's gifts are certain. The words "it will be given to him" speak of certainty. In verse 16 James says "do not be deceived" or misled about this. God will give generously to His children.

It is reported that Sir Walter Raleigh was constantly submitting requests to Queen Elizabeth on behalf of convicts. Once the Queen said to him: "Sir Walter, when will you stop being a beggar?" Raleigh responded, "When your Majesty ceases to be a giver."

A LITTLE HUMOR: Snoopy is getting dog food for his Thanksgiving Day dinner, and he is aware that everyone else in the family is inside having turkey. He meditates and talks to himself: "How about that? Everyone is eating turkey today, but just because I'm a dog I get dog food?" He trots away and positions himself on top of his doghouse and concludes: "Of course, it could have been worse. I could have been born a turkey."

OCTOBER 23

FOR THOSE WHO STUMBLE

"We all stumble in many ways." (James 3:2, NIV)

Does the name Vinko Bogataj ring a bell? No? Well, let me give you some hints about who this very famous person is. He drives a forklift in a factory that manufactures anchor chains. He lives a quiet life with his wife, two daughters, and mother-in-law. In his spare time, he paints and carves wood.

Any guesses yet? None? Well, let me give you a couple more hints. Vinko Bogataj lives in Lesce, Yugoslavia, and is probably the most famous retired ski jumper in history. Still no guesses?

Well, even if you don't recognize his name, you've probably seen Vinko Bogataj. You see, Vinko happens to be the poor "agony of defeat" guy of ABC's "Wide World of Sports" fame. He was the one who took an incredible head-over-heels fall while in a ski jump competition in Oberstdorf, Germany, in 1971. Unfortunately for Vinko, "Wide World of Sports" was there to capture every inglorious second of his spectacular fall. They broadcasted Vinko's fall at the opening of their show every week for years, permanently immortalizing him in the "Sports Hall of Shame." Jim McKay, the voice of "Wide World of Sports" for the past thirty years it has been on the air, said that perhaps the single most-asked question about the show concerns this poor skier from Lesce.[99]

In James 3:2 we find these words, "For we all stumble in many ways." What is he saying? To stumble is normal, a fact of life, an act that guarantees our humanness. When Italian glassblowers of the Middle Ages discovered a flaw in a beautiful piece of glassware, they converted that failure into a common wine flask. The flask was called in Italian a fiasco.[100] That word has come to mean any type of failure. Perhaps you have just stumbled, creating a fiasco. You opened your mouth and devastated someone with a bitter remark. Or maybe you did something you wish a thousand times over that you had not done. You feel guilty; you feel like a failure. You wish like crazy you hadn't done what you did or responded like that. You're miserable, discouraged, and you'd like to hide.

Failures are not final if you have the persistence to begin again. In his book,

---

[99] *Dynamic Illustrations*, January-March, 1999

[100] *Pulpit Digest,* Jan-Feb, 1987, page 49.

Starting Over, Charles Swindoll writes, “Stumblers who *give up* are a dime a dozen. In fact, they’re useless. Stumblers who *get up* are as rare as rubies. In fact, they’re priceless.” We all stumble; we all fail at something some time or another. Poor Vinko. His fall was shown to the world every week for years. He couldn’t get away from it. You may find that someone who saw you stumble and will not let you forget it either. They will bad-mouth you or hold you down for as long as they can get by with it. I like what Charles Swindoll suggests as to how to handle such people: “Ignore them completely! They have forgotten that James 3:2 includes *them*. The only difference is that you didn’t get to see them stumble. But they have, believe me, they have.”

When you stumble, try to learn from it, but don’t crawl off and die. Climb out of your canyon of self-pity, brush off the dirt with the promise of God’s forgiveness — and move on.

A LITTLE HUMOR: A pastor had been trying in every way possible to increase worship attendance. One Monday he handed his secretary some church stationery, a list of ten members who were absent the most often and asked her to write each of them a letter concerning their absence. Within a few weeks, the minister received a letter from a prominent physician who apologized profusely for having been absent so often. He had enclosed a check for $5,000 to cover contributions he would have made had he been in attendance. He promised to be there the following Sunday and every Sunday after that unless providentially hindered. The usual complimentary closing with his signature was given. However, the following note was at the bottom of the page: "P. S. Please tell your secretary there is only one "t" in dirty and no "e" in skunk."

OCTOBER 24

THIS DOG WON’T HUNT

“Clothe yourselves with the Lord Jesus Christ, and do not think about how to gratify the desires of your sinful nature.” (Romans 13:14, NIV)

A man who liked to shoot pheasants bought a dog he thought would help him as he hunted. However, he was soon disappointed to learn the dog was addicted to chasing skunks. No matter how hard the owner tried to retrain that dog, and no matter how well it first behaved after retraining, it was usually not long until it was distracted by another skunk. The owner even fed the dog some pheasant, and the old dog liked it. It was the finest food the hound ever ate. Despite that, he soon forgot the good life his master showed him. The next time he had a chance, that dog took off after a skunk again. As if that were not bad enough, the dog caught the skunk. The skunk caught the dog too, and the dog came home stinking. The displeased dog-owner declared, “I need a bird dog and you ain’t nuthin’ but a hound dog!”

It is hard to teach an old dog new tricks. As hard as that man tried to retrain his dog to be a bird dog, even after being sprayed by the skunk the dog showed no signs of change. Finally, there was only one solution to the problem. The hunter became determined to leave his hound in the doghouse and go off hunting alone.

Why is it that we try to do good things and end up doing bad things? It is because there is an "old dog" inside each of us called the "fleshly nature." Until Jesus comes, that old dog will continue to hound us. The fact that he has tasted the best the Master has to offer does not change him. If we are not alert, we will be distracted by the skunks that are hiding everywhere around us. We will spend our time in pursuit of things we are better off without, and we will miss the best there is for us.

Life does not need to be like that. The good news is, that in the meantime, we are not left alone with only our own power. By putting on Jesus we can find strength to leave the old dog behind and live more and more like our Master. Paul said, "Clothe yourselves with the Lord Jesus Christ, and do not think about how to gratify the desires of your sinful nature." (Romans 13:14, NIV).

A LITTLE HUMOR: With high-definition TV, everything looks bigger and wider. Kind of like going to your 25th high school reunion.

OCTOBER 25

TRAVEL LIGHT

"Blessed is he whose transgressions are forgiven, whose sins are covered."
(Psalm 32:1, NIV)

Every year, about 1500 "thru-hikers" set out to walk the entire Appalachian Trail in a single season. Only ten percent complete the 2,160 miles of challenging terrain stretching from Georgia to Maine. One reason some people drop out early is that they haven't learned to travel light.

One individual launched his "thru-hike" carrying a seriously overloaded backpack. He had a cassette player and six tapes of bird calls, air pistol to keep the varmints away, a camera, a radio, and an alarm clock.

At his first stop, an experienced hiker helped him go through his pack and decide what to keep and what to send home. Each item was placed on a gram scale with the question, "Is it worth it? Do you want to carry this for the next 2,000 miles?"

He discovered that his biggest problem was an accumulation of little things. Most of his extra weight was in ounces, not pounds. He didn't need half of what was in his first-aid kit nor the extra tube of toothpaste. His heavy multi-tool knife was replaced with one weighing only an ounce. A metal knife-fork-spoon set gave way to a single plastic spoon. He sent home twenty-six pounds of unnecessary weight.

How many of us are trying to walk the trail of faith in Christ weighed down by an accumulation of little things — anger, bitterness, worry, envy, jealousy, lust, and selfishness? Instead of enjoying the beauty of life with Jesus, we complain about how hard it is to follow Him.

Psalm 32 is for anyone who's ready to shed the weight of sin and regain the joy of walking with the Lord. "Blessed is he whose transgressions are forgiven, whose sins are covered" (Psalm 32:1, NIV). The word *forgiven* means literally, to be taken up and carried away. The word *covered* means it has been put out of God's sight. No wonder the psalmist begins Psalm 32 with a happy shout of joy: "Blessed." A person whose sin have been forgiven is a happy person. He travels light!

A LITTLE HUMOR: A pastor was talking to one of the "shut-ins" of his church. She was never healthy enough to come to church. Finally after much encouragement, she came to a worship service. Greeting her at the door, the pastor expressed his pleasure in seeing her. "Pastor," she said, "I had to take two pain pills to get through that sermon today."

OCTOBER 26

PLAYING THE BLAME GAME

"When tempted, no one should say, 'God is tempting me.' For God cannot be tempted by evil, nor does he tempt anyone; but each one is tempted when, by his own evil desire, he is dragged away and enticed." (James 1:13-14, NIV)

In one of the Peanuts cartoon strips, Lucy is talking to Charlie Brown. She says, "My teacher's mad at me. She's mad because I called our field trip dumb." Charlie Brown asks, "What are you going to do?" She replies, "I'm trying to figure out how I can put the blame on you!"

Do you blame others for the messes that you get yourself into? It is always easier to blame others rather than learning to take responsibility for our own mistakes.

I read about a manager of a minor league baseball team who was fed up with the poor performance of his center fielder. The manager was so disgusted that he took the center fielder out of the game and went out to play the position himself. The first ball hit to the manager took a bad hop and smashed him in the mouth. The second, a high fly ball, bounced off his forehead when he lost it in the sun's glare. The third ball was a hard line drive. It flew between his outstretched arms and hit him right in the eye. He was furious! He ran back to the dugout, grabbed the center fielder and shouted, "You idiot! You've got center field so messed up that even I can't do a thing with it!"

Will Rogers once said that history could be summarized into three great movements: (1) the passing of the buffalo, (2) the passing of the Indian, and (3) the passing of the buck. Someone else has said, "To err is human. To blame it on the other guy is even more human."

It's easy to blame others and make excuses for evil thoughts and wrong actions. Excuses include (1) it's the other person's fault; (2) I couldn't help it; (3) Everybody's doing it; (4) It was just a mistake; (5) Nobody's perfect; (6) The devil made me do it; (7) I was pressured into it; (8) I didn't know it was wrong; (9) God is tempting me. A person who makes excuses is trying to shift the blame from himself or herself to something or someone else. The Bible reminds us that every person is responsible for his or her own mistakes and sin: "When tempted, no one should say, 'God is tempting me.' For God cannot be tempted by evil, nor does he tempt anyone; but each one is tempted when, by his own evil desire, he is dragged away and enticed" (James 1:13-14, NIV).

Each person must accept responsibility for his or her wrongs, confess them, and ask God for forgiveness. Only then will he or she be able to learn from their mistakes and grow so that the same mistakes will not be made again.

A LITTLE HUMOR: A pastor was digging around under his bed looking for something, when he found a box with $2,000 and two eggs in it. Concerned about what this might be since he didn't know why his wife would have this large sum of money, he finally asked his wife what it was. A little bit embarrassed, she replied, "Well, Honey, whenever you preach a bad sermon I put an egg in a box." He was a little bit relieved to think that he had only preached two bad sermons, until she continued and said . . . "and then when I have a dozen eggs, I sell them."

OCTOBER 27

WHY WINNING THE LOTTERY WON'T MAKE YOU HAPPY

"Watch out! Be on your guard against all kinds of greed; a man's life does not consist in the abundance of his possessions." (Luke 12:15, NIV)

At the age of 41, Bud should have been the happiest man alive, for he had won the first $2 million Georgia State Lottery. After telling the local media he would not change his lifestyle in any way, he went on a spending spree that included buying a new Corvette, a new house, a whale-shaped swimming pool, and ordering 23 new credit cards with a total credit limit of $210,000. When he opened the envelope containing his first lottery check, he found a check for only $70,000. Only then did he realize what the limits of his new cash flow would be. Instead of happiness, he went into what psychologists call "fiscal funk."[101]

Conversations are often punctuated with, "When I win the lottery, I'll . . ." — as if winning the lottery will instantaneously solve all our problems. Experience has taught us that winning the lottery often creates as many problems as it solves.

Why do we seek so diligently for more money only to discover, when we get it, that money is not the answer? Jesus provided some insight on this dilemma in one of his most famous stories, the story of the fortunate but foolish farmer (Luke 12:13-21).

The farmer in Jesus' story had a very successful year. In fact, the crop was so plentiful he had no place to store it. He needed new barns. Unfortunately, the farmer attributed to his vocational success more value than it actually had. He was convinced his future was secure. "Take life easy," he said to himself. "Eat, drink, and be merry" (v. 18, NIV). Clarence Jordan has published a paraphrase of the Bible called *The*

[101] Jerry Benson, "Pennies from Hell," *Omni* (June 1991), 112.

Cotton Patch Version of Luke and Acts. In that paraphrase he renders the expression this way, “Recline, dine, wine, and shine!”

But the farmer didn’t have a long life of leisure ahead of him. Instead, his life was over that night. He thought he had it make, but God called him a fool (v. 20).

Money, which is material, cannot satisfy our deep life needs, which are spiritual. Happiness comes only when we have peace with God, when we are at peace with ourselves, and when we live in peace with other people. Money simply cannot provide those things. That’s why Jesus said, “Watch out! Be on your guard against all kinds of greed; a man’s life does not consist in the abundance of his possessions” (Luke 12:15, NIV).

A LITTLE HUMOR: A preacher was driving out in the country when his car broke down. He knocked on a farmhouse door and asked to use the telephone. As he was sitting in the living room, a three-legged pig walked through. The farmer said, "This is the most incredible pig you have ever seen. He saved my daughter from drowning, my son from a burning house, and my wife from a fall." The preacher said, "Man, that is some kind of pig, but why does he only have three legs?" "The farmer replied, "Mister, you don't eat a pig like that all at once!"

OCTOBER 28

GOING TO THE EXTREME!

“Then He said to them all, ‘If anyone desires to come after Me, let him deny himself, and take up his cross, and follow Me’.” (Luke 9:23, NKJV)

A high school drama class was performing at a local theater. Somehow an accident occurred and a hole was cracked in the stage floor. Carefully the performers avoided the damaged area until Joey, jugging bowling pins, accidentally stepped through the hole up to his knee. He apologized to the audience for his clumsiness which caused a heckler to shout, “Don’t worry, Joey . . . It’s just a STAGE you’re going through!”

We all go through stages, don’t we? One of the stages that some sports enthusiasts enjoying going through is a fondness for extremes. Note the popularity of extreme sports — sky diving, ice climbing, skateboarding, paragliding, and who knows what’s next.

The people known as Generation X introduced us to extreme fashions. Not only extreme clothes — but also ornaments attached to the body. All kinds of body parts are pierced including eyebrows, navels, tongues, and more private parts. All that sounds a little extreme to me, but that’s the point, isn’t it?

Going to extremes is nothing new. Some of the greatest people who have ever lived have been risk-takers. Think of people who have placed footmarks on our history. People like John Glenn, Alan Shepherd, Krista McAulliff, Charles Lindbergh, Amelia Earhart, Christopher Columbus, Martin Luther, Galileo, Augustine, and Saint Paul.

Think what risk-takers Jesus' followers were in those first centuries after His ascension into heaven. They faced the possibility of death daily for their faith. But they still persisted. If there is any sin that you and I are guilty of, it probably is that we play it too safe when it comes to our faith. We have made being a Christian so convenient and so comfortable that our faith has lost its edge. A faith that demands too little will not grab hold of the passion that many people need in their lives.

A missionary society wrote to the great missionary, David Livingstone, deep in the heart of Africa and asked, "Have you found a good road to where you are? If so, we want to know how to send other men to join you." Livingstone wrote back, "If you have men who will come only if they know there is a good road, I don't want them. I want men who will come if there is no road at all."

Christ is still looking for men and women like that today, people who will come if there is no road at all. Better than extreme sports — more exciting than extreme fashions. God is looking for men and women who have extreme faith.

A LITTLE HUMOR: A man and his son were shoveling their driveway after a heavy snowfall when their dog, Lady, wandered away from them. The man, fearing the dog might be hit by a car, shouted angrily: "Lady! Lady! Get over here right now!"

The dog charged happily back to them, accompanied by a commuter who had been standing at the bus stop. "Yes, sir, what can I do for you?" she asked.

OCTOBER 29

LISTEN

"God spoke to the three disciples and said, 'This is my Son, whom I love. Listen to Him!'" (Mark 9:7, NIV)

One of the best known comedians of today is Steve Martin. He is a "wild and crazy guy!" A few years ago he made a movie, *The Man With Two Brains* — a movie that took no brains to watch. In this movie he plays a brain surgeon, Dr. Herfarrerer, who has fallen in love with an evil and conniving temptress. Standing before the portrait of his late wife, Martin asks for guidance. "Just show me a sign. Should I marry her or not? Please show me just a little sign."

Suddenly a cold wind begins to blow, sending an icy chill throughout the room, and a voice wails, "Noo, Nooo, don't do it." The wall splits in two, and the portrait spins eerily on the wall faster and faster, saying, "Nooo," while the furnishings crash around the room. Suddenly everything is still and Steve Martin slowly picks himself up and says, "Since you won't show me a sign, I guess it's okay to marry her." And he goes on his way.[102]

Would it be safe to say that Martin's character had already made up his mind to remarry — that he really had no intention to listen to his late wife? Many of us have

[102] *Dynamic Preaching,* (January-March, 2000, Vol. 15, No. 1), 57.

selective listening, don't we? We hear what we want to hear.

A ninety-one year old fellow went to the doctor and had a checkup. Two days later, the doctor saw his patient, smiling, with a 30-year-old woman on his arm. "Thanks, Doc," the old man said, "I did what you said." The doctor asked, "For heaven's sake, what did I say?" The ninety-one - year-old man replied, "You said, 'Find a hot mamma and be cheerful." "No," replied the doctor. "I said, "You have a heart murmur and be careful."

On one occasion Jesus was on a high mountain with three of His disciples (Mark 9:2-9). God spoke to the three disciples and said, "This is my Son, whom I love. Listen to Him!" Are you listening to Jesus when He says, "I love you?" Are you listening to Jesus when He says, "You must be born again?" Are you listening to Jesus when He says, "I want to give to you a meaningful life?" Are you listening to Jesus when He says, "I will give you peace?" Are you listening to Jesus when He says, "I will give you eternal life?"

The word *listen* in Mark 9:7 means not merely hearing, but the hearing that leads to obeying what is heard. Jesus talked about how important it is to obey as well as to hear (Matthew 7:24-27). Are you listening?

A LITTLE HUMOR: A Sunday school teacher asked her little children, as they were on the way to church service, "And why is it necessary to be quiet in church?" One bright little girl replied, "Because people are sleeping."

OCTOBER 30

THEY'LL CROSS THAT BRIDGE WHEN YOU COME TO IT

"For God has not given us a spirit of fear, but of power and of love and of a sound mind." (2 Timothy 1:7, NKJV)

Have you ever been afraid to drive over a high bridge? If so, you're not alone. In fact, some people are so afraid of bridges that they will drive hours out of their way to avoid them. Others try to cross but have a panic attack in the middle of a bridge and can't go on. They block traffic. Because of this, the operators of some of the longest and highest spans in America now offer a driving service. On request, one of the bridge attendants will get behind the wheel and drive your car over the terrifying expanse.

For example, in 1991 Michigan's Timid Motorist Program assisted 830 drivers across the Mackinac Bridge, which is five miles long and rises two hundred feet about the water. At Maryland's Chesapeake Bay Bridge, which is over four miles long and rises two hundred feet above the water, authorities took the wheel and helped one thousand fearful motorists.[103]

---

[103] *Dynamic Preaching,* (Oct.-Dec., 1998, Vol. 13, No. 4), 5.

Some of you can perhaps relate to that. Fear is a terrible thing. The word *fear* comes from the Old English *faer*, meaning sudden danger. It refers to fright where fright is justified.

There are all kinds of solutions to fear, but the apostle Paul gives us the most helpful one. He writes, “For God has not given us a spirit of fear, but of power and of love and of a sound mind” (2 Timothy 1:7, NKJV). Can you think of a better formula for successful living than this: that God would replace our timidity — our fear — with power, love a sound mind? Self-discipline is a better translation of sound mind. It describes a person who is sensibly-minded and balanced, who has his life under control.

God has not put into our hearts the spirit of fearfulness. That is not God’s way. What time we might be afraid, we can look to the Lord as the Psalmist who said, “What time I am afraid, I will trust in thee” (Psalm 56:3), or better still like the prophet who resolutely took the ground of faith and said, “I will trust and not be afraid” (Isaiah 12:2).

A lady was awakened one morning by a strange noise at the window. At once she saw a butterfly flying around the window on the inside in a great fright, because outside there was a sparrow pecking at the glass, trying to reach it. The butterfly did not see the glass, but it saw the sparrow, and evidently expected any moment to be caught. Yet all the while, because of that invisible sheet of glass, the butterfly was actually safe as if it had been miles away from the sparrow. It is when we forget our Shield, our Protector, that our hearts fail us.

Let us put our trust in the Lord. He will cross that bridge for us when we come to it.

A LITTLE HUMOR — A three-year-old boy put his shoes on by himself. His mother noticed the left shoe was on his right foot and his right shoe was on his left foot. She said, "Son, your shoes are on the wrong feet." He looked up at her and said, "Don't kid me, Mom. I KNOW they're my feet!"

OCTOBER 31

THE INVISIBLE SIN

“Woe to you . . . hypocrites . . .” (Matthew 23:13, NASB)

There are going to be a lot of people running around tonight with masks on their faces. On Halloween people dress up in costumes and put on masks to hide out, to conceal who they really are. Originally the disguises worn on “All Hallows Eve” were supposed to fool the demons and other dark forces roaming the planet on that fateful night. The idea was that good Christians would be left alone by evil spirits if they dressed to look like they themselves were part of Satan’s army.

Masks are interesting things. We all wear them, you know, and not just on Halloween. We put on the brave mask when our hearts are breaking. We put on a gruff mask to keep people at a distance. We put on a wild and crazy mask to get attention or to avoid responsibility. A lot of us dress up and put on our masks when we come to church. We exchange our Friday night "sinner" for our Sunday morning "saint."

In Matthew 23 Jesus used the word "hypocrite" to address people who were pretending to be one thing when in reality they were something else. The word *hypocrite* is taken directly from the Greek word *hypocrites.* Literally it means one who plays a part. In the Greek theater an actor would play many parts. He would have a different mask for each individual character he was portraying. When it came time for him to play another character he would simply lay down his mask and hold up another one in front of his face. Therefore, a hypocrite is one who pretends to be something or someone he really is not.

The late Joseph Bayly wrote, "Hypocrisy is a terrible sign of trouble in our hearts – it waits only for the day of exposure. For as John Milton put it in Paradise Lost, 'Neither men nor angels can discern hypocrisy, the only evil that walks invisible – except to God'."

A LITTLE HUMOR: A hypocrite is one who complains there is too much sex and violence on his DVD player.

NOVEMBER 1

THE ART OF APPRECIATING OTHERS

"I thank my God every time I remember you." (Philippians 1:3, NIV)

While a man was riding a bus to work, a grandmotherly-looking woman who also rode the bus every day sat down beside him. Looking at him, she smiled then opened her pocketbook to the photo section. She said, "You and I ride this bus every day and I've never shown you the photos of my grandchildren." He said, "No, you never have and I really appreciate it!"

One of the lost arts of some people is the expression of appreciation to others. Why should we express appreciation for others? The answer is because it raises their self-esteem. The Bible says we're supposed to do that. First Thessalonians 5:11 reads, "Encourage one another and build each other up." William James has written that the deepest need of individuals is to be appreciated.

As Paul sat in a Roman prison, there were many who took advantage of him. Others were saying negative things about him. Some, no doubt, likely forgot about him. Not the Philippians. They never forgot him as the years went by and even sent a gift to him while he was in prison. Consequently, Paul writes the following words: "I thank my God every time I remember you" (Philippians 1:3). They were Paul's Booster Club, they supported him, standing with him for years. Behind-the-scenes people deserve our appreciation. Some of us have marriage partners who stuck with us through bad times. It may have been financial disaster, a mid-life crisis, a health problem, an affair, a terrible career decision. Some of us have been blessed with someone who has shown wonderful support.

A man was in the hospital recovering from a fall off his roof. He looked at his wife and said, "Wanda, you have always been there for me. When I flunked the tenth grade, you were there. When I wrecked my dad's new car, you were there. When I got fired at the plant, you were there. When I lost my savings on the ostrich farm, you were there. And now, I have broken my arm and leg falling off the roof, and there you were. Wanda, you are nothing but bad luck!"

I challenge you this week to give a compliment to every person in your family or in your office. People blossom under affirmation.. They wilt under criticism. Every time you appreciate the people around you, you raise their value. And while you're at it, don't forget to express your appreciation to God for all He has done for you in Christ.

A LITTLE HUMOR: A woman went into a Post Office to buy stamps for her party invitations. "What denomination?" asked the clerk. "Oh, goodness! Have we come to that?" asked the woman. "Well, give me 30 Baptist, 20 Methodist, 10 Catholics and 5 Presbyterian!"

NOVEMBER 2

THE GREAT BURDEN BEARER

"Give your burdens to the Lord. He will carry them. He will not permit the godly to slip or fall," (Psalm 55:22, LB)

A man was carrying a heavy load of grain down a country road. Sweat dripped from his brow and soaked his worn shirt, while the dusty air and scorching sun burned his face. A man in a passing wagon noticed his struggle, and, judging the sack to weigh at least fifty pounds, he gently tugged on the reins and slowed his horses. "Mister, you need a ride. Get up here with me, and I'll take you."

Relieved, the tired man climbed up onto the seat and settled in for the remainder of the trip to town. However, he did not remove the loaded sack from his shoulder.

After a moment of silence, the compassionate driver said with consternation, "Why don't you put that down and relax?" To his surprise, the first man replied, "Oh no! It's enough to ask you to carry me without having you carry this also."

Have you ever done that to God? When you're tempted to carry your burdens by yourself, stop and think about whom you are dealing with. He is God the Creator and Sustainer of the universe! No crisis — whether health, financial, relational, etc. — is a challenge for Him, so why handle it yourself. Psalm 55:22 reads, "Give your burdens to the Lord. He will carry them. He will not permit the godly to slip or fall" (LB).

In his devotional book on the *Psalms, Prayer, Praise and Promises,* Warren W. Wiersbe writes this about burdens: "The Lord gives us the burden, and then He says, 'Now give that burden back to Me. But don't stop there; give Me yourself as well.' If we try to give Him our burdens without giving Him ourselves, He really can't help us. It's like stepping onto an elevator with many heavy packages and failing to put them down on the floor until you reach your destination. Let the elevator carry both you and your packages."[104]

Our great God offers you his amazing power. Take hold of it today!

A LITTLE HUMOR: A little boy opened the big family Bible with fascination, looking at the old pages as he turned them. Then something fell out of the Bible, and he picked it up and looked at it closely. It was an old leaf from a tree that had been pressed in between the pages." Momma, look what I found," the boy called out. "What have you got there, dear?" his mother asked. With astonishment in the young boy's voice he answered, "It's Adam's suit!"

[104] Warren W. Wiersbe, *Prayer, Praise, and Promises* (Grand Rapids: Baker Book House, 1992), 152.

NOVEMBER 3

ONE PERSON

"Do not fear therefore, you are of more value than many sparrows."
(Matthew 10:31, NKJV)

A little girl about five years old strolled along the midway at the State Fair of Texas. She held in her hand a fluffy pile of cotton candy that was about as big as she was. The humorous picture of such a little person attempting to eat something so big caught the eye of a man passing by. He said to her, "How can a little girl like you eat all of that candy?" Without a moment's hesitation, she replied, "It's easy, Mister. You see, I'm really much bigger on the inside than I am on the outside."[105]

What a great truth to discover about ourselves! We are bigger on the inside than on the outside. How much better to feel like this little girl than to feel like the women pictured in a cartoon who were standing next to a sign that read, "The Low Self-Esteem Glee Club," and singing, "If you're worthless and you know it, say 'amen!'"

Many people today are singing that song and saying amen! with great gusto. They feel worthless. They don't believe they can make a difference in the world. We need to realize that we are bigger on the inside than we are on the outside.

Charles Wesley was only one person, and what's worse, he had to live under the shadow of his more popular brother, John. Still, two hundred years after he died, Christians all over the world are singing Charles' songs.

Ethel Andrus was just one person, but at the age of seventy-two she started an organization that in half a century has become one of the most powerful lobbying forces in America, the American Association of Retired Persons (AARP).

Every significant accomplishment in life started the same way, with one person who conceived an idea, one person who started a movement that eventually involved others. There are no unimportant people. Every person, no matter how small or seemingly insignificant, can make a difference in this world.

Jesus underscored how important just one person is in the parable of the talents (Matthew 25:14-30). Jesus gives each of us a talent to use. He expects us to put it to work for our good and His glory. The one-talent person is just as important as any other multi-talented person. Don't hide behind your talent. Don't surrender to an inferiority complex. You are important!

A LITTLE HUMOR: A teacher of small children were listening to some of them as they were telling her about their brothers and sisters. "My brother takes horseback-riding lessons," bragged one little girl. "My sister takes gymnastics," said another. Not to be outdone, the youngest piped up, "My sister takes antibiotics."

[105] Brian L. Harbour, *Jesus the Storyteller* (Macon, Georgia: Smyth and Helwys Publishing, Inc., 1999), 18.

NOVEMBER 4

WHAT ARE YOU TIED TO?

"I am the vine; you are the branches." (John 15:5, NKJV)

Two men, walking through the woods, come across a big deep hole. "Wow, that looks deep," says one. "Sure does," says the other. "Toss a few pebbles in there and see how deep it is." They pick up a few pebbles and throw them in and wait. No noise. "Hey, that is really deep," says the first man. "Here, throw one of these great big rocks down there. That should make a noise." They pick up a couple of football-sized rocks and toss them into the hole and wait. Nothing. They look at each other in amazement. One gets a determined look on his face and says, "Hey, over there in the weeds is a railroad tie. Help me carry it over here. When we toss that in, it's gotta make some noise." The two drag the heavy tie over to the hole and heave it in. Not a sound comes from the hole. Suddenly, out of the nearby woods, a goat appears, running like the wind. It rushes toward the two men; then right past them, running as fast as its legs will carry it. Suddenly it leaps in the air and into the hole. The two men are astonished with what they've just seen. Then, out of the woods comes a farmer who spots the men and ambles over. "Hey, have you two guys seen my goat out here?" One of the men says, "You bet we did! Craziest thing I ever seen. It came running like crazy and just jumped into this hole!" "Nah," says the farmer, "That couldn't have been my goat. My goat was chained to a railroad tie."[106]

That poor goat was tied to something that pulled him down, way down. What are you tied to? It's one of the most relevant questions that can be asked of us. Everyone has something pulling on him. Are you tied to your work? Are you tied to a comfortable lifestyle? Are you tied to alcohol or drugs? Or are you tied to Christ?

Jesus says in John 15:5, "I am the vine; you are the branches." What is Jesus saying? Isn't He saying, "You are tied to me. Here is where you draw your strength. Here is what sustains you when life is tough. You are connected to me."

The purpose of being tied to Christ is to live a productive life (John 15:4) and find true joy (John 15:11). And what is the key for staying connected to Christ? Obedience! Jesus said, "If you love Me, keep my commandments" (John 15:15). Stay connected to Christ. Learn the principle of loving obedience. Bear much fruit. Enjoy life in Him.

A LITTLE HUMOR — A little boy was in a relative's wedding. As he was coming down the aisle, he would take two steps, stop, turn to the crowd, put his hands up like claws and roar. So it went, step, step, ROAR, step, step, ROAR, all the way down the aisle. As you can imagine, the crowd was near tears from laughing so hard. The little boy, however, was getting more and more distressed from all the laughing, and was also near tears by the time he reached the platform. When asked what he was doing, he sniffed and said, "I was being the Ring Bear."

---

[106] *Dynamic Preaching*, (April - June, 2000, Vol. 15, No. 2), 55.

NOVEMBER 5

MUCH WORSE THAN BAD BREATH!

"When words are many, sin is not absent, but he who holds his tongue is wise."
(Proverbs 10:19, NIV)

It's estimated that 60 million Americans suffer from "halitosis" — bad breath! Dealing with it is an $850 million industry in the United States. Contrary to popular myths about bad breath, dental research suggests that the tongue may be the cause of the odor — not the stomach or something you ate. A recent article in the Journal of the American Dental Association cited six studies and concluded that in 85 percent of those with bad breath, the odor originated in the mouth. Is your tongue causing people to flee from you?

Americans spend a fortune to guarantee that a sweet, sweet spirit comes from our mouths. If you've ever been close to someone with halitosis, you're acquainted with the need to clear the air.

But what if we spent that much time and attention dealing with the sour, noxious words that come out of our mouths? Bad breath may offend for a moment, but a few harsh words can have an impact on the hearer that never fades.

Solomon provided some insight into the problem of the tongue. He said that too many words give rise to sin: "When words are many, sin is not absent, but he who holds his tongue is wise" (Proverbs 10:19, NIV).

Do you talk too much? Say more than you should? Leave an unpleasant aroma lingering in the air? Can you hold your tongue?

The real problem with the tongue, of course, is what it's connected to: the mind. When we dwell on thoughts of bitterness and judgment of people, those thoughts will escape in verbal form sooner or later. To purify your breath, cleanse your tongue; to purify your tongue, trust God to cleanse your thoughts.

A LITTLE HUMOR: A preacher decided to skip services and head to the hills to do some bear hunting. As he rounded the corner on a perilous twist in the trail, he and a bear collided, sending him and his rifle tumbling down the mountainside. Before he knew it, his rifle went one way and he went the other, landing on a rock and breaking both legs. That was the good news. The bad news was the ferocious bear charging at him from a distance, and he couldn't move. "Oh, Lord," the preacher prayed, "I'm so sorry for skipping services today to come out here and hunt. Please forgive me and grant me one wish. Please make a Christian out of that bear that's coming at me." That very instant, the bear skidded to a halt, fell to its knees, clasped its paws together and began to pray, "Dear God, bless this food I am about to receive."[107]

[107] *Stand Firm,* (Nashville: LifeWay Press, January 13, 1999).

NOVEMBER 6

MALICE TOWARD NONE!

"Rid yourselves of all malice." (1 Peter 2:1, NIV)

Peter wrote, "Rid yourselves of all malice" (1 Peter 2:1, NIV). The word *malice* connotes a spirit of ill will with the desire to get even. This sin is extremely malicious and destructive. When wronged, the malicious heart quickly, but thoughtlessly, assents, "I will pay back. I will get even." Many people live in spiritual defeat because of this sin of malice. Rather than forgetting unkindnesses by returning good for evil, they are possessed by an underlying, diabolical desire to get revenge.

The story is told that Leonard da Vinci, while painting his great work, "The Last Supper," vowed he would get even with a bitter enemy by painting him as Judas. There was a sense of gratification in his heart as he yielded to this selfish temptation. But later, as the famed artist tried to paint the face of Christ, he was forced to give up in despair. Realizing that such a task demanded a pure heart, he put away his animosity, admitted the folly of his vindictiveness, and quickly painted out the face of his enemy. Only then, it is said, was he able to paint the face of Christ.[108]

So long as there is a vengeful spirit, no believer can effectively serve God. He may be extremely busy for the Lord and his labors may be many, but they will be hopelessly fruitless. Only the heart which overflows with God's love for others can be useful in exalting the name of the Lord Jesus Christ. To this end, God's plea to every Christian is, "Do not take revenge, my friends, but leave room for God's wrath, for it is written: 'It is mine to avenge; I will repay,' says the Lord" (Romans 12:19, NIV).

A LITTLE HUMOR: A little boy's new baby brother wouldn't stop crying and screaming. "Where did we get him?" he asked his mother. "He came from Heaven, dear," the mother replied. "I can see why they threw him out!" the boy exclaimed.

NOVEMBER 7

RESISTING THE DEVIL

"Resist the devil, and he will flee from you." (James 4:7b, NKJV)

Like many sheep ranchers in the West, Lexy Fowler has tried just about everything to stop crafty coyotes from killing her sheep. She has used odor sprays, electric fences, and "scare-coyotes." She has slept with her lambs during the summer and has placed battery-operated radios near them. She has corralled them at night, herded them at day. But the southern Montana rancher has lost scores of lambs — as many as fifty in one year.

---

[108] J. Allen Blair, *Living Peacefully: A Devotional Study of the First Epistle of Peter,* (Neptune, New Jersey: Loizeaux Brothers, 1959), 92-93.

Then she discovered the llama — the aggressive, funny-looking, afraid-of-nothing llama. "Llamas don't appear to be afraid of anything," she said. "When they see something, they put their head up and walk straight toward it. That is aggressive behavior as far as the coyote is concerned, and they won't have anything to do with that. Coyotes are opportunists, and llamas take that opportunity away."

Apparently llamas know the truth of what James writes: "Resist the devil, and he will flee from you" (James 4:7). The moment we sense the devil's attack through temptation is the moment we should face it and deal with it for what it is.

The word *resist* is a military term that means to stand against another's onset. We cannot fight the devil. He is too strong for us. But while we cannot take the offensive, we can stand our ground in the face of Satan's attacks. The devil is like any bully; he retreats when he is gallantly and bravely resisted in the strength and the company of Jesus Christ.

Peter says we are to "resist steadfast in the faith" (1 Peter 5:9). The word *steadfast* describes something as firm, hard, solid, and compact, like a rock. A Christian should stand firm and unyielding like granite in resisting Satan. Victory over the devil lies in the death of Jesus on the cross where He defeated the devil (John 12:31-33). In Christ, Satan is now a defeated foe. Someone told a reformed alcoholic: "I see you have mastered the devil at last." "No," came the quiet answer, "but I do have the Master of the devil." That is our hope also.

A LITTLE HUMOR: After a long, dry sermon, the minster announced that he wished to meet with the church's board following the close of the service. The first man to arrive and greet the minister was a total stranger. "You misunderstood my announcement. This is a meeting of the board members," explained the minister. "I know, said the man, "but if there is anyone here more bored than I am, I'd like to meet him."

NOVEMBER 8

GETTING RID OF DECEIT

"Rid ourselves of all deceit." (1 Peter 2:3, NIV)

The apostle Peter exhorts us to "rid ourselves of all deceit" (1 Peter 2:3, NIV). *Rid yourselves* is also translated put away or put off. The phrase is used to indicate removing one's former life of sin as one would take off a garment. While we cannot become completely sin-free in this life, no matter how hard we try to put aside sin, we are commanded to get rid of sin in order to become more like Christ.

God's people are to be true blue, stalwart men and women of the faith, honest and trustworthy at all times. "For we are taking pains to do what is right, not only in the eyes of the Lord but also in the eyes of men" (2 Corinthians 8:21, NIV). Under no circumstances should a child of God endanger his testimony by stooping to little tricks of deceit or falsehood.

It is said of Abraham Lincoln that he would accept no case in which the client did not have justice on his side. One time a man came to employ him. Lincoln stared at the ceiling, yet listened intently as the facts were given. Abruptly, he swung around in his chair.

"You have a pretty good case in technical law," he said, "but a pretty bad one in equity and justice. You will have to get someone else to win this case for you. I could not do it. All the time while pleading before the jury, I'd be thinking, 'Lincoln, you're a liar!' I might forget myself and say it out loud."[109]

"A righteous man hates lying" (Proverbs 13:5, NKJV). Lying and all forms of guile grieve the heart of God. No Christian should lie or deceive, regardless of consequences to himself. If he does, he will never advance the things of God.

The late Dr. Will Hougton used to tell of a soldier who became a Christian through watching a believer who was also a serviceman. The thing that impressed him was the fact that although the other men of the regiment made fun of this Christian, they always left their money in his possession for safe keeping.

How important to provide things honest in the sight of all men! Say, does your Christian walk square with your Christian talk?

A LITTLE HUMOR: A very wealthy individual died and left a half million dollars to each of his relatives. At the cemetery, the minister noticed among the well-dressed mourners was a shabby young stranger who cried as though his heart was breaking. After the service, the minister walked over to the young man and said, "I notice you crying. Were you related to the deceased?" "No," the man responded, "I wasn't related at all." "Then, why are you crying?" the minster asked. The man replied, "I just told you — because I wasn't related!"

NOVEMBER 9

YOU SHALL NOT WANT

"The Lord is my Shepherd; I shall not want." (Psalm 23:1, KJV)

David, the author of this beautiful psalm was not saying he was self-sufficient and didn't need anything. Rather, he was saying, "Because the Lord is my Shepherd, He provides everything thing I need. Having Him as my Shepherd, consequently, I lack nothing."

Recently I preached a series of sermons on Psalm 23. During that time one of our church members, Charlotte Wooton, sent me a copy of "You Shall Not Want" by Roy Lessin. I was blessed by it and want to share it with you.

---

[109] J. Allen Blair, Living Peacefully: A Devotional Study of the First Epistle of Peter, (Neptune, New Jersey: Loizeaux Brothers, 1959), 93.

"You Shall Not Want"
To the lost sheep, He is the seeking Shepherd;
To the needy sheep, He is the providing Shepherd;
To the hurting sheep, He is the comforting Shepherd;
To the bruised sheep, He is the healing Shepherd;
To the anxious sheep, He is the peaceful Shepherd;
To the wandering sheep, He is the guiding Shepherd;
To the fearful sheep, He is the protecting Shepherd;
To the lame sheep, He is the carrying Shepherd;
To the discontented sheep, He is the fulfilling Shepherd;
To the parched sheep, He is the anointing Shepherd;
To the timid sheep, He is the reassuring Shepherd;
To the fallen sheep, He is the merciful Shepherd;
To the nervous sheep, He is the quieting Shepherd;
To the heavy laden sheep, He is the restful Shepherd;
To the lonely sheep, He is the ever-present Shepherd;
To the weary sheep, He is the restoring Shepherd;
To all His sheep, He is the Good Shepherd.

The psalmist said, "The Lord is my Shepherd." The word "my" speaks of a personal relationship with the Lord. Can you say that the Lord is your Shepherd? If not, why not invite the Lord Jesus Christ into your life? He longs to be your Savior and Shepherd.

A LITTLE HUMOR: A church member whose business was real estate said, "This house has both its good points and its bad points. To show you I'm above board, I'll tell you both. Its bad points are that there is a chemical plant one block north and a slaughterhouse three blocks south." "Tell me the good points," asked the prospect. "The good point is that you can always tell which way the breeze is blowing."[110]

NOVEMBER 10

A TRIP TO GOD'S WOODSHED

"Those whom I love I rebuke and discipline." (Revelation 3:19, NIV)

A young man went off to a rather expensive university. The bills were coming in monthly to his parents. They were struggling to keep their heads above water. One day his mother received a letter from their son that read like this: "I'm writing to

---

[110] Leslie Flynn, *A Sourcebook of Humorous Stories* (Grand Rapids: Baker Book House, 1973), 74.

inform you that I have flunked all of my courses. I had an accident and totally wrecked my car. I owe the clothing store in town $2,000. I have been suspended for the next semester because of misconduct. I am coming home. Prepare Dad." His mother wrote a one line letter back to him. It read: "Dear Son, Dad is prepared. Prepare yourself."

God is prepared to deal with His children when they sin. God has a woodshed, and if you are one of His children, before you get through this life you will make more than one trip to it. The author of the *New Testament Book of Hebrews* talks about God's woodshed: "Endure hardship as discipline; God is treating you as sons. For what son is not disciplined by his father? If you are not disciplined (and everyone undergoes discipline), then you are illegitimate children and not true sons" (Hebrews 12:7-8, NIV).

There are three ways God could deal with us when we sin. First of all, God could condemn us. Even after a person is saved, the first time he sins God could send him to hell. But God cannot do that, for the Bible says, "There is now no condemnation for those who are in Christ Jesus" (Romans 8:1, NIV).

Then again, God could condone us. God could stick His head in the sand and ignore our sin and overlook it. But God cannot and will not do that. God is a holy and just God that lets no sin go unpunished.

The third way God could dead with us, and does deal with us is, He can correct us. If God condemned us after we sinned, that would be pure legalism. If He condoned our sin, that would be liberalism. But the third way is God's way and that is the way of love. The Lord Himself said, "Those whom I love I rebuke and discipline" (Revelation 3:19, NIV).

We need to remember that the purpose of discipline is not to discourage us. Hebrews 12:5 reminds us that God's discipline is meant to encourage us. It is for our good (Hebrews 12:10) and it enables us to be productive in righteousness and peace (Hebrews 12:11).As His children we are to be holy, and He will discipline us when we are not, and He will discipline us until we are.

A LITTLE HUMOR: A country boy went a courtin' . . ."Why, I think you're cute as a speckled pup in a little red wagon. I care so much for you, I'd climb the tallest mountain, swim the deepest ocean, cross the hottest desert just to see you. And if it don't rain come Saturday, I'll be over."

NOVEMBER 11

WHAT'S BUGGING YOU?

"Resist the devil and he will flee from you." (James 4:7, NKJV)

Have you ever wondered about all those bugs that get electrocuted every summer night in those big lights in backyards? Those bugs must be deaf not to hear the bugs before them getting zapped, or blind not to see all the dead insects that have fallen around the light. On the other hand, maybe they do hear and see all the warning signs, but every bug thinks he is different from the rest, stronger, and more able to avoid the danger of the light. But in the end, he winds up dead like all the other bugs. If he could fly around that light without getting too close to it, he would be fine. However, all the bugs who have gone before him prove that it just doesn't work that way. The more bugs are around the light, the closer they want to get to it, until they finally get too close and are shocked to death.

Humans are a lot like that. We, too, can hear all the warnings and see all the negative results of sin, but that won't always keep us away from temptations. James 1:14-15 describes temptation as being enticed by our own evil desires. Such desires attract us, just as the light attracts the bugs, but we think we're different from anyone else and can handle the temptations that cause others to sin. Yet every person who has lived before us is proof that it just doesn't work that way.

How can we overcome temptation? Let me suggest four steps.

Request. Each believer has the privilege of prayer in overcoming temptation. James says, "If any of you lacks wisdom, let him ask of God, who gives to all men generously" (1:5). Do you need help in overcoming your weakness? Ask God. Do you need deliverance from the power and temptation of sin? Ask God.

Resist. James urges Christians to "lay aside all filthiness" (James 1:21, NKJV). He charges us to get rid of moral filth. Joseph refused temptation (Genesis 39). We must "run" from temptation.

Receive. Jesus met and overcame temptation by quoting Scripture (Matthew 4:4, 7, 10). We, too, can win over temptation if we "in humility receive the word implanted, which is able to save your souls" (James 1:21).

Rely. Rely on God's ability. "Submit therefore to God" (James 4:7). John reminds us, "Greater is He who is in you than He who is in the world" (1 John 4:4).

In your hour of temptation, remember God is faithful. He knows your capacity. He will give you all the strength you need to overcome, or He will make a way of escape.

A LITTLE HUMOR: When a customer left his cell phone in my store, I strolled through his saved numbers, stopped at "Mom" and pushed send. His mother answered, and I told her what happened.

"Don't worry," she said, "I'll take care of it."

A few minutes later, the cell phone rang. It was "Mom." "Martin," she said, "you left your cell phone at the convenience store."

NOVEMBER 12

HEAVEN'S ROYAL WEDDING

"Let us rejoice and be glad and give the glory to Him, for the marriage of the Lamb has come and His bride has made herself ready." (Revelation 19:7, NASB)

The Royal Wedding of Kate Middleton and Prince William of London filled the news media with every imaginable detail. It was the wedding of the century. Weddings are meant to be beautiful and full of joy.

There is another wedding that is to take place any time now. I am referring to the future wedding of the Lamb of God, the Lord Jesus Christ, and His bride, the Church. This future event will be the wedding of eternity, and it will be the most beautiful of all weddings. In his book, *Unveiling the End Times in Our Time*,[111] Adrian Rogers described the future wedding of Christ and His Church under four major headings. I want to use those four headings, combine some of the information about the wedding of Kate and Prince William, and what it will mean for us.

First, the music of this future wedding will be magnificent (Revelation 19:1-6). The music for this wedding will be the "Hallelujah Chorus" (vv. 1,3-4, 6). The word hallelujah means "Praise the Lord." When the day that has been set for this heavenly royal wedding arrives, it will be a glorious day of praise.

Second, the church, as the bride of Christ will be beautiful (Revelation 19:7-8). Verse seven states, "His bride has made herself ready." Kate Middleton spent weeks and months preparing herself for this great event when she would become William's wife. She is a beautiful woman, and her beauty was enhanced by her wedding gown. Likewise the bride of Christ is making herself ready for this future wedding. Verse eight reads, "It was given to her to clothe herself in fine linen, bright and clean; for the fine linen is the righteous acts of the saints."

Third, the guest who will be invited to this future heavenly wedding will be glad (Revelation 19:9). The list of invited guests to Kate and William's wedding will be limited – chosen; by invitation only. No one was allowed into Westminster Abbey whose names were not on the guest list. The royal wedding of heaven also includes a special guest list. Verse nine states, "Blessed are those who are invited to the marriage supper of the Lamb."

Fourth, the Lord Jesus Christ, who is the groom of this heavenly wedding, will be glorified (Revelation 19:6-7, 9-10). At Kate and William's wedding all eyes were focused on Kate. That is also true of most weddings in our culture. At earthly weddings we sing, "Here Comes the Bride!" but at that wedding it will be "Here Comes the Groom!" (v.11). All the attention at this heavenly wedding will be focused on the Groom – the Lord Jesus Christ.

Words and illustrations cannot sufficiently explain or begin to describe what will happen when Jesus comes for His bride. Are you ready?

A LITTLE HUMOR: A doctor said to his patient: "I see you're over a month late for your appointment. Don't you know that nervous disorders require prompt and regular attention? What's your excuse?"

"Well," said the patient, "I was just following your orders, Doc."

"Following my orders? What are you talking about? I gave you no such order," said the doctor.

"You told me to avoid people who irritate me," the patient replied.

---

[111] Adrian Rogers, *Unveiling the End Times in Our Time* (Nashville: Broadman and Holman Publishers, 2004), 206-213.

NOVEMBER 13

LOVE IS AS LOVE DOES

"Love one another fervently with a pure heart." (1 Peter 1:22b, NKJV)

Forest Gump's mother kept telling him, "Stupid is as stupid does." In the same way, the Bible teaches us that "Love is as Love does." The world will have no way of knowing about the love of God if they cannot see His love expressed in the lives of His people.

One evening just before the actress Mary Martin was to go on stage in *South Pacific,* she was handed a note. It was from Oscar Hammerstein, who at that moment was on his deathbed. The note said, "Dear Mary, A bell's not a bell till you ring it. A song's not a song till you sing it. Love in your heart is not put there to stay. Love isn't love till you give it away." Mary Martin gave one of the greatest performances of her career that evening, telling friends, "Tonight I gave my love away." When Oscar Hammerstein wrote those words, he probably didn't realize how scripturally sound they are, yet this is exactly what Jesus is telling us. Love is God's method of winning the world to Christ.

In 1 Peter 1:22-23, the apostle said that we should love one another because this is a part of our new birth. The new nature of God within us gives us the power to love. My old nature is not very loving; it loves the things that are wrong. Paul wrote in Titus 3:3 that once we were "hateful, and hating one another."

A young boy lived with his grandfather on the top of a mountain in the Swiss Alps. Often, just to hear the sound of his own voice echoing back to him, he would go outside, cup his hands around his mouth and shout, "HELLO!" Up from the canyons the reply reverberated, "HELLO . . . HELLO . . . hello . . . hello." Then he would call out, "I LOVE YOU . . . I LOVE YOU . . . I love you . . . love you." One day the boy seriously misbehaved and his grandfather disciplined him severely. Reacting violently, the child shook his fist and screamed, "I HATE YOU!" To his surprise, the rocks and boulders across the mountainside responded, "I HATE YOU . . . I HATE YOU . . . I hate you . . . hate you." Yes, we get in return exactly what we give. It all comes back. What was it Jesus said?

Luke tells us:

> Treat men exactly as you like them to treat you . . . Don't judge other people and you will not be judged yourselves. Don't condemn and you will not be condemned. Make allowances for others and people will make allowances for you. Give and men will give to you . . . For whatever measure you use with other people they will use in their dealings with you. (Luke 6:31, 37-38, Phillips)

When you are born again and receive that wonderful new nature of God, love moves in. Do you know why? "God is love" (1 John 4:8). Since God is love and God is my Father, then I share my Father's nature. So I should experience love, and I should share love. Love is as Love Does.

A LITTLE HUMOR: A little boy had to stand in the corner at school for putting mud in a little girl's mouth. His mother was horrified when she heard about it. "Why in the world did you put mud in that little girl's mouth?" his mother asked. "Well," he said, "it was open."

NOVEMBER 14

WHEN YOU FEEL HELPLESS

"When I am weak, then I am strong — the less I have, the more I depend on him." (2 Corinthians 12:10, LB)

Journalist David Osborne was excited about the purchase of his new home at 58 Glebe Street in the suburbs of Sydney, Australia. Renovations were nearly complete, and he was due to move in within a week. After work, he drove to his new address to check on some of the final details. When Osborne arrived that fateful Monday afternoon, he found a "what's-wrong-with-this-picture" scenario beyond his ability to believe. His dream home had become a nightmare. A huge crane with a wrecking ball towered over his property. Every floor in the house had been removed. Thousands of dollars in renovation materials including a valuable antique fireplace had been transformed into a large pile of debris. Standing in the rubble that was his home was New South Wales Housing Minister Frank Walder. The Housing Minister offered this explanation: "The contractor and demolition crew were told to go to 58 Glebe Point Road, but instead went to 58 Glebe Street." Oops! A minor misunderstanding. Sorry.[112]

Imagine that you are David Osborne standing there peering at that mountain of rubble that was once your home. How would you feel? Angry? Frustrated? Helpless? Some people have experienced what it means to see a home destroyed — by floods, tornados, earthquakes. But that is not the only disaster that can leave us feeling helpless. A health crisis — a tumor or a stroke or a heart attack — or a divorce or a business failure. There are those events that happen in life which we are powerless to avoid and with which we are helpless to contend.

The apostle Paul had a problem he could not conquer. He called it his "thorn in the flesh" (2 Corinthians 12:7). Paul had helped so many others but was helpless to help himself just like you and I are helpless at times to help ourselves. Three times Paul asked God to remove the thorn, but each time God said, "No. But I am with you; that is all you need. My power shows up best in weak people." Paul's response was, "I am glad to be a living demonstration of Christ's power, instead of showing off my own power and abilities. Since I know it is all for Christ's good, I am quite happy about 'the thorn.' and about insults and hardships, persecutions and difficulties; for when I am weak, then I am strong — the less I have, the more I depend on him."

---

[112] *Dynamic Preaching,* July-September, 2000, page 17.

(2 Corinthians 12:9-10, LB).

Is there anything you feel helpless about? A health problem, a problem with one of your children, something at work? Remember, we are never helpless because God is with us. The less we have, the more we depend on Him.

A LITTLE HUMOR: A husband and wife were getting ready for bed. As the wife was standing in front of the mirror she took a hard look at herself. "Look at me," she says, "I look like an old woman – I have wrinkles on my face, my arms are flabby, and my hair is dull and grey." Looking at her husband she smiled and said, "Say something positive about me that will make me feel better."

The poor husband paused for a few moments and sweetly said, "Well, there is nothing wrong with your eyesight."

NOVEMBER 15

A NEW MEANING FOR ASAP

"Men ought always to pray, and not to faint." (Luke 18:1, KJV)

Warren W. Wiersbe has said, "Prayer is not only a wonderful privilege, it is a solemn obligation and a serious ministry. Prayer is not a luxury; it is a necessity." Jesus said "that men ought always to pray, and not to faint" (Luke 18:1, KJV). *The New International Version* of the Bible translates the word *faint* as give up. *The Living Bible* renders it, "keep praying until the answer comes." Another key word in this verse is *always.* Prayer is something that every Christian should be involved in at all times and any time.

We know the letters "ASAP" to mean "As Soon As Possible." Someone sent a special poem to me that gives a new meaning to those letters. The new meaning is "Always Say A Prayer." This is the way the poem reads:

There's work to do, deadlines to meet,
You've got no time to spare,
But as you hurry and scurry,
Always Say A Prayer.

In the midst of family chaos,
"Quality time" is rare. Do your best;
Let God do the rest:
Always Say A Prayer.

It may seem like your worries
Are more than you can bear.
Slow down and take a breather,
Always Say A Prayer.

God knows how stressful life is;
He wants to ease our cares
And He'll respond ASAP;
Always Say A Prayer.

To be praying always doesn't mean that we constantly repeat prayers. Rather, it means to make prayer as natural to us as our regular breathing. Unless we are sick or smothering, we rarely think about our breathing; we just do it. Likewise with prayer — it should be the natural habit of our lives, the atmosphere in which we constantly live.

A LITTLE HUMOR: "Do you say your prayers at night, little boy?" inquired the preacher. "Yes, sir," answered the lad. "And do you always say them in the morning, too?" "No, sir," responded the lad, "I ain't scared in the daytime."

NOVEMBER 16

SUBMITTING TO ONE ANOTHER

"Submitting to one another in the fear of God." (Ephesians 5:21, NKJV)

The captain of the ship looked into the dark night and saw faint lights in the distance. Immediately he told his signalman to send a message: "Alter your course ten degrees south." Promptly a return message was received: "Alter your course 10 degrees north." The captain was angered; his command had been ignored. So he sent a second message: "Alter your course ten degrees south. I am the captain!" Soon another message was received: "Alter your course ten degrees north. I am seaman third class Jones." Immediately the captain sent a third message, knowing the fear it would evoke: "Alter your course ten degrees. I am a battleship." Then the reply came: "Alter your course ten degrees north. I am a lighthouse."

It's not always easy to submit one's self to another person, but it is certainly wise to do so, especially if we realize that the consequences of not doing so could be disastrous. Ephesians 5:21 tells us, "And be subject to one another in the fear of Christ." The word *subject* (or *submit*, KJV) is a military word meaning to arrange yourself under the authority of another person and was used to describe the various ranks in the military ranging from a private to a general.

The idea of submitting to someone else is not a popular concept in our day. Submission often has unpleasant implications because it has been abused in the past and has been used to justify overbearing and self-serving behavior. But submission is a basic ingredient in our society and exists in all levels of relationships.

A man was driving down a country road and came to a narrow bridge. In front of the bridge was a sign posted: "YIELD." Seeing no on-coming cars, he continued across the bridge. On his way back, he came to the same one-lane bridge, now from the other direction. Another sign was posted: "YIELD." A "YIELD" sign was posted on both sides of the bridge. Drivers from both directions were requested to give right of way. It was a reasonable and gracious way of preventing a head-on collision. When the Bible commands us to "be subjected to one another" it is simply a reasonable and gracious command to let the other have the right of way and avoid interpersonal head-on collisions.

Submitting to one another denotes that attitude of reciprocal deference that becomes and marks out those who are filled with the Holy Spirit. It is opposed to rudeness, haughtiness, selfish preference for one's own opinions, and stubborn insistence on one's own rights. It is an attitude that rests on the example of Him who "did not count equality with God a thing to be grasped but emptied Himself, taking the form of a servant" (Philippians 2:6-7).

A LITTLE HUMOR: A lady changed her system for labeling homemade freezer meals. She used to note in large clear letters, "Meatloaf" or "Pot Roast" or "Steak and Vegetables" or "Chicken and Dumplings" or "Beef Pot Pie." However, she would get frustrated when she asked her husband what he wanted for dinner because he never asked for any of those things. So, she decided to stock the freezer with what he really likes. If you looked in her freezer now you would see a whole new set of labels that say: "Whatever," "Anything," "I Don't Know," "I Don't Care," "Something Good," or "Food." Her frustration is reduced because no matter what her husband replies when she asks him what he wants for dinner, she knew that it would be there waiting.

NOVEMBER 17

BE AN ENCOURAGER

"Like apples of gold in settings of silver is a word spoken in right circumstances."
(Proverbs 25:11, NASB)

Bart Starr loves his son and has always encouraged him. Every time he brought home a perfect paper from school he would write on his paper: "Bart, I really believe in you. I'm proud of you and what you are doing. Love, Dad." He would tape a ten cent coin on the paper. The ten cent coin became a symbol to Bart, Jr. that his dad believed in him and loved him. In 1965 Bart, Sr., who was the quarter back for the Green Bay Packers football team, went to St. Louis to play a game against the Cardinals. He played the worst game of his life. He had three interceptions. He lost the game for his team. He was discouraged. He was really down. When he got home he walked into his bedroom and over to his chest of drawers where he found a note from his son: "Dad, I watched you play football today on television. I thought you played a great game. Love, Bart." He taped a ten cent coin onto the note.

All of us like to be encouraged. All of us need to be encouraged at times. The Bible says in 1 Thessalonians 5:11 that we are to "encourage one another, and build up one another" (NASB). One of the highest of human duties is the duty of encouragement. Many a time a word of praise or thanks or appreciation or cheer has kept a man on his feet. Charles Swindoll defines encouragement as "the art of inspiring others with renewed courage, spirit, or hope." When we encourage others we spur them on, we stimulate and affirm them.

Did you know that a man was once court-marshaled and sentenced to a year's imprisonment for being a discourager? It happened during the Boer War at the siege of Ladysmith. The fortunes of the town and garrison were hanging in the balance. This civilian would go along the lines and speak discouraging words to the men on duty. He struck no blow for the enemy, not one. He was just a discourager, and that at a critical time. The court-martial judged it a crime to speak disheartening words in an hour like that.

We can encourage one another by speaking a kind word to a person when we see them; by praying for others when we know they need it; by writing a note to express our concern or gratitude; or by just being with them in a time of crisis. Proverbs 25:11 says, "Like apples of gold in settings of silver is a word spoken in right circumstances" (NASB). Strive to be an encourager.

A LITTLE HUMOR: A man was being examined for an insurance policy. He answered the questions about his sisters and brothers. But when he came to the question about his father, his face took on a long look. He said, "My father is dead." He was asked the cause of his father's death. Being afraid that he might lose the insurance, he replied, "I don't know just what it was that killed him, but it wasn't nothing serious."

NOVEMBER 18

THE POWER OF EXAMPLE

"Be imitators of God, therefore, as beloved children; and live a life of love, just as Christ loved us and gave Himself for us." (Ephesians 5:1, NIV)

In his autobiography, Benjamin Franklin tells of the time he wanted to convince the citizens of Philadelphia to light the streets at night as a protection against crime and as a convenience for evening activities. Failing to convince them by his words, he decided to show his neighbors how compelling a single light could be. He bought an attractive lantern, polished the glass, and placed it on a long bracket that extended from the front of his house. Each evening as darkness descended, he lit the wick. His neighbors soon noticed the warm glow in front of his house. Passersby found that the light helped them to avoid tripping over protruding stones in the roadway. Soon others placed lanterns in front of their homes, and eventually the city recognized the need for having well-lighted streets.[113]

That is the power of example. Samuel Johnson once wrote, "Example is always more effective than teaching." Albert Schweitzer said, "Example is not the main thing

---

[113] Max Anders, *Holman New Testament Commentary: Galatians, Ephesians, Philippians, and Colossians, Vol. 8*, (Nashville: Broadman and Holman Publishers, 1999), 169.

in influencing others. It is the only thing." Children become like parents; churches become like pastors; students become like teachers — all because of the power of example. There may be no greater power on earth to change the behavior of others.

Ephesians 5:1 is an appeal to this great principle: "Be imitators of God, therefore, as beloved children; and live a life of love, just as Christ loved us and gave Himself for us" (NIV). The word *imitate* comes from the word *mimeomai*, from which we get our word mimic. It means "to act like." To imitate God in this context means to walk in love (Ephesians 5:2). Love denies self. It is willing to give up self-interest for God's sake. Since Jesus gave himself up for us, we ought to give ourselves up for Him. To give oneself up means to follow, to obey, to live in relationship with. When we live with this attitude toward God, we please Him just as a pleasant aroma pleases the one who smells it. Jesus has set the example in love. Let's follow His example.

A LITTLE HUMOR: A new business was opening and one of the owner's friends wanted to send him flowers for the occasion. They arrived at the new business site, and the owner read the card, "Rest in Peace." The owner was angry and called the florist to complain. After he had told the florist of the obvious mistake and how angry he was, the florist replied, "Sir, I'm really sorry for the mistake, but rather than getting angry, you should imagine this: somewhere there is a funeral taking place today, and they have flowers with a note saying, 'Congratulations on your new location'."

NOVEMBER 19

THE POWER OF A WITNESS

"But you will receive power when the Holy Spirit comes on you; and you will be my witnesses." (Acts 1:8, NIV)

A Chinese farmer, after having cataracts removed from his eyes, made his way from the Christian compound to the far interior of China. Only a few days elapsed, however, before the missionary doctor looked out his bamboo window and noticed the formerly blind man holding the front end of a long rope. In a single file and holding to the rope behind him came several blind Chinese whom the farmer had told about his operation. They all knew the farmer had been blind, but now he could see. He told them of the doctor who had cured him; naturally, all these other blind people wanted to meet the doctor who had cured the blind man.

The cured man could not explain the physiology of the eye or the technique of the operation. He could tell others he had been blind, the doctor had operated on him, and now he could see. That was all the others needed to hear. They came to the doctor.[114]

So it is in our Christian lives. We need not all be trained theologians. We need

---

[114] Kenneth O. Gangel, *Holman New Testament Commentary: Acts* (Nashville: Broadman and Holman Publishers, 19989), 7.

not understand all the intricacies of God's mysteries, nor be perfect example of flawless Christian living. We can all tell everyone what Christ has done for us. We may not all be teachers. We may not all be like Mother Teresa. We can all be witnesses.

That's what Jesus was saying in Acts 1:8, "But you will receive power when the Holy Spirit comes on you; and you will be my witnesses" (NIV). Notice the progression: (1) they would receive the Holy Spirit, (2) He would give them power, and (3) they would witness with extraordinary results. When you are on the witness stand in court, the judge is not interested in your ideas or opinions; he only wants to hear what you know. Our English word *martyr* comes from the Greek word translated witness, and many of God's people have sealed their witness by laying down their lives. We are not called to debate or argue, but to be a witness. Witnessing is not showing what we can do for God. It is showing and telling what God has done for us. Every Christian is a witness.

A LITTLE HUMOR: A middle-aged bachelor found himself in love with a pretty lady. One night they were driving along, and on an impulse, he turned to her and said, "Will you marry me?" The woman said, "Yes." This was followed by a long silence until she asked the man, "Won't you say something more?" He answered, "Ah, I think I've said too much already."

NOVEMBER 20

WHEN THE GOING GETS TOUGH

"My brethren, count it all joy when you fall into various trials." (James 1:2, NKJV)

Two country boys, Zeke and Zeb, decided to build a Bungee Jumping tower down in Mexico to see if it would make them some money. After they got it set up, they noticed that the crowds gathered around but nobody was buying tickets. Zeke said to Zeb, "Maybe you should demonstrate it to them so they get the idea." After Zeb was strapped on, he jumped and fell almost to the ground before springing back. As he came back up Zeke noticed that Zeb's clothes were torn and wondered what that was all about. Zeb went down again and this time when he came back up Zeke noticed that he was bleeding. Zeke thought, "Wow, what's going on here?" Zeb went down the third time and this time when he came back up Zeke noticed he had blood, contusions and cuts all over his body. Zeke pulled Zeb in and said, "Zeb, what happened?" Zeb groaned, "I don't know, but what's a piñata?"

There have been times in my life when I have felt like a human piñata, haven't you? Times when I have been jabbed from every side. But then I read about the Apostle Paul, in chains — not gold chains like some men wear today — but heavy prison chains, languishing in jail. And his only crime was being a follower of Jesus. When I contrast them with Paul's situation, my problems seem quite trivial.

I like something that Barbara Johnson wrote in one of her books. Barbara is a

Christian writer and speaker who runs a ministry for people in pain. Tragedies in her own life have given Barbara and her husband special insight into suffering. Over thirty years ago, Barbara's husband was involved in a car wreck that left him severely and permanently injured. Their oldest son was killed in the Vietnam War, then their next son was killed by a drunk driver and for many years they were estranged from their third son, who was living a self-destructive lifestyle. Yet in spite of all this, Barbara and her husband have never lost their faith in a loving God. Whenever she meets someone who is in despair, she shares with them a few words of wisdom she lives by. These words will particularly resonate with those of you who are football fans. "God didn't promise we'd be leading at the half, but only that we would win the game!" What a grand message for anyone feeling like a human piñata.

A LITTLE HUMOR: A lady wrote her son and said, "The pastor came to call on me the other day. He said at my age I should be thinking of the hereafter. I told him, 'Oh I do it all the time. No matter where I am, in the parlor, upstairs, in the kitchen, or down in the basement, I ask myself, 'Now, what am I here after?'"

NOVEMBER 21

WHEN YOU CAN'T TURN LOOSE

"No temptation has seized you except what is common to man. And God is faithful; he will not let you be tempted beyond what you can bear. But when you are tempted, he will also provide a way out so that you can stand up under it."
(1 Corinthians 10:13, NIV)

Maybe you heard about the two mountain boys who spotted a bobcat up a tree and decided to have some fun. One said, "I'll shinny up that tree and chase him down, and you put him in a sack."

The other agreed, and the first fellow climbed up the tree. When he reached the right limb, he started shaking and the cat came tumbling down. The other fellow grabbed the varmint by the back of the neck and tried to put him into a sack. There was a terrible commotion. Dust and fur and skin were flying in all directions. The fellow in the tree called down, "What's the matter, you need help catching one little ol' bobcat?"

"No," replied his friend. "I don't need help catchin' him. I need help turnin' him a-loose!"

The problem with sin is that it is easy to get in but it's a terror sometimes to get back out. But think of this promise God revealed to Paul: "No temptation has seized you except what is common to man. And God is faithful; he will not let you be tempted beyond what you can bear. But when you are tempted, he will also provide a way out so that you can stand up under it" (1 Corinthians 10:13, NIV).

That's good news! That verse says at least three things: (1) wrong desires and temptations happen to everyone, so don't feel you've been singled out; (2) others have resisted temptation, and so can you; (3) any temptation can be resisted because God will help you resist it.

We've all seen load-limit signs on highways, bridges, and elevators. Knowing that too much strain can cause severe damage or complete collapse, engineers determine the exact amount of stress various materials can safely endure. Posted warnings tell us not to exceed the maximum load.

So when temptations press down on you, take courage! Remember, your heavenly Father knows the limits of your ability to stand up under life's pressures. Draw upon His strength. No temptation will ever be greater than that! Remember, if you give in to God, you won't cave in to sin.

A LITTLE HUMOR: After being away on business, a man thought it would be nice to bring his wife a little gift. "How about some perfume?" he asked the cosmetics clerk. She showed him a bottle costing $50.00. "That's a bit much," he said. The lady returned with a smaller bottle for $30.00. "That's still quite a bit," he complained. Growing annoyed, the clerk brought out a tiny $15.00 bottle. "What I mean is, I'd like to see something really cheap." The clerk handed him a mirror.

NOVEMBER 22

A HOLIDAY FOR EVERY DAY

"Enter into His gates with thanksgiving, and into His courts with praise. Be thankful to Him, and bless His name." (Psalm 100:4, NKJV)

Thanksgiving just goes by too fast. What we need to do is to set aside one day for complaining and griping and 364 days to be thankful. Okay, I'll give you two days to gripe and complain. Okay, one week, but that's it.

You see, Thanksgiving isn't just a once-a-year celebration. Thanksgiving is an attitude. That's why I believe we must make Thanksgiving a holiday for every day. But how do we do that?

First, **we must learn to rejoice always.** 1 Thessalonians 5:16 reads, "Be joyful always" (NIV). Gratitude has always involved rejoicing. Rejoicing somehow puts us in a better position to be thankful. Rejoicing is more of an inward experience. Continuous rejoicing can only occur on the inside. It is an attitude of the heart. If the Bible tells us to rejoice always, it stands to reason that we should be glad to do it in the midst of the bad as well as the good. When we learn to rejoice, we will soon discover that being thankful is not so bad.

Secondly, **we must learn to pray without ceasing.** 1 Thessalonians 5:17 reads, "Pray continually" (NIV). Prayer and thanksgiving are also soul mates. Show me a prayerful person and I will show you a thankful person.

There was a pastor who had a parrot. All the parrot would say was, "Let's pray, let's pray." The pastor tried to teach him other things but to no avail. The pastor learned that one of his deacons had a parrot. The deacon's parrot would say, "Let's kiss, let's kiss." The pastor decided to invite the deacon and his parrot over to his house. When the deacon arrived, the pastor put the parrots into the same cage to see what would happen. The deacon's parrot said, "Let's kiss, let's kiss." The pastor's parrot said, "Thank you Lord, my prayers are answered."

Thirdly, **we must learn to be thankful in everything.** 1 Thessalonians 5:17 reads, "Give thanks in all circumstances, for this is God's will for you in Christ Jesus" (NIV). Here is yet another counsel from God we do not believe we can live up to. A few things, yes; in good things, yes; but in everything, that's another matter. Fortunately, the Scripture says in everything and not for everything. It is hard to be thankful for cancer, AIDS, the loss of a loved one, senseless killings and other horrible things that happen in this life. However, we can give thanks for God's comfort, care and love in the midst of those experiences. When we give thanks in everything, it helps us to focus on the unlimited resources of God.

Do you know what is the greatest hindrance to being thankful? Not thinking. In the old Anglo-Saxon language, *thankfulness* means thinkfulness. The more we think the more thankful we will be. Take a moment and think about what you have and how God has blessed you. You see, it works. Count your blessings and thanksgiving will fill your heart.

A LITTLE HUMOR — Thanksgiving Day was approaching, and the family had received a card picturing a Pilgrim family on their way to church. Grandma showed the card to her young grandchildren and remarked, "The Pilgrim children liked going to church with their parents." "Oh, yeah?" her grandson replied, "Then why is the dad carrying that rifle?"

NOVEMBER 23

THE LORD BLESS YOU

"The LORD bless you, and keep you; the LORD make His face shine on you, and be gracious to you; the LORD lift up His countenance on you, and give you peace."
(Numbers 6:24-26, NASB)

God loves to bless His children. He provided this wonderful prayer of blessing to Aaron and the priests of Israel to be used when praying over His people. It can and should be used by Christians today. How should we pray for God to bless us?

Bless Us with Your Protection. "The LORD bless you, and keep you." *Keep* means to watch over, protect. It is actually translated *bodyguard* on one occasion in the Old Testament. God promises to defend and guard us as we walk with Him through this life. He will be our strong shield against the enemy.

Bless Us with Your Presence. "The LORD make His *face* shine on you (and) lift up His *countenance* on you." The greatest blessing for the Jews was for God to look on them favorably. His "face" refers to His presence, which gives us joy (Psalm16:11).

Bless Us with Your Pardon. "The LORD . . . be *gracious* to you." Israel was prone to wander rebelliously into sin. Apart from God's grace, none of them would have entered the Promised Land. God's grace saves (Ephesians 2;8-9) and sustains us as well.

Bless Us with Your Peace. "The LORD . . . give you *peace*." God gave Israel peace when He rescued them from Egypt and from the Canaanites they fought in the Promised Land. He continues to grant peace to His people today. When we pray and walk in faith, He gives us His peace that passes all understanding (Philippians 4:6-7).

The Lord desires to bless you. He has given you this prayer to guide you as you pray. Ask Him to bless you and others with His protection, presence, pardon, and peace. He has been answering this prayer for a long time. He will answer it for you today!

A LITTLE HUMOR: The Episcopalian minister was promoted. That night when his young son was being tucked into bed, he asked his mother, "Now that Daddy is a canon, does that make me a son-of-a-gun?"

NOVEMBER 24

THE GRATEFUL SAMARITAN

"Now one of them, when he saw that he had been healed, turned back, glorifying God with a loud voice, and he fell on his face at His feet, giving thanks to Him. And He was a Samaritan." (Luke 17:15-16, NASB)

Everyone knows about the Good Samaritan. He is one of the best-known characters in history. We know he belonged to a despised people — Samaritans — people who did not keep the laws in the prescribed way and who had intermarried with foreigners. We know he was the surprise hero in Jesus' parable that bears his name (Luke 10:30-37).

Everybody knows about the Good Samaritan, but let's not forget the story of the Grateful Samaritan (Luke 17:11-19). This Samaritan was a member of a group of ten lepers who asked Jesus for mercy. Leprosy was such a dread disease that those who were inflicted with it were not even allowed to come close to those who were well. All they could do was cry out from a distance, "Jesus, Master, have mercy on us." Jesus had mercy on them and healed all ten. One of the ten, when he saw that he was healed, turned back, and with a loud voice glorified God, and he fell down on his face at Jesus' feet, giving Him thanks.

Seeing this, Jesus said, "Were there not ten cleansed? But where are the nine?" We know, don't we? They were off celebrating, reuniting with family or friends. They were too preoccupied living out their good fortune to think about its origin. That's life. That's realism. Every one of us has been blessed beyond measure, but probably only about ten percent truly live grateful lives.

Don't you imagine that from that day forward, the grateful Samaritan lived his life in gratitude to Jesus? Wouldn't you? If you had lost everything, and you encountered someone, who out of the goodness of his heart gave it all back to you, wouldn't you live from that day forward mindful of that gracious act? Are you, then, among the ten percent who are truly grateful? Does your life bear witness to your gratitude?

A LITTLE HUMOR: A minister delivering the children's sermon in church asked, "Boys and girls, what lives in a tree, eats nuts, and has a long, bushy tail?" One little boy responded, "Preacher, I know the answer is Jesus, but it sure sounds like a squirrel to me."

NOVEMBER 25

ON JUMPING TO CONCLUSIONS

"Judge not, that you be not judged." (Matthew 7:1, NKJV)

Some persons seem to be born in the objective case — objecting to this, questioning that, accusing here, criticizing there. The only mental exercise some people take is jumping to conclusions. This can be a dangerous practice, as the quip indicates:

There was a dog named August,
He was always jumping at conclusions;
One day he jumped to the conclusion of a mule,
That was the last day of August.

One example from Scripture of someone who jumped to false judgments was Aaron and Miriam, the brother and sister of Moses (Numbers 12:2). The Lord's anger was kindled against Aaron and Miriam. Miriam was stricken with leprosy for seven days. She was guilty of evil-speaking against Moses, whom she had watched over when he was a baby.

When David came down to bring food to his brothers who were engaged in battle against the Philistines, he saw Goliath strutting forth to defy the Israelites and wondered why no one of the army of the Lord had gone to fight him. But David's brothers falsely charged David with coming haughtily to observe the battle.

Secular life, as well as Scripture, abounds with examples of jumping to conclusions. Six-year-old Steve had picked up some swearwords, which caused his mother much anguish. One day he was invited to a playmate's birthday party. His mother's final word of warning as he went out was, "Stephen, I've asked them to send you straight home the minute you use a bad word." Fifteen minutes later Steve walked in the door. His mother was furious. Steve was ordered to bed. His attempts to explain were ignored. Later his mother mellowed, and she went upstairs to see how he was taking it. Sitting at his bedside, she asked, "Tell me honestly, Steve, just why you were sent home. What did you do." Little Steve, humiliated but still angry, replied, "I didn't do nuttin'. That party ain't till tomorrow!"

Jesus warns against the practice of always judging and jumping to conclusions: "Judge not, that you be not judged" (Matthew 7:1, NKJV). Not all judgment is wrong. You can judge methods, but not motives; means, but not minds. Be careful in jumping to conclusions. It could mean the last day of August for you!

A LITTLE HUMOR: A group of senior adults were sitting around talking about their ailments. "My arms are so weak I can hardly hold this cup of coffee," said one. "Yes, I know. My cataracts are so bad I can't even see my coffee!" replied another. "I can't turn my head because of the arthritis in my neck," said a third, to which several nodded weakly in agreement. "My blood pressure pills make me dizzy," another went on. "I guess that's the price we pay for getting old," winced an old man as he shook his head. Then there was a short moment of silence. "Well, it's not that bad," said one woman cheerfully. "Thank God we can all still drive!"

NOVEMBER 26

CHARACTER IS IMPORTANT

"We know that suffering produces perseverance; perseverance, character; and character, hope." (Romans 5:3, NIV)

I watched the inaugural ceremony for George W. Bush and appreciated his inaugural address. I listened to the remarks by one of the news commentators for CNN as the platform party exited. Making reference to Bush's comments about character he said, "Character is a word used by preachers, not politicians."

I don't believe his comment was true, but nonetheless, if the word *character* is not used by politicians, it's high time they did. All of us should recognize the importance of having a good character. I believe President Bush is correct: "If we do not turn the hearts of children toward knowledge and character, we will lose their gifts and undermine their idealism." Remember the old saying, "What you are speaks so loudly I can't hear what you are saying." Character does matter. It is important.

Webster's Dictionary defines character as the attributes or features that make up and distinguish the individual. Someone else has defined it as the sum and total of a person's choices. Abraham Lincoln said, "Character is like a tree and reputation like its shadow. The shadow is what we think of it; the tree is the real thing."

Character can be either good or bad, and such is the dilemma of life. Who will we be? Character is the result of our everyday choices. Unfortunately, people emphasize doing rather than being, action rather than character. Being must come first. We must know who we are before we can excel. There is nothing wrong with action, but it is more important to decide what to be than what to do.

I agree with what Sidney Greenberg has said: "Character is distilled out of our daily confrontation with temptation, out of our regular response to the call of duty. It is formed as we learn to cherish principles and to submit to self-discipline. Character is the sum total of all the little decisions, the small deeds, the daily reactions to the choices that confront us. Character is not obtained instantly. We have to mold and hammer and forge ourselves into character. It is a distant goal to which there is no shortcut." I agree also with what the Bible says: "We know that suffering produces perseverance; perseverance, character; and character, hope" (Romans 5:3, NIV). President Bush also said, "Our public interest depends on private character." Let all of us strive to develop the best character possible.

A LITTLE HUMOR: Two elderly widowed people decided to marry. They wanted to keep things simple and arranged with their pastor to get married at the end of the worship service the following Sunday. The next Sunday, at the end of the service, the pastor announced: "Now, would those who wish to be married please come forward." As he waited for the elderly couple to come forward, eleven members from the Singles Group came down to join them.

NOVEMBER 27

YOU DON'T HAVE TO WORRY

"Do not be anxious about anything, but in everything, by prayer and petition, with thanksgiving, present your requests to God." (Philippians 4:6, NIV)

Worry is one of the biggest problems we face in life, and it tends to get worse as we get older. Its destruction is sure. Charles Mayo of the Mayo Clinic in Rochester, Minnesota, said, "Worry affects the circulation, the heart, the glands, the whole nervous system, and profoundly affects the health." Corrie Ten Boom knew the destructive force of worry when she said, "Worry does not empty tomorrow of its sorrow; it empties today of its strength." Its destruction starts like a little trickle through the mind and cuts out a furrow until it becomes a Grand Canyon, and all other thoughts drain into it. Warren Wiersbe has said, "Most Christians are being crucified on a cross between two thieves: yesterday's regret and tomorrow's worries."

The apostle Paul wrote, "Do not be anxious about anything, but in everything, by prayer and petition, with thanksgiving, present your requests to God" (Philippians 4:6, NIV). The Greek word translated *anxious* means to be pulled in different directions. Our hopes pull us in one direction; our fears pull us the opposite direction; and we are pulled apart! The Old English root from which we get our word *worry* means to strangle. If you have ever really worried, you know how it does strangle a person! In fact, worry has definite physical consequences: headaches, neck pains, ulcers, even back pains. Worry affects our thinking, our digestion, and even our coordination. Worry is the greatest thief of joy.

But it is not enough for us to tell ourselves to quit worrying. Worry is an inside job, and it takes more than good intentions to get the victory. The antidote to worry is the secure mind: "And the peace of God . . . will guard your hearts and your minds in Christ Jesus" (Philippians 4:7, NIV). When you have the secure mind, the peace of

God guards you and the God of peace guides you! With that kind of protection — why worry?

A LITTLE HUMOR: A radio commentator covering an important news event was at the point of cracking from strain. A colleague, observing him tensely gripping the microphone, suggested he take a tranquilizing pill. "I can't," he replied. "If I'm not tense, I get nervous."

NOVEMBER 28

HOPE BEYOND HOPE

"Blessed is the man who trusts in the Lord, and whose hope is the Lord."
(Jeremiah 17:7, NKJV)

A few years ago the daily devotional guide, *Our Daily Bread,* printed the story of a terminally ill young man who went to a medical clinic for his usual treatment. A new doctor who was on duty said to him casually and cruelly, "You know, don't you, that you won't live out the year?" As the young man left, he stopped by the director's desk and wept. "That man took away my hope," he blurted out. "I guess he did," replied the director. "Maybe it's time to find a new one."

Commenting on this incident, Lewis Smedes wrote, "Is there a hope when hope is taken away? That question leads us to Christian hope, for in the Bible, hope is no longer a passion for the possible. It becomes a passion for the promise."

Because God is the God of hope (Romans 15:13), He alone keeps hope flowing when its spring dries up in the human heart. As someone has said, "The secret of coping is hoping in God."

Wherever Jesus went, he brought hope. It was His calling-card. He brought hope to the leper, exiled from his home and community. He brought hope to the paralyzed man who was unable to care for his family. To people who felt worthless, or lost, or broken, or rejected, or beyond saving, Jesus brought the message that God loved them — that they had a purpose in life. Even in Jesus' last moments, when He was dying in agony on the cross, He offered the hope of eternal salvation to the thief dying beside Him. This was Jesus' first act in life and his last act before death — the giving of hope.

In the ancient classic, titled *Inferno,* Dante, the author imagines that the entrance to Hell is marked by a sign, "Abandon all hope, ye who enter here." Dante can't be far off the mark. Where God is, there is hope; where God is absent, there is no hope. That was the message Jesus came to share with us.

A LITTLE HUMOR: A first-time father was taking a turn at feeding the baby some strained peas. Naturally, there were traces of the food everywhere, especially on the infant. His wife comes in, looks at the infant, then at her husband staring into space, then says, "What in the world are you doing?" He replied, "I'm waiting for the first coat to dry so I can put on another."

NOVEMBER 29

SETTLED IN HEAVEN

"Forever, O Lord, Your word is settled in heaven. Your faithfulness continues throughout all generations; You established the earth and it stands. They stand this day according to Your ordinances." (Psalm 119:89-91, NASB)

There are six words in these three verses that refer to the permanency of God's Word: forever, settled, faithfulness, continues, established and stands. The word *settled* means fixed, unmovable, permanent.

Washington, D. C. is the home of the National Bureau of Standards. The National Bureau of Standards was established in 1901 and became a part of the Department of Commerce in 1903. Every weight and every measure that is used in the USA is a copy of the standard that is kept inviolate by the Bureau in Washington. In that Bureau there is a perfect inch, a perfect foot, a perfect yard, a perfect gallon, a perfect pint, a perfect millimeter, a perfect milligram. Every weight and measure that we have finds its standard in that Bureau in Washington, and all are judged by that standard. They follow the rule held inviolate in Washington.

The Bible in the original manuscripts is a copy of that which is "fixed" in heaven. The Bible is God's Word. It is neither fickle nor uncertain; it is settled, determined, fixed, sure, immovable. Man's teachings change so often that there is never time for them to be settled; but the Lord's Word will remain unchanged eternally.

In his book, *Why I Preach That the Bible is Literally True,* Dr. W. A. Criswell writes, "I believe that the Bible is literally true because it partakes of the nature of God, who is eternal, who is the same, yesterday, today, and forever. The Bible is not *a* book; it is *the* book. It is the indestructible, undestroyable, ever-living, eternal, enduring Word of God . . . God's Word and God's book is a living Word and a living Book . . . It is impossible for God's Book to die."[115]

To quote the late Dr. A. Z. Conrad:

Century follows century – There it stands.
Empires rise and fall and are forgotten – There it stands.
Dynasty succeeds dynasty – There it stands.
Kings are crowned and uncrowned – There it stands.
It outlives, out-lifts, out-loves, outreaches, outranks, out-runs all other books.
Trust it, love it, obey it, and Eternal Life is yours.
The Bible stands and we believe it.

---

[115] W. A. Criswell, *Why I Preach That the Bible is Literally True* (Nashville: Broadman Press, 1969), 76.

A LITTLE HUMOR: Here are some signs that you may not be reading your Bible enough:

1. The preacher announces the sermon is from Genesis...and you check the table of contents.
2. You think Abraham, Isaac, and Jacob may have had a few hit songs during the 60s.
3. You open to the Gospel of Luke and a WWII Savings Bond falls out.
4. You think the Pentateuch is the headquarters for the US Department of Defense.
5. Your favorite Old Testament Patriarch is Hercules.
6. You become frustrated because Charlton Heston isn't listed in either the concordance or the table of contents.
7. Catching the kids reading the Song of Solomon, you demand, "Who gave you this stuff?"
8. The kids keep asking too many questions about your usual bedtime story: "Jonah the Shepherd Boy and His Ark of Many Colors."

NOVEMBER 30

JESUS IS COMING BACK

"This same Jesus, who has been taken up from you into heaven will come in just the same way as you have watched Him go into heaven." (Acts 1:11, NASB)

On November 30, 1954, a meteorite struck Elizabeth Hodges. Sleeping on her couch in her Sylacauga, Alabama home, a meteorite crashed through the roof of her house and into her living room, bounced off a radio, and struck her on the hip. The space rock was a sulfide meteorite weighting eight and one-half pounds and measuring seven inches in length. It was the first modern instance of a human being struck by a meteorite, although ancient Chinese records tell of people being injured or killed by falling meteorites. Mrs. Hodges was not permanently hurt but suffered a nasty bruise along her hip and leg.

As believers, there are certain things we want to see come "from heaven", but a meteorite is not one of them. Acts 1:9-11 speaks of the ascension and return of Jesus Christ. Verse 11 states, "This Jesus, who has been taken up from you into heaven, will come in just the same way as you have watched Him go into heaven." Jesus will return to this earth. Several observations of His return are obvious from Scriptures.

Jesus will return PERSONALLY – "This Jesus . . ." In John 14:3 Jesus said "I will come again." In 1 Thessalonians 4:16, Paul wrote, "For the Lord Himself will descend from heaven."

Jesus will return VISIBLY – "Behold, He is coming with the clouds, and every eye will see Him" (Revelation 1:7). A child asked her mother, "If Jesus is so wonderful, why doesn't He show Himself?" That is precisely what He will do.

Jesus will return SUDDENLY – "Therefore be on the alert, for you do not know which day your Lord is coming" (Matthew 24:42). Mrs. Hodges was not expecting to be hit by a meteorite, but she was. Many people never give thought to the fact that Jesus will return, but He will.

Jesus will return TRIUMPHANTLY. There were those who stood at the cross and watched Jesus die who thought they would never see Him again. But Jesus is not dead. He is alive. He has conquered sin, death and the grave and one day soon He will return as the conquering Savior that He is.

A LITTLE HUMOR: The older a man gets, the more ways he learns to part his hair. Some men pull what little bit of hair they have around on their head to cover their baldness. However, as a man gets even older, he realizes there are basically only three ways to wear your hair – parted, unparted, and departed.

DECEMBER 1

THE JOY OF SINGING

"O come, let us sing for joy to the Lord, let us shout joyfully to the rock of our salvation."(Psalm 95:1, NASB)

Sing Sing Correctional Facility is a maximum security prison operated by the New York State Department of Correctional Service in the town of Ossining, New York. Ossining's former name, "Sing, Sing," was derived from the name of a Native American tribe, "Sinck Sinck" (or "Sint Sinck"), from whom the land was purchased in 1685. As a humorous way of challenging the congregation of my home church to sing, my pastor would say to our congregation: "A person who can sing and won't sing ought to be sent to Sing Sing until he does sing."

The month of December is filled with music and singing about the birth of our Savior. Between now and December 25 many Christmas carols will be sung. Churches will be filled with programs and singing devoted to celebrating Christ's coming. It is a joyful time for all of us who love our Lord. Someone has said that singing is the language of the heart and indeed it is.

In Psalm 95, the word *come* appears three times (vv. 1-2, 6) and is an invitation for us to be in the Lord's presence. As we enter the Lord's presence in worship we are to do so joyfully (verse 1), thankfully (verse 2), and humbly (verse 6).

The late evangelist, Vance Havner, once wrote: "Saving grace is singing grace and if we are not singing, at least in our hearts, we had better check on our state. Beware of a Christian profession that is words without music, mandates without melody. Your salvation, standing and service should be accompanied by a song."[116]

I know what some people say when asked why they don't sing: "I just can't sing. I can't carry a tune." Well, I understand what they are saying. Most people fall into one of four different groups of singers: (1) those who really can sing, (2) those who can somewhat sing – at least they can stay on key, (3) Those who think they can sing, but can't, and (4) those who wish they could sing, and we wish they could, too.

Donald Hustad, former music professor at The Southern Baptist Theological Seminary in Louisville, Kentucky, and frequent organist for Billy Graham crusades, wrote in the Winter, 1982 issue of *Leadership* magazine: "Singing is for believers. The question is not, Do you have a voice? but Do you have a song?"

Christmas is in the air. Singing ought to be in our hearts!

---

[116] Dennis J. Hester, Compiler, *The Vance Havner Quote Book* (Grand Rapids: Baker Book House, 1986), 216.

A LITTLE HUMOR: A church had a man in the choir who couldn't sing. Several hinted to him that he could serve in other places, but he continued to come to the choir. The choir director became desperate and went to the pastor. "You've got to get that man out of the choir," he said. If you don't, I'm going to resign. The choir members are going to quit, too. Please do something." So the pastor went to the man and suggested, "Perhaps you should leave the choir." "Why should I get out of the choir?" he asked. "Well, five or six people have told me you can't sing," the pastor said. "That's nothing," the man snorted. "Fifty people have told me that you can't preach!"[117]

DECEMBER 2

LOVING GOD

"Love the Lord your God with all your heart, with all your soul, with all your mind and with all your strength." (Mark 12:30, NIV)

Glynn Wolfe died alone in Los Angeles at the age of 88. No one came to claim his body; the city paid to have him buried in an unmarked grave. This is sad, but not unusual. It happens all too often in large cities where people tend to live disenfranchised lives.

Glynn's situation was unique, though, because he was no ordinary man. He held a world record. The Guinness Book listed him as the Most Married Man, with 29 marriages to his credit. This means 29 times he was asked, "Do you take this woman to be your lawfully wedded wife . . . forsaking all others do you pledge yourself only to her, so long as you both shall live?" Twenty-nine times Glynn Wolfe said, "I do," but it never quite worked out that way.

He died leaving behind children, grandchildren, great grandchildren, a number of living ex-wives, and innumerable ex-in-laws — and still, he died alone. He spent his entire adult life looking for something he apparently never found — and he died alone.

Glynn Wolfe is an extreme example of how people spend their lives drifting in and out of marriage, in and out of relationships, only to find themselves isolated and alone. Even worse, there are others who spend their lives married to the same person and still end up feeling isolated and alone.

The fact is, if we look for ultimate fulfillment in marriage, or romance, or friendship, or family, we will never be satisfied. As important as these relationships are, they cannot take the place of the ultimate relationship for which we have been created.

Our primary purpose is to love God. When we allow secondary relationships to take God's rightful place in our lives, we become dissatisfied and frustrated. The

---

[117] Tal D. Bonham, *The Treasury of Clean Church Jokes* (Nashville: Broadman Press, 1986), 42.

result is, like Glynn Wolfe, we end up isolated and alone.

When Jesus was asked what is the greatest commandment of all, he responded by saying, "Love the Lord your God with all your heart, with all your soul, with all your mind and with all your strength" (Mark 12:30, NIV). Part two of this commandment is to "love your neighbor as yourself." Our success in loving others is dependent upon our willingness to love God above all else, with all that we have.

A LITTLE HUMOR: Ron Dentinger said: "Some couples can't even agree before they get married. I heard one couple talking in the shopping mall. They couldn't agree on two rather picky little details for a wedding. She wanted the bridesmaids to wear long blue gowns, and he didn't want to get married."

DECEMBER 3

GET A LIFE!

"For Demas has forsaken me, having loved this present world . . ."
(2 Timothy 4:10a, NKJV)

One of the greatest talents ever to play baseball was a Native American named Louis Sockalexis. He signed with the Cleveland Spiders in 1897. In his first year he amazed the baseball world with his tremendous arm, his impressive speed, and his .331 batting average. Sockalexis made such an impact, his team changed its name from the Spiders to the Indians in honor of him.

Sockalexis was bright and well educated. He seemed to have a brilliant future. But it was not to be, for there was one opponent he could not beat, the opponent called alcohol. In a drunken stupor one night he jumped from the second floor of a brothel and broke his ankle.

That was the beginning of the downfall of Sockalexis. He eventually drifted back to his reservation. At age 42 he died alone in the woods, with old newspaper clippings written about him stuffed inside his shirt.

Sockalexis does not stand alone, but rather is one of a company of thousands who have demonstrated the tragedy of a wasted life.

In the Old Testament, we see it in Solomon. At the beginning of his monarchy, he was so much in tune with God that when God offered to give him anything he wanted, he chose wisdom. But eventually, the affluence and power of his position and the impact of his wives' many gods eroded his spiritual power and robbed him of the life God had planned for him.

In the New Testament character Demas, we see the tragedy of a wasted life. At the beginning of his walk with Christ he was so much in tune with the kingdom, Paul described him as "my fellow worker" (Philemon 24). But eventually, the luster of discipleship was eclipsed by the lure of the world, and Paul wrote that Demas was "in love with this present world" and "deserted me" (2 Timothy 4:10).

The spirit of Solomon and Demas — and Sockalexis — has reappeared in many of our contemporaries. They might go by the name of Tom, Dick, or Harriett, but they carry within them the spirit of Demas. Having been redeemed for life (John 10:10), they live beneath their privileges. The only way to avoid a wasted life is to place our lives in the hands of Jesus Christ through faith and acknowledge Him as our Lord and Savior. To build a life that lasts, we need to build on the right foundation.

A LITTLE HUMOR: Barbara Johnson said it: "I thought I had a handle on life, then it fell off."

DECEMBER 4

ONLY JESUS SAVES

"And there is salvation in no one else; for there is no other name under heaven that has been given among men, by which we must be saved." (Acts 4:12, NASB)

A marshal in Napoleon's army was once supremely devoted to the French emperor and military leader. After this man was mortally wounded in battle, he was carried to his tent where he underwent his death-struggle. He called out the name of the man he idolized, and Napoleon came to the man's tent. The dying man's hero worship was so great that he pleaded with Napoleon to save his life. The emperor looked helplessly at the man and said, "What do you expect me to do?" The dying marshal could not believe his ears! Certainly, the emperor would not let him die! "Save me, Napoleon! Save me!" the man shrieked as the emperor turned his back and walked out of the tent. Napoleon could not help this man. There was nothing divine about Napoleon — he had no power over life and death. Only Jesus does.[118]

Over the centuries, people have called upon other mere mortals for help — all to no avail. If you lack courage, what should you do? You could call out, "Abraham Lincoln! Help me!" But it would do no good. Lincoln was a courageous man, but he can't give you courage. If you lack wisdom, what should you do? You could call out, "Solomon! Help me!" But it would do no good. Solomon was a wise man, but he can't help you. If you lack eloquence, you could call out, "William Shakespeare! Help me!" But no help would come.

Yet for twenty centuries, men and women in desperate need have called out, "Lord Jesus Christ! Help me!" And help comes! Deliverance comes! That is how we know that Jesus is the truth. Jesus Christ is unchanging. He's the same yesterday, today, and forever. Remember that, when you feel defeated, when you are under attack, when doubts come flooding into your mind.

---

[118] Ray C. Stedman, *Spiritual Warfare.* (Grand Rapids: Discovery House Publishers, 1999), 102-103.

A LITTLE HUMOR: The pastor and his family were about to move from one area of town to another. The pastor had to be at the hospital with a church member on the day of the move. The pastor's wife said three times as he left home that morning, "Remember, honey, we won't be living here this afternoon." That afternoon the preacher drove into the driveway as usual, then remembered he didn't live there anymore. He thought for several minutes, "Where did we move?" Seeing boys playing in the street, he thought, "I'll ask one of them." "Hey, young man, could you tell me where the family that did live here has moved to?" The boy replied, "Mom said you wouldn't remember where we moved."

DECEMBER 5

IF ANYONE SINS

"If you sin, there is someone to plead for you before the Father. His name is Jesus Christ, the one who is all that is good and who pleases God completely."
(1 John 2:1, LB)

Billy Sunday, the evangelist once said, "I'm against sin. I'll kick it as long as I've got a foot, and I'll fight it as long as I've got a fist. I'll butt it as long as I've got a head. I'll bite it as long as I've got a tooth. When I'm old and fistless and footless and toothless, I'll gum it till I go home to glory and it goes to perdition."

As believers we should be against any sin and all sin in our life and purpose that we will kick it, fight it, and bite it, and if we have to, gum it till we go home to glory. Our attitude should be that we will not tolerate any sin in our life.

Experience teaches us, however, that in spite of our passion to avoid sin, we still fail the Lord and are guilty of committing sin. The goal is not sinless perfection, but to sin less and less. After saying that we are not to sin, he then says, "And if you sin." So, we do sin. All of us sin.

A minister was walking along a road when he saw a crowd of boys surrounding a dog. "What are you doing with the dog?" he asked. One of the boys said, "Whoever tells the biggest lie, wins the dog." "Oh, my, my, my," exclaimed the minister. "When I was a little boy like you I never told a lie." There was a moment's silence. "Here," said one of the boys, "you win the dog." We may be able to make the claim that we are not guilty of certain sins, but we cannot make the claim that we are totally free from sin. There is no one who can say, "I have no sin."

First John 1:9 reads, "If we confess our sins to Him, He can be depended on to forgive us and to cleanse us from every wrong" (LB). The word *confess* means to say the same thing. To confess is to say the same thing about sin as God says. God has promised to forgive and cleanse our sins if we confess them. The promise of forgiveness is highlighted when John tells us "He can be depended on."

A LITTLE HUMOR: A young boy went into the confessional and told the priest that he had thrown peanuts into the pond. The priest thought this was a strange little sin to confess to, but said nothing. The next small boy also confessed to throwing peanuts in the pond, and the next. Finally a very small boy came in, so the priest went ahead and said, "And did you throw peanuts in the pond?" "No, said the kid, "I'm Peanuts."

DECEMBER 6

COURAGE AND PEACE

"I am leaving you with a gift — peace of mind and heart! And the peace I give isn't fragile like the peace the world gives. So don't be troubled or afraid."
(John 14:27, LB)

A few years ago a tragic event took place as missionaries Jim and Roni Bowers, their two children, and the pilot of their plane were shot down over the Amazon by a Peruvian fighter jet that mistook their plane for drug smuggling. Roni and her newly adopted baby were both killed. At the funeral back in Michigan, Bowers said that he had forgiven the pilots who attacked his family and testified that he and his son were "experiencing inexplicable peace."

Peace is a rare commodity in today's world. The early followers of Jesus gained their courage from the presence of Christ's Spirit within them. And that's good news for us. There are times when you and I need to be courageous — to stand up for those things that are right and good and lasting They received courage, and they received peace. Jesus knew that His disciples would need the assurance from Him that things were going to be okay. And so He said to them, "I am leaving you with a gift — peace of mind and heart! And the peace I give isn't fragile like the peace the world gives. So don't be troubled or afraid" (John 14:27, LB.).

The year was 1887, and a humble music professor named A. J. Showalter received some sad news. Two of his former students had just lost their wives. Both of these men were in despair, and looked to their old music professor for comfort.

Showalter had always been deeply devoted to his students. He had no comforting words of his own, so he turned to Scripture, where he found this verse from Deuteronomy 33:27, "The eternal God is your refuge, And underneath are the everlasting arms." Out of this verse, professor Showalter wrote a chorus to send to his students. You might recognize it:

"Leaning, leaning, safe and secure from all alarms;
Leaning, leaning, leaning on the everlasting arms."

Jesus did not tell his disciples that they would not have problems. In fact, their problems would dwarf most of ours. What he did promise them was peace of mind. He would send upon them the gift of the Holy Spirit to give them courage and peace.

That is the same promise Christ offers us today. There is peace and courage in the midst of troubles.

A LITTLE HUMOR: For years, Shelly's husband denied that he was an aggressive driver. That changed one day when they were out for a drive with their three-year-old son, Matthew. Seeing a teaching opportunity, mom asked Matthew about traffic lights.

"What does a red light mean?" Shelly enquired.

"Stop."

"Good. How about green?"

"Go."

"And yellow?"

In his best deep-voice impression of Daddy, Matthew bellowed . . . "Hang on!"

DECEMBER 7

COMPREHENDING GOD'S LOVE

"For this reason I bow my knees before the Father. . . that He would grant you . . . to be able to comprehend with all the saints what is the breadth and length and height and depth, and to know the love of Christ which surpasses knowledge . . ."
(Ephesians 3:14-18, NASB)

My paternal grandmother, Flora Taft Reed, loved animals. She had cats, dogs, a parrot and a spider monkey. The spider monkey and I didn't get along very well. A spider monkey has a prehensile tail. A prehensile tail enables a monkey to grasp a tree limb and hold on. Every time I went to my grandmother's house that spider monkey would climb into my lap, wrap its tail around my arm and try to bite me. I hated that spider monkey! The monkey had such a grip on my arm it was almost impossible for me to get away.

Our word *comprehend* carries the idea of a person being able to mentally grasp the meaning of something; while *apprehend* suggests laying hold of it for yourself. In our Scripture for today, Paul's concern was that his readers would lay hold of the vast expanses of God's love, allowing it to wrap itself around us and never let go.

The love of God is an inescapable love. Paul spoke of "the breadth and length and height and depth of God's love." In his commentary on the book of Ephesians, Kenneth S. Wuest writes, "The words, 'breadth, length, depth, and height' have no particular significance except to give the general idea of the vastness of the love of Christ. This love is His love for us, not ours for Him."

A father, who was trying to explain to his little girl the vastness of God's love, took her to the top of a mountain and said, "Honey, look to the right as far as you can see; look to the left as far as you can see; look up as far as you can see; look down as far as you can see. That's how much God loves us." His daughter said to him, "In that case, Daddy, we must be right in the middle of God's love." Paul was declaring the unlimited reach of God's love. No one is outside the love of God. No place is outside the reach of God's love. No matter where we are, we are right in the middle of God's love.

May Paul's prayer be our prayer, that an understanding of God's love for us would take hold of us and never let us go.

A LITTLE HUMOR: A Sunday school teacher was telling the little children in her class that God loves them all the time, even when they're grumpy. "And Happy!" exclaimed a three-year-old, adding, ". . . and Sleepy and Dopey and Sneezy and Doc and Bashful."

DECEMBER 8

THE PROMISE OF HIS PRESENCE

"I will not abandon you or leave you as orphans in the storm -- I will come to you" (John 14:18, LB)

Life gets tough sometimes. Even worse, we get the feeling that no one cares. I read an amusing story about a twelve-year-old boy who stood patiently beside the clock counter while the store clerk waited on all of the adult customers. Finally the clerk got around to the youngster, who made his purchase and hurried out to the curb, where his father was impatiently waiting in his car. "What took you so long, son?" his father asked. "The man waited on everybody in the store before me," he said. "But I got even. I wound and set all the alarm clocks while I was waiting. It's going to be a mighty noisy place at eight o'clock."

You can appreciate that young man's feeling of disappointment and frustration. Everyone was having their needs met but him. Nobody was paying any attention. Sometimes you and I feel that way about our lives. Nobody notices. Nobody cares. But we would be wrong to jump to that conclusion. There is someone who is paying attention.

Dr. Norman Vincent Peale was one of the most popular preachers who ever lived. Dr. Peale had an effective technique that he used when counseling someone in distress. First, he let the troubled person tell their story. Every little detail was hashed out. But after the person had explained their problem, then Dr. Peale asked the person to sit in silence for a full three minutes and think of nothing else but Jesus. Just Jesus. This was the moment, Dr. Peale said, when they were to switch their focus from the problem to Jesus. "No matter what your problem might be," said Dr. Peale, "Jesus has the power to help you." He testified that usually, after these three minutes of thinking time, the person being counseled would have an answer to their problem.

Christ promised that He would always be with us. This is an important promise. The critical test in life is not what happens to us. The critical test is how we handle the things that happen to us. Christ's presence can make a difference in how we respond to life. Christ promised us His presence.

A LITTLE HUMOR: There was a man who was trying to get his marriage jump started again so he went out and bought his wife a beautiful bouquet of flowers and attached this note to it: "Darling, flowers will lose their fragrance, but you will smell forever."

DECEMBER 9

NO TIME LIKE THE PRESENT

"What I mean, brothers, is that the time is short . . ." (1 Corinthians 7:29a, NIV)

The most successful people I know have a sense of urgency about their lives. They understand how precious time is and how quickly it gets away from us. They understand the importance of seizing the moment — of not putting off till tomorrow the things that need to be tended to today.

Lorraine Schultz of Brainerd, Minnesota understands the importance of time. An alarm clock rings at 1:00 A. M. in Lorraine's bedroom. Then another alarm clock goes off – and another. Within ten minutes about fifty alarm clocks will have gone off. No, Lorraine doesn't have to get out of bed. She collects clocks. At last count she had six hundred clocks. Clocks that ding, clocks that dong, clocks that beep, buzz, bang, clang, and speak. One even reminds you to wind it, so it can wake you up the following morning. It takes her half an hour to wind up all her spring-driven clocks. And twice a year, once in April and again in October, she spends more than two hours resetting her clocks in the change from standard time to daylight savings time and back again. Lorraine's hobby may seem a little extreme, but she never oversleeps. At least she is aware of the importance of time.

Are you aware of how quickly time is getting away from you? Are you aware of how important those days and weeks and months are to you?

To realize the value of "one month," ask a mother who gave birth to a premature baby. To realize the value of "one week," ask the editor of a weekly newspaper. To realize the value of "one hour," ask the lovers who are waiting to meet. To realize the value of "one minute," ask the person who missed the train. To realize the value of "one second," ask the person who just avoided an accident. To realize the value of "one millisecond," ask the person who won a silver medal in the Olympics. Treasure every moment that you have! And treasure it more because you shared it with someone special, special enough to spend your time. Remember that time waits for no one. Yesterday is history. Tomorrow is a mystery and today is a gift. That's why it's called the present.

God has indeed given us a present. It is the present moment. Use it wisely.

A LITTLE HUMOR: On a continental flight with a very "senior" flight attendant crew, the pilot said, "Ladies and gentlemen, we've reached cruising altitude and will be turning down the cabin lights. This is for your comfort and to enhance the appearance of your flight attendants."

DECEMBER 10

GOD WANTS YOU!

"The Lord is not slow about His promise, as some count slowness, but is patient toward you, not wishing for any to perish but for all to come to repentance."

(2 Peter 3:9, NASB)

Years ago when the army wanted to recruit young men and women to be soldiers, they didn't have fancy television commercials. All they had was a poster. On it was a drawing of a man with a tall hat, a goatee, and a finger pointed outward with these words underneath: "Uncle Sam Wants You!" That meant that the United States government wanted you to be a soldier. But how did Uncle Sam become a symbol for the United States?

There once lived a man in Massachusetts named Samuel Wilson who was around when Paul Revere made his famous ride to warn the American people that the British were coming. Later Samuel Wilson worked for the army stamping the letters "U. S." on barrels of beef for the U. S. government. Since those initials had not previously been used to stand for "United States", the townspeople assumed they meant "Uncle Sam." And, before long, Uncle Sam had acquired a goatee and a tall hat, and people around the world thought of him as a symbol for the United States of America.

Maybe we need a drawing of Jesus with His finger pointing saying, "God wants you!" I've never seen a drawing like that. What I have seen many times, though, is a drawing of Jesus stretched out on the cross showing us how much God loves us. To me that's even better than a pointed finger that says, "God wants you so much that He gave His only begotten Son."

God wants us for salvation. Peter reminds us of this when he wrote, "The Lord is not slow about His promise, as some count slowness, but is patient toward you, not wishing for any to perish but for all to come to repentance" (2 Peter 3:9, NASB). God wants you to be saved. If you have never repented of your sins and invited Jesus Christ to be your Lord and Saviour, I encourage you to do so today.

God also wants us for service. After washing the disciples' feet, Jesus said to His disciples, "If I then, the Lord and the Teacher, washed your feet, you also ought to wash one another's feet" (John 13:14, NASB), and in Matthew 20:27, Jesus said: "Whoever wishes to be first among you shall be your slave." Having been saved, the new believer begins a life time of service for the Lord. Great joy comes to the one who obediently follows the Lord Jesus Christ.

Have you enlisted in the King's army? God wants you!

A LITTLE HUMOR: A little girl asked her father, "Daddy, do all fairy tales begin with 'Once upon a time'?" He replied, "No, there is a whole series of fairy tales that begin with 'If elected I promise . . .'"

DECEMBER 11

BEAUTIFUL FEET

"...how beautiful are the feet of those who bring good news of good things!" (Romans 10:15b, NASB)

Corns and calluses, blisters and bunions, spurs and sprains, ingrown toenails and fungus infections, are just a few of the many ailments the human foot is heir to. Each year, people suffering from one or more of these ailments pay between 40,000 and 50,000 visits to podiatrists in the United States for help.

The human foot, composed of 26 bones, 19 muscles and more than 100 ligaments is one of the marvels of creation. The average American walks an estimated 115,000 miles – almost 5 times around the globe – 38 times across the United States from New York to San Francisco during a lifetime.

But you may be wondering, "Why refer to our feet as being beautiful?" The words "beautiful" and "feet" just don't seem to go together. I have heard people say, "You have beautiful . . . eyes . . . lips . . . hands . . . legs . . . even nails." But never have I heard anyone say, "You have beautiful feet." Dirty feet! Smelly feet! Cold feet! But never beautiful feet. Why are they singled out? It is because of their importance in God's plan for spreading the good news about His Son, the Lord Jesus Christ. It is by means of the feet that the messenger gets to his destination to deliver the good news of Jesus Christ.

Charles H. Spurgeon once said, "The gospel can be summed up in two words – *come* and *go.* "Come unto me..." and "Go ye..." We go on trips all the time. We go on youth trips, ski trips, senior adult trips to Branson and a thousand other places. But the most important going we can do is to go across the street or across the world to carry the gospel of Jesus Christ. Have you signed up for that trip? How beautiful are your feet?

A LITTLE HUMOR: Have you heard about the podiatrist and the manicurist, who met, fell in love with each other and got married? They spent the rest of their lives waiting on each other "hand and foot!"

DECEMBER 12

THEY'RE BOTH THE SAME

"Don't you know me, Philip, even after I have been among you such a long time. Anyone who has seen me has seen the Father . . . I am in the Father, and the Father is in me." (John 14:9, NIV)

A young couple were separated during World War II. While the father was gone, the mother gave birth to a baby girl. The months passed and the mother kept a large picture of her husband on the desk so that the little girl would grow up knowing what her daddy looked like. She learned to say "Daddy" and associated the name with the picture on the desk. Finally the day came when her father returned home from the war. The whole family gathered to watch the little girl when she saw her father for the first time. Imagine their disappointment when she would have nothing whatever to do with him. Instead, she ran to the photograph on the desk, saying, "That's my daddy." Day after day the family had to blink back the tears as they saw the young father on his knees trying his best to get acquainted with his little daughter. But each time she would shake her head, then run to the picture on the desk and exclaim, "That's my daddy." This went on for some time, but one day something happened. The little girl, having gone repeatedly to the picture on the desk, returned to her father and looked carefully into his face. Then she went back to the picture on the desk and studied it. The family held their breath. After several trips the little face lit up as the child exclaimed excitedly, "They're both the same daddy!"

Jesus came to reveal our heavenly Father to us (John 1:14, 18). In spite of the fact that Jesus spent three years with His disciples, they still did not recognize the relationship between Jesus, the Son and God, the Father. Philip asked Jesus to show them the Father (John 14:8). Jesus' response was, "Don't you know me, Philip, even after I have been among you such a long time. Anyone who has seen me has seen the Father . . . I am in the Father, and the Father is in me" (John 14:9, NIV).

Jesus is the visible, tangible image of the invisible God. He is the complete revelation of what God is like. The search for God, for truth and reality, ends in Christ. Look carefully at the face of Jesus. When you see Jesus you will see the Father. They are both the same.

A LITTLE HUMOR: Two young preachers were going door to door. They knocked on the door of one woman who was not at all happy to see them. She told them in no uncertain terms that she did not want to hear their message and slammed the door in their faces. To her surprise the door did not close. In fact, it almost magically bounded back open. She tried again, really putting her back into it and slammed the door again with the same result — the door bounced back open. Convinced that one of the young religious zealots was sticking his foot in the door, she reared back to give it a third slam. She felt this would really teach them a lesson. But before she could act, one of them stopped her and politely said, "Ma'am, before you do that again, you really should move your cat."

DECEMBER 13

A PERSONAL LOVE LETTER

"O how I love Your law! It is my meditation all the day." (Psalm 119:97, NASB)

In 1991, actress Julia Roberts was asked what object she valued most. "I have a letter from my daddy," she replied, "the only letter that I managed not to lose as a child . . . If anybody ever took that away from me, I would just be destroyed. It doesn't mean anything to anybody else, yet I can read that letter ten times a day, and it moves me in a different way every time."

The Bible is a personal love letter from God to us. The first stanza of Philip P. Bliss' hymn about the Bible and God's love reads: "I am so glad that our Father in heaven/Tells of His love in the Book He has given,/Wonderful things in the Bible I see;/This is the dearest, that Jesus loves me."

In this Scripture verse, the author speaks of the object of his love: "Your law." The word *law* refers to the Word of God we commonly call the Bible. The word *love* means desire. It implies an intense love. It is a note of exclamation. It suggests an attempt to express one's feelings for the Bible. We may know God's Word; we may read it, speak it, memorize it, practice it, and yet, not love it.

Notice the word *meditation.* The root meaning of the word refers to the chewing of the cud as a cow chews its food. To mediate on God's word means to reflect or think on; to digest it. Notice furthermore that he mediates on God's Word "all the day." Bible study is not for the lazy person.

Finally, the word "Your" is spelled with a capital letter "Y", an indication that it is the Word of the Lord. A young woman laid aside a certain book she was reading because she thought it was dull. Sometime later she became engaged to be married. One evening she said to her finance, "I have a book written by a man with the same name as yours. Isn't that a coincidence!" The man replied, "That's not a coincidence. I wrote that book!"

That night she sat up until 3 o'clock in the morning reading the book she once found dull. It was not the most thrilling book she had ever read. She had fallen in love with the author.

Is the Bible a dull book to you? Then maybe you should meet the Author. Someone has said, TO KNOW CHRIST, THE LIVING WORD, IS TO LOVE THE BIBLE, THE WRITTEN WORD.

A LITTLE HUMOR: A sick woman church member requested a visit from her pastor. He came, sat by her bed, and listened to her litany of woe. He counseled finally, "I think you will find help from some passages in the Bible which I wish to read to you."

In a syrupy voice she called to her little daughter playing in the next room: "Darling, bring mother that old book she loves so much." Promptly the little girl brought her a copy of a popular movie-TV magazine.

DECEMBER 14

LOVE SETS US FREE

"For God so loved the world, that he gave His only begotten Son, that whosoever believeth in Him should not perish, but have everlasting life." (John 3:16, KJV)

Denzel Washington stars in *The Hurricane,* the true story of professional boxer Rubin "Hurricane" Carter's life. At the height of his boxing career in the 1960's, Carter is falsely accused of murder by a racist police force and sentenced to prison for the remainder of his natural life.

While Carter is in prison, a young black boy, Lesra, who has read Carter's autobiography, befriends Hurricane. Their friendship deepens over time, and the boy introduces Carter to a few of his adult friends who become convinced of his innocence and commit themselves to helping as his amateur lawyers and detectives. After some 20 years in lock-up, Carter, 50 years old, is granted a new trial. While awaiting the verdict in his prison cell, Carter and Lesra share their thoughts.

Lesra says to Carter: "Rubin, I just want you to know...if this doesn't work, I'm bustin' you outta here." "You are, huh?" responds Carter. "Yeah, that's right, I'm bustin' you outta here," insists Lesra. After a moment of silence, Carter changes the subject and states his belief that they were not brought together by chance. Carter pauses and then emphatically continues, "Hate put me in prison. Love's gonna bust me out."

Jesus said that sin would make a prisoner of us (John 8:34) but that as the Son of God He would set us free (John 8:36). Or, to say it as Lesra might, "God will bust us outta here!"

Some years ago James Rowe wrote a song about the love of God delivering us from an imprisoned life of sin. Using the example of a drowning person being rescued, Rowe wrote: "I was sinking deep in sin, far from the peaceful shore, Very deeply stained within, sinking to rise no more; But the Master of the sea heard my despairing cry, From the waters lifted me, now safe am I. Love lifted me! Love lifted me! When nothing else could help, Love lifted me."

The love of God as revealed in the sacrificial act of Jesus Christ, God's Son, dying on the cross of Calvary in our place, demonstrates not only how much God loves us but the power of that love to deliver us from the penalty and power of sin. The best known verse of Scripture in the Bible tells us of that love: "For God so loved the world, that he gave His only begotten Son, that whosoever believeth in Him should not perish, but have everlasting life" (John 3:16, KJV). Thank God for His love. It sets us free.

A LITTLE HUMOR: Stopped by a police officer for driving without a taillight, the driver was visibly distressed. "Don't take it so hard," said the officer, "it's only a minor offense." "That's not the point," replied the troubled driver. "What worries me is, what's happened to my trailer and my wife?"

DECEMBER 15

TURNING TEARS INTO TELESCOPES

"Count it all joy when you fall into divers temptations." (James 1:2, KJV)

When we use the word *temptation* we often use it to speak of a solicitation to do wrong. But James is not talking about seduction, but of suffering and trials. One of the things James tells us is that trials are certain and should be expected in our life. Notice he uses the word "when" not "if."

The word *fall* is only used one other place in the New Testament and that is in Luke 10:30 where we read, "And Jesus answering said, A certain man went down from Jerusalem to Jericho, and fell among thieves, which stripped him of his raiment, and wounded him, and departed, leaving him half dead" (KJV). Trials can come suddenly and without warning. A knock at the door, a phone call, a visit to the doctor can suddenly turn our calm and peaceful sea into a storm. The English word pirate comes from the word translated temptation. Like pirates that ambush the unsuspecting ship, trials can come suddenly.

The word *divers* is interesting. We would call it a technicolor word. It literally means multi-colored. In the Old Testament, the word was used to describe Joseph's coat of many colors. James used the word to describe the diversity of our trials. Shakespeare said: "When sorrows come, they come not in single spies, but in battalions."

In James 1:3 the word *trying* speaks of the purging effect of trials. As George Sweeting said, "A Christian is like a tea bag. He is not worth much until he has been through hot water." Francis Thompson says sorrow, loss and disappointments were "Hounds of Heaven" sent to bring the wanderer back to the haven of peace.

The word *perfect* (James 1:4) means complete or full grown. Trials bring us to maturity. Airplanes take off by overcoming the resistance of gravity and wind. Yet once they become airborne, that wind lifts them higher. Trials have a way of lifting us higher and higher.

The word *count* (v.1) means to think ahead or to look forward. Our joy comes from looking ahead at the end result of our trials. As we go through trials we can anticipate with joy what God will bring to pass as a result of our trials. James is telling us to turn our tears into telescopes. Things may be hard now, but just look down the road!

A LITTLE HUMOR: Nothing makes a long story short like the arrival of the person you happen to be talking about.

DECEMBER 16

WE WIN!

"Sing a new song to the Lord telling about his mighty deeds! For he has won a mighty victory by his power and holiness. He has announced this victory and revealed it to every nation." (Psalm 98:1-2, LB)

One night a little boy was up late reading a murder mystery. It involved a dastardly villain who plotted all kinds of mayhem for the heroine. After a while the boy couldn't stop shivering in dread. He felt so sorry for the heroine — and he became so afraid of the villain himself — that he couldn't stand the suspense any longer. Instead of waiting to finish the book, he decided to skip to the last chapter.

When he found out the villain got his just reward at the end of the book, and the heroine was delivered, he sighed with relief. Relaxed and certain of the end, he could go back and read the remainder of the book. But this time his attitude was different. Every time the villain would plot another evil deed, the boy would say, smiling, "If you only knew what I know, you wouldn't be so proud and cocky right now." You see, he had read the last chapter.

I remember when the Cathedral Quartet presented a concert in our church. The pianist for the quartet had written a song about the Bible and the victory that is ours as Christians. He made the comment that he had read the last book of the Bible and was assured that we had won the victory over Satan. The song he wrote included the words "I've read the last of the book, and we win!"

Friends, as God's children, we already know the last chapter of this life. We know how the story of good and evil is going to end. Satan, the ultimate villain, will get his just reward — for eternity. Therefore, we can rest assured that God has all situations under his control. He has already won the victory! As someone has said, "We don't fight *for* victory; we fight *from* victory!"

As the psalmist wrote, we "sing a new song to the Lord...for he has won a mighty victory." He has won for us victory over temptation, sin, death and the grave. Hallelujah! Jesus Christ is Lord. The Holy Spirit, who is Jesus in the Spirit, lives in us. The apostle John put it this way, "Greater is he that is in you, than he that is in the world" (1 John 4:4, KJV). We win!

A LITTLE HUMOR: If lawyers are disbarred, and clergy defrocked, doesn't it follow that electricians can be delighted, musicians denoted, cowboys deranged, models deposed, tree surgeons debarked, dry cleaners depressed, and computers disputed?

DECEMBER 17

WHAT WAS THAT AGAIN?

"Why do you not understand what I am saying? It is because you cannot hear My word." (John 8:43, NASB)

A woman went to her lawyer to sue her husband for divorce. The lawyer asked, "Do you have grounds?" The woman said, "I own two acres off Walnut Hill." The lawyer asked, "Do you have a grudge?" The woman said, "I have a carport that holds two cars." The lawyer asked, "Does your husband beat you up?" The woman said, "I'm up a half-hour before he is every morning." The lawyer asked, "Why do you want a divorce?" The woman said, "I can't communicate with him."

Communication -- everybody's discussing it, studying it, practicing it. Yet, despite our improved communication skills, we may feel like the author who wrote, "I know that you believe you understand what you think I said, but I am not sure you realize that what you heard is not what I meant."

Good communication involves more than good speaking; it also requires good listening. Jesus, the master communicator, was often misunderstood, as we see in John 8:43, "Why do you not understand what I am saying? It is because you cannot hear My Word." Although He spoke the truth clearly, His hearers jumbled up His message and then rejected it. "Why do you not understand My speech?" He quizzed them. Answering His own question, He replied, "Because you are not able to listen to My Word." Why were they such poor listeners? Not because Jesus failed to communicate, but because they didn't want to hear the truth. And why didn't they? Because it made them face up to their need to change.

Good communication means more than just talking. It means that there is an exchange between two people in which both parties understand each other. One day a man stood on the side of a highway beside his broken-down car. He waved at those who were passing by, and finally a lady stopped to help. He told the lady that he did not have any jumper cables, so she would have to push his car with hers. In that way, he could "pop the clutch" and start the engine. "By the way," he said, "You will probably have to get up to about 40 mph before my car will be going fast enough to start." The lady, who didn't fully understand what he was talking about and did not have a clear concept of what was going on, smiled and said, "OK!" The man got in his car and waited for the lady to pull her car up to his bumper. When she delayed, he looked in his rearview mirror to see what the problem was. She had backed down the road about 100 yards and was bearing down on him at 40 mph. There was a terrible crash!

Lack of good communication can lead to a big mess. Proverbs 25:11 tells us, "Like apples of gold in settings of silver is a word spoken in right circumstances" (NASB). We not only need to say the right thing; we also need to say it at the right time and in the right way.

A LITTLE HUMOR: The day before Christmas was a hectic one. Father was worried with bundles and burdens. Mother's nerves reached the breaking point more than once. The little girl seemed to be in the way wherever she went. Finally, she was hustled up to bed. As she knelt to pray, the feverish excitement so mixed her up, she said, "Forgive us our Christmases, as we forgive those who Christmas against us."

DECEMBER 18

GOD IS FAITHFUL

"God is faithful, through whom you were called into fellowship with His Son, Jesus Christ our Lord." (1 Corinthians 1:9, NASB)

The late Norman Vincent Peale told the story of a struggling businessman who reached a turning point in life after seeing a picture of a boat stuck in sand. The caption said, "The Tide Always Comes Back."

There are two mistakes we make in life. When things are good, we tend to think they will always be good. When things are bad, we tend to think they will always be bad. Both ideas are wrong. Life, and all it consists of — our marriage, our work, our relationships, our finances, etc. — tend to go up and down in cycles. As the old hymn says, there is an ebb and flow to life.

There is one constant in all of this: God is faithful. We see His faithfulness everywhere we look. The very center of God's creation is built around His faithfulness. Psalm 119:90 says, "Your faithfulness continues through all generations; you established the earth, and it endures" (NIV). Joshua, looking back on his career as a military leader, gathered all the people of Israel together. He told them to look at what God had done for them and he said, "You know with all your heart and soul that not one of all the good promises the Lord your God gave you has failed. Every promise has been fulfilled; not one has failed" (Joshua 23:14, NIV). God cannot fail. He is faithful.

We are experiencing difficult and dangerous days as a nation. But even in times like this, God, who cannot lie, is faithful. Whether I feel it or not, His faithfulness is great. That's why Christian people face tragedy and death and difficulty like no other people on this earth — because when they cannot feel, they know. God is faithful whether you feel like He is or not, whether you think He is or not, whether you observe His faithfulness or not. God is faithful.

One of my favorite hymns is *Great is Thy Faithfulness,* written by Thomas O. Chisholm. The first stanza reads, "Great is Thy faithfulness, O God, my Father, There is no shadow of turning with Thee; Thou changest not, Thy compassions, they fail not; As Thou has been, Thou forever wilt be." God's faithfulness truly is great.

Today, whether your tide is in or out, lean on the faithfulness of God. Be thankful for His goodness; be thankful for His mercy. Most of all, remain faithful to Him.

A LITTLE HUMOR: A few days before Christmas two ladies stood looking into a department store window at a large display of the manger scene with clay figures of the baby Jesus, Mary, Joseph, the shepherds, the wise men, and the animals. Disgustedly one said, "Look at that. The church trying to horn in on Christmas!"

DECEMBER 19

PASSING THE TEST OF FAITH

"Consider it all joy, my brethren, when you encounter various trials, knowing that the testing of your faith produces endurance." (James 1:2-3, NASB)

A juggler with a circus was pulled over for speeding. The officer was suspicious when he looked in the back seat and saw several large knives. "What are you doing with those?" he asked. "I'm a juggler with the circus," said the man. "To make it more exciting I juggle those large knives." "Well, show me," said the officer. So the juggler started juggling six of these large knives all at once. Knives were flying everywhere, though amazingly all of them were expertly under his control. While he was performing, another car passed by. The driver of this car did a double take when he saw the juggler throwing six knives up in the air at one time and catching them. He turned to his wife and said, "That's it. I'm through drinking. Why, if I ever got stopped, I could never pass one of those new sobriety tests!"

There are times when your faith will be tested. This testing usually comes in the form of problems or trials. There are three classes of people: (1) those who have problems, (2) those who are just coming out of a problem, and (3) those who are getting ready to have a problem. How can I profit from my problems? What can I expect to happen when problems put my faith to the test?

First, problems will purify your faith. The word *testing* means to purge from impurities as one would heat metal until it melts so its impurities rise to the surface and can be removed. A ship built in dry dock is not proven seaworthy until it hits gale-force winds. A raw recruit with six weeks of boot camp is not really ready for battle until he faces the enemy. Faith will prove to be genuine once it has been tested.

Second, problems will produce patience. The word *endurance* means fortitude, steadfastness, staying power, or patience. A scuba diver has an air tank that allows him to stay under water and breathe while under pressure. The only way for patience to be produced is to subject it to trials.

Third, problems will perfect your character. We should allow patience to run its course and have its full effect on us. It will lead us to maturity. Remember that the devil wants to use problems to defeat you; the Lord wants to use problems to develop you.

Would your faith pass the "sobriety tests" of life? Having problems may not be so bad after all. There's a special place for folks who have none — it's called a cemetery!

A LITTLE HUMOR: A young preacher boasted that all the time he needed to prepare his Sunday sermon was the few minutes it took him to walk to the church from the parsonage next door. After a few weeks of hearing his sermons, the congregation bought a new parsonage five miles away.

DECEMBER 20

'TIS THE SEASON TO BE JOLLY — OR MELANCHOLY

"But the angel said to them, 'Do not be afraid; for behold, I bring you good news of great joy which will be for all the people'." (Luke 2:10, NASB)

Christmas is a time to be merry. It is a time for parties, good food, gifts, carols and happy expressions of peace on earth. During the Christmas season we think about shepherds rejoicing, angels announcing "good tidings of great joy," and Mary "magnifying and praising God" for the coming of the Christ child. Enthusiastic anticipation, exciting activities, pleasant memories, and warm feelings all merge into something called "the Christmas spirit." But for a great number of people the Christmas season is a very difficult time of the year. For them the season to be jolly is a season to be melancholy!

What can be done to combat this melancholy feeling during what is supposed to be the happiest time of the year?

For one thing, we can recognize that God is in control of our lives and because He is, we don't have to be afraid or depressed. Mary recognized this. When the angel addressed her, he said, "Do not bc afraid" (Luke 1:29, NIV). She responded, "I am the Lord's servant. May it be to me as you have said" (Luke 1:38, NIV). She placed her faith in the Lord and trusted Him to work things out for her good and His glory. We should do the same. God loves us and cares for us, and we can rest assured that He is in charge. We do not have to face the Christmas season alone. His name is *Immanuel* which means God with us.

Recognizing the true meaning of Christmas will help, too. Christmas is more than just a time for parties and food and fun and Santa Claus. Christmas is the birthday celebration of Jesus Christ. It is a time for rejoicing in the fact that God came in the flesh of His Son and dwelt among us. (Luke 2:29-32). It is a time for recognizing that we are individuals of worth whom God loved so much that He sent Jesus to die for us and save us from our sins.

Finding ways to help others is another way to keep this holiday. A Sunday School teacher was telling her class of fourth-graders the Christmas story about the three Wise Men bringing gifts to the baby Jesus. A little girl who had recently become the big sister of a brand-new baby brother said: "Well, I guess gold and all that stuff are all right, but I'll bet Mary really wished somebody had brought some diapers."

Instead of feeling sorry for ourselves we should get out and mix with people. Find someone you can help and encourage and to whom you can be a friend to. Joseph went to Mary. He married her. In doing so he was saying, "I love you. I'll stand with you. I'll protect you. We'll see this through together." Surely you can find someone who could use a helping hand and an encouraging word during this season. Helping them will help you.

Christmas was meant to be a time of joy. It still can be.

A LITTLE HUMOR: Did you hear about the father who suggested that his family get him a Christmas gift that the whole family could get something from? They did. They bought Dad a new wallet!

DECEMBER 21

NO CHRISTMAS WITHOUT THE CROSS

". . . For this I have been born, and for this I have come into the world . . ."
(John 18:37, NASB)

It was a Christmas pageant presented by a class of four-year-olds – and it was an evening to remember. It began with the three virgin Marys marching out onto the stage. As they stood there, they, of course, were waving to their parents. It's not every Christmas pageant that has three virgin Marys but over the years the school had acquired three Mary costumes, and so, quite naturally the script was revised. This gave a chance for more children to be involved and kept down the squabbling over who has the starring roles. The two Josephs walked up behind the Marys.

Then twenty little angels came out. They were dressed in white robes and huge gauze wings. They were followed by twenty little shepherd boys, dressed in burlap sacks. They carried an array of objects that were supposed to be shepherds' crooks.

It was at this point that the problem occurred. During the dress rehearsal, the teacher had used chalk to draw circles on the floor to mark where the angels were supposed to stand and crosses to mark the spots of the shepherds. But the children had practiced with their regular clothes on. So, on the night of the pageant, the angels came walking out with their beautiful gauze wings and stood on their circles. However, their huge wings covered the crosses of the shepherds as well. So when the time came for the shepherds to find their places, they did not know where to go because the angels took up all their space. There was one little boy who became extremely frustrated and angry over the whole experience. He finally spied his teacher behind the curtains and shocked everyone when he said in a loud stage whisper heard by everyone, "Because of these blankety-blank angels, I can't find the cross!" He didn't say, "blankety-blank," but this is a religious article and I can't tell you what he really said, but you get the idea.

I wonder if that can't happen sometimes? The romantic elements of Christmas – the shepherds, the wise men, the angels, the star in the East – not to mention the commercialism of Christmas – have a tendency to obscure the important meaning of it all, and particularly the message of the cross. It was difficult for Mary and Joseph to find room in the inn and it's difficult to find room for the cross in the Christmas story. But we must find room for the cross.

Billy Graham once wrote, "Christmas is not Christmas without a message on the cross of Christ. This is why He was born. Christmas says that grace is greater than all our sins. Christmas says that the sin question was answered at the cross." Jesus said, ". . . For this I have been born, and for this I have come into the world . . ." (John 18:37, NASB). To Christians the joy of Christmas is not limited to His birth, gloriously supernatural as that was because of His virgin-birth. It is built even more on the triumph of His death. It was His death that gave meaning to His birth. We must find room for the cross for this and every Christmas.

A LITTLE HUMOR: A concerned little girl approached her father one day and said, "Daddy, I just don't believe it's right to ignore Jesus." The father, more than a little confused, answered, "I agree with you. We shouldn't ignore Jesus. But what made you think of that?" "Well, it's that Christmas song we sing at church. You know, the one that says, 'O come let us ignore Him'."

DECEMBER 22

DON'T MISS CHRISTMAS

"There was no room for them in the inn." (Luke 2:7b, NKJV)

On December 17, 1903, Orville and Wilbur Wright made their first flight of a self-propelled, heavier-than-air aircraft which stayed aloft for twelve seconds and covered 120 feet on its inaugural flight near Kitty Hawk, North Carolina.

Wilbur rushed to the local telegraph office and sent the following message to their sister, Katherine: WE HAVE FLOWN FOR 12 SECONDS – WE WILL BE HOME FOR CHRISTMAS! Upon receiving the telegram, Katherine went to the newspaper office, told the editor of her brother's new flying machine, and informed him they would be home for Christmas, if he would like to set up an interview.

The editor told Katherine that the news was nice, and he would be sure to put something in the paper regarding the boys. On December 19th, the local paper placed the following headline on the sixth page of the paper: "WRIGHT BROTHERS HOME FOR CHRISTMAS." The most important story of the year – man's first successful flight – and the editor missed it!

In his book, *Sign of the Star,* R. Earl Allen wrote: "On that first Christmas, three different kinds of people missed the promised one, the longed-for Messiah, the Son of God. He was missed by secular people, like the innkeeper. He was missed by political leaders, like Herod. He was even missed by those supposed to be the most spiritual, the priests in the Temple. We may say that he was missed in the home, the state, and the church. All of these missed the Messiah."[119]

I wonder if the same could be said about us when it comes to Christmas. Look around . . . the trees are decorated, the music is festive, the Season is right – it's Christmas. In all of our rushing around, in all of our gift buying, in all the things we have to do during this season – HAVE WE MISSED THE MOST IMPORTANT THING ABOUT CHRISTMAS – JESUS HAS COME TO THIS EARTH!

Will Christ be in your heart, in your church, in your home this Christmas? The Saviour is born: do you have room for Him? Will you make room for Him?

A LITTLE HUMOR: Grandma had just arrived at her daughter's house for Christmas. The little grandson rushed out to greet his grandmother with a big hug. "I'm so glad to see you, Grandma!" he said. "Now maybe daddy will do the trick he has been promising us." Grandmother was curious. "What trick is that my dear?" "I heard daddy tell mommy that he would climb the walls if you came to visit us again!"

---

[119] R. Earl Allen, *Sign of the Star* (Nashville: Broadman Press, 1968), 90.

DECEMBER 23

ALONE, BUT NOT LONELY

"I will ask the Father, and He will give you another Helper, that He may be with you forever...I will not leave you as orphans; I will come to you."

(John 14:16, 18, NASB)

As difficult as it may be for you and me to believe, not everyone gets all that excited about Christmas. In the "Bah, Humbug department," no Scrooge could ever beat the outrageous comedian, William Claude Dunkenfield, better known as W.C. Fields.

Born In Philadelphia, Fields began earning a living as a juggler at the age of fifteen. He went on to become a famous magician and vaudeville entertainer and even performed for King Edward VII at Buckingham Palace. He perfected two roles in his career: that of a small time gambler and con man and the bumbling henpecked husband. Fields hated Christmas. Writer Will Fowler, who knew Fields well, asked him why.

Fields responded, "It's because those days point up a thing called loneliness. An actor on the road – as I was for so long – finds himself all alone on days when everyone else has friends and companionship. It's not so good to be in some foreign country, as when I was on tour, all alone on Christmas Day." Then he added, "I was born lonely! But Christmas and New Year's and Thanksgiving and all the rest made me even more lonely. So I observe only one day – April First. That's my day!" Ironically, Fields died on Christmas, a day he always claimed to hate.

Can you imagine celebrating April Fool's day and not Christmas? Even if Fields was engaging in a little hyperbole, his sentiments come through loud and clear. Christmas is a very sad season if you are lonely.

But of all the holidays we celebrate, we ought to rejoice all the more during the Christmas Season because Christmas means you don't have to be alone. One of the names of Jesus is "Immanuel" which means "God with us." In addition to Jesus being with us, the Holy Spirit is also our constant companion. Jesus said, "I will ask the Father, and He will give you another Helper, that He may be with you forever...I will not leave you as orphans; I will come to you" (John 14:16, 18). Today, give thanks for the presence of the Lord in your life. You may be alone, but you don't have to be lonely.

A LITTLE HUMOR: A little girl was always being rushed to dinner with the words, "Hurry up and wash your hands and come in here for the prayer." After a while the refrain irritated her. She remarked to her mother, "Germs and Jesus, germs and Jesus! That's all I ever hear from you, and I can't see either one of them!"

DECEMBER 24

LOVE'S PURE LIGHT

"...the people living in darkness have seen a great light; on those living in the land of the shadow of death a light has dawned." (Matthew 4:16, NIV)

A man from Little Rock, Arkansas named Osborn decided to decorate his house for Christmas with lights. It got a little out of hand by the time he was finished — he had put up three million lights. It was spectacular; it was so spectacular that they had to move in extra power lines just to generate enough electricity to run the lights. People came from everywhere to see it, even people from out of state. The lines were so long the neighbors sued Mr. Osborn. It went to the Arkansas State Supreme Court. The judge said, "I think you need to scale it down a little bit." Lights definitely attract. When you ride through your neighborhood you are attracted to the houses with the most lights.

West Virginia folklore carries a tale about a couple that called for a doctor late one night when the wife was ready to deliver a baby. The country physician turned the rustic farmhouse into a makeshift delivery room. The husband was handed a lantern and instructed to hold it up so the doctor could see. After a healthy boy was born, the man lowered the lantern. The doctor shouted for this new father to get the lantern up as he delivered another baby — this time a girl. The father was thrown into shock when the doctor once again insisted that the light be held up. He said, "We can't stop now, it looks like there's another one." The shaky father then asked the doctor, "Do you think it's the light that's attracting them?"

Unfortunately, sometimes we are more afraid of the light than attracted to it. That first Christmas when the light was so bright, the shepherds were afraid. Why are we afraid? Perhaps it's because light exposes who we really are. Do you ever wonder why people say, "Candlelight is so romantic?" Candlelight is romantic because you can't completely see the other person.

A lady who was late with her rent saw her landlord coming to her door. Thinking he was about to evict her, she turned off all the lights and hid in the darkness. Later in the week, he passed by her on the street in broad daylight. He told her that a friend of hers had paid her rent. The light of day was not a light of punishment but of pardon.

When God knocks on your door it is not to evict you but to welcome you into His eternal light. Don't hide in the darkness this Christmas. Celebrate the light, the eternal light. Jesus entered our dark world. He voluntarily entered the dark room of death but when He left, He left the light on for us.

A LITTLE HUMOR: On one Christmas, a church bulletin gave exciting ecclesiastical authority to "Sing, choirs of angels, sin in exultation."

DECEMBER 25

A BIRTHDAY CELEBRATION

"Today in the city of David there has been born for you a Savior, who is Christ the Lord." (Luke 2:11, NASB)

A mother took her three-year-old daughter to church for the first time. The church was having a special candlelight service. The church lights were lowered; then the choir came down the aisle, carrying lighted candles. All was quiet until the three-year-old started to sing in a loud voice, "Happy birthday to you, happy birthday to you . . ." It was only a candlelight service, but it seemed liked a birthday party to her. She's right about Christmas. It is a celebration of Jesus' birthday.

I heard someone say the other day that instead of calling Christmas the birthday of Jesus, they wanted to refer to the activities that accompany this season of the year as a "Festival of Lights" because they didn't want to offend anyone who may not be a Christian. Well, I'm not for offending anyone either, but neither am I in favor of calling this season of the year something it's not. No matter what we may believe or feel about this season of the year, it has always been, is, and always will be the celebration of the birth of Jesus Christ, the Son of the Living God!

At one time Della Reese, the actress and performer, was known primarily for her singing. Today she is known as one of the co-stars of the television program, *Touched by an Angel.* When she was co-starring in an earlier television show, she was asked if she would be giving up her singing career altogether. Her answer was no. She said, "I don't work on July 6 and December 25 — my birthday and Jesus' birthday — but outside of that I have to sing." Those are two good exceptions — her birthday and Jesus' birthday.

A five-year-old was showing his Christmas presents to Grandma when she asked, "Did you get everything you wanted for Christmas?" The little fellow thought for a moment before answering, "No, I didn't Grandma. But that's okay. It wasn't my birthday."

Remember the reason for the season is to celebrate the birth of Jesus Christ, the Son of God and our Lord and Savior. "Joy to the world! The Lord is come; let earth receive her King; let every heart prepare Him room, and heaven and nature sing." Happy Birthday Jesus!

A LITTLE HUMOR: A man said his wife had not spoken to him since last Christmas. He asked her what she wanted for Christmas, and she said, "Oh, just surprise me." So, at three o'clock Christmas morning, he leaned over and went, "BOO!"

DECEMBER 26

INTERVIEW WITH A GERBIL

"Seek peace and pursue it." (Psalm 34:14, NASB)

With appealing humor, Ron Hutchcraft, busy author, speaker, and counselor, tells about his battle with stress. One day Ron decided to "interview" the family gerbil. "Tell me, Gerbie," Ron asked, "what do you have planned for today?" "First, breakfast," he replied, "and then get started." "Doing what?" Ron asked. "Why, the same thing I did yesterday, and the day before that." "What's that?" Ron asked again. "The wheel." And sure enough, Gerbie climbed on his little wheel and started running in circles. Hours later, he was still running.

The more Ron watched that gerbil, the more he saw himself. He had his own personal "wheels" — demands, deadlines, aggravations, ambitions. He felt as if he was running in circles, and he longed for peace. In his search, he made this discovery in Psalm 34: Peace isn't automatic or passive; it must be pursued. Not only that, but peace is also a result of a right relationship with the Lord. As never before, Ron enthroned the Lord as the Shepherd of his life. As he did, peace instead of the stressful wheel, became normal.

In Psalm 34:14, the word *seek* means to strive and the word *pursue* means to hunt. We are to strive for and hunt for peace as one would hunt for game. Different comments are made about the pursuit of peace. "One should follow after it" is one comment. Another is, "make it an object of your desire." Still another one is, "Don't be discouraged if it should need prolonged effort to overtake it."

Seeking peace doesn't deny the fact that peace is a gift from God. Jesus said, "Peace I leave with you; My peace I give to you; not as the world gives, do I give to you. Let not your heart be troubled, nor let it be fearful" (John 14:27, NASB). In John 16:33, Jesus said, "...in Me you may have peace. In the world you have tribulation, but take courage; I have overcome the world" (John 13:33, NASB). Notice, Jesus said peace was to be found "in Me." Jesus is the Prince of Peace who gives us that peace which surpasses all comprehension (Philippians 4:7). Having received God's peace, I am to be a peacemaker (Matthew 5:9) seeking to live in peace with everyone (Hebrews 12:14). May we seek peace and pursue it with all diligence.

A LITTLE HUMOR: At the Little Brown Church, the Christmas Eve service included a candle-lighting ceremony in which each member of the congregation lit a candle from his neighbor's candle. At the end of the ceremony, the minister rose to announce the concluding hymn and was taken completely by surprise when his invitation evoked laughter: "Now that everyone is lit, let's sing 'Joy to the World'."

DECEMBER 27

LET US COME

"Let us therefore come boldly unto the throne of grace, that we may obtain mercy, and find grace to help in time of need." (Hebrews 4:16, KJV)

Hebrews 4:16 is one of my favorite verses of scripture. The important word in the verse is *come.* There are several questions which we can ask here in connection with the word come.

Let us come – WHO? Who are invited to come? The answer is we. We are to come. We may come. Every believer is to come. Unworthy though we are, we are to come.

Let us come – HOW? We are to come *boldly* ("with confidence," NASB). *The Amplified Bible* reads, "Let us then fearlessly and confidently and boldly draw near." This does not mean we can come carelessly or flippantly, but it does mean we can come with absolute assurance that for Jesus' sake, God will accept us and help us.

Let us come– WHERE? The answer is – *unto the throne of grace.* We do not come to the throne of judgment. We come to the throne of grace, to the place where God is gracious.

Let us come – WHEN? – The answer is *in time of need;* that is, in every time of need. I especially like the translation of *The Amplified Bible*: "in good time for every need – appropriate help, and well-timed help, coming just when we need it."

Let us come – WHY? – *That we may obtain mercy, and find grace.* We are always in need of mercy and grace but we must come to the throne of grace in order to find or receive the grace we need. Dr. Alexander Maclaren says that this reference to "obtaining mercy" and "finding grace to help" suggests a significant metaphor. The one expresses the heart of God (obtaining mercy), and the other expresses the hand of God (finding grace to help). Because we have such a great and glorious High Priest (Jesus Christ), let us come boldly and frequently to the throne of grace, that we may find out more and more of His loving heart and the help of His powerful and mighty hand!

A LITTLE HUMOR: A preacher, after describing all the glories of heaven, called for a show of hands of all who wanted to go there. All but one meek little fellow promptly responded. The startled preacher asked the holdout, "Do you mean to tell me you don't want to go to heaven?" "Sure, I want to go, but I thought you were trying to get a load for tonight!"

DECEMBER 28

FOOTPRINTS TO FOLLOW

"You were not redeemed with perishable things like silver or gold from your futile way of life inherited from your forefathers, but with precious blood, as of a lamb unblemished and spotless, the blood of Christ." (1 Peter 1:17-18, NASB)

Not long ago I read of a boy who appeared at a mission hospital in Kenya with a gaping wound in his foot. He had been accidentally injured while cutting grass far out in the jungle. Somehow he had stepped into the path of the long, sharp knife of a friend working with him. Part of his heel was cut off. Without waiting to inform anyone of the mishap, the two boys set out across country to find the mission station where they had heard medical help was available. Every time the little foot touched the sandy earth it left a faint trace of blood. The journey was long and difficult, but as last they arrived.

After a time the boy's mother appeared. The doctors were surprised that she had been able to find the way. There were no well-defined trails, and she had never made the trip before.

"How did you do it?" she was asked. The dear woman, overjoyed to be with her child, replied, "Oh, it was easy. I just followed the blood!"[120]

In a much more profound sense that is how we come to God. The path is sometimes rough and may lead through many trials, but we need not fear getting lost. All we have to do is follow the footprints of Jesus. They are easy to find, for each one is stained with blood. The blood will always lead to the Father and home.

I must needs go on in the blood-sprinkled way,
The path that the Savior trod,
If I ever climb to the heights sublime,
Where the soul is at home with God.

The way of the cross leads home,
It is sweet to know as I onward go,
The way of the cross leads home.
Jessie Brown Pounds

A LITTLE HUMOR: Traveling through New England, a motorist stopped for gas in a tiny village. "What's this place called? he asked the station attendant.

"All depends," the native drawled. "Do you mean by them that has to live in this ugly, moth-eaten, dust-covered dump, or by them that's merely enjoying its quaint and picturesque rustic charms for a short spell?"

---

[120] Robert E. Coleman, *Written in Blood*, (Old Tappan, New Jersey: Fleming H. Revell Company, 1972), 15-16.

DECEMBER 29

SHOW A LITTLE KINDNESS

"And be kind to one another, tender-hearted, forgiving each other, just as God in Christ also has forgiven you." (Ephesians 4:32, NASB)

A recent survey by the research group Public Agenda said that "most of us think the rest of us are rude – and getting ruder." Nearly 80% of the 2,013 adults surveyed by telephone in January said a lack of respect and courtesy in American society is a serious problem. Sixty-one percent think things have gotten worse in recent years.

Kindness is the antidote for rudeness. Paul admonishes us to "be kind to one another." I remember a quote by Mark Twain. He said "Kindness is a language the deaf can hear and the blind can see."

We should be kind in what we say. The old saying, "Sticks and stones may break my bones but words can never hurt me" just isn't true. Words can be used to hurt others. On the other hand, Proverbs 25:11 says, "A word fitly spoken is like apples of gold in pictures of silver." Also, Isaiah 50:4 reads, "The Lord God hath given me the tongue of the learned, that I should know how to speak a word in season to him that is weary." There never has been an overproduction of kind words.

We should be kind in what we do. The Apostle Paul wrote that "we are His workmanship, created in Christ Jesus for good works" (Ephesians 2:10). Such acts of kindness as holding a chair for someone or opening a car door or saying, "Please" or "Thank you," writing a note of appreciation, saying nice things about a person, not contradicting someone telling a story, holding a lady's coat, saying how much you enjoyed being with someone – and the list could go on and on – these so-called little things do make a difference in people's lives. William Penn wrote: "I expect to pass through life but once. If therefore there be any kindness I can show, or any good thing I can do to any fellow-being, let me do it now, and not defer or neglect it, for I shall never pass this way again."

The poet Longfellow wrote:

Kind hearts are the gardens,
Kind thoughts are the roots,
Kind words are the flowers,
Kind deeds are the fruit.

Take care of your garden,
And keep out the weeds;
Fill it up with sunshine
Kind words and kind deeds.

A LITTLE HUMOR: When asked to give a testimony, a couple who had been married over fifty years, shared the following: The wife said, "On our wedding day, we decided the husband would make the major decisions, and the wife would make all the minor decisions. For our marriage, this arrangement has worked wonderfully. So far there have been no major decisions."

DECEMBER 30

WRAPPED IN GRACE

"For the grace of God has appeared . . ." (Titus 2:11)

All God's gifts come wrapped in grace, but there are different kinds of grace for our different needs. According to Titus 2:11-15, there is:

1. Saving Grace – "For the grace of God has appeared, bringing salvation to all men" (v. 11). God the Father *planned* our redemption. God the Son *purchased* it, and God the Spirit *performs* it within us. Grace has its *source* in the heart of God; its *scope* encompasses all human needs, and its *sufficiency* meets every need.

2. Schooling Grace – "instructing us to deny ungodliness and worldly desires and to live sensibly, righteously and godly in the present age" (v. 12). The grace of God teaches us to *leave* the old life, to *live* the new life, and to *look* for the return of the Lord Jesus Christ.

3. Sanctifying Grace – "Christ Jesus, who gave Himself for us, that He might redeem us from every lawless deed and purify for Himself a people for His own possession . . ." (v. 14). Grace *sanctifies* or sets us apart from sin and *keeps* us pure in this present world.

4. Serving Grace – "These things speak and exhort and reprove with all authority..." (v. 15). God's grace *enables* us to faithfully serve the Lord Jesus Christ.

I heard about a man who wanted to buy a Rolls Royce automobile. After several years, he contacted the dealership to determine some pertinent facts about the particular model he wanted. He learned the price and proceeded with some thorough questions about the vehicle. Only one remained unanswered. "What is the horsepower of this particular engine?" The salesman could not find that information in the brochures. Finally, the sales manager cabled the company in England with the inquiry. The answer came back, just one word, "ADEQUATE!"

No matter the need, the trial, the weakness, God's grace is adequate. When the infinite God and Savior Jesus Christ, to whom is given "all power in heaven and on earth" (Matthew 28:18), promises, "My grace is sufficient for you," you can bank on it. God's grace keeps pace with whatever we face.

A LITTLE HUMOR: A boy got his old father to see a football game between two rivals. As they sat down, the boy slapped his father on the back and said, "Dad, for three dollars you are going to see more fight, more life, and more enthusiasm than you ever saw before." The old man smiled and replied, "I am not so sure about that, Son. That's what I paid for my marriage license."

DECEMBER 31

COMMITMENTS FOR THE NEW YEAR

"I urge you therefore, brethren, by the mercies of God, to present your bodies a living and holy sacrifice, acceptable to God, which is your spiritual service of worship. And do not be conformed to this world, but be transformed by the renewing of your mind, that you may prove what the will of God is, that which is good and acceptable and perfect." (Romans 12:1-2, NASB)

When Luciano Pavorotti was a boy, his father, a baker, introduced him to the wonders of song. He urged him to work hard to develop his voice. Arrigo Pola, a professional tenor in his hometown of Modena, Italy, took him as a pupil. He also enrolled in a teacher's college. Upon graduation, Pavorotti asked his father, "Shall I be a teacher or a singer?"

Luciano's father said to him, "If you try to sit on two chairs, you will fall between them. For life, you must choose one chair."

Pavorotti said, "I chose one. If took seven years of study and frustration before I made my first professional appearance. It took another seven years to reach the Metropolitan Opera. And now I think whether its laying bricks, writing a book — whatever we choose — we should give ourselves to it. Commitment, that's the key. Choose one chair."

A New Year is about to begin. We do not know what this new year will bring — peace and prosperity we hope, but we can't be sure. Whatever lies ahead of us can be faced and handled if we have the right kind of commitments. May I suggest several.

First, we need to be committed to **the Son of God.** We Christians believe that the Son of God is Jesus Christ. According to John 3:16, He is the "only begotten Son." That means there is none other like Him. As we live our lives through this new year, may it be with a renewed commitment to live for Him. We don't know what the future holds, but we know Who holds the future!

Second, we need to be committed to **the Word of God.** Several years ago telephone directories carried the slogan "Look in the Book First" on the front cover. It was a reminder to check for numbers before calling the operator. Before we meet any challenge or seek the Lord's blessing on our lives, we should look first in His Book — the Bible — for His instructions. His word will be our guide (Psalm 119:105).

Third, we need to be committed to **the House of God.** In his book, *The Church Today,* Paul W. Powell writes: "The church is the only movement Jesus left on this earth to represent Him. Anyone who wants to be on the cutting edge of what God is doing in the world today needs to be vitally involved in a local New Testament church." Don't neglect the church (Hebrews 10:24-25). People flocked to churches the day after September 11. May our attendance and involvement with the church be an on-going commitment.

Fourth, we need to be committed to **the Work of God.** Jesus said the harvest was great, but the laborers were few. He encouraged us to pray for more workers (Matthew 10:37-38). There is much to be done for the Lord. Time is running out. We must work for Him while we still can. Be involved in the Lord's work.

Eva B. Lloyd wrote, "Come, all Christians, be committed to the service of the Lord. Make your lives for Him more fitted, tune your hearts with one accord. Come into His courts with gladness, each His sacred vows renew, turn away from sin and sadness, be transformed with life anew."

A LITTLE HUMOR: The first graders were attending their first music lesson. The teacher was trying to begin at the beginning. She drew a musical staff on the blackboard and asked a little girl to come up and write a note on it. The little girl went to the blackboard, looked thoughtful for a minute and wrote, "Dear Aunt Emma, just a short note to tell you I'm fine."

HOW TO BECOME A CHRISTIAN

1. Realize God's Love for You.

"For God so loved the world, that He gave His only begotten Son, that whoever believes in Him shall not perish\, but have eternal life." (John 3:16)

"In this is love, not that we loved God, but that He loved us and sent His Son to be the propitiation for our sins." (1 John 4:10)

2. Realize That You Are a Sinner.

"For there is no difference; for all have sinned and fall short of the glory of God." (Romans 3:22b-23)

"For the wages of sin is death, but the gift of God is eternal life in Christ Jesus our Lord." (Romans 6:23)

3. Realize That God Desires to Save You.

"Say to them: 'As I live,' says the Lord God, 'I have no pleasure in the death of the wicked, but that the wicked turn from his way and live. Turn, turn from your evil ways! For why should you die, O house of Israel?'" (Ezekiel 33:11)

4. Realize That Jesus Christ Paid the Penalty for Your Sin.

"But God demonstrated His own love toward us, in that while we were still sinners, Christ died for us." (Romans 5:8)

5. Realize That You Must Repent of Your Sin.

"Repent therefore and be converted, that your sins may be blotted out, so that times of refreshing may come from the presence of the Lord." (Acts 3:19)

"The Lord is not slack concerning His promise, as some count slackness, but is longsuffering toward us, not willing that any should perish but that all should come to repentance." (2 Peter 3:9)

6. Realize That You Must Receive Jesus Christ as Your Saviour.

"But as many as received Him, to them He gave the right to become children of God, to those who believe in His name." (John 1:12)

"That if you confess with your mouth the Lord Jesus and believe in your heart that God has raised Him from the dead, you will be saved. For with the heart one believes unto righteousness, and with the mouth confession is made unto salvation." (Romans 10:9-10)

WOULD YOU RECEIVE JESUS CHRIST AS YOUR SAVIOUR NOW?

If so, pray a prayer like this:

"Lord Jesus, I confess to you that I am a sinner. I believe that you died for me. Please forgive me of my sins. Please come into my heart. I accept you as my personal Lord and Savior. Thank you for forgiving me of my sins. Take control of my life. Amen.

NOW THAT YOU HAVE RECEIVED CHRIST[121]

The moment you received Christ by faith, as an act of the will, many things happened, including the following:

1. Christ came into your life (Revelation 3:20; Colossians 1:27)

2. Your sins were forgiven (Colossians 1:14)

3. You became a child of God (John 1:12)

4. You received eternal life (John 5:24)

Can you think of anything more wonderful that could happen to you than receiving Christ? Would you like to thank God in prayer right now for what He has done for you? By thanking God, you demonstrate your faith.

To enjoy your new life to the fullest . . .

SUGGESTIONS FOR CHRISTIAN GROWTH

Spiritual growth results from trusting Jesus Christ. "The righteous man shall live by faith" (Galatians 3:11).A life of faith will enable you to trust God increasingly with every detail of your life, and to practice the following:

G – *Go* to God in prayer daily (John 15:7).
R – *Read* God's Word daily (Acts 17:11); begin with the Gospel of John.
O – *Obey* God moment by moment (John 14:21).
W – *Witness* for Christ by your life and words (Matthew 4:19; John 15:8).
T – *Trust* God for every detail of your life (1 Peter 5:7).
H – *Holy Spirit* – allow Him to control and empower your daily life and witness (Galatians 5:16-17; Acts 1:8).

---

[121] *Have You Heard of the Four Spiritual Laws?* © 1965-2012 Written by Bill Bright - Copyright Bright Media Foundation ®. All rights reserved. Used by Permission. No part of this booklet may be changed in any way or reproduced in any form without written permission from Bright Media Foundation.

SCRIPTURE INDEX

Old Testament Date

New Testament

ABOUT THE AUTHOR

Allen Reed has been the pastor of First Baptist Church, Nacogdoches, Texas, since 1981. He received his B.A. degree from East Texas Baptist College, Marshall, Texas, and his M.Div. and D.Min. degrees from Southwestern Baptist Theological Seminary, Ft. Worth, Texas. He and his wife, Linda, have three children and seven grandchildren.